THE STATE OF THE EUROPEAN UNION

VOLUME   8

A project of the European Union Studies Association

The State of the
European Union

*Making History: European Integration and
Institutional Change at Fifty*

VOLUME 8

edited by

SOPHIE MEUNIER and KATHLEEN R. MCNAMARA

OXFORD
UNIVERSITY PRESS

OXFORD

UNIVERSITY PRESS

Great Clarendon Street, Oxford OX2 6DP

Oxford University Press is a department of the University of Oxford.
It furthers the University's objective of excellence in research, scholarship,
and education by publishing worldwide in

Oxford New York

Auckland Cape Town Dar es Salaam Hong Kong Karachi
Kuala Lumpur Madrid Melbourne Mexico City Nairobi
New Delhi Shanghai Taipei Toronto

With offices in

Argentina Austria Brazil Chile Czech Republic France Greece
Guatemala Hungary Italy Japan Poland Portugal Singapore
South Korea Switzerland Thailand Turkey Ukraine Vietnam

Oxford is a registered trade mark of Oxford University Press
in the UK and in certain other countries

Published in the United States
by Oxford University Press Inc., New York

British Library Cataloguing in Publication Data

Data available

Library of Congress Cataloging in Publication Data

Data available

Typeset by SPI Publisher Services, Pondicherry, India
Printed in Great Britain
on acid-free paper by
Biddles Ltd., King's Lynn

ISBN 978–0–19–921867–7 (Hbk.)   978–0–19–921868–4 (Pbk.)

1 3 5 7 9 10 8 6 4 2

PREFACE

This volume, the eighth in the *State of the European Union* series under the auspices of the European Union Studies Association, comes at a particularly opportune time for reflection on the European project. It is now fifty years since the 1957 signing of the Treaty of Rome, the document that established the foundations for what is today the European Union (EU). At the same time, our reflections occur in the aftermath of the failure of the proposed European Constitution—an effort to complete the process begun in Rome five decades ago that floundered in two key referenda in France and the Netherlands. As politicians and citizens take stock in Europe, this volume places the analysis of European integration in broader historical perspective, probing the sources of stability, crisis, and change across the Union as a whole as well as within all the key policy arenas the EU now encompasses.

The theoretical approach best suited to this goal, we believe, is that of historical institutionalism. Throughout the volume, leading scholars of European integration situate a wide variety of policy issues, from citizenship to competition policy to foreign policy to the stability of the EU as a political system, within the historical institutionalist approach. All of the accounts are united in stressing the role of temporality, in addition to formal and informal institutional contexts, in mediating political struggles and outcomes. Thus, even as there is great diversity in the empirical area each chapter surveys, we believe that readers will find the volume to be a remarkably coherent theoretical assessment of the trajectory of European integration over time.

We are grateful to the many individuals and organizations who contributed to making this project possible. Early memos were presented at a workshop at Princeton University in September 2005. For their incisive comments on the memos and for stimulating discussions, we are very grateful to Christina Davis, Harold James, Robert Keohane, Jan-Werner Mueller, Mark Pollack, Kim Lane Scheppele, and Joshua Tucker. We were fortunate to receive financial and institutional support from the European Union Studies Association and its Executive Director Joe Figliulo, the European Union Program at Princeton, the Princeton Institute on International and Regional Studies, the Law and Public Affairs program at Princeton, and the Liechtenstein Institute on Self-Determination at Princeton. Jayne Bialkowski made the efficient organization of the workshop possible. Our appreciation goes to Elizabeth Grimm at Georgetown University for expert and cheerful assistance with the final manuscript preparation and to Lisa Camner at Princeton University for help with the index. We also would like to thank our children, Idir and Ines Aitsahalia, and Theo and Henry Montgomery, for never letting their mothers' preoccupations with scholarship interfere with their enjoyment of their summer vacations.

Finally, we dedicate this volume to the memory of all who struggled to overcome the ravages of war across the European continent, and found a remarkable path forward to peace and prosperity instead.

Sophie Meunier and Kathleen R. McNamara

CONTENTS

III. Law and Society

IV. The EU as a Sovereign State in World Politics

LIST OF FIGURES

LIST OF TABLES

LIST OF ABBREVIATIONS

ACP	African, Caribbean, and Pacific
ALMPs	Active Labor Market Policies
AMM	Aceh Monitoring Mission
ASEM	Asia–Europe Meeting
AU	African Union
CAP	Common Agricultural Policy
CCP	Common Commercial Policy
CFI	Court of First Instance
CFSP	Common Foreign and Security Policy
DG Comp	Directorate General Competition
DG	Directorate-General
DRC	Democratic Republic of Congo
DTEU	Draft Treaty establishing the European Union
EC	European Community
ECE	East Central European
ECHR	European Convention on Human Rights
ECJ	European Court of Justice
ECS	European Company Statute
ECSC	European Coal and Steel Community
EEC	European Economic Community
EES	European Employment Strategy
EFP	European Foreign Policy
EMS	European Monetary System
EMU	Economic and Monetary Union
ENP	European Neighborhood Policy
EP	European Parliament
EPAs	Economic Partnership Agreements
EPC	European Political Cooperation
ERM	European Exchange Rate Mechanism
ESDP	European Security and Defense Policy
EU	European Union
EUPM	The EU Police Mission
EUPOL-COPPS	Coordination Office for Palestinian Police Support
FCC	German Federal Constitutional Court
FDI	Foreign Direct Investment

FESE	The Federation of European Securities Exchanges
FIPP	Fair Information Practice Principles
FSPG	Financial Services Policy Group
GATT	General Agreement on Tariffs and Trade
GDP	Gross Domestic Product
HA	High Authority
HI	Historical Institutionalist
ICTY	International Criminal Tribunal for the former Yugoslavia
IGC	Intergovernmental Conference
ISAF	International Stabilization Force in Afghanistan
ISD	Investment Services Directive
ITA	International Trade Administration
JHA	Justice and Home Affairs
KEDO	Korean Development Organization
MC	Monetary Committee
MEPs	Members of the European Parliament
MRA	Mutual Recognition Agreement
NATO	North Atlantic Treaty Organization
NTA	New Transatlantic Agenda
OECD	Organization for Economic Cooperation and Development
OMC	Open Method of Coordination
PA	Palestinian Authority
QMV	Qualified Majority Voting
SEA	Single European Act
SEM	Single European Market
TPA	Trade Promotion Authority
UNICE	Union of Industrial and Employers' Confederations of Europe
USTR	US Trade Representative
WTO	World Trade Organization

LIST OF CONTRIBUTORS

KAREN J. ALTER is an Associate Professor of Political Science, Northwestern University.

TIM BÜTHE is an Assistant Professor, Department of Political Science and a Faculty Associate, Center for European Studies, Duke University.

MARY FARRELL is a Senior Research Fellow, CERI, Sciences-Po.

ORFEO FIORETOS is an Assistant Professor of Political Science, Temple University.

ROY H. GINSBERG is a Professor of Government, Skidmore College.

DOROTHEE HEISENBERG is the S. Richard Hirsch Associate Professor of European Studies, Johns Hopkins University School for Advanced International Studies.

AILISH JOHNSON works in the Privy Council Office, Government of Canada, and is a Sessional Lecturer at the Norman Paterson School of International Affairs, Carleton University.

R. DANIEL KELEMEN is an Associate Professor of Political Science, Rutgers University.

WILLEM MAAS is an Assistant Professor of Political Science, Glendon College, York University.

KATHLEEN R. MCNAMARA is an Associate Professor of Government and in the Edmund Walsh School of Foreign Service, Georgetown University.

SOPHIE MEUNIER is a Research Scholar in Public and International Affairs, Woodrow Wilson School, Princeton University.

ANDREW MORAVCSIK is a Professor of Politics and the Director of the European Union Program, Princeton University.

ABRAHAM NEWMAN is an Assistant Professor at the Edmund Walsh School of Foreign Service and a Member of the BMW Center for German and European Studies, Georgetown University.

JOHN PETERSON is a Professor of International Politics, University of Edinburgh.

ELLIOT POSNER is an Assistant Professor of Political Science and International Affairs, George Washington University.

BERTHOLD RITTBERGER is a Junior Professor in Comparative Politics, Kaiserslautern University of Technology.

FRANK SCHIMMELFENNIG is a Professor of European Politics at ETH Zurich.

MICHAEL E. SMITH is a Reader, School of International Relations, University of St Andrews.

DAVID STEINBERG is a Doctoral Candidate in Political Science, Northwestern University.

MILADA ANNA VACHUDOVA is an Assistant Professor, Department of Political Science, University of North Carolina at Chapel Hill.

AMY VERDUN is a Professor of Political Science and Jean Monnet Chair at the University of Victoria, Canada.

ALASDAIR R. YOUNG is a Senior Lecturer in International Politics, University of Glasgow.

1

Making History: European Integration and Institutional Change at Fifty

SOPHIE MEUNIER AND KATHLEEN R. MCNAMARA

Fifty years ago, on March 25, 1957, the leaders of six European states signed the Treaty of Rome, creating the European Economic Community (EEC) and launching the process of European integration. Since then, this innovative institution has evolved to encompass a much broader array of responsibilities than originally planned, its membership has widened to twenty-seven countries through successive enlargements, and its legislation and jurisprudence has come to supersede national law.

The European Union (EU) has now become the most successful example of voluntary, institutionalized political integration in the world. Most of the original goals for which it was created have been reached: ensuring peace in Europe, fostering freedom and democracy on much of the continent, and securing economic prosperity for its inhabitants. Additional countries are still knocking at the door to demand membership, and its model of integration is now being explored by countries around the world. This innovative institutionalized cooperation has also prompted scholars to turn their attention to the political, economic and social dynamics at work in the construction of the EU, creating a field of EU studies alongside the union itself.

The EU's successes and the incremental encroaching of European integration on national sovereignty have occurred, not surprisingly, in tandem with expanding public criticism and political contestation. Accusations of democratic illegitimacy have increased over the past decade, both in political and in intellectual circles, especially as the EU was perceived to be responsible for policy areas, such as immigration and outsourcing, highly sensitive to voters. While many observers viewed the enlargement of the EU to the east as one of its most important successes, fears of further enlargement likewise seemed to stir up concern among EU citizens. This contestation culminated in an intense debate over the EU Constitution throughout the course of 2005. It revealed deep divisions between and within European countries around issues such as economic liberalism, enlargement and immigration, and national sovereignty. It has also prompted scholarly observers of the EU to reflect on and sometimes rethink their assumptions about the nature and causes of integration.

The failure of the Constitution has not provoked, however, the expected cataclysm and collapse of the foundations of the EU, at least not so far. It seems to be business-as-usual in Brussels. From the environment to competition policy, from television broadcasting to food safety, the Commission, the Council, and the Parliament are busy regulating the internal market, while the European Central Bank continues its management of the euro. As always, the EU is engaged in intense trade talks at the bilateral and multilateral levels. And it continues to seek a coherent position on various foreign policy matters, from development aid to peacekeeping.

Despite these important markers of continuity, the crisis of 2005 can arguably be considered a turning point. The EU today may be at a crossroads, not because of the failed referenda, but because of the unresolved tensions in European governance not banished with the Constitution's defeat. Can the EU continue to expand, both geographically and in terms of its political ambitions, without imploding? What are the sources of continuity or change in key policy areas across the Union? These are the questions that now engage EU scholars, and are central to this volume. Our goal in this book is to illuminate the deeper roots of stability or turmoil in the EU, going beyond the latest headlines and current events.

Fortunately, there is a well-established theoretical approach, historical institutionalism, which provides a set of useful tools for such an analysis. Historical institutionalism's emphasis on asking big, real world questions, on highlighting temporal sequences and historical trajectories, and on situating political events in their broader social and institutional contexts is uniquely appropriate for our examination of the EU fifty years after the Treaty of Rome. The chapters that follow situate various key issue areas of European integration historically and draw on the historical institutionalism approach to analyze them. In so doing, our authors paint a portrait of the EU today that reveals a robust, but not invulnerable, set of institutions and practices. The EU may not be in crisis, but it certainly faces a series of key challenges that will determine the shape of its future.

In the rest of this introductory chapter, we outline the historical institutionalist (HI) approach and suggest ways in which its analytic tools, increasingly employed by scholars of the EU in recent years, can shed light on the past and future political and institutional trajectory of the EU. We then take stock of the specific political challenges and questions facing the EU today and in the years to come and identify four areas as crucial: the robustness of EU institutions, European identity, the European economy in a globalized world, and the role of the EU as a world power. We evaluate the potential outcomes of these challenges, informed by the insights of historical institutionalism. Finally, we introduce the chapters in this volume which, while diverse in the range of issues and policies studied, are united in seeking to explain change and continuity in Europe's institutions in historical perspective.

Explaining European Integration through Historical Institutionalism

The definitive answers to the question of how the EU will cope with its current set of political, economic, and social challenges lie, of course, in the future. But suggestions of what might lay ahead can be found in the past, in the trajectories already followed by European integration and in the paths not taken. In order to understand how the EU came to face such challenges and whether they may be overcome in the future, we have chosen to step back and place our analysis of European integration in historical and theoretical perspective, drawing on the insights offered by historical institutionalism. In so doing, our broader scholarly aim is to refocus EU theoretical scholarship on wider debates about the nature of the integration process.

Academic study of the EU, like any other area of inquiry, has proceeded in recognizable waves. The first wave of theorizing about the EU focused largely on the relative weights of neofunctionalism and intergovernmentalism in explaining the path of integration (Hass 1958; Lindberg 1963; Hoffmann 1966; Taylor 1983; Sandholtz and Zysman 1989; Moravcsik 1993). More recently, a new wave of theorizing has sought to connect EU processes and outcomes to broader patterns of political life and larger theoretical traditions. To name but a few, studies drawing from the theoretical assumptions of rational choice institutionalism can be placed in this wave (Scharpf 1985; Tsebelis 1994; Mattli 1999; Egan 2001*a*; Pollack 2003*a*), as can works from the perspective of comparative federalism (Nicolaïdis and Howse 2001; Kelemen 2004), as well as those drawing on constructivist theory (Christiansen, Jørgensen, and Wiener 2001; McNamara 2001; Parsons 2003; Risse 2003*a*; Schimmelfennig 2003*a*; Checkel 2005*a*). In all these theoretical approaches, the EU is viewed as a political entity whose exact form may be unique, but whose underlying political processes reproduce patterns of policymaking and contestation that readily exist at all levels of governance.

This volume provides the opportunity to engage productively in a new, unified set of theoretical debates, pulling from disciplines outside EU studies, while building on the empirical advances the field of European integration studies has made. Historical institutionalism represents a rich and productive vein of such theorizing, as Paul Pierson's groundbreaking article first argued (Pierson 1996) and as the fertile contributions of many scholars of the EU have made clear (Pollack 1996; Aspinwall and Schneider 2000; Dowding 2000; Alter 2001; Lindner and Rittberger 2003; Jupille 2004; Pollack 2004). Below, we outline the basic foundations of historical institutionalism before assessing how it contributes to understanding the current state of the EU.

Historical Institutionalism

Our definition of historical institutionalism is simple and echoes Steinmo and Thelen's: 'an attempt to illuminate how political struggles are mediated by the institutional setting in which they take place' (Steinmo, Thelen, and Longstreth 1992). In other words, institutions affect policy outcomes, rather than simply reflecting the distribution of political power and preferences. They can have an independent and/or intervening effect on the policy paths chosen. Institutions in our definition comprise both formal organizations (such as the Council and the Commission) and informal shared rules and social institutions (such as the practice of consensus and the informal veto right). Once in place, these institutions can take on a life of their own and contribute to determining and explaining subsequent developments in European integration.

The wide range of scholarship that constitutes historical institutionalism is diverse, emphasizing at times material and in other instances ideational factors, and is found across fields of comparative politics, international relations, American politics, economic history, and sociology. However, there are clear commonalities across this scholarship, shared theoretical and empirical commitments that create a coherent approach. Steinmo and Thelen originally identified historical contingency and attention to path dependency as key shared features of this scholarship. Pierson and Theda Skocpol subsequently emphasized three key elements binding HI studies: big real world puzzles, temporality, and context (2002). Together, these three features create a set of strategies for asking and answering the central question of how, once established, institutions constrain and influence over time the behavior of political actors—making this approach clearly distinct from other approaches in political science, most notably behavioralist or rational choice modeling.

First, as Pierson and Skocpol note, the substantive agendas of HI scholars engage squarely with big, real world questions of interest far beyond the academy. Questions like 'how do stable democracies develop?' or 'when do ethnic identities become important in politics?' have an immediacy and clearly constitute real world puzzles not driven by methodological or narrow theoretical concerns. Likewise, our authors ask fundamental questions about the nature of the EU, its past and future. To name but a few, Daniel Kelemen probes the very sustainability of the EU as a system of governance, while Milada Vachudova asks why a remarkably large number of enlargement countries are on track to join the EU. Several contributors investigate the fundamental shifts in economic governance that have occurred in the course of European integration, such as Tim Büthe who traces the surprising movement of power to the European Commission from national authorities in the regulation of European firms' activities and Orfeo Fioretos who examines the development of the European Company Statute (ECS). In keeping with the HI tradition, our authors trace developments in a host of policy arenas with great importance to the citizens of Europe and, as Roy Ginsberg and Michael Smith remind us in examining the EU as a foreign policy actor, increasingly to the rest of the world.

A second key commonality of HI works is that they have a distinctive temporal dimension: they take time seriously. Historical processes are central to HI studies, as the particular sequencing of events is posited to be causally consequential, and transformation over time is often an essential variable in explaining substantive outcomes (Büthe 2002; Pierson 2004). Early HI studies established the general idea of path dependence, noting that what happens at an earlier time is likely importantly to shape and sometimes definitively constrain what happens in the next time period.[1] Over time, studies have addressed with increasing precision how time and path dependence matter. Work by Pierson and others on the EU detailed the many cases of unintended outcomes in institutional development, such as in the case of EU gender equality law, originally initiated for largely symbolic reasons but subsequently used strategically by women's groups to achieve concrete policy goals at the EU level that were previously unattainable within the domestic sphere (Pierson 1996; Cichowski 2002). These empirical findings contrast with the rational efficiency view of institutions as coordinating mechanisms that simply solve functional problems, and instead put forward a more contingent view of institutions and their effects. In this contingent view, institutions emerge from and are embedded in concrete historical time (Thelen 1999: 382). In this temporal setting, institutions may also shape identities, in contrast to the rational choice view that actors only adjust strategically to a changed environment. For HIs, institutions have the potential to reverberate back on actors, changing their identities and, ultimately, preferences, instead of just changing their strategies as might be the case from a rationalist viewpoint. This potential is important for thinking through the evolution of European identity as well as the entire spectrum of EU actor preferences over time.

A further consequence of temporality important in this tradition comes from Douglass North and others (North 1990). Many scholars have found that institutions, once constructed, over time may have dynamics of increasing returns that make them quite 'sticky' and resistant to change. These reinforcing tendencies occur as 'adjacent institutions and groups become connected to the institution and dependent on it for their own functioning' and those invested politically,

---

[1] See Thelen (1999) for good discussion of the limits of the idea of path dependency. She cautions against the tendency of some work to be too apolitical, reminding us that choices at the time of creation are rarely random, as they were in the QWERTY keyboard story, but rather the result of political contestation and power.

economically, and socially in the institution have strong interests in its maintenance (Ikenberry 2001: 69–70). Others have pointed to sources for change despite
this potential reinforcing dynamic, highlighting the role of ideational innovations
(Steinmo, Thelen, and Longstreth 1992) or external shocks or displacing events
such as war (Ikenberry 2001). In addition, others have focused on the potential
role for 'critical junctures' decisively to determine the path of policymaking
(Katznelson 1997). These various elements of temporality are specified more
closely in Pierson's *Politics in Time*, which outlines the mechanisms that shape the
trajectory of institutional change, drawing out the logics behind path dependence
(Pierson 2004).

This *State of the EU* volume offers ample examples of the benefits of such
emphasis on temporality. The central question asked by the contributors is the
following: Did European integration create path dependencies and lock in commitments over time? Chapters situate institutional development in concrete temporal terms, and demonstrate how sequencing and historical situations impact
outcomes, giving a range of answers to this overall question. For example, Elliot
Posner focuses on the role of sequencing in demonstrating how small incremental
changes may accumulate over time in ways that set up opportunities for policy
entrepreneurs to promote change when exogenous shocks occur, in his example,
in the area of financial reform. Orfeo Fioretos traces the development of the ECS,
which allows some companies to operate under one set of EU rules—the first and
only truly transnational corporate legal status in the world. But the Statute is also
notable for having languished the longest of any of the EU's legislative proposals,
and for taking nearly four decades before it was adopted. Fioretos's explanation
of the law's eventual creation as a complex hybrid of EU rules that preserved key
national prerogatives hinges decisively on both historical contingency and on historical variations in national economic institutions. Similarly, Berthold Rittberger
and Frank Schimmelfennig find path dependency, or what they call 'internal
coherence', in two constitutionalization processes that have taken place in the EU
over the years: the development of a representative parliamentary institution and
the codification of fundamental rights at the EU level. By contrast, the chapter by
Karen Alter and David Steinberg finds that there were little path dependencies in
the case of the European Coal and Steel Community (ECSC), ironically the policy
area which gave rise to the neofunctionalist literature on European integration.

A third feature of historical institutionalism is the role that 'contexts and configurations' play in producing outcomes (Pierson and Skocpol 2002). Obviously,
institutions themselves are central to these studies, but it is a particular type of
institutional approach that distinguishes this scholarship from the other forms
of institutionalist study, such as rational choice institutionalism and sociological
institutionalism (Hall and Taylor 1996). The HI studies tend to analyze macro
processes and look at the combined effects of institutions. As in Polanyi's well-
known argument, policy arrangements cannot be understood in isolation from the

broader political and social institutions in which they are embedded. Institutions overlap and bump up against each other in ways that can be the source of tension or provoke change, visibly impacting outcomes and moving institutions in decisively different directions. This focus has commonalities with neofunctionalism, the first wave theory pioneered by Ernst Haas and still influential today in studying European integration (Haas 1958). Historical institutionalism tries to spell out clearly the mechanisms by which such interactions produce outcomes, for example by highlighting how distributional effects create reinforcing tendencies once institutions are set up as interest groups form and act. This institutional complexity is illustrated in every chapter that follows, as the authors do not shy from analyzing their particular realm, be it monetary union as Amy Verdun discusses, or in Ailish Johnson's assessment of social policy. A specific form of institutional embeddedness is explored in Abraham Newman's chapter on data privacy policy, namely feedback effects. Here, national regulatory agencies, the product of administrative feedback loops, have created European networks that have become remarkably decisive coalitions shaping the content and timing of the EU's data privacy laws.

The attention to context carries with it some theoretical pitfalls that need to be carefully attended to, however, by scholars working in this tradition. Capturing the empirical complexity creates a rich account, but it can result in underspecification of the key causal mechanisms at work in the institutional context. Attention to the precise mechanisms of both temporality and institutional effects is critical to fruitful research on European integration. In addition, the emphasis on institutional context should not crowd out attention to agency, that is, the role of particular political actors in shaping outcomes. Historical institutionalism, like any predominantly structural theory, can at times lack such an account of agency. Likewise, theorizing and predicting change can be challenging to theories that focus squarely on institutions, but it need not be. For HI, clues in the tendency toward change might be found in tensions in the space where institutions overlap, or in the competing cultures or norms that are embedded in different institutions but come newly into contact over new emerging issues. Finally, HI theorizing at the national level can provide content for understanding preferences of national actors, which when projected onto the EU level, open up avenues for understanding the sources of change in the path of integration. It is the potential for such change that we take up in the next section.

Central Political Challenges Facing the EU Today

Looking back at the fifty years since the Treaty of Rome, and twenty years since the Single European Act (SEA), one is tempted to take the progress of European integration for granted, as somehow inevitable. As historical institutionalism's emphasis on contingency and historic specificity suggests, taking such a teleological view of the EU would be a mistake. At many junctures over the past decades, the challenges facing the European Community (EC) and then the EU could have been insurmountable: the 'empty chair' policy, the entry of Great Britain, the end of the cold war, the referenda on the Maastricht Treaty, the introduction of the euro, and the enlargement to ten new countries at once. Yet a closer look at this historical evolution suggests, in keeping with the historical institutionalism approach, that the progress of integration was in fact the result of high stakes leadership, hard-won battles, and political creativity, not inevitability.

Today the EU is once again confronted with ubiquitous challenges, from sluggish economic growth in most European countries and competition from Asia to the integration of European Muslims both within the current borders of the EU and in Turkey. This time, some analysts say, the challenges truly are insurmountable. In a way, the EU might be the victim of its own success: because the hardest political tasks are often left for last, the most controversial issues are coming up now as the EU becomes a mature polity. Of these many challenges facing the EU today, we highlight four that have the potential for significantly shaping European integration into the future. Here, our discussion raises a series of questions for readers to consider as they examine key policy areas in the following chapters. We also point to how the historical institutionalism approach delineated above might help in shedding light on the future resolution (or not) of these challenges. Historical institutionalism is well equipped to tell us where to look to answer these questions, and what sort of factors come into play in shaping the future of European integration.

1. **Robustness of EU institutions**: One of the most persistent questions facing the EU almost since its inception is whether its institutions are up to the task of supporting 'an ever closer union' as proscribed in the preamble of the Treaty of Rome. The governance architecture of the EU has grown slowly over time, incrementally evolving in ways that, to put it mildly, do not always conform to the dictates of functional efficiency. From the development of highly complex and administratively cumbersome agricultural subsidies to convoluted methods of weighted voting and a patchwork of allowable vetos, the EU institutions clearly are the product of hard-won political bargains embedded within specific institutional settings. Yet somehow the EU's leaders have continued to move forward with integration along a multitude of policy dimensions, and its institutions have proved dynamic at adjusting both to new tasks and to changing political realities.

The most recent round of institutional contestation has been arguably different, however, in its visibility and in the political stakes involved. In the late 1990s, many analysts and politicians argued that the EU institutions, set up to govern over six states originally and last amended by the Amsterdam Treaty in 1997, were not going to be able to withstand the addition of ten new members in 2004. An EU of twenty-five members seemed certain to strain the institutional machinery, and some of the central features of the EU institutional system, such as the rotating presidency and the informal veto right, were simply not feasible given the sheer number of countries involved. The general consensus was that the EU institutions simply had to be reformed, preferably before the big eastward enlargement. However, the Nice negotiations, which took place in 2000, proved both tedious and controversial, resulting in a treaty with limited ambitions.

Given all the outstanding issues left unresolved in the Nice Treaty, the member states agreed to change methods and convene a Convention on the Future of Europe to address the impasse over institutional reform. Among the unresolved issues to be addressed in the Convention were the division of labor between the member states and the EU, the role of national parliaments, the simplification and transparency of the EU policymaking process, the rotating presidency, the status of the Charter of Fundamental Rights, and the external representation of the EU. An additional rationale for this move from intergovernmental bargaining was to bolster the democratic character of the EU through open deliberation during the Convention and then popular ratification of the Convention's results, either through parliamentary procedures or through referenda.

The Constitution that emerged out of the Convention was designed more to fix the faults of the European institutional architecture than to give a new impetus to European integration, even if the declared ambitions seemed more far reaching. The ratification of the Constitution was to occur after the EU enlarged to ten new member states rather than beforehand, as adopting institutional reforms after the onset of enlargement seemed more prudent than jeopardizing the European project by trying to force premature revisions.

The rejection of the Constitution in the May 2005 French and Dutch referenda led to immediate doomsday predictions that the EU would suffer a massive institutional crisis from which it could not recover. Indeed, the institutions still needed to be fixed, and the defeat of the Constitution seemed to mean a defeat of institutional reform. And second, the referendum campaigns made highly visible the issue of democratic legitimacy in the EU. Political elites could not, at least in the short term, push the reforms through anyway over popular rejection, as they had in the past. Nevertheless, these dire predictions have failed to materialize as the EU's institutions continue to govern despite its twenty-seven members.

Two central sets of questions remain unanswered for the future. First, is the EU indeed still facing a crisis of institutions given the recent enlargement? Are the failed referenda a threat to the very existence of the EU, now entering an extended period of drift? On the contrary, can the rejection of the Constitution be turned into a political opportunity? Have predictions of the impending demise of the EU been exaggerated? In short, is the current institutional structure a stable equilibrium?

A second set of questions have to do with the democratic legitimacy of the EU. Empirical studies have demonstrated that people are more likely to accept and follow laws if they believe the overall process of decision-making is fair. Is the EU politically and democratically legitimate? Is it about to implode or to explode as a result of popular disapproval in at least two member states? Can European integration proceed, as it has in the past, as an elite-driven process with tacit popular support (or disinterest) in spite of the recent referenda? Or, on the contrary, should the EU invent a new form of democracy beyond the nation-state? These foundational questions continue to be debated even as the day to day activities of the EU continue.

Here, the general orientation of historical institutionalism would direct us to look at the fit between the institutions and the underlying preferences of key political actors. Have the EU institutions outlived their usefulness for the most powerful states? Are there certain sunk costs built up over time that would make these institutions sticky, even if the underlying preferences might be diverging? What about the normative ideas and values inherent in the existing institutions—do they fit the political culture and social institutional setting of contemporary Europe? It seems that these questions can be generally answered in the positive: the EU, not the least of which its single market and various regulatory regimes, clearly continues to serve the interests of all of its members, although differentially and incompletely. Moravcsik (2005*a* and this volume) has made a convincing case for the continued functionality of its institutional framework, even despite what many would argue is a new level of public demand for democratic accountability. While clearly a union of twenty-seven presents more complexity in governance, it is far from clear that it tips the balance toward an implosion absent comprehensive reform. We should look to see incremental institutional change agreed to and acted on over the next years, as the institutions of the EU evolve instead of being radically transformed.

2. **The elusive European identity**: A second, related foundational issue concerns the question of European identity. Can European integration continue to proceed even in the absence of a clear European identity? Can the recent evolution of the EU, in particular enlargement and economic liberalization, threaten European identity so much that it will eventually halt the process of European integration?

Both political theory and practical experience suggest that governance cannot be sustained without some common political identity among the governed, which helps to construct legitimate political authority and undergird the exercise of power. A European identity need not be monolithic, unproblematic or completely consolidated (Risse 2003*a*), but some sense of shared community binding the citizens of Europe is likely to make the entire institutional apparatus of the EU work better. Acceptance of policies that may not be in the direct interest of particular societal actors is more likely if there is some feeling of overall political community. Actors sharing some identity are likely to have an increased sense of diffuse reciprocity (i.e. a belief that in the long run they will benefit even if they do not win on a particular issue). A European identity that legitimizes the legal- and regulatory-based governance structures of the EU is surely an important part of a stable EU system.

European institutions and European identity are linked together by a feedback loop. In order to be legitimate, the EU institutions should embody the peculiarities of European political identity: a dose of federalism, centralization, parliamentarism, and so forth. However EU institutions not only reflect but also fashion European identity. In contributing to the erosion of the main prerogatives of the nation-state, they socialize European citizens in a new way and thereby create a new European identity (Checkel 2005*a*).

The question of European identity has critical practical implications for the domestic governance of increasingly heterogeneous populations. Across the EU, tensions and violence have flared over the treatment of racial and religious groups, as most dramatically seen in France and the Netherlands. Whether the EU offers a way to solve some of these tensions, as may be the case with certain regional political actors such as the Scots and the Basques, is unclear.

The question of European identity also comes into play in the issue of enlargement. The debates over the Constitution in several countries exposed the discontent with the recent pace of the EU's eastbound expansion (Mayhew 1998; Vachudova 2005). Between 1973 and 1995, such expansion had taken place gradually, seemingly leaving enough time in between each enlargement for the new entrants to be absorbed and assimilated into the EU culture. The 2004 enlargement was perceived as different, with so many countries coming in all at once, raising doubts about whether they would not transform the culture of the EU instead of absorbing the culture of the EU (Cameron 2003). This enlargement, and future enlargements, also raises the central question of where the ultimate borders of Europe lie. Does changing the geographical center of Europe with each successive eastward enlargement also change the identity of the EU? Is there a 'natural' border beyond which one country cannot be considered for membership? Does one even have to be on the European continent in order to become a member of the EU?

These questions obviously lead to the difficult debates surrounding the entry of Turkey into the union. In addition to the potential disruptions to the functioning of the EU institutions caused by the sheer number of Turkish citizens, the question of Turkey's adhesion to the EU directly intersects with the issue of how religion, most notably Islam, factors into European identity. During the deliberations of the Convention, the question of the EU's Christian character and heritage was widely debated. The issue of the place of Islam in contemporary European politics has been particularly thorny in recent years, especially in light of the Danish cartoons controversy.

Over the next few years, Europeans will have to decide between two distinct definitions of Europe's identity (Berman 2006). Should European identity be determined on the basis of history, culture, and heritage? One of the roles of the EU should therefore be to protect this identity from outside threats, whether coming from globalization or from immigrants with different religions. This backward and inward-looking definition assumes a lot of commonality between Sweden and Greece, between Ireland and Bulgaria. In this case, on the basis that it does not share this common cultural heritage, Turkey should not be granted membership, because it would threaten Europe's identity and unity. Alternatively, should European identity be determined by shared values and goals? In this case, Turkey should be embraced as a member of the EU if it can demonstrate that it shares its goals. In any case, the question of European identity is one that will not be easily solved but instead has the potential for splitting further European publics about the future of the EU.

Scholars of European politics have begun to piece together a portrait of increasing European political identity, drawing on polling data and case study work (Hooghe 2003; Hermann, Risse, and Brewer 2004; Morgan 2005). It is clear that the EU does exercise its authority with substantial legitimacy, but that does not keep scholars and citizens alike from pressing the important issue of whether the EU's governance reach outstrips its collective democratic legitimacy. Much of this work is informed by social constructivism theory, but historical institutionalism also has insights that would be useful to draw out. Questions about the ways in which ideas and meanings get embedded into institutions, and how this institutionalization changes with social interactions over time, are all part of the broader HI agenda. Here, the key is to infuse the study of institutions with a more social understanding of how shared meanings structure action, and how actors' experiences with the political institutions of the EU change those institutions.

3. **A European economic malaise?** A continual challenge for the EU is the management of the European economy, both in terms of concrete policies and in terms of the political tensions that arise as markets for goods, capital, and labor are knitted more tightly. Three related areas in particular are of concern: how to deal with slow growth and unemployment in certain parts of the EU; public fears of low cost labor from other EU countries displacing national workers; and the more diffuse question of how to manage the process of globalization.

First, many observers inside and outside Europe focus on persistently low levels of economic growth and a failure to create enough employment as markers of poor economic performance, particularly relative to the USA. The sluggish growth and high unemployment in the past five years, especially in old member states, have led to fears about European competitiveness in the future, and in turn about the preservation of the European social model. These fears prompted the adoption in

2000 of the 'Lisbon strategy' by the EU, with the objective of making Europe the world's most dynamic and competitive knowledge-based economy by 2010. It will clearly be a challenge for Europe to meet these self-imposed, wishful-thinking objectives.

However, others note that we should be very cautious in assessing European economic welfare on the basis of only a few macroeconomic indicators, such as economic growth and employment. Surveys of citizen's health and well-being may provide a more positive view of Europe than the USA. Many analysts argue that the EU's productivity, an indicator some believe is crucial to the health of any economy, is actually quite high. Kenneth Rogoff (2004) even argues that the EU may in fact be the rising economic power of the next few decades:

... the notion that European firms and workers are much less productive than those in the United States is simply uninformed. The main reason why Europe's output per capita stands at only seventy per cent of U.S. levels is that Europeans work less than Americans—a lot less. Europeans work fewer hours per week, take longer vacations, and retire earlier. When it comes to leisure, it is the Americans, Japanese, and even the Chinese who have plenty of catching up to do.

In addition, there remains significant variation in economic performance across the EU members, as well as heterogeneity in the institutional configurations and policy models that authorities follow in each EU nation. This variation within Europe, as well as the strong overall quality of life and substantial economic welfare and income equality experienced by many EU citizens, should make us wary about general pronouncements about a widespread European economic malaise.

Nonetheless, it is certainly the case that perceptions of economic insecurity, particularly fears of cheap labor from new EU member states, have at times been highly salient in national politics across the EU. The example of the 'Polish plumber' undercutting French workers was a cornerstone in the 'No' camp during the French constitutional referendum campaign in 2005. These fears have also been invoked in arguments against Turkey's entry into the EU. The image of rampant 'insourcing' from cheaper labor parts of the enlarged EU (not outsourcing to the developing world) has become a powerful frame for political contestation, whatever merits of arguments about the overall benefits from labor integration for aggregate European welfare.

Some national governments have joined this debate by blaming the EU for its inability to protect their national economies against the vagaries of globalization. In particular, the recent acceleration of cross-border mergers and acquisitions activity has led many countries to recourse to 'economic patriotism', a term coined by the French government of Dominique de Villepin, to protect their national champions from falling into foreign hands. Does it mean that national governments will increasingly take matters into their own hands in order to manage globalization?

These EU debates are in many ways scaled down versions of similar debates occurring across the globe over the merits and dangers of globalization more broadly. Some groups view market integration as beneficial to their economic circumstances as their skills, economic resources, or price competitiveness create the chance to reap profits from further market integration. Others see a direct threat to their livelihoods as a local factory closes and moves elsewhere within the EU, such that market integration is viewed not as beneficial but rather as imposing serious costs.

The challenges for the EU in navigating these policy debates are manifold. One of them is how to avoid being blamed for policies and outcomes over which it has little or no control. While the EU has some very powerful economic policy tools at its disposal, notably monetary policy and regulatory capacity, other macro- and microeconomic policy realms remain at the national level. The ECB has been accused, with good reason, of taking too tight a monetary stance, slowing growth in key economies in Europe. But most seasoned observers agree that lower interest rates cannot cure all of European unemployment alone, without ongoing national sectoral reforms. The euro's rise against the dollar has been blamed in some quarters for export difficulties, but it is hard to find conclusive statistical proof that the level of the euro is determining the fate of Europe's exports. In addition, fiscal policy remains at the national level, removing a key tool for shaping the economy from the EU's arsenal. All of these examples point toward the political bind of the EU in areas where it has visibility without responsibility. In such instances it may end up being a target for voter discontent over economic circumstances while lacking a full complement of economic policy tools to deal with the challenges of managing the political economy of Europe.

Whether the effects of globalization are positive or negative is the subject of heated debate among academics and political activists worldwide. The debate is particularly virulent in Europe, where the effects of globalization are often hard to disentangle from the effects of Europeanization. On the one hand, Europeanization may appear as just one regional variant of globalization. Most of the effects traditionally associated with globalization have been experienced by European countries in the wake of the implementation of the single market program since the late 1980s. Europeanization can even be conceived as a Trojan Horse of globalization into the heart of Europe. On the other hand, Europe can also be considered as a tool to manage globalization and a shield against its worst effects—when it is not in itself a tool to create and export further globalization. Is Europeanization a facilitator of globalization, or instead a buffer against its worst effects? Did European integration affect the preferences of European citizens toward globalization? More generally, do regional organizations influence the magnitude and the timing of globalization?

Scholars grappling with the political economy of Europe have long used the broader HI approach, particularly the varieties of capitalism literature (Hall and Soskice 2001), to delve into these questions of how national political economies fare in a global market. The clear focus of historical institutionalism on temporality and institutional legacies will help us to ask and answer some of the following questions related to the European economic malaise: Why has the EU not been successful in achieving the sort of reforms that would help spur greater economic dynamism? Is there an optimal socioeconomic model which should be implemented throughout Europe? If there is, why do not states follow strategies to implement it in order to reap the benefits, for instance by transferring economic policymaking and implementation to the supranational authorities? Are national rigidities coming from institutional historical legacies, such as French farmers holding out multilateral trade talks that would benefit French exporters, a central cause of the current economic malaise in Europe? The tools of historical institutionalism should prove fruitful in understanding the sources of economic change in Europe, as well as its constraints.

4. **The EU as a great power?** A final challenge for the EU in the future is the external face it presents to the rest of the world. Today it does not seem far-fetched to ask whether the EU is on its way to becoming a great power, and to probe the very nature of that power and its exercise. Can, and should, the EU aspire to becoming a great power? If it does, what will be its characteristic features? In particular, will it stand along with, or in the way of the USA?

The international system has long been built on the principle, if not always the practice, of sovereign nation-states. The EU's very DNA is a challenge to this mode of international politics. Some have argued that, as a result, the EU can never be a superpower in the traditional sense: it lacks a military force and a common security doctrine, and its current institutions are a cause of its fundamental weakness on the international scene (Kagan 2003).

This traditional view of the EU as a foreign policy dwarf must be tempered for two reasons. First, the key to the EU's influence in the world may precisely lie in its distinctive nonmilitary and noncoercive character—in particular the spreading of its norms and values (Manners 2002; Leonard 2005; Nicolaïdis 2005; K. Smith 2004; Meunier and Nicolaïdis 2006). The EU has already had tremendous influence on many of its neighboring states, most often through the lure of membership, and as such has exercised considerable power on the international scene (Jacoby 2004; Kelley 2004; Vachudova 2005; Grabbe 2006; Vachudova 2006). It also exercises power through example, promoting regional integration arrangements mirrored on its image, as well as through normative suasion.

Second, the capacities of the EU as a foreign policy power have vastly increased in recent years, even though it is a development that has failed to capture the headlines (Whitman 1998; Ginsberg 2001; Winn and Lord 2001; Smith 2004; Elgström and Smith 2006; Ginsberg 2007). As Ginsberg and Smith detail in this volume, the EU's foreign policy initiatives are now directed toward every region of the globe, using an ever-expanding array of diplomatic, economic, and even military tools. It has deployed military and police forces and crisis management personnel to sixteen conflicts, has taken over from NATO in providing security in Bosnia-Hercegovina. It also has a distinct security strategy that provides a guiding framework for its widening foreign policy activity.

Nonetheless, it appears that the EU faces severe handicaps on the road to international power. Divergences between the foreign policy objectives of the various member states make it hard to signal its resolve to the outside world (Ginsberg 2001; Smith 2004). Enlargement does not help in this respect—the greater the number of member states, the greater the wealth of different historical relationships and entanglements with particular countries, and therefore the harder it becomes to find a common, coherent position. For the moment, however, no foreign policy dispute can be blamed on enlargement, since the new entrants fall on either side of the preexisting fault lines (Moravcsik and Vachudova 2003).

Does this new external power of the EU, in turn, reflect on its own institutional and political nature? What does this imply for the EU as a form of political organization? Legally, the EU does have a coherent sovereign status and behaves as a single actor in certain international fora, such as trade and environmental negotiations (Meunier 2005). However its external role as a cohesive entity, which is neither a nation-state nor an international organization, is less clear in areas where it does not enjoy a quasi-federal status. In order to exert power in these areas, the EU needs political will and legitimacy in addition to force and resources. Yet these are hindered by the deep tensions between a number of alternative norms and priorities to which the EU commits simultaneously—such as regionalism and multilateralism, Western hegemony and alternative power, trade liberalization and domestic preferences (Meunier and Nicolaïdis 2006). Since legitimacy is the central pillar of normative power, the EU needs to address what many in the rest of the world perceive as unsustainable contradictions before it can really aspire to becoming a world power.

If we accept the EU as a legitimate sovereign political actor on the world's stage, the next set of questions concerns the relative power and purpose of the EU. In what ways might we expect it to project power internationally, and how might this transform over time? Does the EU even need to build a common defense and security policy? Can it become an international power through other means, such as trade, finance, aid, peacekeeping, and democracy promotion? If the EU does turn into an unorthodox foreign policy power, can it become a counterweight to the USA? Finally, can the EU survive over time even if it does not turn into a great power?

Adopting a HI approach, with its focus both on time sequencing and on institutional inertia, helps us study the nature of the EU as a world actor. A central question is how the past has defined the role of the EU in the world—as a moral rather than a military power. Is the weight of that past too heavy to imagine the EU moving beyond a normative power and becoming instead an international power in the traditional sense? Another question is whether the current institutions enable the EU to exert a foreign policy role in the world, and whether such a role could be eventually achieved even in the absence of approval by the member states. Is there some spillover at play, whereby the EU would develop its own foreign policy, whether the member states want it? Finally, historical institutionalism may help us address the issue of the stickiness of national identities and how this is bound to affect the development of the EU's role in the world.

European Integration and Institutional Change in Historical Perspective

In the chapters that follow, readers find the unifying theme of our inquiry to be how institutions structure change over time. Empirically, the emphasis on historical institutionalism offers a unique opportunity for authors to use the benefit of hindsight to examine the predictions that were made about the future of Europe at various points in time, explain the path that European integration eventually followed, and understand whether and why predictions diverged from reality. As per the purpose of the *State of the European Union* book series, we hope that each chapter will bring readers up-to-date in the issue area under study, while at the same time generating a new set of predictions about Europe's future using tools from the HI approach.

We also asked our authors to answer a unifying set of questions in their policy arenas. To what degree, if any, are policy outcomes the result of path dependence? If path dependence is indeed present, what are the specific transmission mechanisms? What do we know about the preference formation of policymakers and how might we account for variations in preferences? Did institutional developments create new political actors capable of reinforcing and consolidating a certain policy path? Can we spell out the specific ways that previous institutional arrangements mattered in constraining and enabling future decisions? Were there unintended consequences of the policy decisions? How did the time horizon of actors affect their calculations? Are exogenous shocks essential in explaining policy outcomes? Finally, in what scenarios could we imagine things unraveling, instead of incrementally deepening?

Our volume has four sections that seek to give the reader a sophisticated overview of the key political arenas in which these processes are unfolding in the EU today. The first section orients the reader to the big debates over the founding and future of the EU itself as a governance system. The central question addressed by both Andrew Moravcsik and Daniel Kelemen is whether the EU is currently in a state of institutional crisis. While many analysts have surmised that the EU is on the verge of collapse after the failed referenda and the challenges posed by enlargement and immigration, both authors offer a dissenting view. Moravcsik argues that the EU has reached a stable constitutional settlement that reflects the most validated understandings we have about how institutions work, and his chapter offers a detailed empirical description of the contours of that settlement. Kelemen draws on the comparative federalism literature to show that the federal-like safeguards against institutional implosion are strengthening and that the most threatening forms of institutional crisis are highly implausible. Kelemen concludes that rumors of the EU's impending collapse are greatly exaggerated and that the most striking aspect of the EU, from the long-term perspective, is precisely how devoid of institutional crisis it has been. Dorothee Heisenberg's contribution joins the debate about the resilience of the EU's institutional mechanisms. She argues that the predicted legislative breakdown caused by the increasing number of member states has not happened thanks to the practice of consensus decision-making in the Council of Ministers. Karen Alter and David Steinberg revisit the institutional evolution of the ECSC, the case par excellence of neofunctionalism at play. In finding that practice rarely coincided with theory and that the ECSC was merely a paper tiger, they identify a role performed by the ECSC institutions that is rarely highlighted in conventional accounts. The final contribution to this overview of the big contemporary debates on European institutions is provided by Milada Vachudova's chapter on the EU's eastward enlargement, which examines the impact of enlargement's scale on the process of European integration. She argues that its two main but unintended consequences have been the successful promotion of democracy coupled with an erosion in the foundations of the support for European integration.

The second section on the politics of markets provides a comprehensive and cutting-edge analysis of the key issues in European political economy. Abraham Newman turns to an issue on the minds of many individuals, data privacy, and the EU's surprising success in creating a new regime more stringent and more widely emulated than that of the USA. He looks at the role of administrative feedbacks in producing a strong Commission effort in this area, essential to policy development. Elliot Posner explores the critical area of financial integration, outlining the relationship between slow moving, internal EU developments—seemingly unremarkable Commission actions, in particular—and distinct shocks such as the introduction of the euro, in combining to produce institutional innovation and market integration. Orfeo Fioretos looks at the startling innovation of a European level corporate governance law, establishing a new legal entity of the firm at the EU level, the only truly *multinational* firms in the world. Tim Büthe also explores a surprisingly innovative area of political integration: competition policy. Whereas historically states have jealously guarded their ability to shape their national economies through industrial policies, the EU has been remarkably successful at creating and expanding a robust set of institutions to govern competition policy. Büthe argues that an updated version of neofunctionalist theory, stressing the sometimes unintended effects of the pursuit of self-interest over time, can make sense of this outcome. Finally, Amy Verdun offers an overview of the very long and often winding path to EMU, exploring how early plans to have a true economic union as well as a single currency fell by the wayside, producing what many see as a problematically asymmetrical EMU with monetary but no fiscal union. In all the stories told by our authors in this section about the continuing construction of the EU's market, the institutional setting and the accrual of actions, and inaction, over time decisively shape the outcomes we see today.

The third section of the volume explores the legal and social order progressively taking shape in Europe. Berthold Rittberger and Frank Schimmelfennig analyze two processes of constitutionalization in the EU, the development of representative parliamentary institutions and the codification of fundamental rights at the EU level. They argue that such constitutionalization has occurred through a process of 'normative spillover', which arises when supranational integration undermines traditional liberal-democratic norms, leads to a perceived legitimacy deficit, and then corrects the situation through the adoption of new norms. Willem Maas examines the critical historical junctures in the development of a European citizenship. His chapter details the surprising evolution toward common European rights at the EU level and teases out some of the complications of the interaction between 'thick' national rights and identities and the emergent European institutions. He draws attention to the role of political bargains across member states in creating these rights, and cautions us not to view them as inevitable or invulnerable. Ailish Johnson studies social policy in the EU and explains why a strong backlash about the weakness of the EU's role in social policy, evident in the referenda about the European constitution, came at a time when EU governance of social policy had never been greater. Extrapolating from her examination of historical junctures critical to the development of EU social policy, she expects enlargement to make it harder for an activist Commission to build coalitions supporting social legislation at a high standard.

The last group of contributions controversially explores whether the EU is indeed becoming a sovereign state in world politics. Roy Ginsberg and Michael Smith argue that the EU has surprised many by moving forward with foreign policy cooperation, quietly and in spite of the odds, in large part because of institutional dynamics. They marshal an impressive array of empirical data to demonstrate the increasing weight of EU foreign policy in the world, outlining the various civilian and military management tasks currently underway by the EU. John Peterson and Alasdair Young turn to the EU as a unitary economic actor on the world stage, studying the deep economic ties between Europe and the USA. They contend that there is a profound and potentially destabilizing mismatch between the quality and quantity of trade and investment interdependence across the Atlantic and the policy institutions currently governing those relations. This chapter provides a cautionary warning about the ways in which informal institutional ties may outstrip formal structures, a potentially costly development in times of stress or crisis. In the last chapter, Mary Farrell examines EU efforts to replicate the European model of regional integration elsewhere in the world. Pinpointing the particular role of the Commission and the institutional path dependencies, she analyzes three ways in which the EU attempts to influence regional integration processes: enlargement, normative suasion, and interregional agreements. If these strategies are successful, maybe the world will be one day made of a multitude of EU-like regional unions, but Farrell carefully shows the constraints and obstacles along the way.

This volume presents not a snapshot of the state of the EU today, but rather a three-dimensional study that richly portrays the past and suggests the future of European integration. Drawing on a fruitful theoretical tradition, systematically collecting and assessing extensive empirical materials, and writing forcefully about the nature of European integration today, our authors provide a uniquely comprehensive and informed overview of the EU. The richness of their scholarship is testament to the reach and depth of the EU, a remarkable political entity whose policies fifty years after its founding are immensely consequential, not only for Europeans but for people around the world.

I

The Past and Future of European Institutional Integration

2

The European Constitutional Settlement

ANDREW MORAVCSIK

Over the past half-century the EU has successfully expanded its substantive mandate and institutional prerogatives to a level without parallel among international organizations. Today this process has reached what appears to be, barring large exogenous shocks, a stable constitutional equilibrium. The EU may expand geographically, reform institutionally, and deepen substantively, but all this currently seems set to take place essentially within the contours of the existing European constitutional structure. The time has come to acknowledge the existence of the 'European Constitutional Settlement'—a plateau in the process of European integration unlikely to be upset by medium-term trends.[1]

The EU's constitutional evolution since the Treaty of Maastricht illustrates this phenomenon. The institutional balance has evolved only slowly. The powers of the Council and Parliament have increased slowly at the expense of the Commission, intergovernmental cooperation outside the core 'first pillar' of EU institutions has been reinforced, adjustments have been made to voting weights, and the membership has enlarged to twenty-five members. The period has also been one of substantial, perhaps unprecedented, achievements, with the 'completion of the single market', expansion of foreign, defense, immigration and internal security powers, the single currency, and enlargement. But all this was launched at Maastricht or before and completed with remarkably little further constitutional reform. From this perspective, the recent draft constitutional treaty, like Amsterdam and Nice before it, was a conservative document that consolidated rather than transcended the constitutional status quo. Its ambitions for substantive and institutional reform were modest. And there is no immediate reason to believe any of this will change.

Yet most scholars and commentators do not see it this way and, as a result, writings on the EU reveal considerable tension between reality and rhetoric. On the one hand, they remain wedded to the goal of 'ever closer union', culminating in a European federal superstate. Few explicitly acknowledge holding such a view, of course, but it is implied in the widespread tendency among those

---

[1] I have referred to this previously as the 'European Constitutional Compromise' (2005*a*, 2005*b*).

who study or support the EU to emphasize, even exaggerate, new steps toward integration. On the other hand, an equally prevalent tendency is to criticize the lack of substantive progress in the EU and a purportedly debilitating 'democratic deficit' in the EU, which is judged responsible for a crisis of legitimacy. Without fundamental reform, it is argued, the process of European integration may well falter or collapse. The EU is failing to achieve what it could with greater public legitimation. It must move forward, yet it is in crisis.

This combination of ambition and alarm spawned the EU's recent, ill-fated constitutional project. If one believes that the EU can and should move forcefully toward more centralized governance *and* that the major impediment is the lack of direct democratic legitimacy, a democratic constitution and a grand public debate over 'finalité politique' may seem an obvious recourse. Yet it is now clear that this effort to legitimate the EU through constitutional engineering failed—and did so for reasons that go far beyond a few mismanaged referenda. The decade of debate over the EU's constitutional future—probably the broadest and deepest such debate in human history—failed from the start to create an attentive, informed and engaged public. It was dominated from the start by a handful of 'symbolic extremists' of a Euroenthusiastic or Euroskeptic persuasion. Both groups cast the debate as a vital one for the future of Europe—Euroenthusiasts because they aspire to much more, and Euroskeptics because they aspire to much less. The unhealthy ideological codependence between these groups fueled exaggerated and cloudy rhetoric about the purposes of European integration. Such views belie the modest content of the constitutional treaty, which reaffirmed rather than fundamentally reformed the existing scope of European integration. The population in the center of the EU political spectrum, whose interests in integration are far more pragmatic, remained either apathetic or, for the few who paid attention, unsettled. There is little disagreement now that, had the reforms been sold as the conservative tinkering they were, surely less time would have been wasted and more achieved.

Obscured in this debate has been a middle position, which the first part of this chapter sets forth. On this view, the EU is quite successful, and its existing constitutional settlement equilibrium is likely to endure, with incremental changes, for the foreseeable future, not least because it serves the interests of Europeans better than any feasible alternative. The constitution was, therefore, an unnecessary and risky political gambit. Throughout, my central thesis is that *the stability of the current equilibrium, and its precise terms, follows from the best—by which I mean empirically the most strongly validated—social scientific understanding available about how the EU, and political institutions more generally, actually work.*

This chapter explores the substantive, institutional, and ideological dimensions of the European Constitutional Settlement. The first dimension is *substantive*. The primary motivations behind European integration have almost always been functional. The EU moves forward when formal policy coordination helps manage cross-border policy externalities stemming from transnational interdependence. Today no functional 'grand projet' of this kind exists. European social policy is a chimera, while a stronger, yet viable, foreign and defense policy would not require constitutional change. The second dimension is *institutional*. The EU remains, despite a few federal elements, essentially a confederation of nation-states: the most ambitious and successful among international organizations, rather than a federation aiming to replicate and supplant European nation-states. Its limited 'state capacity', whether from a political, coercive, fiscal, or administrative perspective, appears a permanent structural characteristic impervious to all but an unforeseeably great exogenous shock. The third dimension is *ideological*. Because the EU handles issues of low salience, relative to national ones, publics are unlikely to mobilize in response to European issues, whether in spontaneous opposition or in response to official encouragement. The constitutional project failed to shake this ideational equilibrium by mobilizing greater popular support for the EU, because the basic premise on which it was based—namely that expanding institutional opportunities for public participation generates greater participation, deliberation, and legitimacy—is inconsistent with our best understanding of how modern democracies actually work. Bad social science makes bad policy. I conclude by briefly examining some ways in which scholars of political science, political philosophers, and legal academics have been complicit in propagating a view of the EU that is inaccurate, and the biases in the existing literature that have resulted—including insufficient attention to the existence of the European Constitutional Settlement.

The Substantive Dimension of the European Constitutional Settlement

Historically, the main impetus toward European integration has been functional. Major steps in the development of European institutions have rested on 'grands projets' such as the customs union, common agricultural policy (CAP), single market, single currency, or Eastern enlargement. In each case, historians increasingly agree, pressure to manage substantive policies stemming from new forms of socioeconomic interdependence motivated governments to undertake new institutional commitments. To be sure, ideological and geopolitical objectives—such as realizing European federalism, avoiding yet another Franco-German war, opposing Communists abroad and at home—played an important subsidiary role, particularly in defining the institutional form integration took. Its substantive content was shaped primarily by functional imperatives (Moravcsik 1998). Most of those imperatives were those of a continent of relatively small but highly developed nations undergoing an unprecedented postwar economic boom, thereby creating the regional intra-industry flows of trade and capital that rendered coordinated regulation attractive (Milward 1984, 1993, 2000). From the 'relaunching' of European integration after the failure of the European Defense Community and the ECSC, if not well before, even the most ambitious proponents of European integration concluded that integration without the functional imperatives was impossible—and little has changed since.[2]

This functional focus helps explain why individual governments have generally embraced European-level governance schemes only after exhausting domestic policy alternatives. The Coal and Steel Community was a response to a crisis in postwar French and German economic planning (Milward 1984). A decade later, the EEC was an instrument to shape multilateral trade liberalization that had come to be viewed as inevitable. France promoted the CAP in the 1960s and single market liberalization in the 1980s only after subsidized domestic alternatives had reached their fiscal limits. For decades, in the face of increased capital mobility and declining credibility of domestic macroeconomic management, governments resisted a single currency in favor of domestic policy alternatives (Moravcsik 1998).[3]

Decisions to accede to the EU, from that of Britain in the early 1960s to those by central and eastern European countries in the past, rested similarly on the widespread conviction that there is no unilateral alternative to integration. Individual governments weighed the benefits of coordinated policymaking against the costs imposed by adjusting diverse policies and social structures to common policies. Time and again, it was the uniquely high levels of socioeconomic interdependence among many European countries, and the corresponding negative externalities to uncoordinated policies, that outweighed the maintenance of distinctive national systems.

The limited substantive mandate of the EU, which remains perhaps its most striking constitutional characteristic vis-à-vis national governments, reflects the unevenness of functional imperatives. Recent academic studies suggest that 15–20 percent of European national laws stem from the EU—not much higher figures one often encounters (see Töller 2003). It could hardly be otherwise, given the narrowness of the EU's formal legal mandate.

To illustrate this, current European policymaking can usefully be divided into three categories. The first contains areas of centralized EU discretion or inflexible

---

[2] Already in 1949–50, and even more clearly after 1954, Jean Monnet understood that integration could only be conducted by functional means. Yet even Monnet underestimated the dominance of functional market-driven forces. His firm belief was that functional integration would best take place within highly regulated sectors of the economy like nuclear and transport, and with strong central authority, rather than through markets. This is why he passionately opposed the formation of the plan for a European Economic Community, secretly begging German Chancellor Konrad Adenauer to kill it, until he finally bowed to a fait accompli imposed by German economic interests (Moravcsik 1998).

[3] See McNamara (1997) for case of policies where material interests are less clearly defined, material interests may often be mediated by policy ideas.

EU rules, including monetary policy, antitrust policy, and restrictions on internal tariffs and quotas. The second contains areas of joint decision-making by EU member states within common institutions, as in external trade; industrial standardization; agricultural pricing and export policy; a subset of regulatory issues in environment, consumer and other policies; fisheries policy, and certain rules regarding service provision. In many of these matters, the EU is now clearly the primary source of European law—though even in apparently integrated areas such as agriculture, the environment and other regulatory issues, the bulk of policy discretion may well still be national.

A third category accounts for some 80 percent of legislation and rule-making that remain almost entirely outside the mandate of direct EU policymaking. Issues within this category include the power to set tax rates and fiscal priorities, police law and order, manage national defense, provide local and national infrastructure, set cultural goals and educational priorities, and, above all, and provide health care, pensions, labor market regulation, and social welfare. These functions, many of which focus on redistribution, are today the primary functions of the modern European nation-state. Yet the EU has almost no direct impact on such policies, except through light and sporadic EU regulation under unanimity rule or, in a small handful of cases, through indirect spillover from regulation in other areas.

None of this appears to be changing. Indeed, perhaps the most striking characteristic of recent EU constitutional deliberations since Maastricht, as it was of Amsterdam and Nice, is how little substantive expansion has been seriously considered. The member states agreed upon incremental changes essentially within existing constitutional mandates, or sought to reinforce intergovernmental cooperation in areas such as defense, asylum, law and order, fiscal policy, social policy, or tax harmonization, outside the classic EU institutions. As the constitutional convention convened, the EU had just completed its most successful decade ever, counting among its recent achievements monetary union, two rounds of enlargement, greater transparency, more foreign policy coordination, movement toward EU policies on energy, services deregulation, and other issues. Entirely absent from the constitutional draft was any significant expansion of the EU's substantive mandate. Even in the constitutional convention itself, a forum in which European federalists had a disproportionate influence, less than two days were devoted to consideration of proposals for new policies, during which few were considered and none adopted. What proposed changes were there could surely have been obtained through piecemeal implementation over the five years during which the unwieldy draft was debated. From a substantive perspective, the promulgation of a new constitution was, and remains, unnecessary.

This situation appears stable. The truth is that today no plausible 'grand projet' for Europe can be found—nothing, at least, on the projects that powered major constitutional reform in the past, such as the CAP, the single market, the single currency, or the recent enlargement. Polls show that most Europeans are broadly satisfied with the current scope of the EU.[4]

Most of the proposals for inclusion of new issues are more style than substance. Consider, for example, the issue most commonly mentioned as a possible candidate for future communitarization: social policy. The absence of a 'social Europe' today is not the happenstance consequence of short-sighted political decisions, but an inevitable result of the structure of national and social interests. No wonder the French and Dutch referenda, like the convention, were devoid of any serious discussion of what a concrete European social policy would look like. To see why European social policy is, and must remain, a chimera, consider four possible meanings for such a policy. None appears viable, and they contradict one another.

Transnational Transfers from Rich to Poor?

Following the egalitarian rhetoric of European socialism, one might expect that a pan-European social policy should mandate resource transfers from rich to poor. This would mean, in the EU context, a system dominated by payments from taxpayers in richer member states, such as Germany and France, to the less advantaged citizens of Europe, most of whom are found in new member states such as Lithuania, Slovakia, and Cyprus. Or, if indirect means were favored, it might mean transfers via the suppression of any barriers to the free movement of workers, goods and services emanating from these countries.

There are almost no concrete proposals for a Europe-wide social policy of this kind, and the governments of richer countries have made clear that they do not wish to increase transfer payments beyond current levels.[5] Existing national systems remain sacrosanct. The absence of concrete proposals and political support for cross-national distribution is often attributed to a lack of a common transnational culture, language or sense of political identity (demos) among Europeans.[6] A more fundamental reason is probably that redistribution is simply not in the material interest of citizens in the richer polities of Europe: Large

---

[4] Poll data is difficult to interpret. Recent polling reveals that the issues where Europeans would most like to see more EU activity tend to be those where there is already action: terrorism, democracy promotion, law and order, R&D, the environment, and health and safety, whereas those where they would least like to see increased EU activity include unemployment, social rights, economic growth, and agriculture, even though the first three of these issues are consistently salient. It also reveals that whereas the new member states would favor social welfare harmonization, this is less popular in the old member states (see European Commission 2006*d*, 2006*e*). Foreign and defense policy have consistently rated high as well.

[5] To be sure, it is often forgotten that existing EU transfers via structural funding and market liberalization involve a far greater commitment to transnational redistribution than any other advanced industrial democracy—notably the USA—is able to contemplate.

[6] A comparison of European and German reunification—the former privileging national boundaries, while the latter ultimately granting East Germans social rights as nationals—does suggest that there may be some truth to this.

transfers would impose wrenching distributional shifts and threaten universal national systems that currently enjoy broad domestic support.[7] Absent a strong functional case for international cooperation—that is, a plausible argument why maintenance or improvement of most existing national policies requires transnational policy coordination—it has never been possible to push European integration forward, and it does not seem to be possible here.

A Coordinated Defense against Globalization?

Some other advocates of a European social policy imagine the opposite of transnational transfers, namely a European social policy designed to defend the current prerogatives of the working class in richer 'old' member states against 'globalization'. Most Europeans appear to favor maintaining current levels of welfare spending, as demonstrated by the opposition encountered by national governments that seek to consolidate spending and its impact on attitudes toward the EU. Prominent among perceived threats are the fiscal erosion of domestic social protection, increased domestic labor flexibility, and immigration of low-skilled workers from 'new' member states. Many speak of a regulatory and fiscal 'race to the bottom', whereby regional trade, immigration, and investment create strong incentives for countries to reduce welfare expenditure and regulatory standards.

Yet an EU policy designed to meet these challenges cannot claim support either among policy analysts or among governments—for three fundamental reasons. First, there is little empirical evidence of a 'race to the bottom' induced by regional integration. To be sure, there is downward pressure on standards in some areas of social policy (pensions, medical care, and labor market policy), but the most important factors driving it appear to be domestic: the shift to a postindustrial economy, lower productivity growth, shifting demand for less-skilled workers, and rising costs of health care, pensions and employment policies, exacerbated by increasingly unfavorable demographic trends (Pierson and Leibfried 1995; Iversen, Pontusson, and Soskice 1999; Scharpf 1999; Rhodes, Ferrera, and Hemerijck 2001; De Grauwe and Polan 2005; Pontusson 2006). Second, current levels of social protection and economic growth are manifestly unsustainable—and thus a defense of existing social policy does not address the true policy challenge facing European governments. There is a near-consensus—accepted at least rhetorically by all member state governments and embodied in the EU's nonbinding 'Lisbon Process'—that some reduction in benefits, increase in immigration, and expansion of labor flexibility are required to render domestic systems viable. In this context, any effort to harness the EU to protect current systems of social protection would be futile, if not counterproductive. Third,

---

[7] Social welfare systems, which undergird class compromises in European polities, are locked in by historical processes (Pierson 1994).

given the diversity of existing national social welfare systems, national reform is more appropriate than EU reform. Even advocates of social policy admit that with proper national reforms, social democratic welfare states are compatible with high levels of interdependence—but the reforms required are politically delicate and nationally specific (Scharpf 1999). There is little political or technocratic justification for a 'one size fits all' centralized social policy, the costs of which would surely outweigh the benefits.

Offsetting the EU's Neoliberal Policy Bias?

More nuanced social democratic advocates of a European social policy, aware that neither transnational redistribution nor a centralized defense of the status quo is feasible or desirable, argue that an explicit EU social regulation might help offset specific, particularly undesirable or inequitable developments in social policy resulting from existing EU policy. Fritz Scharpf (1999) offers the most subtle, rigorous, and empirically informed formulation of such a position. In this view, unfettered market competition tends to degrade regulatory protection in particular areas. The EU cannot respond effectively to such tendencies, despite overwhelming support for the maintenance of current social protection, because there is a neoliberal bias in the EU's constitutional structure. Unanimity voting dampens redistributive policies, European courts and regulators favor market liberalization ('negative integration') over social protection ('positive integration'), and in certain areas, effective national responses may be blocked either by EU law or by market competition. While reform must be essentially national, the EU should establish legal standards that render national responses more effective and more just. Scharpf points to the need to offset the potential of future ECJ jurisprudence to undermine national public service provision, as well as a tendency to increase the share of taxation on labor. The EU regulation might also help assure that necessary welfare reforms are just as well as sustainable, for example by mandating intergenerational equity (Schmitter 2000).

This argument for an EU social policy is at least plausible, yet it falls short of a compelling case. First, while EU policy biases exist, there is little evidence that they drive social protection downward. The EU often permits, even encourages or mandates, high regulatory protection (Vogel 1993; Joerges and Vos 1999; Scharpf 1999). Scharpf asserts that the member states are trapped in a suboptimal equilibrium, due to supermajoritarian rules—yet he provides no plausible examples of this phenomenon. (Old arguments about agriculture are empirically incorrect (Moravcsik and Sangiovanni 2002; cf. Scharpf 1991, 1999).) Second, even Scharpf concedes that any serious consequences EU law may have for, say, domestic public service regulation, lie in the future. Today there is little reason for a social democrat to fear the piecemeal evolution of European law— indeed, less so than might have been the case five or ten years ago (Scharpf 1999: 121–86). Third, given the failure of national governments to pursue sustainable social welfare policies, an offsetting neoliberal bias at the EU level may well be justified—as we are about to see. Overall, an EU social policy to block excessive neoliberal reform would be, at most, an extremely modest policy, and is probably premature (Moravcsik 2002).

Neoliberal Reform?

A final conception of EU social policy is one of a neoliberal EU imposing reform, thus counterbalancing unsustainable generosity of current national social welfare and regulatory policies.[8] In this view, the EU should not defend national social welfare and labor market systems, but bolster international competitiveness and long-term sustainability by compelling states to reform. This view has the virtue of being consistent with current national policies and expert policy analysis, as well as the ongoing 'Lisbon process' of EU information coordination in social policy.

While these are worthy goals, there is little reason to believe that the EU has any comparative advantage in achieving them. First, as we have seen, the diversity of national social welfare systems and the national social compromises they embody means that the regulatory requirements of reform are different in each member state. From a technocratic point of view, there is widespread agreement that national governments should take the lead in this matter—and that such efforts can be successful (Scharpf 1999). Second, even if pan-European social welfare reform could work technically, it would be perceived as illegitimate—as was the case with the pan-European distributive schemes considered above. This is surely why the member states have opted in this area for the 'Open Method of Coordination' (OMC), which provides technical assistance, but no binding central regulation (Zeitlin, Pochet, and Magnusson 2005).

If social policy appears to be unpromising as an avenue for substantive co-operation, an area with a stronger functional justification may well be foreign and defense policy. The EU already coordinates European foreign policies with regard to most civilian international organizations, including the World Trade Organiza-tion (WTO) and the UN—in the latter case only Security Council matters are largely exempt. The EU enlargement is a major tool. Yet national foreign policies on other matters can be uncoordinated or contradictory, as the oft-cited cases of Bosnia and Iraq illustrate. In defense affairs, in particular, EU member states maintain redundant, suboptimally sized, and uncoordinated procurement and deployment policies. European governments—with over 100,000 troops deployed out of their home countries—are stretched tight (Everts et al. 2004). Centralized EU policymaking is often proposed as a way to support a larger global role for Europe. Even if the most ambitious plans currently on the table for a European force were fully realized—which few expect to see—the EU would oversee only

---

[8] As early as 1995, Pierson and Leibfried noted that this would be the likely content of any European social policy.

2 percent of European NATO forces. To many, this constitutes a prima facie case for greater coordination, perhaps through the EU.

Yet the binding constraint on more effective foreign and defense policy coordination appears less to be unwillingness to coordinate policy and share sovereignty per se (though such inhibitions surely exist), but rather the lack of sufficient functional incentive for individual governments to devote resources to effective national policies. Europeans are constrained at the margin more by the willingness to deploy coercive forces than their availability or coordination of such forces.[9]

There are a number of reasons for this lack of enthusiasm. First, traditional external military threats are perceived to be modest. Even the cold war created an insufficient motivation to coordinate military spending; today the pressure is far less. The EU declaratory policy speaks of humanitarian, peacekeeping, and peacemaking intervention, yet we may doubt how important this goal is to European governments. Europeans reject greater coordination of foreign and defense policy not simply (or even at all) because the issue area is essential to national identity and sovereignty, but because the benefits are insufficient to justify costly domestic adjustment—even if there are good policy arguments in their favor. Second, costly transformation of domestic military establishments—the shift to all-volunteer forces, more efficient procurement, reorientation toward new scenarios for the use of forces and, for some, an ideological shift away from neutrality—is slow and difficult. Third and most important, Europeans have strong ideological and institutional reasons to remain skeptical of military solutions to global problems. They prefer to invest in civilian power: expanding the EU, promulgating trade policy, dispensing foreign aid, promoting international law and organization, and focusing on low-intensity military operations. There is substantial cooperation in these areas, and European civilian power is arguably more cost-effective than military might. Since the end of the cold war, for example, enlargement of the EU has proven itself the most cost-effective instrument for spreading peace and security available to Western nations (Moravcsik 2003).

Even where European governments do face strong incentives to coordinate military policies, the argument for major constitutional reform appears weak. Intergovernmental cooperation backed by bi-national efforts appear to work well. In this regard, the oft-cited case of Iraq is quite misleading. Would European policy have been substantially different with greater coordination? In fact, there are few, if any, examples since (perhaps) the decision to recognize former Yugoslavian states in the early 1990s when EU member states would have voted by qualified

---

[9] A failure of domestic adjustment, not of international coordination, appears to be the critical constraint. National procurement policies are flatly inconsistent with supposed military strategy. France, for example, though a strong supporter of European defense cooperation, procures nuclear weapons, fighter jets, aircraft carriers, and other expensive weapons suited to unilateral responses to cold war threats.

majority, or even simple majority, for more effective policies than those they actually pursued through existing unilateral or intergovernmental means. Recent diplomacy over Iran or Lebanon may be more appropriate exemplars. Military planning within the intergovernmental Council is proceeding. This is why realistic proposals currently under consideration to develop a EU defense or foreign policy identity take the form of strengthening intergovernmental cooperation within the Council of Ministers, rather than radical constitutional change to import the classic 'community method' into this area. Had the draft constitution been adopted, it would in fact have centralized decision-making and shifted power from the Commission to the more intergovernmental Council, not the reverse.

We have seen that there is currently little functional pressure for major constitutional change in areas like social and foreign/defense policy, beyond the incremental change currently underway.[10] To be sure, future exogenous shocks, or even unforeseen spillovers from existing policies, may create opportunities for 'grands projets' that decisively expand the substantive scope of European cooperation.[11] It is not unlikely that, for example, certain aspects of defense or immigration might someday generate pressures strong enough to motivate governments to expand the scope of integration. Today, however, neither a severe unmet need for centralized regulation in Europe nor even significant movement in favor of concrete steps to deepen functional cooperation is in evidence. The trend is rather toward a stable substantive division of labor between national and European competences.

The Institutional Dimension of the European Constitutional Settlement

Stable limits on the substantive scope of EU policymaking do not simply reflect the absence of appropriate functional imperatives. They are reinforced by the basic constitutional structure of the EU. The Treaty of Rome has long provided the EU with a de facto constitution, defining the relationship between member states and Brussels, the separation of powers among institutions, a stable process of legislation and adjudication, and the interaction between citizens and political institutions.

In most particulars, the EU's existing constitutional structure is confederal, rather than federal—at least in the classic sense we recognize from national

[10] For an analysis of immigration policy, which appears equally unpromising, see Guiraudon (2004) and Moravcsik (2006: 225).

[11] Promising issues surely exist. Perhaps fiscal policy coordination among Euro countries, antiterrorism policy, or the General Services Directive would be useful places to seek unintended or unwanted spillovers of significant size. Yet even in these areas, few analysts see a medium-term prospect of centralizing policy in Brussels, and even if they did, it is unclear that a major change in the treaty basis of the European Union would be either desirable or practical.

governmental experience (Elazar 2001; Majone 2005). These confederal characteristics of the EU run deep, and are deepening over time. In the historical process of state formation, adequate state capacity has been an important prerequisite for policy innovation. Yet the EU does not (with a few exceptions) enjoy the power to coerce, administer, or tax (Moravcsik 2001). Most of the important substantive areas of modern governance remain firmly in the hands of national governments, to be extended only by unanimous vote of the member states. Nation-states dominate the relationship between citizens and the EU, and impose extremely tight institutional constraints on political decision-making in the EU—deciding only by concurrent supermajority (in practice, near consensus). These narrow institutional constraints render almost impossible any expansion of centralized EU decision-making into most of the significant new issue areas, which would require substantially greater state capacity. Let us consider political, coercive, fiscal, and administrative capacities in turn.

Political Capacity

The EU's ability to act, even in those areas where it enjoys legal competence, is constrained by the checks and balances between member states and Brussels, and among the Brussels institutions themselves. The EU is not a system of parliamentary sovereignty but one of separation of powers, with political authority and discretion divided ('horizontally') among the Commission, Council, parliament and court, and ('vertically') among local, national, and transnational levels. For legislation to pass, the Commission must propose (by majority or consensus), the Council of Ministers must decide (by supermajority vote), European parliamentarians must assent (by absolute majority of members), national parliaments and officials must transpose directives into national law, national bureaucracies must implement them, and, if the result is challenged, the domestic and European courts must adjudicate. Formally, this makes everyday legislation in the EU as difficult to enact as a constitutional amendment in the USA. For EU constitutional change, unanimity is required, often with ratification by referendum in at least some of the member states, and by at least parliamentary vote in all—a standard higher than any modern democracy except perhaps that of Switzerland.

Such a system is deeply resistant to any fundamental transformation without consensus among a wide variety of actors. As a result, the EU tends to tolerate internal diversity, rather than forcing common solutions. Thus the single currency, the Schengen arrangement, and foreign policy cooperation—to name just three examples—tend not to bind all members of the EU to a common standard, but to permit a level of internal flexibility unheard of in modern national governance. One sees this even in everyday legislation, where carefully crafted compromises and local implementation tend to generate considerable flexibility.[12] Radical change in such a system is unlikely.

Coercive Capacity

Traditionally, the preeminent international characteristic of a state has been its capacity to coerce. Yet the EU has no police, no army, no significant intelligence capacity—and no realistic prospect of obtaining any of them. This constraint restricts the EU's autonomous ability, without the active and, in some cases, unanimous, support of the member states, to conduct external coercion or internal policing. The EU forces could be employed only for a narrow range of peacekeeping tasks, and with the unanimous consent of the participating national governments engaged in the operation. This 'coalition of the willing' approach is no different than that of NATO, a classic international organization. To be sure, coordinated military planning and some rationalization of defense procurement are possible, and the EU may be helpful here—but almost no one envisages the EU thereby gaining control over military action or spending. Similarly, although the EU helps to coordinate efforts to combat international crime, the structure of national police, criminal justice, and punishment systems remains essentially intergovernmental. The convention revealed little significant support for a more centralized defense structure.

Fiscal Capacity

Redistributing wealth by taxation and spending is the preeminent activity of the modern state, yet the EU does little of this. Its ability to tax is capped at about 1.3 percent of the combined GNP of its members—representing only about 2 percent of European public spending (as compared to the US federal government, which collects 70 percent of American tax revenue). The EU funds are transfers from national governments, not direct taxation; their disbursement is directed to a small range of policies like the CAP, structural funding, and development aid. Little room exists for discretionary spending by Brussels technocrats, or spontaneous shifts in funding by the member states. Unanimous consent is required to change any of this, and in recent years, wealthier member states have blocked efforts to expand EU fiscal capacity. Even in areas of the EU's greatest fiscal activity, most public funding remains national. Agriculture is often thought of as a purely EU

---

[12] Consider e.g. the controversial EU directive on chocolate, finally agreed several years ago after twenty-seven years of discussion. It permits chocolate products with up to 5 percent vegetable oil to circulate within the EU, yet countries are allowed to alter the labeling of such products (e.g. 'chocolate', 'family milk chocolate', or 'pure chocolate'), which reportedly have a considerable impact on consumer behavior. Implementation is expected to be slow (Confectionery News 2005; Stiff 2006).

function, carried out by the CAP. Yet even in France, the largest beneficiary of the CAP, national sources provide more than half of French farm spending—often enough to counteract EU influence where desired. The EU is thus condemned to remain what Giandomenico Majone has termed a 'regulatory polity'—a political system with instruments of regulation, but little fiscal discretion (1996).

Administrative Capacity

The essential power of the modern state resides not just in its capacity to coerce and to tax, but also in its capacity to administer—that is, in the discretion officials and politicians wield over detailed regulatory implementation and adjudication. Though European bureaucrats can be as frustrating to deal with as any others, the notion of a European 'superstate' swarming with Brussels bureaucrats is a delusion (or a deception) of Euroskeptics. In Europe, the power to administer remains largely national, even in areas where European regulation is extensive—outside a few exceptional areas. The EU simply lacks the capacity to do so, since its workforce numbers less than 30,000, of which only around 5,000 are genuine administrative decision-makers—employment no larger than that of a medium-sized city government. This constitutes about one-fortieth of the civilian federal workforce in the USA, even with its smaller population and lower level of government employment. With so little manpower, the task of implementing EU regulations therefore necessarily falls to national parliaments and officials.

The EU trend is not toward centralization, but instead toward a 'pillarized' structure, in which new issues have tended to be handled by bureaucratic networks centered in the Council of Ministers and the European Council. In traditional EU issues, the Commission's agenda power has increasingly passed to the European Parliament (EP) and the Council, acting jointly. Important exceptions to the norm of administrative decentralization are limited to a handful of independent EU functions, including constitutional adjudication in the European Court of Justice (ECJ), monetary policy in the European Central Bank, and prosecutorial activities of the Commission in competition policy. These exceptions are important, but we would nonetheless do well not to exaggerate their importance. These are areas where, for good policy and normative reasons, power is customarily insulated even in national settings.

Recent constitutional deliberations underscored the stability of existing constraints on political, coercive, fiscal, and administrative capacity. Notwithstanding its high-minded Philadelphian rhetoric, the proposed draft consolidated, rather than fundamentally reformed, the 'European constitutional settlement'. Few in recent constitutional debates called the EU's essentially confederal structure into question. The claim that Europe would need a radical overhaul to avoid gridlock with twenty-five rather than fifteen members was always more pretext than reasoned motivation. Some claimed a simplification of existing treaties would render them more popular, yet the notion of a simple 'American-style' constitution barely survived the first day of constitutional deliberation. (And rightly so, since there is little reason to believe it would have been perceived as more legitimate.) Some claimed that more democratic participation was required, yet in the draft did little more than prolonging an incremental shift in intrainstitutional power that has been underway for over two decades by modestly extending involvement by the EP and the Council of Ministers involvement at the expense of the Commission. Absent a redesign of its structure far more fundamental than anything seriously proposed by even the most radical critics during the recent episode of constitutional debate, EU institutions are likely to remain essentially what they are today.

The Ideological Dimension of the European Constitutional Settlement

In recent years, Europeans have come to believe that the EU, even if functionally and institutionally secure, may be ideologically unstable. In this view, the central danger facing the EU stems from its lack of popular support, trust, and legitimacy. Advocates of this view refer to the modest decline over the past decade in poll support for the EU, and the slowing pace of expansion of EU policymaking into wholly new substantive areas. Public skepticism might be understood as yet another reason why the EU is unlikely to undertake more 'grands projets' in the near future. But many fear also that the EU will become unstable and ungovernable, thereby calling into question not simply the capacity for further integration, but its current achievements. This unpopularity is often attributed to the EU's lack of direct democratic mandate.

This formulation of the 'bicycle theory'—the folk wisdom that if the EU does not continue moving forward, it will collapse—was the primary argument underlying the constitutional project, which otherwise had little substantive or legal justification.[13] The constitution was, from this perspective, primarily an exercise in *public relations*. Its main purpose was to surmount the perceived ideological crisis of legitimacy in the EU by increasing trust and support among the general European public, which it sought to achieve by bolstering the EU's democratic credentials. As the mandate to the European convention of the 2001 Laeken Declaration stated: 'Within the Union, the European institutions must be

[13] The reforms contained in the draft constitution were, to be sure, pragmatic and desirable adjustments to the existing EU constitutional structure. They would have clarified bureaucratic responsibility for foreign policy, streamlined presidential leadership, reweighted national voting in favor of larger countries, expanded the use of majority voting and parliamentary codecision, and altered procedures for further enlargement. Yet these are modest improvements in the existing structure, not major reforms—much less anything that amounts to a wholly new 'constitution'.

brought closer to its citizens'(Ludlow 2002). The alternative, critics hinted darkly, would be stagnation, disintegration, or collapse. Supporters of the constitution continue to this day to argue for this course. Europeans must now earnestly engage in an extended 'reflection period', await elections and political renewal in Germany, France, and Britain, then relaunch the draft constitution (Duff 2006).

The claim that the constitution would help combat ideological disaffection was widespread, yet rarely analyzed in detail. Closer inspection reveals that it rests on three premises, none of which appears to be empirically valid:

1. The EU has lost popular trust and legitimacy;
2. The EU is now irrevocably politicized and thus faces the danger of a populist backlash; or
3. Further democratization of the EU would increase public deliberation, and thus restore popularity, trust, and perceived legitimacy.

Let us analyze each (this section follows Moravcsik 2006).

Is the EU Perceived Today as a Particularly Untrustworthy or Unpopular Institution?

Many believe that the EU, by virtue of its purported distance and unfamiliarity for the average citizen, its supposed lack of direct democratic deliberation, and its apparently elitist and technocratic style of governance, is widely viewed as untrustworthy and illegitimate. Citizens who voted no in the referendum, it is argued, must have thus been opposed to the specific content of the constitution or the general tendency of European integration.

Yet polls do not support this view. A strong and stable majority of Europeans supports EU integration, something that the constitutional process appears to have obscured, even undermined, rather than reinforced. For the last decade, just over 50 percent of Europeans have felt EU membership is a good thing, about 30 percent have been neutral, and only 15 percent have felt it is a bad thing. This number has declined, though modestly, over the past five years. Support for the constitution initially declined in the wake of the referendum, though it has now increased: 63 percent of Europeans continue to support the idea of a constitution, compared to 21 percent who oppose the idea—stronger support than in the spring of 2005, before the referendum. In no country do opponents outnumber supporters. And an even larger majority of Europeans supports the most important substantive reforms contained in the constitution such as the strengthening of foreign policy coordination (European Commission 2006d, 2006e).

Nor is there empirical evidence that Europeans in large numbers are fundamentally dissatisfied with EU institutions. The French and Dutch referenda, like every other election or referendum ever held on the EU, were dominated by

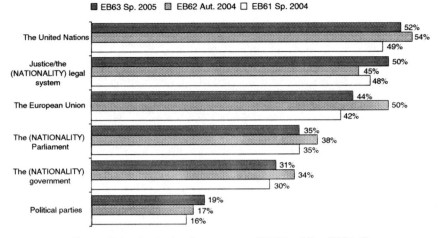

■ EB63 Sp. 2005   ▨ EB62 Aut. 2004   ☐ EB61 Sp. 2004

GRAPH 2.1.   Institutional trust among EU-25 publics (2004–5).
Note: Percentage 'Tend to Trust'.
Source: Eurobarometer 61, 62, 63.

extraneous issues. An apparently pro-constitution, pro-EU majority on the issues did not assert itself. Motivations for opposition appear to have had little to do with the constitution's content or, for the most part, with the EU at all—but overwhelmingly expressed general concerns about social spending, fears of globalization, dislike of the sitting government, opposition to third-country immigration, and perhaps skepticism about future Turkish accession.[14] This 'disconnect' between issue preferences and electoral behavior has been consistently evident in patterns of support for or opposition to the EU. This, we shall see, is generally in situations where the issues handled by the institution are not highly salient, or run parallel to other existing institutions and cleavages.

The underlying claim that EU institutions lack political legitimacy, and are thus unpopular, is also belied by the evidence. The closest proxy for legitimacy is probably 'trust'. Poll data reveal a level of skepticism about both the EU and about political institutions in general, but the EU and the EP (as well as the United Nations) are clearly more trusted by Europeans than national parliaments and governments (Graph 2.1). Political parties, those essential intermediaries of any modern electoral process, score the lowest trust and popularity of any political institution.

In sum, there is little evidence that whatever legitimacy crisis may exist in Europe attaches particularly to the EU, or is in any way related to levels of democratic participation.

[14] Debates on this issue are continuing. It is agreed, however, that the content of the constitution played almost no role in voting, and EU matters a secondary role. For a range of views, see the symposium edited by Sbragia (2006).

Is EU Policymaking Irrevocably Politicized, such that it Faces the Danger of a Populist Backlash?

Critics of the EU's 'democratic deficit' often invoke the specter of a populist backlash against the EU. In this view, the expansion of EU policies over the past two decades has irrevocably politicized the organization.[15] The public has taken an interest, and now it must be satisfied. If the EU does not undertake major constitutional reform, and in particular redress the 'democratic deficit' by increasing participation, many argue, it will regress or collapse.

The available empirical evidence disconfirms this view. Far from being incensed and mobilized about Europe, citizens are largely apathetic—as they always have been. Over the years, European citizens have resolutely refused to avail themselves of existing institutional opportunities to participate in EU politics. Not since farmers deserted Charles de Gaulle during the first round of the French presidential elections in 1965–66 has an EU issue played a decisive role in the national election of a west European member state. (Even then, the effect lasted only a few weeks.) This is not because they ignorantly underestimate EU influence. Polls tell us citizens are fully aware of—indeed perhaps exaggerate— the increasing importance of the EP, and yet they turn out for European elections in low and declining numbers—something many scholars find baffling (Blondel, Sinnott, and Svensson 1998). Some interest groups do mobilize mass protest around EU policies (with protest directed largely at national governments) but their propensity to do so has not increased with increases in the perceived impor-tance of the EU (Imig and Tarrow 2001: 235). Thus it should have come as no surprise that the EU—at least until the misguided referendum at the end—did not engage or mobilize European publics.

To judge whether this apathy is likely to persist, or whether it is likely to change suddenly into organized angry opposition, as supporters of democratizing the EU assert, we must understand its root causes. There are a number of reasons why European citizens fail to participate or seriously deliberate about EU politics. Here I consider only one such reason—arguably the most important among them— namely that the issues dealt with by the EU are far less salient to the public than issues dealt with by national governments.

Political scientists accept that political learning, mobilization, deliberation, and participation are expensive for rational citizens, and thus the bulk of the electorate holds only a small number of major issues in their minds at a time. The resulting number of salient partisan cleavages in Western democracies is relatively few. Any mass politicization of the EU would require first that existing national (or personal) concerns, currently of greater importance in the minds of citizens, be swept aside to make room for EU issues.

---

[15] An intelligent, if not entirely consistent, statement of this position has been advanced by Hooghe and Marks (2006).

It is hard to see why rational European citizens would want to do this. The issues the EU deals with most intensely—trade, industrial regulation, technical standardization, soft power projection, foreign aid, agricultural policy, infrastructural, and general foreign policy—are not salient issues for the mass public. Data on the fourteen most salient issues in the minds of European citizens reveal that only one issue, the environment—which ranks only twelfth in salience, with 3–4 percent of the public placing it among the top two issues—is a major focus of EU legislation.[16] Even in environmental policy, the EU is involved in only a subset of policies.

The issues publics care about most remain overwhelmingly national. On the list of the fourteen, six (health care, pensions, taxation, education, housing, and transport) provide little role for the EU. Another seventh area, law and order, is subject only to modest intergovernmental information sharing and coordination. Two more issues, foreign and defense policy, remain traditional intergovernmental issues dominated by national policymaking and hedged with unanimity and opt-outs, rather than areas of genuine EU competence. (And their role remains relatively minor, as we have seen.) Yet another issue, third-country immigration, may become a potentially important EU activity in the future, but it is not today.[17]

This leaves three highly salient macroeconomic issues: unemployment, inflation, and 'economic conditions'. At first glance these concerns seem to be closely related to the EU, due to the activities of the European Central Bank. They could potentially also be the subject of action under the so-called 'Lisbon strategy' and the OMC. Yet this does not make them potential catalysts for electoral mobilization against the EU. The link between monetary policy and macroeconomic outcomes remains obscure, and in any case, the ECB (like EU national central banks) is an independent body. For both reasons, its proper connection to political participation is unclear. Short of a crisis, in which withdrawal from EMU becomes a serious option, it is hard to imagine monetary policy becoming a salient electoral issue in any national polity—nor even precisely what it would mean if it did. Most policy analysts believe instead that today the most influential and most policy-relevant instruments for influencing macroeconomic performance (unemployment and 'economic conditions', if not necessarily inflation) are instead fiscal, labor market, and education policies—all of which remain essentially national. Certainly these policies are also more visible and controversial among voters. Fiscal policy lies outside the EU's mandate, while labor market policies—with

---

[16] The top fourteen issues in the minds of European citizens are in declining order of importance: unemployment, the (macro-)economic situation, crime, health care, inflation, immigration, pensions, terrorism, taxation, education, housing, the environment, transport, and defense/foreign affairs (Eurobarometer 63).

[17] The case of asylum—a hot-button issue in countries such as the UK, and thus somewhat exaggerated in EU scholarship—involves obligations under international law adjudicated, insofar as the mechanisms are regional, largely by the Strasbourg court of the Council of Europe.

the odd exception of gender policy—are subject only to discussion under the OMC. Yet, as we shall see below, there is no evidence that the OMC has had any significant impact on national policy. Meaningful discretion over macroeconomic management remains an essentially national affair.

As long as voters view the matters handled by the EU as relatively obscure, they have little incentive to debate or decide them. The limited time, money, and energy of European citizens do not permit a wholesale shift of attention and attachment to EU matters.[18] There is little evidence that this will change on its own. Spontaneous mobilization against Europe is therefore unlikely to occur. Publics are likely to become involved only if efforts are made to frame issues in a way calculated to mobilize them—and the results of that, we are about to see, are perverse.

Would Further Democratization of the EU Increase Its Popularity, Trust, and Legitimacy in the Eyes of European Publics?

The ideal of the constitutional project as a public relations exercise aimed at 'bringing Europe closer to the people' rested on the belief that it would trigger a mass constitutional debate, which would inform and engage citizens, thereby transforming the EU's symbolic politics, rhetorical framing, and political culture. Rather than seeking public support by securing mutually beneficial economic and regulatory advantages, the EU should mobilize publics to debate the 'finalité politique' of Europe. In doing so, citizens would come to understand and appreciate the EU more fully, thereby reshaping the content of public debates and reversing the EU's sagging popularity. Some participants—not least a number of European parliamentarians—also viewed the constitutional convention as an optimal opportunity to exercise behind the scenes influence in a profederalist direction (Interview 2003).

Those who remain committed to the constitutional project say that mistakes were made. The constitution failed because it was insufficiently inspirational, or because it fell victim to opportunistic national politicians. Referendums were opportunistically called, ineptly waged, and, in two cases, decisively lost. For some, this demonstrates the validity of the basic premise underlying the constitutional project—namely that the EU is crippled by its 'democratic deficit', 'legitimacy crisis', and lack of a common vision of its 'finalité politique'.

Yet this is to miss the central lesson of the constitutional debacle. Judged by the goal of inspiring citizens to informed deliberation and generating political support, the constitution was a failure from the beginning. And failure was

---

[18] This is not to deny that EU issues are important, normatively or positively. In an ideal world, we would surely wish citizens to participate in EU politics, and every other kind of politics, more enthusiastically. But the real world imposes trade-offs—a fact of pragmatic and normative importance.

inevitable because the basic strategy on which it was based is inconsistent with our *basic empirical knowledge of modern democratic politics in general.* For such a strategy to work, three premises must be correct:

1. Expanded institutional opportunities for political participation must generate more popular participation;
2. More participation must generate more informed public deliberation; and
3. More deliberation must generate greater political trust and legitimacy.

None of these three claims is generally valid, and each is least likely to obtain in political environments resembling the EU (this section follows Moravcsik 2006).

Again, the critical structural factor is the absence of salient issues, which renders a 'public relations' approach to the EU futile, because publics have little rational incentive to pay attention or mobilize. The problem in the EU is not the absence of political opportunities to participate. National elections, EP elections, rules requiring regulatory input, and support for interest groups exist. Cross-national research reveals that EU regulatory procedures are as transparent and open to public input as the best practices of national governments (Zweifel 2002, 2006). The EU officials have limited scope for arbitrary discretion. Elected national governments and elected European parliamentarians increasingly dominate EU policymaking. Disputes and voting within the EU reflect the same national interests and left–right cleavages visible in national politics. The issues the EU handles are roughly those that European publics would like to see handled. The erroneous view that the EU suffers from a greater 'democratic deficit' than its constituent member states, a foundational presumption of the constitutional project, stems largely from the fact that it deals disproportionately with issues commonly delegated or insulated in modern democratic politics. The problem is not that citizens cannot influence the EU; it is rather that *they do not choose to become involved.* (For a detailed analysis, see Moravcsik 2002).

Forcing the issue onto the agenda via a constitutional convention and referendum is counterproductive. This is the deepest lesson of the constitutional episode: from the very beginning with the Laeken Declaration—not simply at the end in a set of mismanaged referenda—the constitution utterly failed to inspire, engage, and educate European publics. The absence of any necessary link between institutional opportunities, informed political participation, and political legitimacy will defeat any effort to mobilize support for the EU in this way. In the end, if forced to be involved, the response of a public without rational incentives to participate, is likely to be ignorant, irrelevant, and ideological.

- *Ignorant* because individuals have no incentive to generate sufficient information to render concrete interests and political behavior consistent. As we see from the fifty-year track record of EU referenda, elections, and conventions, the result is an information-poor, institutionally unstructured, and unstable plebiscitary politics. Ignorance about the EU remains stubbornly high. Few citizens were aware of the 200 conventionners' deliberations, and at the end of the process, few could state what was in the resulting document. Constitutional aspirations and democratic reform seemed to have little effect on public knowledge (Brouard and Tiberj 2006; Norman 2003).

- *Irrelevant* because publics are likely to react to efforts to stimulate debate on nonsalient issues by 'importing' more salient national and local (or global) issues with little to do with the matter at hand (in this case, EU policy). Elections to the EP are routinely turned into 'second order' elections in which concerns about national governments—or, more recently, issues handled by national governments—are aired. No wonder the referendum debates were dominated by issues unrelated to ongoing EU policy, including third-country immigration, the exchange rate at which the Dutch government had decided to enter EMU, social welfare reform, and general fears of globalization. Even the few EU issues that were discussed, such as Turkish membership, had little to do with the constitution itself.

- *Ideological* because intense efforts to stimulate electoral participation in EU matters tend to encourage symbolic rather than substantive politics. Polls show that, absent strong preferences about EU policies, feelings about the 'idea' of EU (i.e. general pro- or anti-Europe sentiment) dominate the European sentiments of many voters. The result is that electoral politics, insofar as it is focused on the EU at all, is quickly dominated by symbolism and rhetoric. This, in turn, plays into the hands of small bands of active Euroenthusiasts and Euroskeptics, who are likely to dominate any popular debate with ideological appeals to nationalist or antinationalist sentiment.

None of this is conducive to the sort of informed discussion sought by European constitutionalists—and deliberative democratic philosophers. It only made manifest the paternalistic utopianism underlying the continued insistence by advocates of pan-European democracy that citizens will pay the high costs of informed participation, even though they do not share the dedicated policy wonk's enthusiasm for the EU's relatively arcane and obscure set of concerns. It is thus unsurprising—and was indeed predicted by some—that the effort to achieve legitimacy through constitutional engineering on the basis of these premises would fail, and that advocates of constitutional reform have been consistently disappointed by the apathy, and the subsequent hostility, of national publics toward the constitutional project.

An even more fundamental error was the belief that *even if* citizens could have been induced to participate and discuss EU issues, they would have come to like and trust the EU. This rests on a basic misunderstanding of democratic politics today. *Majoritarian and populist politics is not legitimating.* Publics in almost all advanced democracies distrust and dislike majoritarian, participatory

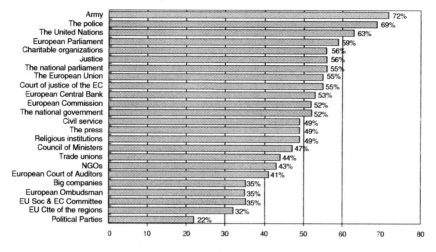

GRAPH 2.2. Institutional trust among EU-15 publics (2001).

Note: Q34 and Q26: 'I would like to ask you a question about how much trust you have in certain institutions. For each of the following institutions, please tell me if you tend to trust it or not to trust it?'

n = 15.939.

Source: Eurobarometer 56.2 (October–November 2001, cited in Norris 2001).

institutions such as legislatures, political parties, and elected politicians; they like and trust *insulated* institutions—armies, police, constitutional courts, and administrative bureaucracies, for example—far more. The same holds for international institutions, which is why European publics trust EU institutions as much—often more so—than national ones (Graph 2.2). The EU's position in the institutional division of labor involves such political functions. Criticizing Commission bureaucrats may be an effective rhetorical tactic, but there is little evidence that the bureaucratic nature of the EU actually generates skepticism of it. Nothing suggests that a 'political' judiciary or administration would be more popular. Even if constitutional deliberations had been more intense, or the resulting reforms more populist and participatory, political legitimacy would be unlikely to have been the result.

The following conclusion is inescapable: To give Europeans a reason to conduct informed debates on EU politics, and to support its activities overwhelmingly, more than expanded institutional opportunities to participate and a public relations offensive is required. In order to inspire the redefinition of existing political identities, familiarity with an entirely new set of institutions, new patterns of cleavages and alliances, and the formation of new civil society organizations, one must overcome the rational disinclination of citizens to attend to politics, educate themselves, or mobilize to construct discourses, institutions and political cleavages. To motivate such a shift, publics must have a salient concrete stake in the outcome—a basic prerequisite that many philosophically inspired discussions of a demos, 'we-feeling', 'community', and 'constitutional patriotism' consistently elide. To deepen public involvement and bolster legitimacy, one needs to introduce into the EU mandate issues that rank among the most important priorities of European citizens. This is how democratization took place in the past, and this is how it is most likely to occur today (Schmitter 2002). So we are back to functionalism.

There are those, notably social democrats like Jürgen Habermas and Philippe Schmitter among them, who believe that the EU should respond to this challenge by incorporating the issue most prominent in the minds of Europeans: social welfare policy. We have seen above that there is little functional case for a centralized EU social policy. Habermas takes a quite philosophical view of that, discussing shared values with little reference to policy proposals at all—as if ideal discourse could effortlessly trump the strongest interests in modern democratic politics (2001, 2005). Schmitter (2002) realizes that something more concrete is required. With the aim of improving EU democracy, he advances three 'modest proposals' to render EU politics more salient:

1. Replace agricultural support and structural funds with a guaranteed minimum income for the poorest one-third of Europeans;
2. Rebalance national welfare systems so as not to favor the elderly; and
3. Grant third-country immigrants and aliens full rights.

With the EU acting as a massive engine of redistribution, Schmitter maintains, individuals and groups would reorient their political behavior on whether they benefit or lose from the system—thereby creating support.

Such proposals for a strong redistributive European social and immigration policy have the virtue of actually addressing the core of the problem, the absence of salient issues. Moreover, they do so—as one might expect from a scholar like Schmitter—in a way informed by what we know from the history of European democratization and political cleavages. There is, moreover, little doubt that such policies would mobilize Europeans. The problem with introducing transnational redistribution, immigration, and generational politics to the EU's portfolio is that, as we have seen above, they lack a functional justification. Thus, such proposals divide Europeans, both within and among nations, more than unite them. It is difficult to see why issues that encounter (currently prohibitive) domestic opposition in national politics could be resolved at the multinational level. Massive redistribution to east Europeans, third-country immigrants, and the young would generate widespread hostility, particularly in richer countries. This would be likely not only to kill any specific policy initiatives, but to introduce an ugly ideological streak to European politics that has not been seen (at least in the center of the political spectrum) in several generations. Schmitter's own presentation of such notions as 'modest proposals' suggests that he may not himself believe they are viable. More generally, such 'cart before the horse' strategies of generating procedural propriety and public popularity by manipulating policies—particularly policies that lack (we have seen) a substantive justification for communitarization—are difficult to justify either normatively or pragmatically. Even if it were feasible, such a radical break with the existing European constitutional settlement, divorcing the EU entirely from its ostensible purpose of regulating cross-border externalities, would be counterproductive. An ideal deliberative discourse based on shared social values, as Habermas imagines, would emerge in such circumstances only at the expense of comity and consensus among EU member states.

Implications of the European Constitutional Settlement

We have seen that the EU has quietly struck a 'European constitutional settlement'. Barring a very large exogenous shock, it is unlikely to be upset by functional challenges, autonomous institutional evolution, or demands for democratic accountability. Contrary to what Haas and Monnet believed, the EU does not (or no longer needs to) move forward to consolidate its achievements. This is good news for those who admire the European project. When a constitutional system no longer needs to expand and deepen in order to assure its own continued existence, it is truly stable. It is a mark of constitutional maturity. We should celebrate rather than criticize the EU's stability. The EU is now older than most existing democracies. Its multilevel governance system is the only distinctively new form of state organization to emerge and prosper since the rise of the democratic social welfare state at the turn of the twentieth century—and it works remarkably well. We learn far more by viewing the EU as the most advanced model for international cooperation, a vantage point from which it appears as an unambiguous success story, rather than as a nation-state in the making, which encourages cycles of overambition and disappointment. The failure of the constitution is not a failure for Europe as much as a failure to renew an outdated discourse of integration.

The undue attention lavished on constitutional reform in the last five years, and its ultimate failure, signals not only a political failure, but a scholarly one as well. For recent scholarship on the EU has tended to neglect the essential elements and the overall stability of the 'European constitutional settlement', with its deep grounding in the functional preferences of national governments and their citizens, while encouraging students and scholars to think in terms of teleological movement toward 'ever closer union', centralized federal institutions, and a structural democratic deficit that must be overcome.[19] I conclude by briefly considering each.

---

[19] This is not universal, as we see not only from the work of Majone, Weiler and others, but from Kelemen and Heisenberg's sensible contributions to this volume—though even Kelemen cannot resist concluding with a few quibbles about whether federal systems really can be constitutionally stable.

First, recent scholarship *exaggerates teleological tendencies toward 'ever closer union'*. Over the past decade, the successors of Haas have stressed various unintended institutional consequences of the European legal system. Obviously theories about endogenous causality, supranational entrepreneurship, and unintended spillovers offer important insights into European integration. Yet labels, such as 'neo-functionalism' or 'historical institutionalism', suggest general accounts of integration, and thus directly compete with rationalist accounts that stress the intended government responses to exogenously shifting patterns of policy interdependence—even though analyzes of unintended consequences and endogenous causes characteristically lack the empirical power to generalize beyond specific areas to which they have been directed to integration as a whole. Such scholarship also exaggerates the role of institutions. For instance, we learn from the scholarly literature on the ECJ that among the singular preconditions for the evolution of the EU legal system were the existence of autonomous domestic courts with an incentive to recognize the European law, an ECJ that favors further integration, the existence of many economically motivated litigants, and an ability to act without immediate response from the member states—a combination unlikely to be replicated (Alter 2001). In shaping the overall trajectory of European integration, the ECJ, despite its importance, cannot be treated as an institution on par with the Council of Ministers or the European Council. Scholars also stress new policies, even when they have produced few concrete results, because of their purported potential to create unintended spillover. A fine illustration is EU social policy, which has inspired an enormous academic literature and considerable political attention—despite general scholarly consensus that European regulation has had almost no impact on national social policies (outside the juridically exceptional, but much studied, area of gender equality), nor much potential for doing so in the future.

Second, scholarship *exaggerates the centralization of EU governance*. Scholars have tended increasingly to focus on the EU as a unified political system, rather than as a confederal structure for cooperation among nation-states with a limited mandate. Again, scholars tend to 'select on the dependent variable', paying disproportionate attention to situations in which central institutions appear autonomous. Selection bias weighs down the literature on the Commission, where disproportionate scholarly attention has been paid to a relatively small number of categories of policymaking in which the Commission has exploited unexpected autonomy proactively to promote integration within its 'everyday' legislative and regulatory functions. A handful of examples are constantly recycled: some environmental policy directives in the 1970s, telecommunications regulation under Article 90, some parliamentary actions in the mid-1990s, and gender equality. These are peripheral to the overall trend in EU policymaking, and often occurred under conditions predicted by structural theory. A recent case of overemphasis on institutional innovation is the enthusiastic and extensive scholarship on the

OMC, whereby member states exchange information, benchmark policies, and evaluate results. One leading constitutional lawyer views OMC as a striking formal innovation that is ushering in a new form of constitutionalism (De Burca 2003). Policy analysts view it as a fundamental shift in the nature of regulation, if not modern state formation (Zeitlin 2005). Distinguished political philosophers herald a new form of political legitimacy. Social theorists view it as the central element in an emerging European identity, and the basis for balancing the 'neoliberal' tendencies of the EU (Cohen and Sabel, forthcoming). Numerous students of social policy view it as a promising road for future spillover and integration in a 'historical institutionalist' mode. Yet only the most speculative and specialized of empirical evidence suggests that OMC has had any impact on EU policy outcomes. Controlled empirical studies of the process of European social policy cooperation agree that its substantive results to date have been extremely modest, if they exist at all (Zeitlin, Pochet, and Magnusson 2005). In contemporary scholarship, social policy and OMC receive far more attention than the CAP or the common commercial policy (CCP)—though the latter are surely of far greater importance.[20] These may seem like detailed quibbles, but summed across EU scholarship as a whole, they add up to substantial source of misunderstanding.[21]

Third, current scholarship *exaggerates the European democratic deficit and the prospects for redressing it.* Philosophers, political scientists, and legal academics systematically overlook the virtues of the EU's constitutional status quo and exaggerate those of democratic reform (this section follows Moravcsik 2002, 2004). For some this is perhaps because they, unlike the majority of Europeans, are committed to a more federalist future. Yet there is surely another, more influential, utopia at play here as well: Many assert that fully deliberative and participatory democracy is the fundamental philosophical ideal underlying modern democracy and that it ought to serve as a blueprint for applied constitutional engineering. Critics often charge that international organizations like the EU are illegitimate, because they are less intensely deliberative and participatory than sovereign states (Nagel 2005; Rabkin 2005). Yet, as we have seen above, it is inappropriate, impractical, and even counterproductive to hold the EU up to such a standard of pure and direct majoritarian democracy. No modern democracy meets the standard of pure procedural democracy and more importantly, *no*

[20] For an exception, see Meunier (2005).

[21] Similarly, the phrase 'multi-level governance', in fact an accurate description of how the EU functions, has been appropriated to refer to any divergence from the lowest common denominator agreement among states that monopolize access to the EU, even though no respectable theorist holds the latter view of EU policymaking as a whole. A constant search for cases in which policy diverges from member state preferences obscures the fact that such preferences appear to be the major determinate of EU policy. The same can be said for complex institutional models of decision-making. For an empirically convincing demonstration of this, see Thompson et al. (2006).

modern democracy aspires to do so. Recourse to constitutional delegation or insulation is not a flaw, imperfection, or substitute for more broad-based deliberative participation. Nor is it limited to incomplete or imperfect polities, as the EU is often wrongly supposed to be. It is an essential characteristic of modern democracies, which are not populist but constitutional.[22] The justification for delegation and insulation of modern policymaking is not simply pragmatic, but deeply normative. In existing constitutional democracies, popular participation is not an end in itself but one instrument among others to achieve fundamental social goods such as equality, liberty, justice, or nondomination. More participation does not necessarily generate a more desirable outcome in any respect, whether more representative, popular, accountable, or effective policy. The entire enterprise of modern constitutional design and analysis is devoted to the exploitation of 'countermajoritarian' paradoxes—situations where a less 'democratic', in the sense of directly majoritarian, outcome is more desirable normatively. We consistently delegate to legislative representatives and cabinet members, judges, central bankers, government officials, designated experts, political elites, party officials, prosecutors, and public–private partnerships, because we judge these more efficiently and effectively to realize these social goods. We insulate policymaking in order to achieve more informed and expert input (as in many regulatory policies), to protect minority rights (as in human rights policies), to counterbalance powerful special interests (as in trade policy), to block tyrannies of the majority (as in social welfare policies), to resolve time inconsistency problems (as in insurance schemes) and other goals that most normative theorists would applaud.

Once we set aside democratic participation or deliberation—or any other purely procedural norm—as an absolute standard, and instead seek to design constitutional forms to achieve certain social goods, any effort to link normative principles to institutional design must rely heavily on the intermediation of empirical social science about how institutions really work. The relationship between political participation and policy outcomes is complex and often perverse, varying substantially according to the nature of the issue areas, social preferences, institutional settings, and strategic imperatives. Yet the legions of scholarly critics of the EU's democratic deficit have almost universally failed to recognize that their critiques, as we have seen, violate the most elementary among political science premises about the nature of political legitimacy, the motivations for political participation, the varied forms of accountability, and the likely consequences of plebiscitary politics. To the extent this is the case, scholars share the blame for the EU's recent constitutional debacle.

---

[22] With regard to the EU, this point has been advanced most forcefully and consistently by Majone, whose essays of a decade are summarized in (2005). For more recent generalizations of this point to the international domain, see Grant and Keohane (2005) and Moravcsik (2004). For a general philosophical argument consistent with this view, see Pettit (2005).

3

Built to Last? The Durability of EU Federalism

R. DANIEL KELEMEN

Many observers of EU politics viewed 2005 as an *annus horribilis*, and 2006 has brought little relief. Again and again, politicians and pundits of all stripes have proclaimed the EU to be 'in crisis'. Events great and small, from the French and Dutch 'No' votes on the European Constitution, to the stalled budget talks, to threats of Italy quitting the Euro, to the rising tide of protectionism, to alleged strains on the EU's absorption capacity, are routinely portrayed as threats to the very survival of the Union. Many policymakers and scholars maintain that the EU's current institutional arrangements will not function in an EU of twenty-five (or more) member states, and that without significant reform, the EU's institutional machinery will grind to a halt. In June 2005, even Commission President Barroso, whose very position would seem to call on him to serve as Euroenthusiast-in-chief, declared that the EU was facing a 'permanent crisis' (BBC 2005).

Of course, predictions of the EU's imminent demise are nothing new. In March 1982, on the occasion of the twenty-fifth anniversary of the Treaty of Rome, *The Economist* led with a cartoon of a tombstone dedicated to the EEC. The inscription included the dates—born March 25, 1957, moribund March 25, 1982—and an epitaph borrowed from Tacitus—*Capax imperii nisi imperasset*. (It seemed capable of being a power, until it tried to be one.) Noting the weakness of EEC institutions, growing disenchantment among European citizens, Greenland's secession and the looming threat of a UK secession, *The Economist* declared the EEC to be in a near-death coma, at risk of collapsing into prolonged crisis or total stagnation. Yet as we know today, the twenty-fifth anniversary was not the beginning of the end, but merely the end of the beginning. Three years later, Jacques Delors became Commission President and launched the Single Market program that breathed new life into the EEC and paved the way for the SEA and Maastricht's Treaty on EU. In the ensuing years, the EEC (later the EC and then the EU) both widened—adding fifteen member states—and deepened—extending majority voting, enhancing the powers of the Parliament and the ECJ, gaining new powers in existing areas of economic policymaking and extending its authority to a host of new areas outside the purely economic realm.

As we approach the fiftieth anniversary of the Treaty of Rome, we again confront the question of whether the EU is on its last legs. Are today's dire predictions any more credible than those made twenty-five years ago? Are the EU's institutional arrangements fragile? Are they in danger of collapsing under the weight of enlargement, as today's reports of 'crisis' suggest? Or instead, as Andrew Moravcsik (2005*b*) has suggested, is the EU's current 'constitutional settlement' actually quite stable? In short, is today's EU a fragile house of cards, or is it built to last?

Unfortunately, too many scholars and commentators address these questions on the basis of intuition and conjecture, rather than theory and systematic comparative analysis. As in so many areas of EU studies, the EU is treated as a unique case. which by definition cannot be compared to other political systems. This approach is the wrong way forward. We do not need to reinvent the wheel in order to identify the likely sources of instability in the EU and to assess the prospects for the Union's survival. A conceptual framework for analyzing the durability of EU institutions lies at hand, in the literature on stability and instability in federal systems.

Some observers reject the comparison out of hand, maintaining that because the EU lacks some crucial elements of statehood it cannot rightly be viewed as a federal system. However, in recent years more and more EU scholars have applied the lens of comparative federalism to the EU polity (see McKay 2001; Nicolaïdis and Howse 2001; Börzel and Hosli 2003; Kelemen 2003, 2004; Ansell and Di Palma 2004; Fabbrini 2005; Swenden 2004; Trechsel 2005; Schain and Menon 2006; Thorlakson 2006). Building on the work of earlier pioneers of the comparative federalism approach (such as Cappelletti, Seccombe, and Weiler 1986; Scharpf 1988; Sbragia 1992), these studies make it clear that the EU polity can operate as and be analyzed as a federal system even if it lacks necessary attributes of statehood. Indeed, the fact that the EU is not a state has not stopped scholars of comparative federalism from examining it. Unencumbered by the prejudice that the EU is *sui generis* and uncomparable, federalism scholars now regularly treat the EU as a case in their comparative studies (Friedman-Goldstein 2001; Filippov, Ordeshook and Shvetsova, 2004; Rodden 2005; Bednar 2006). For the purposes of the present analysis, the EU has the necessary minimal attributes of a federal system[1] and, crucially, the EU is riven with many of the same tensions that afflict federal systems.

This chapter explores the durability of the EU, asking what comparative federalism suggests about the prospects for the EU's survival. Drawing on recent work on self-enforcing federalism and on institutionalist insights into 'self-reinforcing' institutions, the chapter suggests that while the safeguards of EU federalism remain weak, they are strengthening. The paper also explores the range of forms of crisis that EU institutions might confront and suggests that the most threatening

---

[1] See definition of federalism below.

forms of crisis are highly implausible. As a result, the EU is, it would seem, built to last. While EU institutions are likely to prove durable, they will by no means remain static. The EU may have arrived at the broad outlines of a constitutional settlement with regards to its basic institutional design as Moravcsik (2005*b*) suggests; however, the allocation of authority between levels of government will continue to shift incrementally, with the EU continuing to gain power at least in the medium term.

The remainder of the chapter is divided into four sections. The first section explains why federalism is inherently, but not insurmountably, unstable. The second section identifies the safeguards of federalism that the literature on comparative federalism suggests are crucial for enabling federal systems to withstand centrifugal and centripetal pressures. This section also assesses the extent to which these safeguards can be found in the EU or appear to be emerging. The third section connects the first two, exploring various scenarios in which the absence of necessary federal safeguards might lead to some form of breakdown of EU federalism and assessing their plausibility. The fourth section concludes.

Why Federalism is Unstable

Federalism is inherently unstable, and most federations fail (Lemco 1991). Federalism can be defined as an institutional arrangement in which (*a*) public authority is divided between state governments and a central government, (*b*) each level of government has some issues on which it makes final decisions, and (*c*) a high federal court adjudicates disputes concerning federalism (Kelemen 2003). In some sense every federal system is a house divided. Each level of government may have powerful incentives to undermine the federal system, and as a result, all federal systems (the EU included) face 'two fundamental dilemmas' (Riker 1964; Bednar, Eskridge, and Ferejohn 2001; De Figueiredo and Weingast 2005). The first is federal overreach. Federal governments may undermine federalism by aggrandizing their authority and usurping competences that the federal bargain had reserved for states. Taken to the extreme, this could transform a federal system into a de facto unitary system, in which state governments are mere administrative appendages. The second dilemma is state shirking. Constituent states may shirk on their commitments by refusing to comply with federal law, failing to contribute required resources (i.e. taxes) to the center or infringing the rights of neighboring states. Taken to the extreme, such behavior could lead to the breakdown of the system, with state governments splitting apart to form entirely separate polities. Unfortunately, institutions that help to resolve one of the dilemmas of federalism often exacerbate the other.

One might attempt to wish away these dilemmas by simply including detailed 'competence catalogues' in federal constitutions and mandating norms of 'federal comity'. However, such parchment barriers are inadequate (Swenden 2004; Thorlakson 2006). Constitutions do not enforce themselves, and ultimately the institutional arrangements that underpin federalism must provide state and federal political actors with incentives to abide by the rules of the federation. In practice there is a continuous 'ebb and flow' of authority between states and the center (Donahue and Pollack 2001; Filippov, Ordeshook, and Shvetsova 2004). The danger is that these ebbs and flows may quickly turn into torrents and healthy tensions may explode into hazardous conflict. To be durable, a federation must provide for a rigid enough division of authority to prevent one level of government from usurping the authority of the other, while remaining flexible enough to allow for shifts in the division of authority in response to economic, technological, sociocultural and political developments (Nicolaïdis 2001).

Federations that fail to provide the necessary mix of rigidity and flexibility can collapse in one of two ways: *implosion* or *explosion*. With implosion, centripetal forces undermine the autonomy of state governments and the federal system transforms into a unitary state. Implosion is quite simply not a threat to the EU. The notion that Brussels will usurp the authority of national governments and create a unitary European superstate is the fear and rallying cry of Euroskeptics across Europe. However, this is utterly implausible. Andrew Moravcsik is quite right in declaring that, 'the European superstate is an illusion' (2005*a*: 370). While the EU may continue to expand its authority in existing policy areas and extend it to new ones, even the most extreme cases of deepening would rely on a federal structure that preserved a central role for member state governments in both policymaking and implementation. In other words, the federal balance in the EU might in years to come tip further toward Brussels, but the EU could never become a unitary state.[2]

The more plausible routes to collapse would involve various forms of explosion. With explosion, centrifugal forces undermine the authority of the federal center and pull apart member states, to the point where the federal system fragments. In practice, explosion can take many forms, from extreme forms that lead to the total collapse of the federal system to relatively minor forms of fragmentation that loosen the ties of union but leave the edifice intact. While it may be easy to dismiss suggestions that the EU is on the verge of total collapse, less catastrophic forms of 'explosion' are plausible. In order better to understand the prospects for the EU's durability, we must first assess the strength of the 'safeguards' of federalism in the EU and then explore whether and how failures of these safeguards might lead to some form of collapse.

---

[2] Paradoxically, however, centralization might itself give rise to some form of explosion if, for instance, the growing concentration of authority in Brussels leads one or more recalcitrant governments to exit the union. I return to this possibility below.

Federal Safeguards and Pitfalls

To understand whether the EU is likely to prove durable, we must first clarify what we think holds it together and next consider whether we think the sources of the EU's stability are strengthening or weakening over time. The literature on federalism explores the conditions under which federal institutions are likely to prove durable and identifies a number of sources of stability in federations, often termed *federal safeguards*. It is important to distinguish such ongoing federal safeguards from the factors that provide the original motivation for the formation of a federal system. An extensive literature on comparative federalism has also examined the essential preconditions for the emergence of federalism (Deutsch 1957; Riker 1964; Wheare 1964) and some scholars have usefully applied this literature to the EU (Riker 1996; McKay 1999; Eilstrup-San Giovanni 2006). However, a federation can continue to thrive long after the initial conditions that gave rise to it have passed. For the purposes of this chapter, it is more important to explore the sources of the EU's ongoing stability (or instability) than to query its foundations. In this section, I review the leading sources of institutional stability identified in the literature on comparative federalism—including structural safeguards, partisan safeguards, judicial safeguards, and sociocultural safeguards—and assess both what role they play in sustaining EU federalism and whether they are strengthening or weakening.

Federal safeguards are fixed in the short term but are subject to change in the long term. The EU federalism can only be durable in the long term if its ongoing operations encourage behaviors that serve to strengthen its federal safeguards over time. In the language of institutional analysis, these dynamics are captured by the notion of self-reinforcement. Self-reinforcement is an extension of self-enforcement. A self-enforcing federal system is one structured such that the center and the states have incentives to fulfill their obligations to the federation, given their expectations about one another's behavior (de Figueiredo and Weingast 2005). To be self-reinforcing, the system must encourage behaviors that serve to expand the range of situations in which, or degree to which, it is self-enforcing.[3]

Structural Safeguards

As Madison recognized in the Federalist Papers (No. 45), participation of state governments in federal policymaking can provide an important structural safeguard against federal overreach (see also Wechsler 1954; Bednar, Eskridge, and Ferejohn 2001). Giving representatives of state interests a voice in the federal

---

[3] A self-undermining institution, by contrast, is one that is self-enforcing in the short term, but encourages behaviors that undermine its foundations in the long term.

legislative process puts them in a position to defend their prerogatives against self-aggrandizing federal authorities. The most powerful means by which to safeguard state interests structurally is to represent state governments in a powerful upper legislative chamber. This is the approach taken, for instance, in the German Bundesrat. Other structural safeguards may involve giving states a role in the appointment of federal officials, such as federal judges or bureaucrats, or simply overrepresenting small states in the lower legislative chamber.

The EU has extremely powerful structural safeguards. Member state governments are directly represented in the EU's 'upper chamber', the Council of Ministers. Member state governments appoint the European Commission President and the College of Commissioners (now subject to the approval of the EP). Member state governments also appoint ECJ justices. Finally, member state governments both monitor the implementation of EU policies by the Commission (through the comitology system) and control the implementation of most policies at the national level.

These powerful structural safeguards for state interests make Euroskeptic fears of a European superstate utterly implausible. However, the structural safeguards that limit federal overreach offer little protection against state shirking and the explosion of the federation.[4] To identify federal safeguards against explosion, we must turn to the judiciary, political parties, and culture.

Judicial Safeguards

Federal courts are relied on both to police the division of authority between the federal and state governments and to enforce state government compliance with federal law. In other words, they are expected to prevent both implosion and explosion. While federal high courts can and do police both forms of opportunism, empirical studies (Bzdera 1993; Bednar, Eskridge, and Ferejohn 2001) have demonstrated that they are more effective in policing state cheating than in restraining federal overreach. In policing the division of authority, federal courts tend to be biased in the direction of the center, both because this is often in their institutional self-interest (if doing so expands the scope of federal law) and because the federal government will typically be in a stronger position to apply political pressure on a federal court than will states. By contrast, when policing state compliance, federal courts will have little to fear from backlash in an isolated, recalcitrant state.

The EU has a powerful supreme court in the form of the ECJ, and all indications suggest that the ECJ is growing more powerful. The strength of the ECJ is rooted

---

[4] Structural safeguards may discourage fragmentation in an indirect sense: states that enjoy effective 'voice' at the federal level may be less inclined to 'exit' the federation. A counterexample illustrates the point: the weak structural safeguards of Canadian federalism were blamed for stoking secessionist sentiments in Quebec, see Bednar, Eskridge, and Ferejohn (2001).

in the EU's fragmented institutional structure. As in other political systems, the fragmentation of power between the political branches empowers the judiciary. Divisions between the Council, the Parliament, and the Commission make it difficult for them to collaborate in reining in the ECJ. Therefore, the ECJ can take an assertive stance in enforcing EU law against noncompliant member states with little fear of backlash. Also, knowing that the ECJ and many national courts are independent and assertive, EU lawmakers invite them to play a central role in the policy process, encouraging the Commission and private parties to enforce Community law in court (Kelemen 2004).

The history of EU legal integration has witnessed a steady tightening of EU control over member state compliance. The development of the EU legal system has benefited from a dynamic in which member states encourage the EU to crack down on states who seek to free ride by shirking on their legal obligations. Though individual member states attempt to shirk in particular cases, the member states acting collectively have encouraged the Commission to take a strict line with lawbreakers. Thus the Commission has strengthened its enforcement activities radically over the past twenty years and now makes frequent use of its power to impose financial penalties on member states that disregard EU rulings (Börzel 2001; Kelemen 2006).

Judicial safeguards against member state shirking have also been strengthened by the development of decentralized enforcement of EU law by private parties before national courts (Alter 2001). Decentralized enforcement is based on the Article 234 preliminary ruling procedure, which provides that whenever a national court is hearing a case involving an unresolved question of EU law, that court may refer the case to the ECJ to ask for the proper interpretation of the law.[5] The procedure has encouraged the development of a dialogue between the ECJ and national courts that set in motion a self-reinforcing process that steadily strengthened the ECJ and EU law (Burley and Mattli 1993; Stone Sweet 2000; Alter 2001).

By allowing national courts at all levels to refer cases to the ECJ, the procedure enlists national courts as partners and generates a steady flow of cases that has enabled the ECJ to build up a body of case law that it can then refer to in justifying subsequent judgments (Stone Sweet 2000). Furthermore, many judges see the ECJ as a potential ally in battles with other branches of government, or higher courts, domestically (Alter 2001). Many litigants use the procedure to leverage EC law in the service of domestic policy battles (Alter and Vargas 2001). With national courts applying EU law, governments that seek to resist European law may be forced to disobey their own judiciaries; something they are loath to do. The key to this process has been that the preliminary ruling procedure allows the

---

[5] All national courts have the option of making such references, and final courts of appeal are obligated to do so.

self-interested behaviors of the ECJ, national courts and private litigants to re-inforce one another and continually to strengthen the EU legal system.

Partisan Safeguards

Party systems affect the incentives of state and federal politicians in several ways that may work to sustain federal systems. Riker (1964) emphasized how the decentralized structure of political parties (as in the USA) may play a vital role in defending state interests and maintaining federalism in the face of great centralizing pressures. Bermeo (2002) highlights the opposite dynamic, whereby the incorporation of regional interests into national political parties can help maintain federalism in systems threatened by centrifugal pressures. Turning to the EU's fragmented polity, the relevant question is whether the emerging European-level party system has the potential to safeguard EU federalism against centrifugal pressures?

A number of EU scholars have noted the growing power of party groups in the EP (Kreppel 2002; Hix, Noury, and Roland 2006). While MEPs increasingly toe the party line of their European party groups rather than voting along national lines, for the time being these nascent party groupings remain too weak to restrain behavior by national parties that might imperil the Union. In a recent comparative federalism study, Thorlakson (2006) highlighted how the lack of congruence between the national party systems in EU member states and the emerging European party system makes it difficult to build linkages between national parties and party groups in the EP.[6]

While the European party groups do not yet provide an effective safeguard against explosion, are there reasons to believe they will become more effective in years to come? In their historical, comparative study of federations, Chhibber and Kollman (2004) find that party systems track the shifting allocation of power in federations. Applying their insights to the EU, one would predict that the increasing transfer of authority from the national to the EU level will be accompanied by a strengthening of the role of European-level parties. Indeed, Kreppel's work (2002) suggests that the increasing legislative power has led to increased centralization of party groups in the EP. From this perspective, Euro-pean parties will not build Europe, but if European leaders build it, they will

---

[6] The recent dispute between the British Conservative Party and the European People's Party both hints at how partisan safeguards of EU federalism might operate in the future and demonstrates that they are not yet effective. When Conservative leader David Cameron pledged to break away from the EPP and form a new coalition of Euroskeptic parties in the European Parliament, he came under severe pressure from leading figures in the EPP (such as Angela Merkel, Nicolas Sarkozy, and EPP Chairman Hans-Gert Pöttering) who threatened to isolate the Conservatives should they pull out. However, Cameron brushed off these threats and went ahead with his plan—recently announcing an agreement with the Czech Civic Democratic Party to form a Euroskeptic group after the 2009 European Parliament election.

come. The experience of other federal systems suggests that if the EU continues to gain authority at anything like the pace it has in recent decades, we should expect European-level parties to strengthen and gain influence over their national counterparts.

Sociocultural Safeguards

The sociocultural approach to federal durability suggests that the stability of federal institutions must be grounded in a shared sense of identity and political culture of federalism. Most of the major scholars of federalism including Tocqueville, Beer, Elazar, Stepan, and Riker have suggested, in one way or another, that 'a culture of federalism' is vital for the survival of a federation. Conceptualizations of federal culture vary, with some scholars viewing it in terms of common identity at the level of mass publics (Riker 1964; Elazar 1987; Stepan 2001), others viewing it as a shared sense of commitment to the federal project among political leaders (Franck 1968; Friedrich 1969; Elazar 1987) and others viewing it more as a shared understanding—or focal point—concerning the division of authority between states and the federation (de Figueiredo and Weingast 2005).

Without a healthy mixture of complementary identities, the routine infighting that is part and parcel of federal politics may degenerate into conflict that threatens the very survival of the polity (Franck 1968). Bednar (2006: 180) captures the essence of the danger, explaining that 'If citizens identify primarily with one government then they may forgive or ignore (or even reward) opportunistic behavior by it.' Similarly, Stepan (2001: 326) emphasizes how the lack of a sufficient shared sense of identity can increase secessionist threats in fragmented polities. If one level of government senses that it will not be punished by voters for openly defying the other—and that it may in fact be rewarded—then it may have an incentive to do so.

Turning to the EU, we must ask whether EU mass publics and elites have a sense of common identity sufficient to hold together the Union. There is sharp disagreement among EU scholars as to what degree of common European identity is necessary to support existing and future transfers of authority to the EU level, and whether such common identity exists or is emerging. Let us begin with mass publics. As in other federal polities, a sense of 'Europeanness' may be a complex hybrid mixed with national and subnational identities (Choudhry 2001; Risse 2001; Nicolaïdis 2004). Can we say anything about the current level and trajectory of this common identity? Eurobarometer surveys suggest that while slightly more Europeans feel at least some sense of European identity mixed with their national identities, there has been no long term increase in European identity over the last thirty years (Duchesne and Frognier 1995). Graph 3.1, which presents some recent Eurobarometer data (for 1992–2004), shows great stability in respondents' senses of national and European identity.

Question: In the near future do you see yourself as...?

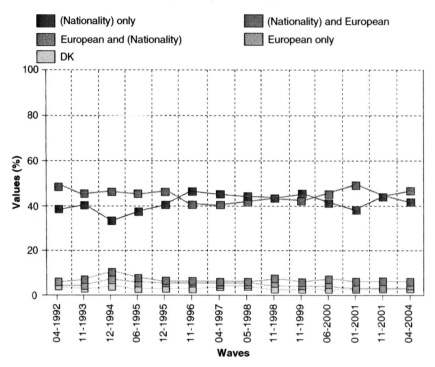

Country: EU period: from April 1992 (EB37.0) to April 2004 (EB61).

GRAPH 3.1.   Hybrid identities.

Source: http://ec.europa.eu/public_opinion/cf/waveoutp

Ultimately, whether the lack of a stronger common identity may prove trouble-some depends on one question: just how much common identity is necessary to underpin the EU? We cannot answer that question with any precision. However, given that EU competences have expanded dramatically while levels of 'European identity' have remained rather static, the likelihood that the EU's power has grown to the point where it exceeds the necessary basis of 'identity' safeguards must necessarily have increased.

Turning to political elites, there is greater evidence of a long-term increase in shared identities and a culture of federalism. Pioneering work on European integration by Haas (1958) and Friedrich (1969) emphasized how the development of shared identities and among national representatives at the EU level greased the wheels of EU politics. More recently, a great number of studies of EU policymaking in a wide variety of areas have found evidence that deliberative policymaking in European fora has led national representatives to develop shared norms and identities (Christensen, Jørgensen, and Wiener 1999; Checkel 2005*b*).

While some important studies have found that EU socialization pressures have at best weak influence on preference change of elite decision-makers (Egeberg 1999; Hooghe 2005), we can still accept the qualified claim that at least under some conditions, processes of socialization and deliberative policymaking can lead to some forms of collective identity formation among elite decision-makers engaged in European fora.

Though multinational federations can prove robust (e.g. Switzerland, Canada, and, so far at least, Belgium), most have proven unsuccessful.[7] Where federal institutions are imposed on divided societies in which political elites and mass publics lack adequate commitment to federalism, the system will be prone to fragmentation. For the EU to resist centrifugal pressures over the long run, the EU citizens and leaders may need to develop a stronger sense of common, albeit hybrid, identity.

Breakdown Scenarios and Their Plausibility

While observers of EU affairs are quick to declare the EU to be in crisis, they are typically far less clear as to what exactly a crisis of the EU might entail. Many analyses of EU crisis seem to be premised on some version of the 'bicycle theory': if the EU does not continue rolling forward it will fall over. Leaving aside for the moment the fact that the bicycle theory lacks conceptual or empirical foundations, it is still worth clarifying precisely what people mean with the idea that the EU will 'fall over'. What exactly would constitute a breakdown of EU federalism? Would we recognize one if we saw it?

The formal renunciation of the Treaties by all member states and the vacating of the offices in Brussels, Strasbourg, and Luxembourg would constitute an indisputable breakdown of the EU. But, short of such a dramatic and unlikely scenario, it not self-evident precisely what sort of behaviors or institutional changes should be viewed as indicators of the breakdown of EU federalism. This section explores the range of variation on our dependent variable—the durability of EU federalism—by highlighting the behavioral and institutional changes that could be taken as indicators of the breakdown of EU federalism.

Dissolution

Formal dissolution constitutes the most complete form of breakup for a federation. In this case, the federation dies when all of its constituent states agree to end their union. Total dissolution is more likely in a federation with a small number of states, in which they simply break up the federation and decide to go their separate ways. Czechoslovakia's velvet divorce and most recently the dissolution of Serbia

---

[7] However, as Bermeo (2002) notes, all the failed federations of the 20th cent. have been ones imposed by an outside power.

and Montenegro illustrate this dynamic. As the number of states in the federation increases, so does the likelihood that some subset of states will maintain existing federal institutions, even if others have torn away from the federation. (We discuss this outcome—*limited secession*—below.)

While formal dissolution would constitute the most complete form of breakup of the EU, it is also the least likely. The current Treaty contains no provisions allowing for its termination. Formally, if all the member states agreed to end the EU, they would need to sign a new treaty detailing how and when to dissolve the Union. This treaty, like any EU Treaty, would need to be ratified, in some cases via a national referendum.

For the foreseeable future, it is difficult to imagine any plausible scenario in which the EU's twenty-five member states would agree to dissolve the Union. Sociocultural safeguards provide the strongest bulwark against dissolution. Even with today's modest levels of European identity, far more citizens across the EU think EU membership is a good thing than thinking it is a bad thing. Eurobarometer surveys over the past decade, supposedly a period of public disenchantment with the Union, show that consistently approximately 50 percent of respondents felt that EU membership was 'a good thing' while only approximately 13 percent felt that it was 'a bad thing'. Even in the most Euroskeptic countries, such as the UK and Sweden, those who view EU membership is a good thing consistently outnumber those who view it as a bad thing. (In 2006, 34 percent good vs. 28 percent bad in the UK and 39 percent vs. 32 percent in Sweden. See Eurobarometer 64: 9–12.) In this climate of public opinion, it is difficult to imagine politicians aggresively pursuing moves to dissolve the EU, or to imagine publics supporting such moves, either directly through referenda or indirectly through elections. If the EU is someday formally dissolved, this would most likely only come at the endpoint of a long series of partial breakdowns along the lines we outline below.

Limited Secession

The secession of one (or a small number) of member states would constitute a limited form of explosion. Though rare, such voluntary secessions are not unprecedented in federal systems. For instance, the Malaysian Federation continued (and continues) to operate after Singapore's exit in 1965. The EU itself has experienced secession. Though a full-fledged member state has never seceded, Greenland did secede from the Union in 1985 after achieving home rule from Denmark. The EU's draft constitutional treaty specifically establishes a mechanism for secession (Article I-60). Secession of a member state would clearly signal a crisis of the Union, but it might not prove catastrophic. Indeed, while any secession would be traumatic in the short run, one can imagine scenarios in which the exit of a 'preference outlier' might eventually facilitate strengthening of the Union. For instance, if a state with strong sovereignty concerns, such as Denmark or the UK, left the Union, it might free up remaining members to pursue deeper integration in areas that had been blocked.

The secession of a member state would signal a failure both of the Union's structural safeguards, partisan safeguards, and sociocultural safeguards. Secession would be likely only where a member state felt that it could not adequately assert its interests through the Council of Ministers or its influence in other EU fora. If a member state found itself repeatedly outvoted in the Council on issues of core national concern and was unable to block such decisions at the ECJ as violations of subsidiarity or to mitigate their impact through the implementation process, then one can imagine (however unlikely) scenarios in which a member state would decide to quit the Union. Secession would also mark a failure of partisan safeguards, as the European partisan counterparts of the government in question would have surely tried to dissuade it from exiting. Finally, governments are only likely to quit the Union if such a move enjoys the approval of their electorates, which would itself indicate a clear failure of sociocultural safeguards.

Atrophy

Another form of breakdown would involve gradual atrophy. In this scenario, EU institutions would continue to exist in more or less their current form, but would be increasingly ignored by governments and interest groups, who might instead turn their attention inward or to other supranational organizations. Over time, the EU would cease to be a significant forum for policymaking. This type of atrophy would be unprecedented among truly federal systems. However, a number of empires and international organizations provide useful illustrations of this process. For instance, the Holy Roman Empire experienced a slow death through atrophy. Formally, the Holy Roman Empire existed for nearly a millennium (843–1805). In practice, the conflict between Protestants and Catholics in the sixteenth century initiated a downward spiral from which the empire never recovered. Over the next 200 years, the Holy Roman Empire devolved from a powerful, quasi-federal arrangement into an empty shell. By the eighteenth century, Voltaire famously quipped that the Holy Roman Empire was 'neither Holy, nor Roman, nor an Empire'. As Tim Garton Ash put it recently, might a future French philosopher, surveying a weak, loose agglomeration spanning into Asia Minor, the Caucasus, and to the edge of the Urals one day point out that the EU is 'neither European nor a Union' (2006)?

Atrophy would result most likely from an erosion of the Union's judicial safeguards. Though the EU enjoys strong judicial safeguards, these cannot be taken for granted. Defenders of national sovereignty and economic protectionists regularly rail against the ECJ's intrusions into national affairs. National politicians of all varieties complain of 'red tape' emanating from Brussels, and EU policy-makers increasingly profess commitment on the use of flexible, non-binding 'new modes of governance' such as the Open Method of Coordination (see Kelemen and Idema 2006 for a critique of the OMC). Thus far, such methods have been limited to peripheral areas of policymaking such as social policy. However, if they spill over into core areas of EU competence, such as the Single Market and the protection of individual rights, they could erode the EU's judicial safeguards. Were the EU to travel too far down this path, it might atrophy into something like the OECD (Organization for Economic Cooperation and Development)—a weak international forum for the comparison of 'best practices' and the dissemination of policy ideas—a far cry from the powerful EU we observe today.

Growth of Variable Geometry

The least obvious form of collapse would involve the growth of variable geometry. Some degree of variable geometry constitutes no threat to the Union. Variable geometry already exists in the EU, for instance with the variable memberships in the Eurozone and Schengen, voluntary opt-outs in areas such as immigration and asylum and plans for 'enhanced cooperation' in European Security and Defense Policy (ESDP). Variable geometry exists in many federations, where it is labeled 'asymmetric federalism', and is typically tailored to allow some states—for instance those with particularly distinct cultural identities—greater autonomy in policymaking.

Like other federations, the EU can operate effectively with some forms of variable geometry. To date, variable geometry has served primarily to facilitate deepening of European integration, allowing pioneers to move ahead and generating pressures to follow (Labeta 2005). However, taken to an extreme, variable geometry could vitiate the Union (Leslie 2000). Some observers fear that the exercise of opt-outs in sensitive areas—for instance a large state quitting the Eurozone—could initiate a great unraveling, leading more states to opt out of more policy areas. If voluntary opt-outs and opt-ins became the norm, the EU might come to constitute more of an inchoate assemblage of overlapping clubs than a formal federal-type organization with a legal order. As Schmitter (1996) pointed out in his analysis of potential Euro futures, this outcome (which he labeled *Condominio*) would be the most unprecedented path for the EU to take.

Greater reliance on variable geometry, if it is to emerge, is most likely to result from an effort to steer clear of two less attractive outcomes: limited secession and atrophy. In order to discourage skeptical member states from either seceding or grinding EU operations to a halt, those who wish to push ahead will be tempted simply to allow them to opt-out.

Civil War

A civil war, in which federal forces are deployed against a member state's forces or in which one member state's forces are deployed against another's would constitute a breakdown of the federal system. Federal systems are designed to function as communities based on a shared rule of law. Where federal-state or interstate relations become violent, this rule of law is, at the very least, temporarily shaken. Such conflicts, by their very nature, signify a lack of common identity and the breakdown in the sociocultural safeguards of federalism.

Ultimately, the impact of a 'civil war' on a federal system depends on the outcome of the conflict. If state based rebels prevail, a federal system may collapse or at least lose one or more states to secession. If, on the other hand, federal forces prevail, the federal system may well emerge strengthened. Indeed, as Brian Taylor (2006) has argued, in practice many federal systems regularly rely on some degree of coercion. Similarly, Horowitz (1985) has argued that coercion may be crucial to deterring secessionist threats and helping federations to succeed.

Is a European civil war plausible? While a war pitting the EU as a collective actor against one of its member states is highly implausible, a variety of other civil war scenarios are easier to imagine. For instance, looking some years into the future, one could imagine a newly admitted member state in the Balkans requesting EU assistance in suppressing an armed insurgency by a minority ethnic group. They might in fact be eager for EU involvement, both to benefit from material assistance and to multilateralize the conflict so as to avoid potential charges of human rights abuses by domestic troops. If the EU mounted a successful 'peacemaking' and 'peacekeeping' operation, such a civil war might in fact strengthen the Union. By contrast, any violent conflict between two member states—for instance involving a border dispute or intervention by one member state to protect its ethnic compatriots in a neighboring state—would prove far more threatening to the Union. Fortunately, violent conflict between member states is highly unlikely for the foreseeable future.

Conclusion

Rumors of the EU's impending demise are greatly exaggerated. The EU is not in a 'permanent crisis' as Barroso put it in June 2005, nor is it in a particularly 'deep crisis' as Jean Claude Juncker put it days later. The EU is certainly not facing an institutional crisis. The EU's legislative machinery continued operating effectively throughout 2005 and 2006, coping well with enlargement and continuing to make policy on everything from telecommunications to financial services, to environmental and consumer protection. Recently, the member states have backed the strengthening of EU powers in controversial areas such as counterterrorism and policing (with the Data Retention Directive, the European Evidence Warrant and proposals to give Europol new investigatory powers), and they have reached a compromise on the controversial services directive. The ECJ has continued to take a strict line enforcing EU law against errant governments and has expanded the reach of EU law into sensitive areas including health care policy (*Yvonne Watts*, Case C-372/04) and taxation (*Marks & Spencer*, Case C-446/03). In 2005, when the *Lega Nord*, a partner in Berlusconi's coalition government, raised the prospect of Italy quitting the Eurozone, some observers worried about the currency's future. The Euro has taken such threats in its stride, maintaining its strength on international currency markets.

In short, the EU still works, and it is extending into new policy arenas despite its supposed crisis. Though the EU lacks significant fiscal resources and has developed only a weak common foreign and defense policy, it has amassed an impressive array of powers at a rapid pace, with relatively few hiccups (such as the empty chair crisis and the Danish No Vote on Maastricht) along the way. From the long-term perspective, therefore, what is surprising is not that voters in two member states rejected the constitutional treaty, but that the EU does not experience more frequent clashes over its aims and direction.

Moravcsik suggests that we view the impasse over the EU constitution not as a sign of crisis, but as a sign that the EU has arrived at a stable constitutional equilibrium. He explains, 'The EU's current constitutional status quo appears stable and normatively attractive. Beyond incremental changes in policy, it is difficult to imagine functional pressures, institutional pressures, or normative concerns upsetting the stability of the basic constitutional equilibrium in Europe today' (2005a: 351). While one might agree with Moravcsik that today's constitutional status quo is normatively appealing, the notion that the EU is likely to remain in some type of stasis belies the experience of other federal systems. To be fair, Moravcsik does expect 'incremental changes in policy'. However, the experience of federal systems suggests that the cumulative effect of such incremental changes may yield significant changes in the division of authority between member states and the federal system. Even where they are self-enforcing and durable, federal systems are inherently unstable. They never stand still: rather the division of authority ebbs and flows between the center and the states in response to social, economic, and political change. To put it another way, if the EU achieves any sort of stable endpoint, it will be the first federal system in history to do so.

If the EU is facing any crisis, it is an existential crisis, driven more by anxiety and a panicked search for meaning than on any objective failings of the system. As with any existential crisis, so long as the victim does not commit suicide, they go on living. Indeed, the collective dialogue concerning the objectives of the EU that this crisis has sparked is surely good for a Union that has long failed to inspire much interest or passion on the part of its citizens. Perhaps the greatest danger in the current stalemate is that EU leaders seek to solve nonexistent problems, by introducing potentially destabilizing reforms to institutions that are operating quite well.

4

Informal Decision-Making in the Council: The Secret of the EU's Success?

DOROTHEE HEISENBERG

Introduction

The EU suffered a major public relations defeat in May 2005 with the French and Dutch rejection of the Constitutional Treaty. The fact that two founding member states' populations rejected a Treaty that had been laboriously negotiated over three long years (and mainly codified the status quo) suggested that the very idea of the EU itself was in question. Behind the scenes, however, in the EU's day-to-day dealings, the EU continued to legislate and conduct business in very much an ordinary way. Naturally, there are lingering questions about the status of the Constitutional Treaty, but there is no evidence of an EU decision-making crisis. Elites continue to work in the Commission, Council, and Parliament, and decisions are made on large and small integration items. The suggestion that the EU is at a crisis point because of a lack of political will or the enlargement or the lack of citizen support is not borne out by empirical evidence. It appears that the EU is capable of functioning indefinitely under the terms of the existing Nice Treaty (2003). This fact is somewhat of a puzzle for all those who championed the Constitutional Treaty as essential to prevent legislative gridlock in an enlarged EU.

To understand why this is a puzzle requires understanding how worried analysts of the EU were with each enlargement about the chances of decision-making gridlock unless the decision-making institutions themselves were adapted to the new EU size. Probably the most important impetus for each Intergovernmental Conference (IGC) after the Maastricht Treaty (those resulting in the Amsterdam, Nice, and Constitutional Treaties) was the need to change the decision-making process to accommodate enlargement. The received wisdom was that the institutions that had worked well with six member states in 1958 could not function effectively for twenty-seven in 2007. The old system of qualified majority voting (QMV) was problematic for several reasons: it overweighted the small countries significantly relative to the large. Moreover, it set a fairly high threshold for a supermajority (71–74 percent) and thereby cut down on the number of proposals likely to pass. Table 4.1 highlights the changes over time to the EU's QMV

TABLE 4.1. *Voting weights, population, and majority thresholds*

	1958	1973	1981	1986	1995	May 1 04	Nov. 1 04	Constitutional EU-27	Treaty	Population
B	8	5	5	5	5	5	12	12	1	10,396
Fr	32	10	10	10	10	10	29	29	1	61,685
Ge	32	10	10	10	10	10	29	29	1	82,532
It	20	10	10	10	10	10	29	29	1	57,888
L	1	2	2	2	2	2	3	3	1	452
N	7	5	5	5	5	5	13	13	1	16,258
DK		3	3	3	3	3	7	7	1	5,398
Ir		3	3	3	3	3	7	7	1	4,028
UK		10	10	10	10	10	29	29	1	59,652
Gr			5	5	5	5	12	12	1	11,041
P				5	5	5	12	12	1	10,475
Sp				8	8	8	27	27	1	42,345
A					4	4	10	10	1	8,976
Fi					3	3	7	7	1	5,220
Sw					4	4	10	10	1	8,976
Cy						2	3	3	1	730
Cz						5	12	12	1	10,212
Es						3	4	4	1	1,351
H						5	12	12	1	10,117
Lv						3	4	4	1	2,319
Lt						3	7	7	1	3,446
M						2	3	3	1	400
Pl						8	27	27	1	38,191
Sk						3	7	7	1	5,380
Sl						3	4	4	1	1,996
Bu								10	1	7,965
Ro								14	1	22,300
QMV	67/90	41/58	45/63	54/76	62/87	88/124	232/321 with 13 MS 62% pop.	255/345 with 14 MS 62% pop.	15 MS, 55% MS 65% pop.	488,864
QMV %	74%	71%	71%	71%	71%	71%	72%	74%		

Source: Adapted from Hayes-Renschaw et al. (2005).

weights and thresholds. Thus, in each IGC, a great deal of negotiation time was spent on reweighting the member states' votes and redrafting the threshold for QMV or drafting a new method that would be seen as more equitable and effective.

On the face of it, it did seem to be important to make decision-making easier not only from the perspective of the EU federalists. Even to Euroskeptics the prospect of legislative gridlock was not attractive, since even the most mundane proposals needed to conduct the daily business of the EU would need to pass the Council. Certainly, there was a logical reason to worry: more member states meant more opportunities for blocking legislation. The Treaty of Nice, originally designed to simplify decision-making, required a three-part test for each piece of legislation: a qualified majority of states, a majority of states (thirteen of the current twenty-five) and, if contested, more than 50 percent of the EU's population. Thus, mathematically, in an EU of fifteen states, any randomly chosen legislative act would have a passage probability of 8.2 percent, but with an EU of twenty-seven, that probability falls to 2.1 percent (Giavazzi et al. 2001).

Moreover, the inclusion of ten new very diverse member states with dissimilar economies, young party systems and different levels of development would lead one to expect policy differences in the Council undermining the EU's ability to pass legislation. Finally, the EU-25 includes more overweighted (Council votes relative to population) small states, very different postwar political histories and a reflexive urge to assert long-subjugated sovereignty.

In light of these mathematical and historical calculations, it is somewhat surprising that the feared legislative gridlock has not materialized to date. Even at the time of this writing with an EU of twenty-five, legislation continues to be churned out of the Council in significant numbers per year. To put these statistics in context, between 1999 and 2005 there were an average of forty-six directives, slightly less than the 1974–95 yearly average of forty-eight directives cited by Golub (1999: 738), but hardly a harbinger of legislative gridlock.[1]

There are two possible interpretations for the absence of a decision-making breakdown: the first hypothesis is a realist interpretation which argues that the dynamics in the Council were always based on power considerations (e.g. the Franco-German motor of integration), and that this trend continues with the addition of ten states. A cohort of large countries dominates the Council and achieves their objectives, while the others acquiesce, accept side payments, and agree to a 'consensus', knowing they could not stop the powerful states' agenda anyway.

The second hypothesis for the absence of breakdown is that the Council's method of decision-making is informal, not the formal Treaty-prescribed method, and that this informal practice is the secret of the EU's success. The informal process of consensus decision-making is *institutionally unique* and has its roots in EU history. It is the result of path dependencies developed early on in the Council,

---

[1] Golub counts only directives, and not regulations or Council decisions because 'although important issues are sometimes dealt with through regulations, separating these cases from the more numerous trivial and often routinized bundles of proposals presents an intractable methodological problem. By contrast, with directives the frequency of routinized legislation is quite low' (1999: 738). The statistics for the number of directives for 1999 through 2005 are 36, 39, 56, 54, 53, 48, and 38. The first five months of 2006 had fifteen directives, compared with eight in the same months of 2005, suggesting that the decline in the number of directives in 2005 was not due to enlargement gridlock.

which in turn have self-reinforcing properties. Over time, new member states in each enlargement have found it more useful, and more consistent with earlier practice, to adopt consensus than insist on voting.

This chapter argues for the second hypothesis, based on empirical accounts of the negotiation style in the Council, supporting sociological explanations that the negotiations in the EU Council of Ministers are institutionally unique and a HI adaptation that veers away from a realist interpretation of power dynamics in the Council of Ministers.

The rest of this chapter is organized as follows: the next section describes consensus decision-making in the EU, and analyzes its advantages and disadvantages. The second section briefly compares the decision-making methods used in the General Agreement on Tariffs and Trade (GATT)/WTO setting to those used in the EU Council of Ministers. The following section analyzes the summaries of Council acts from the last two years to see if the ten new member states are adapting to the institution of consensus or whether they are behaving differently in Council bargaining. The final section examines the question of how we observers would know that the institution is changing, and what kind of system might take its place.

Consensus Considered

One of the most unusual features of EU decision-making is its ability to pass legislation in the Council without a formal vote. Although many international and supranational organizations act on the basis of consensus (e.g. NATO, WTO, and International Standards Organization), the Council's legislative acts are binding without another vote, and thus the Council is institutionally closer to a parliament than a supranational organization. The Council of Ministers is transparent only insofar as a member state would like to present its views to the public. Formally, of course, the treaty-prescribed method of decision-making is QMV in the Council, but only approximately 20 percent of decisions are actually made that way.

The system of consensus decision-making has its roots in the 'empty chair crisis' and the Luxembourg compromise of the mid-1960s. Recalling that the Treaty of Rome had stipulated a move from unanimity voting to QMV in 1966, French President Charles de Gaulle used the battle about the CAP to protest the elimination of the national veto. Other states, while not necessarily happy to give up unanimity voting, understood that a state's important national interests were unlikely ever to be overruled, and refused to give in on the issue of QMV (Dinan 2004a). The constitutional crisis was resolved by the Luxembourg compromise in 1966, essentially a four-part agreement to disagree:

1. When issues very important to one or more member countries are at stake, the members of the Council will try, within a reasonable time, to reach solutions which can be adopted by all the members of the Council, while

respecting their mutual interests and those of the Community, in accordance with Article 2 of the Treaty.

2. The French delegation considers that, when very important issues are at stake, discussions must be continued until unanimous agreement is reached.
3. The six delegations note that there is a divergence of views on what should be done in the event of a failure to reach complete agreement.
4. However, they consider that this divergence does not prevent the Community's work being resumed in accordance with the normal procedure (Lambert 1966).

Two enduring features that put the Council of Ministers on the current path of consensus decision-making are illustrated in the communiqué.

- *Respecting their mutual interests and those of the Community*: the idea that each member state must respect serious political constraints of other states when negotiating is highlighted by empirical observers. No acts or issues are 'crammed down the throats' of other member states and a certain flexibility is shown when a particularly sensitive issue is negotiated.
- *Discussions must be continued until unanimous agreement is reached*: this has been modified slightly and now means that discussions must be continued until no significant objections have been raised. The issue under discussion is negotiated until all real objections have been met, or the issue is withdrawn.

The Luxembourg compromise legacy was a new system of decision-making that was accepted by the new entrants when they joined the EU. The system proved robust and self-reinforcing, and although several calls for changing to QMV were delivered by such EU luminaries as Leo Tindemans (1976) and Hans-Dietrich Genscher and Emilio Colombo in their plan (1981), consensus remained the norm. Even the attempt to repeal the Luxembourg compromise in the internal market in the SEA 1986 did not change the practice of consensus decision-making.

Advantages of Consensus

What accounted for the lack of change over time and numbers of decision-makers? Below, I argue that the advantages of consensus outweigh the disadvantages, and that historical experience has reinforced to the member states that consensus decision-making is rationally optimal as long as the parameters of decision-making remain at the status quo.

The empiricists claim that actual observation of the Council negotiations contradicts the realists' interpretations outlined above, and thus a sociological explanation of the Council decision-making process is more accurate. Lewis (2005: 942–5) suggests four measures by which Council negotiations are unique:

1. Noninstrumental self-restraint in demands and arguments,
2. Self-enforcing adherence to informal decision-making norms without threats of external sanctioning,
3. Empathy and other-regarding behavior not linked to calculative reasoning, and
4. Limits on instrumentalism through the collective legitimation of arguments.

There is a tacit agreement between the member states about the rules of the negotiations, which include reciprocity, thick trust and a genuine commitment to reach an agreement (see Hayes-Renshaw and Wallace 1997; Lewis 2000, 2005; Sherrington 2000). Strong preferences trump weak preferences and member states which have specific political problems domestically with a proposal are given some leeway or some ambiguous language to help cover their actions with the domestic constituencies. The role of QMV is more a deterrent to obstructive behavior than an actual shadow decision-making device. These characteristics are all empirically observable and would be more well known if the Council were more transparent.

This lack of transparency, however, provides the opportunity to trade off issues and legislative acts against each other which, it could be argued, is the secret of the EU's lawmaking success as well as the most compelling rationale for why a state against a specific proposal would capitulate and join the consensus. If a state has a number of legislative priorities and others which are less salient, then it can trade off progress in one area for concessions in another. In the aggregate, this means that the decision-making method in the EU is actually a decentralized system of strong preferences and priorities being exchanged for weakly held preferences. States can use their bargaining chips in the areas which mostly correspond to that state's priorities, enhancing sovereignty. The system of consensus essentially devolves into a very decentralized structure of preference voting. For example, hypothetically Germany and Finland could trade off fisheries policies against car recycling directives, allowing both Finland and Germany to reach an acceptable bargain as well as giving the EU two legislative successes.

The institution of consensus decision-making has enabled sovereign states to continue to compromise and integrate for almost fifty years by setting up a system where potential bargains across time and issue areas can be tabled and thereby create the impulse for further integration along quasi-neofunctional methods.[2] Although it gives a great deal of negotiation power and leeway to member state

---

[2] Neofunctionalists argued that the impulse for new areas to integrate was functionally necessary, whereas I argue they are necessary only as the counterpart to another bargain, not as some solution to a problem at the supranational level.

ministers, it is centralized enough to allow for vote swapping and temporal trade-offs, especially when one considers the role of the permanent representatives, COREPER. The negotiation style also explains how integration has been able simultaneously to deepen and widen, as different member states have preferences to integrate new issues.

The second, major advantage of consensus decision-making over voting is that ministers have the leeway to acknowledge 'special circumstances' or political constraints in their decision-making. There is, in essence, peer review that member states do not abuse the system. The informal negotiation dynamic, brought about by weekly or monthly meetings with the same partners and organized by COREPER, leads to a strong understanding of the other member states' domestic 'win sets' or unusual circumstances surrounding an issue, and the norm in the Council is that when a legitimate domestic problem crops up, the other member states will work around that constraint. This is a key element of the EU's success in not alienating the member states. Consensus tends to temper the overweighting of small states, while still curbing the power of the large.

In addition to the points above, member states might prefer the informal consensus-based decision-making in the Council rather than strict QMV because it gives the unsuccessful minority consideration from the other member states. In contrast to the outvoted minority under QMV decision-making, consensus decisions generated a steady stream of IOU's which expanded exponentially with the expansion of the EU. Thus, the forward momentum of the EU almost demands the continuation of consensus as a dominant decision-making mode. Interestingly, this characterization of the EU's decision-making style is consistent across methodologies, with spatial model theorists (König and Proksch 2006) and rational choice institutionalists (Farrell and Heritier 2003*b*) describing the negotiation style in similar fashion. Over time, new member states have chosen to participate in this system, preferring it to more confrontational, winner-take-all legislating styles.

Disadvantages of Consensus

There are five sets of problems that result from consensus decision-making:

1. Issue self-censorship and issue-area truncation,
2. Sloppy lawmaking,
3. Legitimacy and agent control,
4. Possibly lagging implementation of EU directives, and
5. Increasing marginalization of the Commission.

Because consensus has proved to have so many advantages over voting, however, these negative consequences have been more or less accepted over time as the price to pay for functioning EU governance.

The first drawback is relatively straightforward: if member states cannot simply outvote any minority grouping, the issue areas that may be addressed by EU legislation are, by definition, more truncated than they would otherwise be. Fewer legislative areas can be addressed because a minority does not want to transfer them to the EU. It is, of course, an open question whether by hindering EU action in sensitive national issue areas, the Council has actually contributed to the fifty years of positive integration. Having a brake on the EU legislation based on national sensitivities as defined by the member states' foreign ministers is perhaps a good thing, promoting the overall legitimacy of the EU project and keeping the member states engaged.

The second problem is one that has a long history in the EU—that of bad lawmaking. When consensus decision-making in the Council is the norm, the machinations required to get the required consensus often lead to flawed compromises on the substance of the issue. This is true not only of the legal parameters but also of the economic logic of some directives. The legal problem with consensus-driven directives was highlighted by the Council's legal service in 2004. When member states add statements to the Council record, they intend to influence the public perception and ECJ interpretation of the directive. However, the Council's legal service was sufficiently worried about this practice to issue an internal study on publishing statements for the minutes (see 'Study of Council Practice Regarding Statements for the Minutes in Connection with Openness,' May 3, 1995; and also *The Independent*, June 23, 1995). Although admitting that, 'statements in the Council minutes ... have always been a handy negotiating tool,' the report concludes that those 'contradicting or adding to the enacting terms of legislation must absolutely not be made' (ibid.). Noting that these statements would create 'legitimate expectations' on the part of the public despite having no force of law in the ECJ, the Council's legal service foresaw an enormous legal liability. More common are badly worded legal directives that make transposition into national law difficult or have unforeseen consequences. One lawyer compared these elements 'the legal equivalent of pork' and they arise primarily out of the consensus decision-making style.

On the economic front, similar issues arise from consensus decision-making. The history of the European Takeover Directive is perhaps the best known example of consensus in the Council, but other examples exist as well. Briefly, the Council deliberated on the Takeover Directive for fourteen years before it failed unexpectedly in the EP. Subsequently, the Council's new compromise draft passed, but neither the European companies nor the Commission were happy with the hash that consensus (essentially the unwillingness simply to outvote Germany) made of the new directive. Trying to meet the needs of all member states in one directive simply neutered the integrating effect of the directive. Similarly, the Services Directive which ultimately had to omit the 'country of origin' clause in order to appease the French, significantly subverting the intent of the legislation to create a single market for services. Thus, it is fair to say that the unwillingness to outvote minority member states and to appease everyone can make for ungainly or impractical EU laws.

The third problem with consensus decision-making has become perhaps the most damaging: the legitimacy concerns of the citizens of the EU. With so much discretion in the hands of elites without public oversight, the fear of 'a secretive bureaucracy' eroding national sovereignty has been popularized in the member states' press. There are also claims that COREPER, the permanent representatives in the Council, have 'gone native'—meaning they lose touch with the national interests because of the camaraderie of working with the same colleagues for the whole career, and being incentivized to find EU solutions to problems (Lewis 2002; Beach 2004). Over thirty years there have been calls to vote rather than decide by consensus, but the system has remained informal and flexible despite these voices.[3]

As a result of the perceptions of a democratic deficit in the past decade, the Council has tried to make inroads toward greater transparency by releasing some statistics about outcomes of Council acts, but the sensitive negotiations remain out of the public eye. In December 2005, responding to transparency criticisms, the EU Council agreed to some minor changes, but the EU ombudsman indicated that

The [December] decision is limited to the council's first deliberations after the European Commission has presented its proposal and the final vote. The debates in between are still closed to the public.... The intermediate stages of the debates are the more delicate ones, where decisions are hammered out and negotiations take place.... This is something that I believe citizens wish to know about (see *EU Observer*, 20 January 2006. Available at http://euobserver.com/9/20740).

As Desmond Dinan (2004*a*: 244) points out, however, one cannot legislate transparency because it simply drives the substantive negotiations to back rooms and dinner tables: 'the limited openness of Council meetings reveals little of how the

---

[3] Tindemans, 'enhanced coherence, recourse to majority voting, and a strengthening of continuity' (Tindemans Report, EC Bull, 1/76, section V, part C, point 2, paragraphs a. and b.), Prodi, 'From a much broader standpoint, we must carry through to completion the process whereby consensus is replaced by voting, the normal procedure in a democratic system. What we must do is evolve towards a system of decision-making that is based on voting, a system that is both effective and can be understood by everyone.... [W]e must come to embrace a majority voting culture, in which decisions reflect the will of the largest number but apply equally to each and everyone. All too often, we aim for consensus even when there is none to be found, and progress grinds to a halt. To overcome reservations in some quarters, there is only one solution: to put the matter to the vote.' 'For a Strong Europe, with a Grand Design and the Means of Action.' Speech by the president of the European Commission, Romano Prodi, at the Institut d'Etudes Politiques, May 29, 2001 in Paris. Available at http://europa.eu.int/comm/commissioners/prodi/speeches/index_en.htm.

Council really works because ministers restrict themselves while on television to bland, predictable statements.' Indeed, the very first webcast ECOFIN Council meeting in July 2006 yielded very little substantive debate, and controversial questions such as the implementation of the stability and growth pact or the entry by Slovenia into the Euro were debated during an off-camera session. Thus, the EU's legitimacy problem stems partly from the lack of observable debate and positions, as well as the lack of information about how one's ministers have voted. The problem is compounded by member states, which, knowing there is no official record of votes, use opposition to an EU directive for domestic electoral benefit.

A fourth disadvantage of consensus decision-making has been hypothesized by Hayes-Renshaw et al. (2006): perhaps member states which simply go along with the consensus are more likely not to implement those directives in a timely fashion. This question would require more empirical research and actual observation in the Council meetings, so the authors do not draw any conclusions about this point but simply raise it as a possibility. On the more easily researched question of whether a vote against a legislative act correlates with delays in implementation, Falkner et al. (2004: 452) focusing on twenty-six infringement procedures from the area of labor law find that:

...such 'opposition through the backdoor' does occur occasionally. However, we demonstrate that opposition at the end of the EU policy process may also arise without prior opposition at the beginning. Additionally, our findings indicate that non-compliance is often unrelated to opposition, and due to administrative shortcomings, interpretation problems, and issue linkage.

Thus, it is fair to say that the jury is still out on whether lack of implementation is a possible consequence of Council consensus decision-making. Hypothetically, however, one should see the same correlation between the silent outvoted minority in consensus and noncompliance as the observable outvoted minority in voting and noncompliance; thus, this is not a drawback specific to consensus decision-making.

Finally, the fifth disadvantage of consensus decision-making is the increasing marginalization of the Commission. Essentially, the Commission takes on more of a technocratic drafting function rather than an agenda-setting role. The European Council has evolved into the central agenda setter, with the Commission relegated to drafting the language of essentially agreed-upon bargains. The fact that so few of the proposed legislative acts ever die permanently, but rather get negotiated and redrafted until they pass, suggests that the Commission sends proposals on which it believes the European Council has reached a consensus in principle.[4]

If there is agreement about the characterization of negotiation as a series of exchanges on issues with greater or lesser salience, there is less agreement about

---

[4] This conclusion is consistent with the conclusions of König and Proksch (2006).

why the decision-making style *persists* over time and member state configuration. Here, the theoretical insights from the HIs (Thelen and Steinmo 1992; Pierson 1996, 2004) can be used to understand the mechanisms by which the existing historical structures constrain and incentivize the member states to maintain the EU's unique decision-making style. To be clear, an alternative arrangement for decision-making exists, has been promoted by prominent leaders, and has certain advantages over consensus decision-making. Had the Council of Ministers adopted it, this would cast doubt on the validity of HI claims. Since, however, the EU continues on the path of consensus decision-making, it is worth examining the variables which account for the continuity.

Path dependence arguments propose that:

1. Small events or decisions early in the time line matter more than later events,
2. Over time, these decisions become reinforced and structure the incentives and disincentives to deviate from the status quo, and
3. The earlier decisions can have unintended consequences later in time.

As the history of the Luxembourg compromise sketched above suggests, the decision to have QMV but to consider a state's vital interests when making decisions at the EU level led to the consensus decision-making style. That method proved highly effective over time, and gave comfort to member states uncomfortable with relinquishing national sovereignty, and was thus reinforced.

Pierson (2004: 35) claims that:

... institutions induce self-reinforcing processes that make reversals increasingly unattractive over time. In contexts of complex social interdependence, new institutions and policies often generate high fixed costs, learning effects, coordination effects and adaptive expectations. Institutions and policies may encourage individuals and organizations to invest in specialized skills, deepen relationships with other individuals and organizations, and develop particular political and social identities.

In the context of the Council of Ministers, the 'complex social interdependence' is perhaps the strongest factor explaining continuity and reinforcement. The ministers can meet as much as forty-two times per year on average (Sherrington 2000: 58) and their interactions are structured by COREPER, a group of member state representatives that spend their career in Brussels working together. The six-month rotation of the Council Presidency provides a significant incentive to cooperate, because every member state understands that obstructionist behavior during another country's Presidency will come back to haunt it during its Council Presidency.

Learning effects are also evident after each enlargement as the new entrants test different behaviors to advance their national interests. Because of the complex social interdependence, however, the new member states are usually incentivized to adopt the norms of the Council. 'Social actors make commitments based on existing institutions and policies. As they do so, the cost of reversing course generally rises dramatically' (Pierson 2004: 35).

Finally, Pierson (2004: 39) highlights the socialization process whereby a collective understanding of the organization's functions are determined and re-inforced. 'Ideas are frequently shared with other social actors in ways that create network effects and adaptive expectations. Sociologists have emphasized that the development of norms or standards of appropriateness is a collective, self-reinforcing process.' Thus, the members of governments are socialized into the norms of the Council's decision-making process, avoiding posturing, making compromises on low-salience issues, allowing exceptions for specific domestic difficulties etc. The understanding of what the EU level is and does is shaped by the negotiation style, and vice versa.

Potential critical junctures in the EU's development—notably various enlargements—have not altered the path of decision-making. The addition of ten new member states and ministers not acculturated to the Council might have been a critical juncture where the path was changed to voting in the Council. However, the existing incentives for continuity of decision-making style (the network of relationships at the Council and in COREPER developed over fifty years and accumulated IOUs and goodwill) mitigated the possibility of significant change.

Finally, a disadvantage of consensus decision-making has been its unintended consequences. Here unintended consequences represent more than simply trade-off decisions made by policymakers. Indeed, many prominent EU supporters have advocated voting to ameliorate or eliminate these disadvantages, but the practice of consensus decision-making has not changed.

How Does Council Decision-Making Differ from Other International Organizations?

Although every analyst of the Council agrees on the fact that there is lim-ited voting in the Council, there is sharp disagreement about what that fact implies. Broadly, there are two schools of thought: the realists and the empiricists. The realists believe that the traditional use of the word 'consensus' ('general agreement or accord') is a useful fiction for any supranational organization com-posed of sovereign governments, and in the EU context it represents no more than 'organized hypocrisy' (Steinberg 2002 uses this term in the context of the WTO). The decisions reached by consensus are actually silent votes where the outvoted minority, realizing it has lost, will capitulate (the 'shadow of the vote') and agree to the consensus. There are various reasons why the outvoted minority would do this: to give the Council an advantage in interinstitutional conflicts, to shore up the supranational decisions vis-à-vis the national level, or to cover up a defeat. For Council rationalists, consensus in the EU is the same as in the WTO or NATO: it helps legitimate decisions of a supranational organization that usurp national sovereignty.

In the GATT/WTO context, powerful countries can coerce a consensus through various mechanisms, according to Steinberg (2002):[5] first, having a large market which can be opened and closed to trade is the measure of power that determines outcomes in the GATT/WTO negotiations. A second form of coercion is the threat to exit the organization that is unable to achieve a consensus, or threatening to move to a different organization where powerful countries are more likely to succeed in their programs. Finally, weak countries are excluded from the initial agenda setting at which powerful countries discuss their preferred outcomes.

Several of the mechanisms cited by Steinberg in the WTO context as enabling the large to dominate, simply do not exist in the Council. In the Council, large countries are deliberately underweighted, and small overweighted in terms of QMV, thus the power differential Steinberg assigns to market size is mitigated considerably. Moreover, member states cannot credibly threaten to exit the EU, and the Commission sets the agenda[6] thus many of the structural advantages that convey power to coerce are absent in the EU context. Furthermore, within the Council, the negotiation style itself is different: negotiations do not stop when the relevant majority has been achieved, and even minority voices are compensated for their assent with either side payments or a proposal on an issue of interest to them.

Enlargement and the Continuity of Consensus

With the disadvantages of consensus decision-making detailed above, why has it proved so resilient? Consensus has been functional for decades and has been able to survive the addition of new members with different histories, interests, and negotiation objectives. Although there has been scholarly acknowledgment that the informal dynamics in the Council matter (e.g. Lewis 1998, 2005), less attention has been focused on how the EU keeps those informal decision-making dynamics and transmits them to new entrants. If a constructivist model is applied, it would be relevant to understand how new Council members interact with existing members and whether they are ever told 'this is how we do things'.

---

[5] Steinberg cites Cox and Jacobson's work (1973) on the UN as the basis for many of the arguments he makes.

[6] There is significant literature on agenda setting in the EU. See Steunenberg (1994), Schneider (1995), Garrett and Tsebelis (1996), and Pollack (1997).

Conversely, do new member states adopt a hard bargaining approach first, and then learn by trial and error that this approach will not yield the anticipated benefits? Anecdotal evidence suggests that at least some of the new member states which shadowed the Council meetings beginning in 2003 became acculturated to consensus by learning that negotiation as opposed to blocking is more successful in the EU.

The data below show that voting patterns in the Council remained similar before and after the big bang enlargement of the EU in May 2004. What accounts for the relatively swift learning of the new member states? One hypothesis might be cultural, that having witnessed the congenial negotiating style and not having a domestic audience for the outcome of the negotiations takes some of the posturing out of the process. Another might be a rational response to the institutional incentives: with the Council negotiations structured in more or less Axelrod (1984) fashion, the best play may be tit for tat, with limited defections. New member states quickly realize that if they buck the institutional incentives, the negative reputation of the member state becomes far more trouble than the single negotiation. The unique historical origins of the EU have created a structure where positive negotiation styles are rewarded and negative ones are isolated. Since there is no domestic payoff for obstruction and isolation, it is possible to assimilate new member states into the existing pattern of cooperation.

In the above acculturation of new member states hypothesis, there is an unspoken assumption that the number of new member states is small enough not to develop its own negotiation logic. Earlier enlargements encompassed only three new states at a time, and thus were a small addition to the old member states. This section of the chapter examines the question of whether the 2004 enlargement comprised a new dynamic because of either the number of new states or the historical legacy of a majority of the new member states.

Before looking at the new member states, a word about the data available is in order. The summary of Council acts that is provided by the Council under the terms of the 1995 transparency guidelines is incomplete in many ways. First, the data only describe definitive legislative acts which are passed, not those proposed. A certain percentage of acts proposed are eventually withdrawn because a consensus cannot be found, and thus these catalogued acts are only those which actually passed. Golub (1999) suggests that approximately 10 percent of proposed acts 1974–95 were withdrawn, but there is no documented evidence that that percentage remains constant. Since proposed legislative acts have increased over time, it is reasonable to presume more have been withdrawn, but the Council does not give those aggregated statistics.

Second, and more important, the data show (and the empirical analysts state) that mainly the acts of smaller importance and budget items on a timeline are subject to contested votes. Generally, issues involving the continuation of agricultural or fisheries subsidies are contested votes (votes with abstentions and votes against). The more significant, transfer-of-sovereignty-to-the-EU-level votes are by and large by consensus. Thus, detailed analysis of contested votes is not really useful if the larger question is about EU integration, since most of those votes are done by consensus and do not figure into the scatter plots (Mattila and Lane 2001).

Historically, about 80 percent of EU legislative acts are approved by consensus, with the other 20 percent being approvals in agriculture, fisheries, and subsidies cases (for more detailed information, see Heisenberg 2005a). The data in Table 4.2 show the average votes against and the member states most likely to contest a consensus. The data also include the first fourteen months of the EU-25 to compare whether the new member states are behaving as the old are in respect to the consensus. The fear among analysts, based on both the argument that there were too many entrants at once to acculturate, or that the state history of these member states requires them to be more independently sovereign of a supranational institution, have thus far proven to be false. The EU-10 which joined in May 2004 have been slightly less likely to contest Council votes, and although Poland is an outlier with respect to its May 2004 cohort, in medium-large member states, it is well below the average and not particularly obstreperous in the Council (Graph 4.1). Thus, the voting record evidence from the first year and a half after enlargement is that the new member states are not particularly predisposed to change the way of conducting business in the Council. There is some variation in the behavior of specific member states—Poland and Lithuania are the two that stand out—but they do not appear to constitute a whole new paradigm of behavior in the Council.

If the Council voting outcomes have remained consistent, has the negotiation style within the Council changed perhaps? On this point, there are some early accounts of changes within the Council that may ultimately change the workings of the Council. Maurer (2006) makes two arguments pointing to changing dynamics in the Council due to the structural changes of moving from fifteen to twenty-five (and next year, twenty-seven) ministers. The first is that due to time and space constraints, complete meetings where everyone speaks are increasingly rare, meaning that sometimes ministers do not even show up, leaving the work to the technocrats. This obviously works to the advantage of states which have a strong technocratic representation or those with particular expertise with a subject. When ministers do speak, it has the effect of making purely political considerations that much more apparent. The second change is that with so many smaller countries, there is less oversight by the presidency of potential deals, and this leaves greater room for the larger countries to 'organize' the groups before the Council meetings. One observer states that usually seven to eight delegations

TABLE 4.2. *Consensus legislation, 1996–2005*

	1996	1997	1998	1999	2000	2001	2002	2003	2004	2005	1994–2005 Average
Total abstentions	14	17	34	9	12	25	30	28	36	13	22
Total votes against	55	56	60	30	22	27	28	48	37	13	38
Total legislative acts with dissent*	44	48	56	30	5	31	37	38	33	21	34
Total legislative acts	229	218	219	199	191	187	192	196	239	133	200
Legislative acts passed by consensus	185	170	163	169	186	156	157	158	206	112	166
Consensus legislation (%)	81%	78%	74%	85%	97%	83%	82%	81%	86%	84%	83.17%

* Is not the sum of abstentions and votes because some legislative acts have both abstentions and votes against.

Note: Data for 2004 masks the fact that only 8 legislative acts were contested after May 1. Before accession, 25 legislative acts were contested.

Source: General-Secretariat of the Council of the European Union: DG F III: Information, Transparency, and Public Relations.

1996–2005

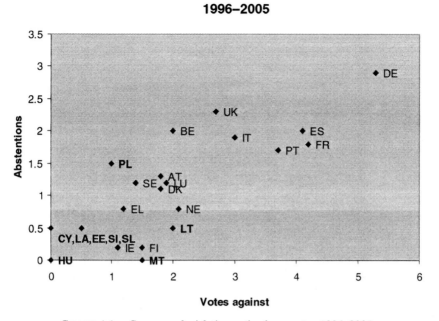

GRAPH 4.1. Consensus legislation voting by country, 1996–2005.
Source: General-Secretariat of the Council of the European Union: DG F III: Information, Transparency, and Public Relations.

monopolize the negotiations and within those delegations the majority is formed.[7] Maurer cites fears that the large countries increasingly block agendas (especially in the internal market) rather than organize them for greater integration. Thus far, however, we do not see changes in the actual outcomes of the Council voting statistics, so these fears of significant Council consensus breakdown may be overblown.

What Would Constitute a Whole New Paradigm?

It has been argued that the EU has benefited from the existence of the consensual decision-making style in the EU. The system has been self-reinforcing and has held up after many different enlargements, indicating its superiority. However, the system relies on certain norms of behavior and institutional understandings, and thus it would be wrong to assume there are no other alternative ways of decision-making. This section looks at the alternatives to consensus and how those observers of the EU decision-making process would be able to discern change. In

[7] Anonymous legal adviser at the Permanent Representation.

particular, two different signs are highlighted: first, if the summary of Council acts suddenly reflected more actual voting, and second, if the institution of enhanced cooperation were suddenly used.

The first of these indicators is self-explanatory. The summary is publicly available monthly, and if one were able to discern an upward percentage of acts passed by voting when the prescribed method of decision-making is QMV, that would certainly be evidence that the benefits of consensus are waning.

A second, less obvious, signal would be the use of the EU's enhanced cooperation procedure. This decision-making procedure has never been used, to date, to create greater integration within a subset of EU member states, but it has been in the *acquis* since the Amsterdam Treaty and has been made easier to use with every subsequent treaty revision.

All three of the IGCs after Maastricht were primarily designed to resolve the outstanding issues on institutional design and in each case, the issues remained unresolved (e.g. the number of Commissioners was not reduced dramatically, the number of Council votes per member state continued to overweight the small countries, and so on). Economists calculated that the Nice treaty council voting procedure with its three tests actually made passing a legislative act *more* difficult than under Amsterdam rules. Thus, the unspoken demand was always that unless institutional changes made decision-making easier, the EU would stagnate. Enhanced cooperation was partially the response to ensure that the forward momentum of consensus continued. It was a signal that stagnation would not become the norm, and that the ideals of 'ever closer union' would continue to drive the EU agenda despite the introduction of more states not really interested in the political agenda. The idea of flexibility had a great deal of intuitive appeal for those states interested in closer integration. Whereas the consensus decision-making model left the speed of integration up to the slowest country or countries, flexibility made it possible to find a group of eight states interested in integrating further and created the possibility of merging into a hard core–periphery arrangement that some (e.g. Lamers of the German CDU) had championed earlier.

The choice of enhanced cooperation, however, is more strategic than simply creating a hard core–periphery arrangement. Implicitly it is a new motor of decision-making integration that can be as effective as the consensus model was in causing an EU-27 to integrate more deeply. Thus, the enhanced cooperation institution serves two distinct purposes (from the perspective of prointegration countries): first, it is an explicit threat to slow or recalcitrant countries on any one issue, 'give us your consent on this issue (and potentially be compensated by having something you care about put on the agenda) or we will go ahead and make an enhanced cooperation issue of it', and second, if states really create enhanced cooperation subgroups, this changes the material and strategic options for the excluded states and may cause them to decide to join even if they originally did not want to (Gruber 2000).

The credible threat of enhanced cooperation is a new weapon in the arsenal of persuasion in the Council of Ministers. It is the 'stick' that may persuade reluctant countries to join a consensus, even when the 'carrots' of side payments or issue linkages will not suffice. Jo Shaw (2004) noted that enhanced cooperation has already been used once in this fashion, in the case of Italy and the European Arrest Warrant in 2001. It remains to be seen how much use will be made of that weapon in the Council, although it will also be difficult, without speaking to Ministers or COREPER members, to assess the full measure of its impact.

The second use is perhaps the more interesting one, since it seems to have a much larger potential impact on integration speed. The hurdle of one-third of member states is not particularly high in a union of twenty-seven countries (requiring at present only nine member states) and it would be fairly easy to construct coalitions on any number of issues that have stalled historically. Thus, the question will be whether the countries at the vanguard of greater federalism will have the self-restraint not to push to create the many potential subgroups that are theoretically possible.

If subgroups are judiciously created, meaning that all member states but two or three are in the subgroup, the impulse to stay out of the enhanced cooperation area will be smaller because the state's strategic options have shifted. This is perhaps most evident in the 'Should Denmark and the UK join the Euro?' discussions. The opt-outs for Euro entry that were given to these countries were permanent and thus EMU should be considered the first case of enhanced cooperation, and yet, ten years after the decision to stay out, both countries have continually to address political pressure to join the Eurozone. The pressure emanates from domestic groups interested in joining the subgroup and links to supranational groups that would prefer to have the member state in the group. As the size of the enhanced cooperation group increases (as, for example, when the CEECs begin to join the euro in 2007), the cost–benefit analysis of the governments outside the enhanced cooperation zone will shift, and it *may* become too costly to be outside the zone of successful cooperation.

Since Britain is no stranger to understanding the role of the outsider, it is not accidental that this feature of enhanced cooperation figured prominently in the UK parliamentary debates over the Nice Treaty (which abolished the national veto over the establishment of enhanced cooperation). The Euroskeptics raised the fear that issues that the British had successfully kept out of QMV voting arena, like taxation for example, would be supranationalized through the use of enhanced cooperation:

It enables a group of states to move ahead, and we must address ourselves to the effect that that would have on other states outside . . . . if benefits were produced for participating countries, non-participants would be motivated to become involved . . . . The pressures on a British Government as a result of the market and of commerce to join such a euro-area of enhanced co-operation in taxation will be considerable .... The Commission has spotted ... a way of outflanking the national veto on taxation.[8]

In the example of monetary union, the centre point is created and a eurozone established. Then all the others are effectively dragged along with it .... Those who are reluctant and are found to be outside the system are then, by a gravitational process, drawn into having to comply with the arrangements.[9]

By late 2005, the Commission had indeed proposed an enhanced cooperation group to deal with harmonizing the corporate tax base in Europe by 2008 because, in the words of one Commission official, 'We don't think we should waste time trying to convince the other five [member states who oppose harmonizing]' (*Financial Times*, October 25, 2005). If this style of decision-making becomes the dominant mode in the EU, adversarial politics may improve the range of issues the EU can legislate, but may ultimately decrease the legitimacy of the institutions.

Conclusion

The institution of consensus appears fairly robust at the time of this writing. The new member states have not disproportionately contested EU legislative acts, and even if new member states such as Poland seem to be contesting the EU status quo in many other fields, the pace of EU decision-making is not under obvious threat at this time.

Although consensus has many advantages that seem to be the key to the EU's unlikely ability to move forward over time, despite more issues and member states, it is too soon to say definitively that this trend will continue indefinitely. In particular, there may be frustration among the EU-25 member states that the number of issues appropriate in the Council is so truncated, and certain states may wish to move forward at a faster integration pace. The other path is a breakdown of the reciprocity and trust in the Council of Ministers, as member states disagree about the desirability of greater integration per se. Finally, a threat to the viability of consensus decision-making would be the greater transparency of Council deliberations, and a change in the negotiating dynamic within that institution to appeal to a domestic constituency more than joint problem solving.

[8] Denzil Davies, Member of Parliament, July 17, 2001, United Kingdom Parliament debate transcript column 211. Available at www.publications.parliament.uk/pa/cm200102/cmhansrd/vo010717/debtext/10717-21.htm.

[9] William Cash, Member of Parliament, July 17, 2001, United Kingdom Parliament debate transcript column 194. Available at www.publications.parliament.uk/pa/cm200102/cmhansrd/vo010717/debtext/10717-17.htm.EU 24.

In any of these scenarios, the signs of a breakdown of consensus would be evident immediately. It is unknowable whether the breakdown would herald a new era of EU decision-making or presage the decline of the EU as we currently conceive of it. As this chapter has argued, consensus decision-making, with its sovereignty enhancing attributes has been a catalyst to the success of the EU, and thus any change from that model should be viewed with trepidation.

5

The Theory and Reality of the European Coal and Steel Community

KAREN J. ALTER AND DAVID STEINBERG[1]

European integration began in 1950 with the Schuman Plan, which launched the ECSC. The Schuman Plan was designed to alleviate concerns that Germany's dominance in coal and steel could be used to harm European reconstruction efforts or to build another war machine. Jean Monnet, the Plan's chief architect, also wanted to shore up the French planning process for reconstruction by Europeanizing the technocratic planning approach. Most supporters of the ECSC project expected integration to expand beyond Coal and Steel, and hoped that it would serve as a first step toward deeper European integration.

European integration theory began with the ECSC as well. Inspired by Monnet's vision that technical functional integration could lead to political transformation, Ernst Haas created a neofunctionalist theory that specified the mechanisms through which integration would be politically transformative. With governance transferred to the European level, Haas expected the stakeholders associated with the sector to come to see their fate as linked to the ECSC's success. He predicted that firms, unions, and workers benefiting from ECSC policies would support the ECSC. Success would breed success. As other industries observed the benefits of supranational coordination, they would demand integration in their sectors, leading to the realization of Haas's hope of moving 'politics beyond the nation-state'(1958, 1964).

After the EEC was launched in 1958, theoretical and practical interest in the ECSC declined. Integrating European economies was a more ambitious goal, and it was clear early on that agriculture—not coal and steel—would be the first large policy nut that had to be cracked for the European project to succeed. Thus by 1958, practically and politically speaking, the success of the coal and steel project was no longer a bellwether for the larger integration efforts. A number of studies of the ECSC were published in the late 1950s and early 1960s, (Haas 1958; Diebold 1959; Scheingold 1965), but then scholarly focus shifted

---

[1] Thanks to John Gillingham and Andy Moravcsik for their very helpful comments on this chapter, and to the editors for their overall guidance.

after the 1960s (see Dudley and Richardson's article (1999) for a noteworthy exception).

This chapter examines the experience of Coal and Steel integration during the ECSC's fifty-year history, focusing on the extent to which practice coincided with theory. Like others, we find that ECSC rules were regularly ignored. Our question is what does it mean for integration theory that the ECSC was mainly a paper tiger? Why did Haas's integration theory not materialize in this case par excellence? Why was the ECJ not the integrating actor in the ECSC that it came to be in the EEC and EU?

We argue that the ECSC failed because the situation for which it was created never materialized, and absent that situation member states actually preferred market segmentation to market integration. Its early failure put to rest the technocratic functional integration approach that inspired the ECSC, and in doing so assured states that integration *did not* mean ceding power to the High Authority (HA). The ECSC did prove useful when external forces created benefits for working collectively. When the USA was concerned about dumping of European steel products, the ECSC assumed its role as foreign representative for the member states. When a global oversupply led to a collapse of the price of steel products, the ECSC was a useful means to manage the painful but necessary market adjustment. However even when the ECSC assumed the role Monnet had envisioned, the ECSC did not trigger a shifting of loyalties, spillover, or an entrenchment of supranational institutions and policies. Instead, the ECSC performed its task and was disbanded.

Section one discusses the ECSC at its founding. The next section divides the ECSC into historical periods demarcated by changes in the economic terms of trade in coal and steel, and thus by critical junctures in which changes in European policy could have and sometimes did occur. Finally, reviewing the entire time trajectory, the chapter evaluates the role the ECSC played in postwar European steel and integration politics.

The ECSC at its Founding

In the immediate postwar period, Germany's European neighbors were concerned that Germany might regain its dominance in steel, and that they would lack the steel they needed to rebuild their economies. While the Allies were occupying Germany, the International Ruhr Authority monitored and controlled Germany's industry. But by 1949 it was clear that the USA planned to create a sovereign Germany largely free of international oversight and control. Schuman proposed the ECSC to avoid German sovereign control of its industry (Milward 1984).

At the time the ECSC was proposed, states were concerned about coal and steel scarcities. In a context of scarcity, Germany could abuse its dominant position in the market affecting other European states' economic rebuilding efforts. Jean Monnet drafted the ECSC treaty with the problem of scarce supply in mind, but with the idea that the ECSC could eventually engage in supranational sectoral planning (Duchêne 1994). During negotiations over the Treaty of Paris, it became clear that countries were not interested in coordinated sectoral planning. Instead, countries wanted resources they could use to rebuild national industries. French producers fought for favorable access to German coal (Duchêne 1994: 221; Rittberger 2001: 686–8). Belgian, Dutch, and Italian firms demanded adjustment subsidies and time to build up their industry (Kipping, Ruggero, and Dankers 2001: 81–5). The Dutch foiled Monnet's plan to have a highly independent supranational planning body, insisting on creating a Council of Ministers to control the HA (Dinan 2004*b*: 51). The end result was a treaty that was far less ambitious than what Schuman had originally proposed (Haas 1958: 251; Milward 1984: 380–420; Groenendijk and Gert 2002: 602).

While the Treaty of Paris ended up an intergovernmentalist bargain, it did establish supranational institutions with real powers, at least on paper. The Council of Ministers, composed of ministers from member countries, had to assent formally to policy measures initiated by the HA, but decisions would originate from the HA, based on a majority vote of the six members. The HA could fine firms and withhold transfer funds to encourage compliance with ECSC rules. There was also a supranational ECJ to arbitrate disputes among participants including member states, European institutions and affected private actors (e.g. firms, unions, and so on). The Treaty also created a 'common assembly' made up of national parliamentarians, and umbrella associations for each industry, for employers, and for unions.

In addition to its institutions, the Treaty created a framework of rules that could be used to shore up the competitive nature of the market. Elements of this framework included:

- *Transparency with respect to prices*: firms were obliged to publish prices, and price discrimination was forbidden.
- *Management of investment*: the HA could help fund or prohibit investments to avoid illegal subsidization of industry.
- *Banning cartels*: cartels were generally forbidden and the HA had to approve that mergers were aimed at increasing efficiency and not at market dominance.
- *Eliminating subsidies*: subsidies were generally illegal, though exceptions were permitted so long as they were gradually reduced.
- *Labor policy*: information provisions aimed to create transparency in labor practices.
- *Transportation*: the same transport rates had to be applied to all steel firms, regardless of nationality, and rates had to be published.

- *Foreign relations*: under the supervision of the Council of Ministers, the HA could negotiate and establish diplomatic relations with foreign governments regarding matters related to coal and steel.
- *Crisis measures*: in the event of a 'manifest crisis', production quotas would be established by the HA.[2]

While Monnet and Schuman had not gotten all they had wanted, the Treaty did establish institutions that could be used to coordinate Europe's coal and steel industries. Monnet saw sectoral planning 'as above all a "method" of mobilizing people for collective effort' and the Schuman Plan as the 'first step to a united Europe' (Duchêne 1994: 157 and 199). Schuman claimed that the ECSC would 'simply and speedily [create] that fusion of interests ... that will be the leaven from which may grow a wider and deeper community' (quoted in Groenendijk and Gert 2002: 602). Analyzing its first ten years of existence, Ernst Haas found evidence of HA influence, of the interpenetration of European steel markets, and of actors below the state organizing to promote common goals. Haas argued that 'political integration is taking place' (Haas 1958: 485). But these interpretations were quite disputable.[3]

Critical Junctures in Coal and Steel Integration

This section assesses the reality of what happened in the ECSC over time. Were the substantive rules followed? Did the institutional mechanisms work as Haas and Monnet expected (e.g. did policy come to be set at the European level, did the peak associations created to oversee Coal and Steel market integration assume the political role of supranationalizing political representation and loyalties)? Our empirical analysis is oriented around four periods, each with a crisis that presented an opportunity to declare a 'manifest crisis' which would trigger the ECSC's provisions to set policy at the European level.

1950–58—Searching for a Raison d'Être

The common market for coal, iron ore, and scraps was officially opened in February 1953,[4] when members agreed to eliminate tariffs and quotas in accordance with the treaty. But in fact there were no tariffs or quotas at the time protecting markets (Haas 1958: 60–2; Gillingham 1991: 268), so this vote was mainly

[2] For a comprehensive and detailed description of ECSC policies and institutions, see Haas (1958), Lister (1960), and Diebold (1959).

[3] For an excellent discussion of problems in Haas's theory, see Moravcsik (2005*b*). For a discussion of how Haas's thinking evolved over time, see Mattli (2005).

[4] A market for 'ordinary steel' opened in May 1953, and after delays the market for 'alloyed steel' opened in August 1954.

symbolic. To create a real common market, the HA would need to tackle the policies and institutions that created barriers to trade, which required Council assent. European governments were most concerned with protecting jobs and facilitating industrial growth—defined exclusively in national terms. These objectives led governments to prefer market segmentation over unleashing competition via market integration. European governments blocked HA's efforts to dismantle barriers to trade, and aided their firms, often in contravention of ECSC rules.

France

The French government granted low interest state-guaranteed loans to help its industry. Convinced that economies of scale would make its industry competitive, the French orchestrated mergers that arguably cut against the ECSC's anti-cartel policies (Daley 1996: 58). While French consumers of steel wanted open markets to gain access to cheaper steel, the government continued to control domestic steel prices, in violation of the ECSC Treaty (Kipping 1996: 16). The government offset high prices with discounted investment credit, but it did so differentially to develop targeted regions; in some places steel prices were higher than prices in neighboring ECSC states, but in other locations prices were lower than what they might have been if there were an integrated European market (Daley 1996: 64).

Germany

Germany was the only country with highly concentrated ownership in the 1940s. While the German government negotiated with Allies regarding deconcentration and complied with ECSC rulings pertaining to German industry, it dragged its feet when it came to implementing the anti-cartel spirit of the ECSC's provisions. Its strategy succeeded. By 1952, efforts to deconcentrate German industry were loosened; by 1958, they were abandoned (Warner 1996: 236). Germany did not have explicit subsidization policies for its steel industry, relying instead on indirect subsidization via special tax credits, relaxed regulatory standards, and favorable credit terms (Esser and Fach 1989: 239). These investment tax incentives were the 'private equivalent to the publicly sponsored heavy industry modernization program of the French Plan' (Gillingham 1991: 284).

Italy

Italy's industry was among the least internationally competitive in Europe, though the high cost of transporting German, Belgian, or French steel provided a buffer for Italian firms. Italy grew its steel industry in the 1950s through a combination of heavy public sector investment, tariffs, subsidization of scrap inputs, and increased concentration of ownership to create economies of scale (Villa 1986: 169; Kipping, Ruggero, and Dankers 2001). The legal authority for these policies was negotiated as part of the ECSC negotiations, where Italy and Belgium won the right to maintain protection during a five-year transition period (Milward

1984: 408). Italy's exceptions to ECSC rules continued, however, past the five-year transition period. Italy was thus able to develop its industry rapidly, increasing production from 3 million metric tons in 1951 to 9 million plus tons in 1961, to 12.7 million tons in 1965 (Kipping, Ruggero, and Dankers 2001: 86).

The ECSC

So what were ECSC institutions doing while its rules and provisions were bypassed? In the 1950s, European countries were not focused on exporting steel. Rather, national industries primarily served national markets. This made it easy for the ECSC to eliminate national policies on the books that were blatantly discriminatory (e.g. formal rules setting different taxation rates or prices for national vs. foreign steel, export subsidies, and so on). The HA also monitored markets and worked to increase transparency in transportation and selling prices, requiring that prices be posted. Despite its efforts, discriminatory railroad rates continued providing a hidden subsidy for local producers (Diebold 1959: 175–7). Firms also continued to sell their product at prices that differed from the advertised price.

The HA also conducted studies and published reports. In a 1954 report the HA admitted that its price transparency efforts were failing as non-compliance with ECSC price policies was more the norm than the exception. Unable to crack down on cheating, the HA instead created the 'Monnet Margin' for prices to deviate up to 2.5 percent from the published prices. William Diebold saw the policy change as a sign the ECSC was unable to implement its rules (1959: 258); Haas by contrast argued that the Monnet Margin showed the ECSC was flexible (1958: 195, 203). French and Italian steel producers did not like the Monnet Margin, and they challenged it in front of the ECJ, which declared the Monnet Margin illegal (Scheingold 1965: 54–70). Indeed many contentious HA decisions were challenged by firms and states, ending up as cases heard by the ECJ, creating an irony—the only actor truly being held to ECSC rules was the HA.

Why were the ECSC policies not enforced? First, as an empirical reality, the problems the ECSC was created to solve quickly disappeared on their own. The 1950s was a sellers market for steel, but supply was not critically scarce. Access to German coking coal—France's main economic motivation for establishing the ECSC—did not prove to be important because technological advances reduced transport costs, and American coking coal became abundant and cheap (Gillingham 1991: 188, 230, 357). While German industry remained cartelized, and implicitly subsidized through cozy relationships with banks (Zysman 1983; Katzenstein 1987), German industry was in no position to dominate the European market. Second, the ECSC was not set up to deal with government policies that created the main sources of market distortions—exchange rate policy, national regulatory rules, and government's low-interest loans to industry. Finally, there was simply no real interest in creating market competition. As long as national policies did not create negative externalities that flowed across borders, member states saw no role for ECSC institutions in facilitating market adjustments.

The political momentum created by the early ECSC was far different than what Monnet had expected. In 1954, France rejected treaties aimed at creating a European Political Community and a European Defense Community, refusing to accept greater supranationalism. The model of technical functional integration was also rejected when proposals for a transport community and an atomic energy union were refused (Moravcsik 1998: ch. 2). Instead, states agreed to build a broader EEC. EEC institutions were weaker than their ECSC counterparts. For example, where the ECSC allowed the HA to create fines for non-compliance, and withhold transfer payments to non-complying states and firms, the Treaty of Rome only allowed the Commission to raise infringement suits, which could lead to a toothless ECJ declaration that a 'member state had failed to fulfill its obligation'. Karen Alter identifies a number of options available to member states had they wanted stronger enforcement mechanisms for the common market. That they chose none of the options, she argues, 'was no accident' (Alter 2001: 8). Member states wanted for the EEC less, not more, supranationalism than they had in the ECSC.

1959–74—National Management of Industrial Modernization

In 1959, the European steel sector entered recession and the European coal sector experienced a severe crisis of oversupply and falling world prices. The HA asked member states to declare a 'manifest crisis' for the coal industry. Belgium, Luxembourg, and the Netherlands wanted ECSC help in dealing with the coal crisis, but Germany, France, and Italy refused to authorize the HA action plan. They agreed to aid measures for Belgium but argued that national governments, rather than supranational actors, should determine the best way to deal with the crisis.[5] Their veto, issued just at the time of publication of Ernst Haas's *The Uniting of Europe*, in some ways was the death knell for the ECSC. The HA could not enforce ECSC rules, nor adjust them, nor could it make itself useful when a European-wide crisis erupted.

In the 1960s, Europe faced more challenges—a continued oversupply of coal, then iron ore, then steel followed by the rise of foreign competition in raw inputs and in steel outputs. At the same time as international competition increased, car firms switched to thinner sheet steel, and concrete construction began using less iron.[6] The ECSC was created for robust demand combined with scarce supply, not falling demand. Member states refused to adapt ECSC institutions to the changing

[5] 'La France, l'Allemagne et l'Italie repoussent définitivement le plan de la Haute Autorité' *Le Monde* 4,451 (May 16, 1959): 1. Available at www.ena.lu/mce.swf?doc=914&Ig=2

[6] 'L'acier casse l'Europe' *L'Express* 799 (October 10, 1996): 62–4. Available at www. ena.lu.mce.swf?doce=1297&Ig=2

market realities. In the face of a proposal to merge the three EEC treaties (the Common Market, EURATOM, and ECSC treaties), the HA published a document, informally known as 'the last will and testament of the ECSC'.[7] Member states responded by declaring the importance of the ECSC, yet refusing to work with the HA to address challenges in the steel industry. Each of the large countries had their own reasons for rejecting a supranational approach. De Gaulle opposed supranational solutions in principle, claiming a preference for different plans for each country. Germany did not want a move toward a centrally controlled economy. Benelux and Italy disagreed about the specific policies and tools the HA recommended, in part because their market competitiveness differed.

France

Despite investments in modernization, French firms entered the European recession uncompetitive compared to their European neighbors. For example, in 1966, French firms took 16.4 hours to produce a ton of steel, but Germany only needed 12.7 hours and Italy 10.0 hours (Daley 1996: 61). Among the sources of French inefficiency were a failure to specialize, a refusal to close plants using outdated technology, combined with an unwillingness to invest in new technologies (Daley 1996: 61–3). Market forces might have forced rapid economic rationalization, but with a growing desire to protect jobs, the French government instead poured more resources into its industry. It kept uncompetitive firms alive with state subsidies or loans, meanwhile it encouraged modest consolidation and rationalization in the industry by orchestrating mergers that closed some uncompetitive production while injecting investment funds into 'national champions' using the latest production technologies (Howell, Noellert, Kreier, et al. 1988).

Germany

The German government generally let the coal and steel industries, in consultation with German banks, work out difficulties they encountered. Government subsidies to industry were fairly low from 1960 to 1970, at least relative to other countries, such as Italy (Harris 1983: 179). The exception to this rule was the German government's rescue of the ailing Krupp firm in 1967.[8] German firms rode out economic upheaval through 'market coordination', which resembled cartel policymaking. Banks would lend to steel industries in times of crisis, and firms signed multiyear arrangements where they agreed to share rather than compete for the market. German firms regularly agreed to reduce or postpone production in return for other firms agreeing to buy from them or withhold production in the future (Shonfield 1969: 256–7).

---

[7] Ibid.
[8] The German federal government provided a loan of DM 400 million and Saar government gave a loan of DM 150 million to Krupp which agreed, in return, to transform itself from a private enterprise into a limited liability company. See Esser and Fach (1989).

Italy

Italy lacked domestic sources of raw inputs for steel, and thus large integrated steel firms. Firms in the north focused on electric furnace technology, creating small 'minimills' that specialized in the production of simple products for local and regional usage.[9] Minimills flourished at the same time integrated steel suffered, because they focused on the most profitable needs of local consumers (Barnett and Crandall 1986: chs. 1 and 2). But consumption demand outstripped supply of steel in Italy in the 1960s (Villa 1986: 169). Italy could have, of course, relied on the international market for this supply. Indeed with a fall in transportation prices, it would have been cheaper for Italy simply to import the products it needed. But with a national demand unmet, the Italian government opted for a more interventionist investment strategy that created jobs and economic growth in the Christian Democrats' political stronghold—the Mezzogiorno South.[10] This decision created an economic liability Italians would be saddled with for the next thirty years (Brusoni and Orsenigo 1997).

The ECSC

If all countries were pursuing their own policies, what was the ECSC doing? The HA developed recommendations to deal with the crisis, but most of its efforts were rejected by member states.[11] It could find support for small, isolated projects. For example in the 1970s, the ECSC helped address a lack of iron ore by helping build private harbors for imports.[12] The HA also found some funds to grant modernization loans, and it created a system of welfare guarantees for workers who lost their job.[13] Its studies on the labor market provided information for unions to use to support their case for retraining programs, worker compensation, and improved worker conditions (Collins 1975: 100–7). According to Gilbert Mathieu, the HA's policies did not affect industrial development, but its coordination (and, one might add, blind eye) arguably made it easier for each country to

---

[9] There are three types of steelmaking plants: basic oxygen systems, open-hearth furnaces and electric furnaces. The first two types are located close to raw materials, and employed by integrated steel plants that produce a great variety of steel products (Barnett and Crandall 2002; Villa 1986). Germany and France had raw inputs sources, and in the 1950s and 1960s focused on creating and innovating around the technology used in integrated plants. Italy did not have raw inputs, thus small northern producers innovated minimill technology in the 1960s. Between 1959 and 1970, minimill production grew in northern Italy by a factor of five (Kipping, Ruggero, and Dankers 2001).

[10] In the 1960s a new steel plant was built in Taranto, owned by Finsider which was 99.82 percent owned by the state holding company IRI (Istituto per la Ricostruzione Industriale) (Howell et al. 1988).

[11] 'La Haute Autorité de la CECA explore toutes les possibilités du traité pour surmonter la crise' *Communauté Européenne*, 11/10 (November 1966): 6.

[12] Based on interviews with the Deputy Head of the Commission Unit for Steel, non-ferrous metals and other materials in the 1970s. Brussels, September 7, 2004.

[13] Op cit. note 11.

obtain supplies when short, while avoiding cutbacks during periods of oversupply (Mathieu 1970).

Beyond these specific policies, the ECSC played two roles in this period. First, from 1953 to 1963 ECSC institutions (mainly the ECJ) provided a forum for actors to challenge policies in other countries that harmed them. In a number of cases, firms or governments of one country were challenging policies that conferred competitive advantages on firms in another country.[14]

Second, the ECSC was the external voice of European countries in negotiations over dumping steel. In the 1960s, declining transportation rates and the rise of new production technologies created problems for all traditional producers of steel (Warren 1975). Responding to the economic distress of US steel producers, the USA pressured Europe and Japan voluntarily to restrain their exports of steel to the USA. The USA negotiated this agreement with the EEC; presumably member states agreed to common representation to avoid a US retaliation that might affect them all (McClenahan 1991).

This period ended with a boom phase (1968–74)—rising prices, rising consumption, extensive expansion plans, and bright horizons for the industry. Countries could well imagine that their intervention had contributed to the recovery. Buoyed by optimistic market projections in the 1970s, national governments redoubled their efforts to invest in and modernize their steel industries, contributing to a vast overproduction and the crisis of the 1970s.

1974–86—The HA (now the Commission) Gets Support for Market Coordination

The international iron and steel industry faced a worldwide crisis starting in 1974, triggered by the rising price of energy, decreased world consumption of steel, and worldwide overcapacity as developing countries created their own steel industries and began exporting cheap steel. Oversupply created a collective problem for European countries, which was exacerbated when the UK joined the EEC in 1973. Firms wanted to protect jobs, and the incremental cost of producing steel was such that firms had an incentive to keep producing even though it contributed further to the collapse in the price for steel. In the first year of the crisis, internal EU

---

[14] German steel producers engaged in a five-year legal battle against Italy for the latter's failure to publish trucking rates—a policy which benefited Italian producers at the expense of German ones (Scheingold 1965: ch. 8). The Dutch Coal Association successfully challenged the German 'miners' bonus' in 1956, which conferred a considerable competitive advantage on this industry relative to others. Still, even after the ECJ ruled the subsidy illegal in 1961, it took years of prodding from the HA before Germany finally repealed the policy in 1964. See Scheingold (1965). The stream of Coal and Steel cases pretty much dried up in the 1960s. The ECJ heard 226 Coal and Steel cases from 1953 to 1963, and an average of 31 cases per year from 1958 to 1963. The ECJ averaged 5.5 ECSC cases from 1964 to 1969, perhaps because the HA was not making much policy worth contesting. See Scheingold (1971).

steel prices fell by 40 percent and export prices dropped 50 percent (Tsoukalis and Strauss 1985: 212).

A number of European countries wanted to follow the US approach to oversupply: setting minimum prices combined with quotas to avoid firms overproducing. Germany opposed strong market intervention, so the ECSC's 1976 'Spinelli approach' mainly monitored the market, with the expectation that the crisis was merely a cyclical adjustment (Tsoukalis and Strauss 1985: 215). Needing a stronger policy, the 1976–77 'Simonet Plan' included regional aids, protection against third countries, and recommended steel prices (Daley 1996: 149; Tsoukalis and Strauss 1987: 199–201).

To help reach price targets, a European Confederation of Iron and Steel Industries, EUROFER, was created in 1976. Working through EUROFER was voluntary, but to create a real power for EUROFER the Commission agreed only to bargain and distribute production quotas via negotiations with EUROFER.[15]

As reality set in that the steel market would not recover to pre-1974 consumption levels (let alone consumption growth), member states came to support a communal approach to deal with oversupply of steel in Europe and the world. EC Minister Davignon's 1977 Plan marked a new era for the ECSC: the steel industry became actively managed at the Community level and the Commission for the first time became a 'relevant actor' from the perspective of national firms and policymakers (Grunert 1987: 233–4).

Davignon's first plan created common external trade barriers; required detailed production, employment, and delivery forecasts from firms; set minimum prices and production quotas; and granted aid on the condition it was coupled with capacity reductions. These efforts were only partially successful. Competitive firms in the Bresciani region of Italy, as well as some French and German firms, refused to follow the restrictions, creating 'rebates' and 'accidentally' delivering more steel than was requested (Jones 1979: 50–1).[16] While national governments voiced support for European policymaking, they continued to bail out their industries, in the hope that the market would recover. In 1980, the USA accused European firms of 'dumping' steel, causing a decline in exports to the USA at the same time that auto companies further reduced the amount of steel in their products to obtain fuel efficiencies. These two events led the European market into another price war (Howell et al. 1988: 80), which prompted the Commission to ask the Council to declare a 'manifest crisis'.

The 1981 vote declaring a manifest crisis led to the second Davignon plan, and the creation of EUROFER II. From a legal standpoint, a manifest crisis authorized the adoption of extensive measures, such as mandatory production

[15] Based on an interview with the director of the European Steel Association (EUROFER). Brussels, September 7, 2004.

[16] The Commission fined about twenty firms in 1978–9 for infringing on price rules.

quotas covering about 80 percent of all steel products and regulations regarding subsidies (Grunert 1987: 235). The resurrection of cartels as a major component of the Davignon strategy shows how far the ECSC strayed from the hopes of Monnet, for whom eliminating cartels was a chief aim (Gillingham 1991: 232; Duchêne 1994: 213).

From a political standpoint, it is not clear what changed with the declaration of a manifest crisis. Compliance with ECSC rules regarding prices, quotas, and subsidies remained problematic because national governments continued to rescue their own industry. According to Kent Jones, only a market readjustment, raising input prices so that firms' profit-maximizing price fell in line with cartel rules, ended the cheating regarding European price policies (Jones 1986: 127–8). Indeed it is quite telling that in a general book on 'Steel and the State', the chapter on 'The European Community' spends forty-eight pages talking about European-level policies and then eighty pages describing the steel policies of the member states that are basically unrelated to ECSC policy. For example, the ECSC, under German pressure, created rules limiting subsidies at the same time as the French nationalized their industry so as to bail it out, and the Italians poured aid into its firms owned by the state holding company IRI (Howell, Noellert, Kreier et al. 1988).

The crisis did not per se make a growing Commission role inevitable. The HA's request that the Council declare a manifest crisis for coal in 1958, its numerous policy suggestions in the 1960s, and even the French request for such a declaration in 1975 had been rejected despite having the support of different member states at different times. Declaring a manifest crisis was easier in 1981 for a few reasons.

First, it had become clear that demand for steel would not recover to its pre-1974 levels both because consumption patterns had changed and because developing countries now could compete in the international marketplace. With this realization came a common diagnosis of the problem and agreement about what was needed to deal with the crisis. All agreed that European production of steel needed to be permanently reduced, and integrated steel production—being no longer economically profitable—was where reductions had to occur (Tsoukalis and Strauss 1985; Grunert 1987; Daley 1996: 148; Dudley and Richardson 1999: 245).

Second, the duration of the crisis meant that governments had a chance to attempt to solve the problem on their own. National policies from 1976 to 1981 were both expensive and ineffective. Governments were frustrated that firms continually undermined their efforts through continued production. With little good news to claim credit for, European governments became more willing to turn the problem over to the European level, which allowed national politicians to pin the blame for the pain inflicted on unelected EEC officials (Tsoukalis and Strauss 1985, 1987).

Third, an international politics of steel had emerged. Falling transportation prices had created a competitive international market in steel for the first time in the late 1960s. When supply outstripped demand in Europe, European firms had looked for international outlets for their goods. They faced strong rebukes from countries that charged European countries with dumping products on their markets. The political bargaining regarding dumping and countervailing duties took place in the context of the GATT. Within GATT, the EEC was treated as a regional organization, which provided EEC states with beneficial exemptions. Its status as a regional organization also put the EEC on the potential receiving end of collective dumping and countervailing duty charges. Within the GATT, the Commission continued its role begun in the 1960s as the interlocutor in negotiations with foreign governments—a role which dovetailed with the general trend to grant trade negotiation authority to the Commission in this period (Meunier and Nicolaïdis 1999; Meunier 2003).

Fourth, there was a sunset clause of the ECSC Treaty that was not too far off. As long as the ECSC Treaty was not extended beyond its original fifty years, states could grant the Commission extraordinary powers without being concerned that the Commission would continue to erode member state authority. In yet another irony, it was not the promised effectiveness of the ECSC's supranational institutions that led to their usage, but nearly the opposite—the fact that the Commission could not be as powerful in the future—that facilitated the granting of extraordinary powers to the Commission.

Europe used its massive intervention in the 1980s to shut down its integrated steel plants, restructure local economies, and develop minimill capacity to produce highly specialized steel products. The interventionist policies continued until 1986, and a bit longer in member states that joined the EEC in the mid-1980s. The bailout was stated as the last and final major subsidy to the industry, and was coupled with privatization policies that allowed governments to extricate themselves from direct involvement in steel production.[17]

1987–94—Downsizing the European Effort

By the 1980s, the ECSC's intervention had finally achieved some of the goals Haas had identified in 1958. There were true EEC-level peak associations representing industry and workers, with real power to negotiate with the Commission to set price and output targets. There were coal- and steel-related labor policies that improved the welfare of workers (Collins 1975: 100–7). Finally, there was momentum behind the ECSC, and coincidentally behind the integration endeavor more generally. Thus, at the conclusion of the crisis, many observers expected the demand for ECSC intervention to continue and for the experience of collective industrial management to spur on supranationalism and European integration (Grunert 1987; Mény and Wright 1987: 91). But this episode did not foment

[17] Based on interviews with the deputy head of the Commission Unit for steel, non-ferrous metals and other materials in the 1970s. Brussels, September 7, 2004.

more of the same. Schuman's expected 'fusion of interests' and Haas's expected 'shifting of loyalties' never materialized despite clear government support for ECSC policies.

When steel once again went into recession in the early 1990s, firms in Italy, Spain, Portugal, and eastern Germany demanded Commission intervention. They were not ECSC converts as much as they were, as always, wanting state support. This time, however, states refused to empower European institutions to act. In the 1980s, Germany had been alone in its opposition to the Davignon Plan's heavy market intervention.[18] But Margaret Thatcher had assumed power in the UK, and François Mitterrand had embraced the market in France, providing Helmut Kohl with political allies. With neoliberal free market ideas in ascent, advocates of free markets, who viewed the supranational interventions associated with the Treaty of Paris as a thing of the past, became dominant in both the Commission and most national governments (Dudley and Richardson 1999). Thus in this crisis the coalition favoring free markets was able to prevail over advocates of supranational interventionism.

In March 1991, the Commission declared that the ECSC would end on schedule in 2002, and the coal and steel sector would be absorbed into the EEC (Groe-nendijk and Gert 2002). National governments gladly assented as they were tired of supporting steel and were looking for a way out of their expensive subsidization policy.[19] By 1994, the ECSC ceased granting loans to industry for investment. By the time the Treaty of Paris reached its fifty year end, little subsisted of it anyway. Its competition policy and external representation in international nego-tiations were fully absorbed into the Common Market structure. Because it no longer gave industry any loans, the ECSC's remaining financial mechanisms were generating funds that were disbursed for research and development, and objectives distantly related to coal and steel. The ECSC disappeared, largely without notice, as member states focused on the monetary union, enlargement, and their many other policy concerns.

What Role Did the ECSC Play in Postwar European Politics?

Assessing the role of the ECSC in European integration is challenging. Ernst Haas noted an increasing interpenetration of coal and steel imports as evidence that a common market existed (1958: 63). But writing on the history of the ECSC up

---

[18] Germany alone had opposed compulsory production quotas in 1981. It withdrew oppos-ition in exchange for a policy on phasing out state aids to steel. See Tsoukalis and Strauss (1985).

[19] Based on interviews with the deputy head of Unit in Trade Defense instruments, and a member of the Commission's DG Enterprise, who was involved with the EC's steel policy in the 1980s. Brussels, September 7, 2004.

until 1958, William Diebold found little evidence that the ECSC per se changed either the pattern of production or the pattern of European trade in coal and steel (1959: 590). Writing on the same topic thirty years later John Gillingham agreed:

[The ECSC] neither reformed prevailing business practices, produced a new relationship between public authority and private power, nor shifted the locus of economic policy, even as regards heavy industry, from national state to supranational agency. The economic impact of the community was slight. Few of its policies had demonstrable effect (Gillingham 1991: 300).

Even after the heavy intervention of the Commission in the 1980s, it is hard to say that the ECSC has left a stamp on the face of the European steel industry that would not exist otherwise. Thus asking the counterfactual question of 'how would EU steel industries look different were there no ECSC' does not reveal a significant institutional imprint.

One can identify several ways in which the ECSC experience mattered. The prime purpose of the ECSC was to assure European countries that Germany would not again become an abusive dominant force on the continent. While there were many factors contributing to Germany's post war industrial and political policies, the assurance the ECSC provided remained politically important. John Gillingham points out that despite the many failings of the ECSC, the 'Schuman Plan . . . ended the competitive bids for heavy industry domination that had wrecked every previous large-scale attempt to reorganize the Continent since 1918, led to *Westintegration* and Franco-German partnership, and resulted in the creation of a new entity, Europe' (Gillingham 1991: 364).

Foundational elements of the ECSC's institutional blueprint also endured. The Treaty of Paris became the 'boiler plate' text in negotiations for the common market. While subsequent agreements tended to strip away elements of the supranational bodies' powers, features of European coal and steel integration endured. For example, the ECJ's preliminary ruling mechanism was transferred wholesale from the ECSC to the European legal system (Pescatore 1981), a transfer that proved extremely important in the development of the EU (Weiler 1991). The legacy of HA failure was also a potential benefit. The ECSC showed that the Council of Ministers could control the HA (now Commission), and that rules would only be enforced to the extent countries wanted them enforced.

The ECSC did become a venue in which policies toward steel were discussed and sometimes implemented. But the ECSC remained throughout its entire history a framework of convenience, to be used when there was a coalition of support for collective responses and ignored when the support faded. Indeed weaving the ECSC into the story of European integration more generally reveals 'critical disjunctures'. The drive to deepen integration signaled by the ratification of the Treaty of Rome was coupled with a decision not to grant the HA's wish to declare a manifest crisis to deal with the coal crisis of 1958. The agreement to declare a manifest crisis in 1981 came well before the Common Market was relaunched, and by the time the SEA was going forward, support for significant ECSC intervention in the economy had evaporated. These couplings represent a shifting over time in the taste for market forces versus government intervention, not for more or less integration. They also reveal that the coalitions of support for integration were not that deep; there was no constituency for integration per se, just a constituency for or against specific policies. These disjunctures may also have been politically significant. The HA's willingness to step back, and look the other way when states did not want intervention may have provided assurance that made further integration more palatable.

The history of the ECSC teaches us two main lessons. First, the actual history of the ECSC highlights the role of external forces in promoting European cooperation. The impetus for the ECSC was internal to European politics. If not for the larger geopolitical concern about German dominance, it is doubtful that states would have been negotiating about the details of a common market in coal and steel. Once the threat of German dominance in coal and steel was gone, there was no impetus to integrate. Firms were quite happy to segment European markets to avoid competition, and European governments were happy to protect and subsidize national production. The HA only came to play its supranational role in response to externally imposed challenges. When the USA wanted a partner to coordinate with to avoid 'dumping' by European firms in its market, the HA assumed its foreign affairs role. When global oversupply created a need to coordinate production and close segments of the industry, the ECSC again played a role. Thus the actual history of the ECSC followed a 'second image reversed' process, where the realization of the ECSC's political structure and policies were caused by forces emerging from the international political economy of the steel sector (Gourevitch 1978).

Second, the existence of multilateral mechanisms cannot be taken as evidence for multilateral politics. Today the active and powerful role of the ECJ in European politics has led many scholars to suggest that European culture and position in the world leads Europeans to like international law and international approaches that Americans do not (Kagan 2002; Rubenfeld 2003). In this light, it is interesting to note the HA did not set European steel policy, nor did the ECJ serve as force of integration. In other words, in a collective polity of liberal democratic European states, with common rules and powerful supranational institutions, law and legal institutions were not an integrating political force. The ECSC's legal and political history suggests that there is nothing uniquely 'European' about the international rule of law working—when it suits them, European countries are quite capable of ignoring common rules, avoiding legal mechanisms, pursuing national interests, and maintaining a reality that is quite distant from what exists on paper.

6

Historical Institutionalism and the EU's Eastward Enlargement

MILADA ANNA VACHUDOVA[1]

The EU's eastward enlargement has taken center stage in the process of European integration over the last decade. Well before the collapse of the Soviet bloc in 1989, however, the EU's institutions were already shaping how enlargement would turn out. The main puzzle is not why EU leaders decided to enlarge eastward: over the medium- and long-term, some enlargement was squarely in the economic and geopolitical interest of EU member states (Moravcsik and Vachudova 2003). Instead, the puzzle is one of scale: how did the EU manage by 2000 to have such a long queue of eighteen officially recognized candidates and proto-candidates, with even more states knocking at the door? In 2006, after the considerable enlargement of 2004, the EU had ten new members, and nine (or ten) officially recognized candidates and proto-candidates. When EU leaders gave the green light for eastward enlargement in 1993, this number of candidates for EU membership was not anticipated.

More than a decade later, two important—and unintended—consequences of the EU's 'magnetism' toward neighboring states are evident. First, enlargement has become a very successful democracy-promotion program: the clear prospect of qualifying for membership creates powerful incentives for successive governments to improve democratic standards and also pursue economic reforms. These incentives are largely a function of the high levels of integration among EU members and the character of the EU's institutions well before 1989, as opposed to the deliberate design of EU leaders to shape the trajectories of postcommunist states. Second, the quantity of new members and the long membership queue have become implicated in the disaffection of EU citizens for the EU's constitutional project and, more generally, for deepening integration. This is chiefly a consequence of concerns about unemployment, wages, and immigration; these are in turn caused by the confluence of many factors including globalization,

[1] For their helpful comments I thank Joshua Tucker and the editors, Sophie Meunier and Kate McNamara. For research assistance as well as insightful comments, I thank Aneta Spendzharova.

but opposition to the EU and its enlargement have become discernible, concrete targets for an array of broader public concerns and fears.

This chapter explores aspects of enlargement that illuminate the different ways that institutions, once established, have shaped outcomes by constraining the behavior of political actors, both within the EU and within prospective member states. Building on the overview of the HI literature set out in the introduction to this volume, I focus on three key mechanisms that institutionalists posit can shape outcomes (and create 'path dependence'): the sequence of institution-building, asymmetries of power in the operation of institutions, and the unintended consequences of institutions designed in a different context and at an earlier time, especially in the event of an unforeseen, exogenous shock (see Hall and Taylor 1996; Pierson 1996). The HI analysis has a very strong temporal component, revolving around the basic question: What happens when existing institutions interact, over time, with successive rounds of political decision-making? (See North 1990; Pierson and Skocpol 2002; Pierson 2004.) This makes it a particularly exciting theoretical tool for analyzing the EU's eastward enlargement. The collapse of communism was an exogenous shock par excellence for the EU, smashing its familiar geopolitical environment. And suddenly, political actors functioning within the EU's fairly static, entrenched institutions were confronted with neighboring states whose fundamental institutional structures—political, economic, social, and international—were, at least in theory, to be completely demolished and built anew.[2]

In the first of four parts in this chapter, I explain how the EU's institutional development since its founding in 1957 set it on a path toward a long membership queue after 1989 by making exclusion costly for neighboring states, and making protectionism difficult to reverse for EU leaders. Second, I consider the collapse of communism and its aftermath as an exogenous shock for the EU, and analyze how the EU responded to this shock. While in the area of external relations this shock elicited two separate institutional responses from the EU—enlargement and an enhanced common foreign policy—these unexpectedly become intertwined as enlargement revealed itself to be the EU's most powerful foreign policy tool.

This brings us to the two most important unintended consequences of the EU's response to the collapse of communism: enlargement as a successful democracy-promotion program, and enlargement as eroding the foundations of European integration by straining EU institutions and diminishing public support. In the third part, I ask why the enlargement process not only attracts more and more candidates, but functions as such a powerful democracy-promotion program. I also ask whether the European Commission has had a hand in constructing

---

[2] Jacoby (2004) offers a groundbreaking analysis that uses historical institutionalism to explain variation across policy areas in the adoption of Western models and rules by postcommunist states.

the preaccession process in such a way as to keep candidates locked into the reform process, keep new states knocking at the door—and keep itself in the enlargement business. Fourth, I discuss the impact of enlargement on the course of European integration, both in threatening an existing equilibrium that enables EU institutions to function and in feeding public resentment of the EU.

Laying the Institutional Groundwork for a Long Membership Queue

Enlargement is fundamentally a product of the high levels of integration among EU member states. These high levels of integration make joining the EU attractive, and exclusion costly. The costs of exclusion are also determined by ways that the EU treats economic actors from non-member states in order to protect domestic producers and labor. Whatever the geopolitical, political, social and cultural attractions of joining the EU (and they are considerable), the lion's share of the EU's power stems from its market (Meunier and Nicolaïdis 2006). For the EU's neighbors, market access for agricultural and other sensitive goods remains restricted, while all other exports to the EU run the continuing risk of being subject to different types of contingent protection. For those states that do not join an enlarging EU along with their neighbors, a steady flow of aid, foreign direct investment (FDI) and know-how is diverted away to states that do. The costs of exclusion can influence relatively rich states as well as poor ones. Walter Mattli has shown that economic integration can cause three kinds of negative externalities for states left outside a regional bloc: trade diversion, investment diversion, and aid diversion. These costs help explain the applications for EU membership of rich West European states as well as relatively poor states from postcommunist Europe (1999).

In the conditions of the cold war and a divided Europe, it is unlikely that EU leaders ever considered that progressively denser integration among EU members combined with high levels of protectionism toward non-member states could someday make virtually every eligible 'European' state seek membership. Yet the membership incentives and the institutionalized nature of the EU, open in theory to all 'European' states and open in practice to new members during the 1970s and 1980s, were creating the conditions for an 'enlargement shock' should the Soviet bloc ever collapse. The long queue of candidates would begin to form after 1989 as the costs of being excluded from an enlarging EU gradually became more and more apparent—and as the EU, with its entrenched formal and informal institutions, would do little to attenuate them.

Before 1989, the EU was laying the groundwork for an enlargement shock in yet another way: through its political and economic success. The revolutions of 1989 in Hungary, Poland, and Czechoslovakia (and elsewhere) were about 'rejoining' Western Europe. This was understood as emulating Western democracy and prosperity. The most Western-oriented East European leaders therefore identified EU membership as the culmination of their democratic revolutions at the very moment of regime change in 1989. The early resolve of Hungarian, Polish, and Czechoslovak dissidents-turned-politicians mattered, because as these three transition 'frontrunners' insisted on joining the EU, they increased the stakes of remaining on the outside for their postcommunist neighbors.

This brings up an elementary but interesting point about enlargement and the sequencing of European integration. If there had been no authoritarian regimes in Europe at the time of the signing of the Treaty of Rome, integration would have likely taken quite a different course due to a different constellation of states shaping EU institutions in the early years. As it happened, authoritarian regimes kept Portugal, Spain, and Greece out of the EU until the 1980s, and twenty other European states (or potential states) behind the Iron Curtain until 1989. By the time the EU began its leap from twelve members in 1990 to twenty-five in 2004 (and rising), EU institutions had become entrenched in important ways.

The aspect of entrenched integration that appears most salient is the high level of protection for certain EU producers. This could be viewed as a path-dependent outcome since it has proved very difficult to change course—even to help small, impoverished, and potentially destabilizing economies on the EU's borders, or to diffuse the pressure for ongoing, increasingly unpopular enlargement. Even member states that overtly wished to head off or slow down a first eastward enlargement found it very difficult to lower the costs of exclusion through improved market access for the EU's most successful postcommunist neighbors.[3] In negotiating the Europe Agreements (signed first with Poland, Hungary, and Czechoslovakia in 1991), the EU insisted on protection for EU producers, and fixed high trade barriers for those products that East European states were most able to export westward: agriculture, textiles, steel, and chemicals. The Europe Agreements were followed by several years of trade disputes, chiefly when the EU chose to invoke various safeguard clauses against imports from the East (for an overview, Vachudova 2005: 82–97). It is ironic that France, the state most interested in stalling EU enlargement in the early 1990s to prevent 'widening' from undermining 'deepening', was also the state that hardened the resolve of East Central European (ECE) governments to attain full membership by insisting on the highest levels of protection from ECE imports. Indeed, in the mid-1990s it seemed easier for EU leaders to accept ECE states as candidates than to grant their goods full access to the internal market (Mayhew 1998: 164). Ultimately, though, this is not surprising as market access threatened to bring at least some immediate political costs while the decision to enlarge deferred visible costs many

---

[3] On the EU's decision to enlarge, see Schimmelfennig (2003*a*), Sedelmeier (2005), and Torreblanca (2001).

years into the future, probably beyond the time horizons of most politicians then holding office in the EU member states.

Responding to the End of Communism and the Yugoslav Wars

The collapse of communism and the disintegration of the Soviet Union between 1989 and 1991 was a considerable exogenous shock that completely transformed the geopolitical environment and the international position of the EU. Throughout the cold war, the question of EU enlargement and, more simply, of the EU's relationship with the economies, polities, and citizens of much of Europe, was greatly simplified by the Iron Curtain that divided Europe in two. Beginning in 1989, the EU was fully exposed to its backyard, and this backyard rapidly became extremely complicated as nine communist states were replaced by some twenty-seven noncommunist states whose diverging political systems, impoverished economies, and regional conflicts demanded attention.

EU leaders responded by tasking the European Commission to develop foreign assistance programs for postcommunist neighbors pursuing a democratic trajectory, and gave it unprecedented powers in building up bilateral relations between East European states and the EU. But as discussed above, the EU's assistance fell short of providing unfettered access to the EU market, even though the scale of economic upheaval and crisis in these new democracies threatened to undermine their fledgling democratic institutions. The prospect of EU membership proved easier to give: in 1993 EU leaders agreed that the EU would expand eastward, someday, and asked the European Commission to design a process through which the region's political and economic frontrunners could qualify to join the EU (Smith 1999). As we see below, this process ultimately enhanced the EU's magnetic attraction: while the costs of remaining outside the EU remained extremely high for neighboring states, the preaccession process designed by the Commission provided a way for states to make progress toward full membership based on the quality of their domestic reforms. Gradually, the EU's preaccession process brought potent if uneven conditionality and socialization to bear on domestic policymaking in a growing number of candidate states.[4]

But the EU was blindsided by the vicious ethnic conflict and war that developed in the Western Balkans as the former Yugoslavia disintegrated in the early 1990s. The wars in Croatia and especially Bosnia-Hercegovina exposed Europe's impotence, and were in many ways a more painful external shock than the fall of the Iron Curtain (see Caporaso 2000: 85–135). The Yugoslav conflicts became an important impetus for strengthening the EU's common foreign policy. Yet even as

---

[4] Recent studies on the EU's impact on domestic policymaking in candidate states include Andonova (2003), Grabbe (2006), Epstein (2006), Jacoby (2004), Kelley (2004), Pridham (2005), Sissenich (2004), Vachudova (2005), and Schimmelfennig and Sedelmeier (eds.) (2005).

the enhanced Common Foreign and Security Policy (CFSP) was being crafted in the early 1990s, the EU was widely seen as having only worsened the conflict in Bosnia-Hercegovina, chiefly by refusing (along with the UN) to label the Bosnian Serbs as the aggressors, and persevering in an increasingly sordid negotiation process. In the end, a tragically bloody war that lasted over four years was over in six short weeks in the autumn of 1995 once US-led military intervention took place under the auspices of the Atlantic Alliance. US-led military intervention was needed again in 1999 to stop Serbia's attacks in Kosovo. The Europeans appeared weak, having twice been unable to prevent or stop violent conflicts directly on the EU's borders.

This led to the EU's choice to expand the membership queue to eighteen candidates by adding the five (now six, soon probably seven) Western Balkan states (see Table 6.1). Keen to establish itself as a credible and powerful geopolitical actor, the EU declared that it would take the lead in the political stabilization

TABLE 6.1.   *The queue to join the European Union, 2006*

EU-15 in order of accession	New Members 2004 in order of application	Candidates in order of application
France	Cyprus 1990	Turkey 1987
Germany	Malta 1990	Bulgaria 1995
Italy	Hungary 1994	Romania 1995
Belgium	Poland 1994	Croatia 2003
Netherlands	Slovakia 1995	Macedonia 2004
Luxembourg	Latvia 1995	
	Estonia 1995	*Proto-Candidates*
UK 1973	Lithuania 1995	*promised membership in 1999 Stability Pact*
Ireland 1973	Czech Rep. 1996	
Denmark 1973	Slovenia 1996	Albania
Greece 1981		Bosnia-Hercegovina
Spain 1986	**= 25 members**	Montenegro
Portugal 1986		Serbia
Sweden 1995		Kosovo?
Finland 1995		
Austria 1995		**= 35 members**
= 15 members		*Past + Future Candidates?* Switzerland, Norway* Ukraine, Belarus, Moldova, Georgia
		= 41 members

* Switzerland's membership application was frozen after Swiss voters rejected participation in the European Economic Area in a referendum in 1992. Norway completed accession negotiations, but Norwegian voters rejected EU membership in a referendum in 1994.

and the economic revitalization of the Western Balkans. Observers as well as EU officials quite sensibly argued that while America would always boast very considerable military superiority, the EU was better suited for the postwar project of reconstructing the states and the economies of the region (see Kopstein 2006). Having previously held enlargement and foreign policy quite separate, EU leaders began to harness the successes of enlargement as evidence of the EU's geopolitical power, and of its potential to act as a unified foreign policy actor. EU leaders and officials acknowledged that the EU's leverage on aspiring members was the most powerful and successful foreign policy instrument at the EU's disposal. Thus enlargement and foreign policy were merged in the EU's policy toward the Western Balkans—the region where the EU's credibility as a foreign policy actor was most at stake. EU leaders made the prospect of EU membership the cornerstone of the EU's foreign policy toward the Western Balkans in the EU-led Stability Pact for Southeastern Europe, launched in 1999 in Sarajevo.

Over the course of the 1990s, the enlargement process shifted in scope and in purpose. I identify three phases. At first, the preaccession process was presented as a way to keep undesirable states out of the EU, while admitting the few that had successfully created Western liberal democracies and market economies. It was not designed to coax and cajole every conceivably 'European' state into making itself desirable. Next, EU leaders declared that countries that had already applied for EU membership would someday join: the question, whatever the setbacks caused by undemocratic leaders, corrupt economic reforms or mistreated ethnic minorities, was 'when' and not 'if'. It was in this period that the preaccession process became a democracy-promotion program. Finally, EU leaders made the foreign policy decision to designate all of the Western Balkan states as credible future EU members in 1999, whether the current governments liked it or not. The regimes of Franjo Tudjman in Croatia and Slobodan Milosevic in Serbia were authoritarian, nationalist, and implicated in genocide during the Yugoslav wars. These regimes, in power since 1990, had never applied, and had no intention of satisfying fundamental membership requirements. Nevertheless, their countries were given, with fanfare, an EU-membership perspective as part of a foreign policy strategy that sought to increase the support of citizens for more moderate, pro-Western opposition parties.

Thus enlargement became the EU's premier stabilization and democracy-promotion program—and quite a successful one. The states that have become credible future EU members over the last decade are making progress toward liberal democracy and a more prosperous, transparent market economy (see Cameron 2005). Although some Western Balkan states still face tremendous domestic obstacles to qualifying for EU membership, there is evidence that political actors are adjusting their political agendas in even the toughest cases such as Serbia, Montenegro, and Bosnia-Hercegovina (Vachudova 2006).

The Unintended Consequence of Enlargement as a Democracy-Promotion Program: Why Does It Work?

The discussion above just begs the question of *why* enlargement has worked as a successful democracy-promotion program, compelling EU leaders to expand its scope to the Western Balkans. Three reasons stand out: First, the high level of integration among EU members produces the sweeping requirements that aspiring members have to satisfy. Second, as discussed above, the benefits of inclusion (and the costs of exclusion) create powerful incentives for states to seek membership and therefore to satisfy these sweeping requirements. They also create a relationship of profound asymmetric interdependence that makes membership conditionality credible (Keohane and Nye 1977; Keohane, Nye, and Hoffmann 1993). The EU can very credibly (at little cost) threaten to exclude a state that does not qualify for membership, since it is (ever) less keen to conclude an agreement on membership than the petitioning state.

But there is a third reason, stemming more from the agency of EU officials after 1989 than from conditions of membership created over decades of integration. The aspects of the EU's leverage that were deliberately designed by the European Commission, including the way that conditionality has been 'delivered' through the preaccession process, have worked remarkably well—not always in absolute terms but certainly in comparison to other democracy-promotion efforts attempted by international actors (Vachudova 2005). The preaccession process has amplified the incentives to comply with the EU's membership requirements, making the EU's threat of exclusion as well as its promises of membership more credible (Kelley 2004; Schimmelfennig and Sedelmeier (eds.) 2005).

What is so remarkable is that so many successive East European governments, in so many countries, would actually be willing to stay the course of political and economic reform, and satisfy the EU's vast entry requirements. One interesting part of this puzzle concerns domestic politics in the candidate states: how do the incentives of membership and the characteristics of the preaccession process interact with divergent domestic conditions in the candidate states? Scholars have explained variation in the speed and content of EU-related domestic reforms among prospective members by analyzing variation in an array of domestic factors (see n. 3). Over time, however, the candidates converge in following a path toward qualifying for membership. One of the key domestic explanations for this convergence is that the condition of being a credible future EU member creates incentives for political actors to make their political agendas compatible with liberal democracy and the state's bid for EU membership (Vachudova 2005).

Another interesting part of the puzzle is why the preaccession process itself helps so many candidate states stay the course of reform and eventually join. If the EU is buckling under the number of countries that want to join it, why did it make the preaccession process so enticing? Here I want to focus on the importance of the meritocracy of the process. So far the EU has adopted a largely merit-based approach to enlargement: an applicant's place in the membership queue has corresponded to the progress it has made toward fulfilling the EU's requirements. While EU members made the decision to enlarge based on interest, the decision when to enlarge to which countries was guided and constrained by this set of rules (Torreblanca 2002). There have been few charges that the Commission's assessments or the Council's decisions have been driven by short-term political interests—for example that a candidate's reforms have been portrayed as lagging behind because (for political, economic, or budgetary reasons) some EU member states would prefer to exclude that country from the first wave of enlargement. Governments would stop expending so much political capital on reform if it were obvious that the quality of preparations for any individual candidate could be trumped by domestic politics in EU member states.

While strict requirements mean a great deal of work for applicant states, they protect those applicants who, for structural reasons, are difficult for EU member states to absorb. For EU electorates, it would be more popular to admit a state with a low potential to export workers, and for the EU budget, it would be more convenient to admit a state with low demands on the agricultural and cohesions funds—irrespective, in both cases, of how well large swaths of the *acquis* had been adopted. At least in principle, a merit-based accession process creates rules which tie the hands of governments not just in aspiring member states, but also in existing ones. Of course, meritocracy could soon go out of the window with the EU's current and future treatment of Turkey—though there is a strong case to be made that the principle has helped Turkey immensely to get this far.

But why has the EU's preaccession process functioned as a meritocracy, at least until now? There is considerable evidence that the European Commission has had a role in creating and defending the meritocratic nature of the preaccession process, and contributing to such a long membership queue for the EU. Already in 1989, the existence of the Commission was important for the EU's response: EU leaders immediately delegated substantial (perhaps unprecedented) authority to the Commission to design the EU's new economic *and* political relationships with its democratizing neighbors.[5] The prospect of developing bilateral policies and aid programs for so many new, unfamiliar states made tasking the Commission to craft a common response attractive to EU members, coming at a time of EU optimism and dynamism thanks to the success of the Single Market Project.

There are three different ways to make the argument that the Commission has had an important role in shaping and channeling the EU's enlargement project. First, the Commission helped member states respond to the tremendous external

---

[5] But for a 'two-level network manager' theory that allows for limited supranational entrepreneurship by the Commission only when the national aggregation of interests fails for a number of reasons, including capture by producer interests, see Moravcsik (1999).

'shock' of the collapse of communism that left many EU governments with confused preferences about EU enlargement. As a policy entrepreneur that supported enlargement, the Commission helped induce cooperation between EU member and candidate states by generating and selling new conceptions of the future of European integration. In this way, it helped set the agenda and exercise control over the preaccession process. Second, it has served as a powerful broker in that process. Third, it has promoted a large enlargement to strengthen its own position. This brings in the debate about whether the role of the European Commission in the eastern enlargement is one of a disciplined agent of the EU governments, as intergovernmentalists would expect (Moravcsik 1991, 1998), or of an independent policy entrepreneur, as neofunctionalists would predict (Stone Sweet, Fligstein, and Sandholtz 2001).

The evidence points to a two-step argument. The European Commission did move on enlargement and design the preaccession process (particularly Agenda 2000) in line with the wishes of the majority of the member states. It also took a careful sounding of member states' preferences at each step. But since dealing with Eastern Europe was such an unexpected, unfamiliar, and confusing issue for many EU member states, the Commission was able to benefit from (and perhaps amplify) some of the unintended consequences of the preaccession process. In particular, the number of candidates that have emerged has made enlargement a very substantial and ongoing project for the EU, and the Commission remains at the heart of the process. It is possible that EU governments did not understand the consequences of a merit-based preaccession process for the scope of the EU's enlargement to Eastern Europe—quite simply, for the potential number of applicants and the difficulties of turning candidates away once they enter the process. This invites further investigation of whether the Commission's role in the accession process really did tip the scales in favor of a large enlargement, and whether this has created a 'gap' in member state control over the course of European integration (Pierson 1996; Caporaso and Stone Sweet 2001).

There are signs that the European Neighborhood Policy (ENP) may turn out to be a successful attempt on the part of the Commission to extend at least part of its enlargement-related authority to a much larger set of the EU's neighbors—and a rather less successful attempt to make democracy-promotion work using similar tools but removing an explicit promise of membership from the equation (see Leigh 2005; Kelley 2006; Weber, Smith, and Baun (eds.) 2007). The ENP can be understood as a way for the Commission to help the EU's new postcommunist neighbors begin the long and laborious preparations for EU membership on the gamble that once they are (more) fit to enter, EU leaders will find it impossible to reject them.

This raises an important question for the future: Will the enlargement framework, including the meritocracy-driven preaccession process, compel EU member states to grant full membership eventually to all states that can jump through all of the hoops of the preaccession process, even though for short-term political reasons they would rather keep some of them out? Or, will the end of meritocracy spell doom for the EU's very salutary impact on domestic reforms in Turkey? Meritocracy encompasses not just fair assessments of the progress of reform, but the ultimate promise of membership once requirements are met. This has already been severely eroded for Turkey with the prospect that Turkey's accession will be decided in a referendum of French voters.

The Unintended Consequences of Enlargement for the EU's Institutions

Does enlargement erode the foundations of European integration by straining EU institutions and diminishing public support? Since 1990, politicians and observers embracing 'deepening' European integration have opposed enlargement (or 'widening') as a threat: increasing the number of EU members and their institutional, political, and economic diversity would surely make it exponentially more difficult to agree on and implement deeper integration. But now the sheer number of new members and candidates has put a more elemental question on the table: Can the EU's institutions that worked with fifteen members continue to function as the number of EU members more than doubles? Putting aside the question of great leaps forward in integration, can the EU's institutions manage current levels of integration with over thirty members?

It is early to judge how well the ten members that joined the EU in 2004 have learned to play by the rules of the EU's institutions—and indeed how well the EU's institutions have adjusted to their presence (see Zielonka 2006). The preliminary record appears quite positive in the sense that the new members have not brought any revolutionary changes. While they sometimes play tough in EU bargaining rounds, in this they are only following the precedent set by other states on acceding, particularly the UK (budget rebate), and Greece, Italy, and Spain (very high structural fund payments) (Moravcsik and Vachudova 2003). Moreover, fundamental divisions within the EU today—such as the war in Iraq, economic deregulation, or international trade interests—are along fault lines that already existed in the old EU.

In terms of importing greater diversity in policy views or institutional approaches, the states still waiting in the membership queue are a greater cause for concern. Indeed, in some respects the more problematic countries are the ones still left in the queue (and of course beyond it). Turkey stands to wield great power in EU institutions because of its size. It is also more likely to import substantially new and divergent positions into the EU on matters of foreign policy and economic development. Romania, Bulgaria, and the Western Balkan states, for their part, suffer from weak state capacity and what are likely to be persistent problems with the quality of public administration. Incompetence may put real strains on a variety of EU institutions, such as the regulation of the internal market (Bignami 2004) or the rotating presidency of the European Council.

Front and center in the public debate about EU enlargement today is not, however, the ability of EU institutions to preserve their current equilibrium: the way that they function has become the object of public mistrust and even contempt. A central argument of HIs is that institutions, once created, are 'sticky': it is very difficult to rehaul them for new context. But enlargement on such a large scale might just be a sufficiently dramatic shock to trigger a useful restructuring of EU institutions. This was the hope, anyway, in the run-up to the negotiation of the Nice Treaty and subsequently the Constitution. The Nice Treaty foundered on classic, entrenched political interests that refused to yield their perceived advantages in the current system in favor of greater efficiency in the future, enlarged EU. The Constitution, tasked with modestly fixing some of Nice's shortcomings, foundered instead on the growing mistrust of EU institutions—their complexity, their lack of transparency, and their poor democratic accountability: Ironically, these were precisely some of the concerns that the Constitution was designed to address by adapting and streamlining EU institutions for an enlarged EU.

Enlargement highlights some of the ways that decision-making about European integration is no longer an elite-controlled project, subject to relatively little attention by EU publics due to lack of interest. During the 1990s, the leaders of the EU member states could quietly agree to add new countries to the EU membership queue, eliciting little public comment and knowing that their successors would have to deal with any political fallout from these countries actually joining the EU. In this sense, the limited time horizons of politicians worked in favor of more countries being admitted to the membership queue. Now, the practice of passing the buck in dealing with the realities of enlargement has caught up with EU leaders. Institutional reform should have been tackled much sooner. And moderate politicians in most EU member states should have made a much greater effort to explain and promote the benefits of enlargement to their citizens. Instead, by staying quiet, they let extreme right political parties set the agenda and link enlargement to immigration, crime, and unemployment.

The long silence about enlargement also contributed to the perception of EU citizens today that the eastward enlargement has taken place very quickly. Like most EU scholars, EU citizens paid little attention to the prospect of enlargement in the 1990s, and the 2004 enlargement seemed to come out of nowhere. For the postcommunist candidates, however, the period that they worked to join the EU— some fifteen years from 1989 to 2004 for the eight frontrunners—did not seem short at all.

Decisions related to enlargement have now become highly politicized as EU citizens link enlargement with unwanted immigration, lower wage levels and higher unemployment (see Table 6.2). Enlargement does have negative economic

TABLE 6.2.   *Public support for enlargement, 2005*

Question: Do you support further enlargement of the EU
to include other countries in future years?

Country	Support for further EU enlargement (%)
Austria	29
France	31
Luxembourg	31
Germany	36
UK	43
Finland	45
Denmark	46
Belgium	47
the Netherlands	48
Sweden	48
Estonia	51
Italy	53
Ireland	54
Spain	55
Portugal	55
Malta	57
Latvia	62
Czech Republic	65
Hungary	66
Cyprus	67
Slovakia	67
Lithuania	69
Poland	72
Slovenia	74
Greece	74

Source: Standard Eurobarometer 2006, 64: 135. Available at http://
ec.europa.eu/public_opinion/archives/eb/eb64/eb64_en.pdf.

consequences for certain economic groups, especially for low-skilled workers
that have to compete with East Europeans willing to work for lower wages. It is
often argued that enlargement helps make the EU as a whole more competitive
in a globalized world economy. But this is an abstract, long-term benefit of
enlargement, while the short-term, concentrated costs are much easier to discern,
or simply to imagine: At a time when Poles could not work freely in France, for
example, there was a vigorous national debate about the threat of France being
overrun by Polish plumbers. This was interwoven with the perception in many
West European states that the EU has expanded to include countries whose culture
is too different, and whose citizens they do not trust.

The highly publicized immigration 'crisis' in certain West European states pertains to unassimilated Muslim populations, public anger against asylum seekers, and illegal immigration—none of which is related to the 2004 enlargement. Unemployment is also primarily caused by factors unrelated to enlargement, such as rigid labor laws and rising manufacturing imports from outside Europe. Indeed, Europe's future demographic difficulties may make enlargement to new countries such as Ukraine or Turkey whose citizens would be likely to move for work a good idea. Yet today enlargement, the Constitution, and the EU itself are all victims of the need for citizens—spurred on by opportunistic national politicians—to find a more concrete target for their discontentment than globalization. And even for moderate national political parties it is easier to blame the EU than to point the finger at current or even past government policies. As many have observed, the referendum provided a perfect outlet for a wide array of groups seeking to protest something, and for politicians ready to benefit from their anger.

The politicization of enlargement is creating a whole new dynamic—and one that is likely to damage the EU's ability to promote democracy. While it appears that using EU enlargement as a democracy-promotion program is undermining public support for European integration, the politicization of enlargement due to low public support in turn threatens to undermine the characteristics that make EU enlargement work as a democracy-promotion program—particularly the meritocracy principle. The erosion of the promise of membership is already slowing down reforms in Turkey, and also threatening the resolve of moderate political leaders in some Western Balkan states. The EU can very justifiably argue that it needs to pause enlargement for a substantial period in order to absorb adequately its new members. Yet this is destabilizing for candidates already in the membership queue that have been promised a timetable based on the progress of their own reforms. More important, the debate on delaying further enlargement has blurred into the one on halting further enlargement altogether, and this has helped call into question the membership promise. The EU may well have the opportunity to bring peace and prosperity to the Western Balkans, a historically very troubled region, and perhaps even to the *entire* European continent. Yet this comes with costs—costs that may be prohibitive if the short-term interests of voters and politicians are at play.

Conclusion

In this chapter, I have examined how three HI mechanisms—the sequence of institution-building, asymmetries of power in the operation of institutions, and the unintended consequences of institutions created to suit a different, earlier context—have shaped the course of EU enlargement since 1989. However unexpected or unintended, the significant enlargement of ten states in 2004 was not particularly surprising: European integration has from its inception evolved in response to external pressures and shocks, without a long-term plan or a clearly defined goal. The post-1989 enlargement process is largely an outcome of the collision between the collapse of the Soviet bloc and the benefits and the requirements of EU membership; these benefits and requirements are in turn an outcome of the gradual institutionalization of the EU over many years. And while there is certainly evidence that the Commission has left its imprint on the preaccession process, so far enlargement appears to be in the geopolitical and economic interest of EU member states—even if it is not necessarily conducive to deepening integration.

Over the next decade, shelving future EU enlargement altogether will be difficult, largely because it has been so successful as a democracy-promotion program. Romania and Bulgaria have already signed their accession treaties, and will enter in 2007 or 2008. For the Western Balkan states of Croatia, Macedonia, Serbia, Montenegro, Albania, and Bosnia-Hercegovina, moving through the process of qualifying to join the EU offers the only real prospect for stability, democracy, and economic revitalization. Integrating the Western Balkan states into the EU is the cornerstone of the long-term foreign policy of all international actors toward the region. Today, strict EU conditionality is the most important (if not the only) reason why the Croatian and Serbian governments are turning over war criminals to the International Criminal Tribunal for the former Yugoslavia (ICTY) in The Hague. For Turkey, Ukraine, Moldova, and other aspiring candidates, however, the current political climate in the EU is a serious setback for their EU membership

TABLE 6.3. *Public support for specific candidates, 2005*

Question: For each of the following countries, would you be in favor or against it becoming part of the European Union in the future?

	Support for future EU membership	
Country	In EU-15 (%)	In new member states (%)
Turkey	29	38
Albania	32	40
Serbia and Montenegro	36	50
Ukraine	38	57
Macedonia	39	51
Bosnia and Hercegovina	39	50
Romania	41	53
Bulgaria	45	64
Croatia	47	70

Source: Standard Eurobarometer 2006, 64: 138. Available at http://ec.europa.eu/ public_opinion/archives/eb/eb64/eb64_en.pdf

prospects. Ukraine and particularly Turkey are large states that, for myriad reasons, would be difficult for the EU to absorb, even if the benefits of doing so would be considerable. Moreover, they would push the EU's borders into some of the world's politically more troubled regions.

Still, it will be not be so easy for the EU to walk away even from Turkey or Ukraine, and forgo the opportunity for the EU to exercise its leverage to promote liberal democracy, minority rights, and the free market. In the case of Turkey, this leverage has already moved mountains in the areas of political and economic reform. Enlargement has turned out to be the EU's most effective foreign policy tool. More by accident than by design, the EU is probably presiding over the most successful democracy-promotion program ever implemented by an international actor. If it can coax the Western Balkan states down the path taken by Bulgaria and Romania, there will be no question that this is true. Abandoning enlargement would have visible costs for the credibility of the EU's emerging foreign policy, and for the geopolitical and economic stabilization of its neighboring regions. Yet to strengthen substantially the EU's foreign policy, national leaders and publics would have to accept, as a matter of course, the immediate domestic costs of pursuing the EU's long-term foreign policy goals—and here the winds certainly do seem to be blowing in the other direction.

This also raises the question of how the EU's ENP will evolve. While in 1993 it was politically easier for EU leaders to offer a membership perspective than to offer complete access to the EU market, this is no longer true. The length and scope of the membership queue has become politicized, and the addition of new candidates unpopular (see Table 6.3). Yet market access remains restricted for the EU's eastern neighbors such as Ukraine and Moldova. Ukraine in particular has pushed very hard to be given a membership perspective. This has not been forthcoming but, during 2006 as part of the ENP, talks began on an EU–Ukraine free trade zone.

The situation is complicated by the EU's twin goals for the ENP. On the one hand, the ENP can be understood as a way to head off further enlargement by attenuating the costs of being excluded from the EU. On the other hand, the ENP is part of the EU's ambitions to become a more powerful geopolitical actor. By offering a 'stake in the internal market' instead of full membership, the EU aims to harness some of the power of the enlargement process in influencing domestic politics in the ENP states. By asking for improvements in democratic standards and human rights as well as for reform of the economy, the EU wants to create a powerful democracy-promotion program that extends beyond its membership queue. The great unknown of the ENP is whether the EU can offer sufficient incentives short of membership to make governing elites comply with its standards.

II

The Politics of Markets

7

Protecting Privacy in Europe: Administrative Feedbacks and Regional Politics

ABRAHAM NEWMAN*

European Leadership in Data Privacy Protection

Advanced industrial societies are awash in personal information. Bank records, credit card transactions, web clicks, mobile phone logs, fingerprints, and now even retina scans leave detailed trails of personal behavior. Governments and businesses use this information to increase efficiency, segment markets, and differentiate risk. At the same time, however, the proliferation of this data raises the specter that personal information will be used to discriminate against individuals and to support Orwellian state surveillance (Newman and Zysman 2006). Societies have responded differently to the privacy challenges raised, relying on quite different public policy solutions.

Over the last three decades, Europe has emerged as the international leader in data privacy protection. Starting in the 1970s, nations including France and Germany enacted comprehensive regulations that establish a basic set of privacy principles for the public and private sectors. These principles are enforced by powerful independent regulatory agencies—data privacy authorities. With the passage of the EU privacy directive in 1995, all member states were required to adopt comprehensive rules.[1] Followed by a set of specific directives in the areas of telecommunications and electronic commerce, European citizens enjoy an internationally unprecedented level of privacy protection.[2]

* I would like to thank Kate McNamara and Sophie Meunier as well as the other participants in the volume for their invaluable comments. Research for this article was made possible by the generous support of the Max Planck Institute for the Study of Societies, Cologne, Germany.

[1] See *The Directive on the protection of individuals with regard to the processing of personal data and on the free movement of such data.* Council of the European Union and the Parliament 95/46/EC, 1995 OJ (L281) 31.

[2] See *The Directive concerning the processing of personal data and the protection of privacy in the telecommunications sector*, Council of the European Union and the Parliament 97/66/EC, 1997 OJ (L24)1; *The Directive concerning the processing of personal data and the protection of privacy in the electronic communications sector*, Council of the European Union and the Parliament 2002/58/EC, 2002 OJ (L202) 37; *The Regulation on the protection of individuals with regard to the processing of personal data by the Community institutions and bodies and*

The construction of a comprehensive regime for data privacy protection within Europe has had far-reaching consequences within Europe and abroad. Because data privacy laws were firmly in place prior to the information technology revolution of the late 1990s, digital marketplaces in Europe have a distinct flair. Consumer information is much less readily available than in comparable sectors in the USA.[3] Similarly, law enforcement and executive agencies within Europe face unique constraints imposed by the stringent privacy regime. The new national security environment brought on by terrorist attacks in the USA, Spain, and the UK has further accentuated these tensions. Despite government efforts to expand police power, privacy protection has proven extremely resilient in the European context.[4]

At the same time, European privacy rules have had far-reaching international consequences. A critical extraterritorial provision of the privacy directive limits the transfer of personal information from Europe to markets that provide 'adequate' protection. Nations without comprehensive systems face the risk that cross-border data flows will be disrupted. This has led to intense negotiations between Europe and many of its trading partners. Over thirty countries including the majority of the OECD have modeled their own laws on European rules. Multinational firms have been forced to reorganize their information collection and processing systems, often barricading European data within Europe. After a period of heated disputes that verged on the first trade war of the information age, even the USA has signed an international agreement that compels US firms active in the European market to comply with European rules.[5] In addition to the obvious implications for international trade, the European data privacy regime has raised a series of security disputes between the NATO allies.[6]

The expansion and resilience of data privacy policy in Europe are particularly striking given the perceived EU market-making obsession. The European Commission, primarily concerned with constructing the internal market during the 1980s, opposed European privacy rules. The Commission repeatedly argued that privacy rules were a public sector issue best dealt with at the national level. Similarly, many of the most powerful states within Europe were skeptical of supranational action in the policy realm. Given this initial resistance, what explains the puzzling entry of the EU into regional privacy debates in the 1990s?

In order to understand the expansion of privacy protection within Europe over the last several decades, this chapter focuses on the innovative role of domestic

on the free movement of such data, Council of the European Union and Parliament 2001/45/EC, 2001 OJ (L) 1.

[3] See Dash (2005), 'Europe Zips Lips; U.S. Sells ZIPs', *New York Times*, August, 7: 1.

[4] See Anderson (2005), 'Major European Institutions Divided on Data Retention', *Telecom Markets*, February 22.

[5] See Jonquieres (1998), 'Bid to Avert Threat of "Cyber Trade War"', *Financial Times*, September, 10: 6. For an academic discussion of the transatlantic dispute, see Farrell (2003a).

[6] See Kochems (2006), 'EU Privacy Directive Could Prohibit Information Sharing with U.S. Law Enforcement', *Heritage Foundation Report 992*, February 14.

regulatory agencies in motivating and maintaining supranational action. I argue that national regulators—data privacy authorities—served to inject policy change into the regional integration process. National regulatory institutions, which were the product of *administrative policy feedbacks*, forged cooperative networks becoming new political actors at the European level. These regulatory agencies have employed their technical expertise and enforcement authority to build powerful coalitions capable of influencing regional political outcomes. Leveraging domestically delegated coercive power and collective interpretive power to frame privacy debates, these regulatory agencies have expanded levels of protection and guarded against retrenchment efforts. The case of data privacy then highlights a more general transformation in European politics brought on by internal market reforms. Europe has constructed a regulatory state (Majone 1996a), in which direct command and control interventions have been replaced by arms'-length oversight, and with it a host of new political actors.

The chapter proceeds in four sections. It first examines existing explanations for European involvement in data privacy that focus on powerful member state preferences and Commission activism. This section is followed by the development of the feedback argument employed in the chapter. The theoretical claim is illustrated in the analytic narrative which examines the passage of the 1995 privacy directive as well as recent attempts to curtail privacy protection in the face of new security concerns. The final section highlights the implications of the argument for European integration and historical institutional debates more generally. In short, the chapter contends that national independent regulatory agencies created as part of the regulatory state have feedback effects on supranational politics within Europe.

Existing Explanations

While scholars have focused a considerable amount of attention on the effect of the 1995 privacy directive for the transatlantic relationship, very little work has investigated the political origins of the EU privacy regime (Long and Quek 2002; Farrell 2003; Heisenberg 2005b). Most explanations point to two theories popular in the European integration literature. The first is a neo-liberal account, stressing the economic interests of firms from the most powerful member states. According to this argument, firms from countries with high levels of privacy regulations including Germany and France pushed their governments to advocate for European action in order to level the regulatory playing field within Europe. Fearing the economic costs of regulatory arbitrage, these governments advocated raising privacy protection standards in Europe to protect their firms.[7]

---

[7] Several historical accounts of the directive suggest that the legislation reflected German and French interests. See Platten (1996) and Wuermeling (1996). The theoretical argument is developed extensively in Moravcsik (1998).

A second argument focuses attention on the role of the European Commission to motivate policy action in critical areas of the internal market. This supranational activism account contends that privacy is just one of many policies that the Commission sponsored to promote the liberalization of the telecommunications market and spur the development of a cutting-edge Information Society. The Commission then used its agenda-setting power to promote supranational data privacy policy.[8]

While these literatures have added considerably to the study of European integration, they cannot explain the emergence of the 1995 data privacy directive. In order for the neo-liberal institutional account to be true, the empirical record would have to demonstrate firm support for supranational action from powerful member states. Quite to the contrary, firms from the largest countries actively lobbied against European involvement in the issue area. The neo-liberal institutional argument seems to suffer further when the statements of the major powers are examined. Both Germany and England called for national action in the policy sphere, and France remained remarkably silent. In short, there was no firm-led member state push for supranational involvement.

Similarly, a supranational activism account would require verification of Commission interest in data privacy policy during the 1980s. Once again, there is no such empirical finding. In fact, the Commission repeatedly rejected recommendations by the EP to take on the issue. Arguing that supranational privacy regulations would create a new trade barrier within the emerging single market, the Internal Market Directorate attempted to forestall European rules. The Commission, instead, called on national governments to resolve the matter.

It then becomes critical to understand why both the Commission and major member states changed their positions and supported supranational intervention in the early 1990s. The following section presents a theoretical argument that explains this switch.

When Regulators Become Actors—The Role of Administrative Feedbacks

The central argument of this chapter builds on historical institutional work that isolates the role that feedback mechanisms play in policy change. Developed primarily in the American and comparative subfields, feedback arguments highlight how government policies affect the resources, goals, and structure of political

---

[8] Heisenberg (2005*b*), e.g., notes that the Commission supported the directive's final passage. Arguments for how and why international organizations motivate international outcomes are presented in Pollack (2003) and Barnett and Finnemore (2004). For additional applications to the European Union, see Sandholtz and Zysman (1989), Jabko (1999), and Weber and Posner (2000).

actors and in turn affect political outcomes (Pierson 1993; Levy 2006; see also the editors' discussion of the broader historical institutionalist literature in Chapter 1).

Much of the existing literature has focused on *client feedbacks*. Studied in the social policy arena, research has identified the ways in which entitlement programs created client groups that then mobilize as actors to protect and promote their political cause (Weir, Orloff, and Skocpol 1988). Andrea Campbell, for example, has examined how the Social Security system in the USA shaped the way elderly Americans identify and organize politically (Campbell 2003). Similarly, Suzanne Mettler has found that participation in veterans' programs such as the GI Bill affected the political involvement of such citizens (Mettler 2002). Policies shape both the organization of interest groups and the participation of individuals in mass politics (Newman 2003).

This chapter identifies a related but distinct causal mechanism. *administrative feedbacks.*[9] In contrast to client feedbacks, where policies create constituents that shape institutional trajectories, the administrative feedback argument scrutinizes the agencies that are constructed to oversee, implement, and monitor a policy regime. While previous research on feedbacks has examined the relationships between policy and the state, this work has focused on issues of state capacity (Ikenberry 1988; Skocpol 1995). The quintessential example is Steven Skowronek's argument that civil service reforms in the US progressive era facilitated the New Deal social policy transformation (Skowronek 1982). Governments are able to conduct certain activities in time $T = 1$ because past governments adopted certain policies in $T = 0$. The administrative feedback argument, by contrast, investigates how policies create new state actors that then influence political outcomes. The goal of this chapter is to examine how and when such administrative feedbacks matter.

Policies shape politics by changing the structure and goals of political actors and the resources that they wield. The creation of an administrative regime transforms advocates into bureaucrats, lawyers, economists, and engineers move from participants in epistemic communities proposing reform to government employees that oversee and implement those reforms. This transition contains an important structural change, whereby policy advocates concerned primarily with establishing basic principles become tasked with carrying out government policy. Administrative agencies and regulatory bodies are embedded within the government. They then act to alert both other government officials and interest groups to emerging policy challenges; as the agency responsible for a particular issue in the government, they guarantee that that issue will be discussed in policy circles.

---

[9] In his review of the literature on feedbacks, Paul Pierson (1993: 603–4) claims that such arguments applied to the state deserve particular attention, 'Yet of all the dimensions of policy influence reviewed in this essay, those linking the resources and incentives generated by existing policies to actions of government elites seem the least well established.'

Once delegation has occurred, however, these agencies often formulate interests distinct from their government principles. While legislative sponsors—both governmental and societal—organize to guarantee adoption, the political agencies that oversee the regime focus on system development and maintenance. This shift from adoption to implementation alters the political discourse. Regime existence is taken for granted, as administrators attempt to expand regulatory authority or carry out their programmatic goals. Far from being simply competency maximizers that relentlessly attempt to expand their authority, regulatory agencies develop a particular organizational culture and beliefs that drive their policy preferences (Carpenter 2001; Barnett and Finnemore 2004).

When legislation creates institutions to oversee and monitor a particular policy regime, the political actors in charge of those institutions receive new resources to affect future policy. Ranging from administrative fines to control over market access, government agencies have delegated authority that allows them to intervene in politics. Official sanctioning authority is backed up by the power of the bully pulpit. Government agencies can use their stature to name and shame their political adversaries and promote an alternative political agenda. Additionally, they develop relationships with their regulatory partners. As they conduct their day-to-day business, they form relationships with private and public sector actors. These constituents may then be mobilized to support the agencies' preferences in future political battles (Goodman 1991).

The effect of these administrative feedbacks is then twofold. First, administrative agencies deploy their resources and position within the political environment to promote their policy goals. Second, agencies protect their administrative authority and therefore work to prevent the retrenchment of that authority.

When then are administrative feedbacks most likely to influence political outcomes? Their success is dependent on two factors: institutional design and reputation. Agencies that are endowed with institutional buffers against political control are more likely to develop unique preferences from their governments (Wood 1988). Staffing (i.e. the mix of civil servants and political appointees), budget independence, and structural independence within the government shape the character of administrative feedbacks. Similarly, the extent of delegated sanctioning authority affects the ability of an agency to promote its preferences. Agencies that have the authority to control market access have more coercive power than agencies that serve merely in an ombudsman role. Powers delegated through institutional design are then complemented by organizational behavior. Through actual policy actions, an agency builds a reputation with the public and its regulatory constituents. A positive reputation augments the institution's bully pulpit with the public and helps build constituent ties. As the reputation tarnishes, the agency's opinion is more likely to be discounted (Carpenter 2001).

Policies do not only affect mass or interest group politics. They also restructure the government. These administrative feedbacks create new political players that

TABLE 7.1. *The fair information practice principles*

Collection limitation: personal information collection should be limited and lawful

Purpose: the purpose of data collection should be disclosed and data should not be used for other purposes without consent

Openness: individuals should be informed about privacy policies

Accuracy: data should be accurate, complete, and current

Participation: individuals may request information about data held by organizations and challenge incorrect data

Security: stored data must be secure from theft or corruption

Accountability: organization must be held accountable to measures that implement the above principles

---

have distinct policy preferences and the resources to assert those preferences. The following section uses the historical narrative of the origins of the European data privacy regime to flesh out the theoretical argument. Data privacy authorities, established in the 1970s to oversee national regulations, used their delegated authority and expertise to press for supranational legislation in the late 1980s.

The Emergence of the European Data Privacy Regime

Planting the Seeds of Supranational Intervention—The Fear of the Computer

Starting in the late 1960s, governments and businesses began looking to new computer technology to assist their daily operations. Proposals emerged to link databanks in order to help organizations reduce fraud, better target customer needs, and increase efficiency. Despite the large potential benefits promised, such proposals quickly met with considerable opposition from groups in society that feared these networks of databanks would be used for nefarious purposes. The information being aggregated was extremely sensitive, ranging from tax rolls to health care records. At the same time, a series of executive branch scandals across the advanced industrial democracies underscored the potential for abuse (Bennett 1992).

Motivated by these concerns, legal scholars developed basic principles of privacy protection. Part of a new generation of socially active lawyers, these privacy experts emerged in the wake of the student movement of the 1960s.[10] Promoted at both the national and international levels, the principles became known as the Fair Information Practice Principles (FIPP). The major components of the FIPP appear in Table 7.1.

---

[10] The motivations of the legal community were described to the author in interviews with members of these early efforts in France, Germany, and the UK, including Spiros Simitis in Germany and Norman Lindop in the UK.

While countries ranging from the USA to Sweden passed legislation to protect privacy in the information age, the scope and enforcement mechanisms of such regulations varied considerably. A number of European countries including founding members of the EU—France, Germany, and Luxembourg—passed comprehensive regulations. These comprehensive rules applied the FIPP to the public and the private sectors. They were monitored and enforced by a new independent regulatory agency—a data privacy authority. Inspired by the New Deal institutions constructed in the USA in the 1930s, the data privacy authorities were among the first independent regulatory agencies in Europe, most set up in the 1970s. Their independence is promoted through long-term leadership tenure, separate housing from other ministries, guaranteed budget lines, and direct reporting requirements to legislatures. While their exact regulatory authority varies across countries, most have some substantial oversight responsibility regarding the use of personal information in both public and private organizations. Additionally, many were granted the power to block the transfer of data to companies or countries that did not comply with national data privacy rules (Flaherty 1989).

Other countries, by contrast, adopted limited rules that covered the public sector and a limited number of sensitive sectors. These limited regimes in countries including the USA and Switzerland did not create a powerful independent agency to oversee these rules, instead delegating enforcement to various executive bodies. Here self-regulation and market mechanisms were emphasized over direct government intervention. Still another set of nations from Belgium to Italy adopted no data privacy rules at all. In these countries, governments and industry had to come to their own solutions regarding the collection and processing of personal information. Europe, therefore, entered the 1980s with a broad spectrum of different privacy rules.

Cross-border Frictions and Supranational Delay

At the same time that legislatures considered national privacy rules, privacy experts were busy discussing cross-border issues at the international level. This epistemic community faced, however, considerable resistance to supranational intervention. Owing to growing economic interdependence, privacy experts argued that personal information could not be contained within national borders.[11] Transnational firms and market integration would result in companies and governments sharing individual data internationally. National privacy experts, therefore, lobbied European institutions to step into the policy area. They scored some initial success with the EP, which passed a series of

---

[11] See Hall (1982), 'Data Havens Threat to Consumer Privacy', *Financial Times*, September, 7: 9.

resolutions calling for pan-European rules.[12] Despite the Parliament's recommendations, the Commission showed little interest in data privacy during the 1980s. Rejecting the Parliament's recommendations, the Commission argued that supranational privacy rules would create heavy regulatory costs for business (Papapavlou 1992; Simitis 1997). Additionally, privacy rules were perceived as largely a public sector issue over which the Community did not have jurisdiction.

The Council of Europe proved to offer a more congenial platform for initial international efforts. Established separately from the EC in 1949 to promote political cooperation among the European states, the Council of Europe has long been active in human rights issues in Europe. In the early 1970s, the Council established a working group of national experts to examine the issue of data privacy. The working group made a set of recommendations to the Council concerning the use of personal information in the public and private sectors (Hondius 1975). These were then elaborated in the Council of Europe *Convention for the Protection of Individuals with Regard to Automatic Processing of Personal Data*, which was passed in 1981 (Council of Europe 1981).

While the Convention promoted the adoption of the FIPP in national law, it did not resolve transborder data privacy issues within Europe. The agreement did attempt to codify a set of standards to permit international data flows, but many loopholes existed. The most dramatic for the community of data privacy experts was that the convention was self-enforcing. Countries had to adopt implementing legislation after ratifying the convention, but there was no sanction for non-compliance. Spain, for example, ratified the convention in 1981 but never passed any implementing legislation. The epistemic community of legal scholars was able to shape the international agenda but had few resources to affect national implementation.

Despite the fact that a third of the EC had failed to adopt national data privacy rules in response to the Council of Europe Convention, the major players in Community policymaking resisted supranational action. In 1981, the European Commission rejected a call by the Parliament for Community legislation. The Commission argued that governments under the auspices of the Council of Europe Convention should adopt national legislation to address transnational frictions.[13] These calls for national action were supported by national governments. The British government consistently argued that data privacy was not an issue to be managed at the supranational level. It carried this position through to its final 'no' vote on the privacy directive. The German and the French governments were similarly reluctant to support supranational rules. The German interior minister,

---

[12] The European Parliament passed a series of resolutions calling for supranational action including those of May 3, 1976 OJ (C100): 27, May 8, 1979 OJ (C140): 147, and March 9, 1982 OJ (C87): 39.
[13] See Commission Recommendation 1981 OJ (L246) 31.

shortly before the development of the first European privacy draft, called on national governments to act to ward off supranational rules.[14]

Interestingly, firms from countries with high levels of regulations did not support pan-European rules. In contrast to arguments stressing the economic interests of corporations to support international harmonization in order to level the regulatory playing field, companies showed no interest in supranational legislation. British firms were the most adamant in their opposition, warning that European intervention would have severe implications for industry. But even German firms, which faced the most stringent rules domestically of any country in Europe, argued that they did not see a need for European intervention.[15] By the middle of the 1980s, the major players in European public policy had rejected the epistemic community's call for supranational intervention, agreeing that national action should be the primary mechanism to resolve data privacy issues.

Administrative Feedbacks—Changing the Stakes

But at the same time that the Commission, member states, and industry resisted supranational involvement, new political players emerged through an administrative feedback process that shifted the policy debate. With the passage of national privacy regulations in the late 1970s and early 1980s, leading privacy experts were appointed to run data privacy authorities in a majority of member states. These regulatory agencies grew increasingly disturbed by the fact that five members— Belgium, Greece, Italy, Portugal, and Spain—had not adopted any privacy rules. The regulators feared that these nations would serve as data havens within the Community. Individuals' rights would be threatened, and their regulatory authority undermined as firms outsourced their data processing operations to countries that had not established data privacy laws. National data privacy authorities began an effort to use their newly acquired political resources to force supranational action.

After the adoption of national laws in France, Germany, and Sweden, data privacy authorities initiated international cooperation at the First Annual International Data Protection Commissioners' Conference in Berlin in 1979. Within the context of this cooperation, data privacy authorities used their expertise to develop a platform for supranational reform. They argued that in order for European integration to progress, European rules on data privacy were necessary. At the

---

[14] For the comments of then interior minister Wolfgang Schaeuble, see Loff (1989), 'Datenschützer warnt vor "Freihafen" der Informationsweitergabe', *Frankfurter Rundshau*, August 8: 1.
[15] See Dwek (1990), 'EC Scheme for Data Protection Stuns UK', *Marketing*, July 12: 3; *Computerwoche*, 1990; 'Wirtschaft fürchtet Nachteile durch verschärften Datenschutz', December 21: online. *European Report*, 1993; 'UNICE Shuns EC Draft Directive', February 13: 1835; Ivor Owne (1993), 'Wider EC Data Controls Opposed', *Financial Times*, October 12: 8.

Annual Conference in 1989 and then again in 1990, data privacy authorities used their bully pulpit to lobby for EC legislation.[16]

With their agenda in place, the data privacy authorities leveraged their coercive power to regulate market access to underscore the importance of their demands. In a series of enforcement moves, data privacy authorities cut off the flow of information within Europe to countries that lacked data privacy regulations. The first, and most high profile, involved the transfer of information between Fiat France and Fiat Italy in 1989. The French data privacy authority (CNIL) blocked the transfer between the two affiliates arguing that the absence of privacy rules in Italy made the transfer illegal. After several weeks of uncertainty, Fiat was forced to sign a contract with the French privacy authority that it would guarantee privacy protection for any information taken out of France.[17]

A second, and potentially more significant event, concerned the passage of the Schengen Convention in the late 1980s. The Schengen Convention was an inter-governmental deal initially between Belgium, France, Luxembourg, the Nether-lands, and West Germany to permit the free movement of citizens between the countries. In order to facilitate this process, the governments set up cooperative immigration controls to share information among the members of the agree-ment. A Schengen Information System was created that promoted enforcement cooperation within the Schengen area. While the Schengen Convention was not Community law, it did fulfill a critical supranational goal: to promote the free movement of citizens within Europe.

This proposal, however, did not sit well with the data privacy authorities who were concerned with the inclusion of Belgium. Belgium did not have data privacy regulations in place and therefore transferring sensitive data to the country com-promised the safety of individuals from countries with privacy rules. The data privacy authority from Luxembourg informed the German and French agencies of the plans for the information system and the three, in turn, demanded action. The authorities argued that the agreement violated national data privacy rules and they would block data transfers to the new Schengen Information System until Belgium had adopted regulations.[18] Once again the data privacy authorities used powers delegated to them nationally in the 1970s to shape European policy.

These incidents convinced the Commission and many member states by the end of the 1980s that supranational action was necessary. The data privacy authorities

---

[16] See the president of the CNIL, Fauvet (1989), 'Privacy in the New Europe', *Transnational Data and Communications Report*, November 17–18; (1990). 'Data Protection Essential to EC 1992', *Transnational Data and Communications Report*, May 5–10.

[17] See (1989), 'No Fiat for Fiat', *Transnational Data and Communications Report*, November 10.

[18] See the comments of the president of the CNIL, Fauvet (1989), 'Privacy in the New Europe', *Transnational Data and Communications Report*, 17–18 November. His argument was confirmed by a German privacy expert, see (1990), 'Simitis Reports Data Protection Chaos', *Transnational Data and Communications Report*, June–July: 26.

had demonstrated that they could disrupt critical Community goals of integrating the European market and creating a European public administration. One Commission official argued that they were held hostage by the actions of the privacy authorities.[19] The major European policymaking institutions switched positions, promoting pan-European rules.[20]

The Commission, with the help of data privacy authorities, drafted a proposal in 1990, which set off an intense period of lobbying. Despite continued industry attempts to stop the directive, the Commission had to meet the demands of the privacy authorities. Industry did win several important concessions, which promoted subsidiarity in national enforcement regimes. Industry in countries with existing rules hoped to minimize adjustment costs. Data privacy authorities supported these efforts, hoping to avoid the creation of a single super-regulator that would replace national oversight.[21] These lobbying efforts by industry and the data privacy authorities had the surprising result of expanding the regulatory powers of national data privacy authorities within Europe. Instead of creating a single European data privacy authority, the directive called on national governments to establish or reform their laws so that national regulators had the powers that their peers enjoyed in other countries. The directive intensified the administrative feedback effect, expanding the role of national regulatory agencies in European politics.

Institutionalizing the Network—The Article 29 Working Party

In addition to requiring the national adoption of data privacy rules, the privacy directive included a critical provision that has further institutionalized the role of national data privacy authorities within the supranational regime. Article 29 of the directive calls for the creation of a Working Party composed of national regulators. The Working Party, which met for the first time in 1997, advises the Commission on emerging data privacy issues facing the EU, oversees the implementation of the directive in the member states, and evaluates the adequacy of privacy regulations in foreign countries. National regulators have been actively incorporated in the rule-development and rule-enforcement process at the supranational level.

The creation of the Article 29 Working Party has consolidated and strengthened regulatory cooperation within Europe. The Commission provides financial and linguistic support for a secretariat for the Working Party, allowing the members

[19] The Commission official responsible for drafting the initial directive explained in an interview with the author.

[20] The importance of the data privacy authorities in persuading the Commission is explained by then Internal Market Commissioner J. Mogg (1994), 'Privacy Protection in the Information Society', *Transnational Data and Communications Report*: 29–32.

[21] Industry attempted to integrate enforcement variation into the directive. See (1991), 'Data Protection: UNICE Calls for Changes in Proposal on Personal Data', *European Report*, 1 February 1651: 3.

to manage many more tasks than they had previously under the International Data Privacy Commissioners' Conference. The Working Party has developed an annual work plan, which covers a broad range of issues from the use of biometric data to Internet Cookies. Each part of the work plan is delegated to teams of national civil servants, who specialize on that issue area. Since 1997, the Working Party has released over 100 recommendations and opinions.[22]

The activities of the Working Party have substantial effects within Europe. The Working Party releases opinions concerning the implementation of the directive by the national privacy authorities (who also comprise the Working Party). While its opinions are not formally binding, firms take its statements seriously. These opinions inform national agency implementation strategies on the ground and signal to industry evolving enforcement patterns.[23] Additionally, national courts have looked to the opinions of the Working Party to uncover the intent of the privacy directive. Companies, therefore, are likely to adopt the positions of the group in order to avoid regulatory uncertainty.

The Working Party has also been active in emerging EU debates concerning privacy. The former chair of the Working Party, Stefano Rodota, contributed to the successful lobbying effort to include data privacy into the catalogue of rights in both the European Charter and the failed draft European Constitution.[24] The Working Party has actively participated in the development of specific privacy regulations for the telecommunications sector, including a directive on electronic commerce and on data retention.

The debate on data retention proves particularly illustrative of the contin- ued role of administrative feedbacks in European privacy politics. As a result of national and European legislation, telecommunications operators found little value in maintaining detailed records of consumer use patterns. Regulations limited their ability to profile consumers, and thus information was stored in some countries primarily to check against fraud or payment disputes.[25] With the rise of transnational terrorism, however, national security agencies have pressed to increase the retention of telecommunications data so as to facilitate police activities. Several governments including the United Kingdom and Ireland called for mandatory data retention of all telecommunications and Internet data for up to four years. This set off a rancorous debate in Brussels over the appropriate level of government surveillance in the telecommunications sector.[26]

---

[22] The opinions of the Group are available at http://europa.eu.int/comm/justice_home/fsj/ privacy/workinggroup/index_en.htm

[23] The power of the Group to affect business behavior was echoed in numerous interviews with European trade associations.

[24] As explained to the author in interviews with members of national data privacy authorities.

[25] Interview with privacy officer from a major European telecommunications company.

[26] See (2005), 'Institutions and Industry Deadlocked on Data Retention Rules', *European Report*, May 5.

The Working Party was among the first groups to respond to the proposal and advocated for a minimal retention period, limited to telecommunications, with identified justifications for use. In short, the Working Party did not oppose retention outright but argued that it should be constructed to pose the least harm possible to individual liberties. The Working Party released several opinions detailing its position (Article 29 Data Protection Working Party 2002; Article 29 Data Protection Working Party 2004). These opinions became an important source of argumentation for the EP, which was also concerned about an overbroad retention policy. While the retention directive has passed, the final compromise reflects many of the concerns raised by the Working Party: retention has been limited to telecommunications data, the minimum mandatory retention period is six months with a maximum of two years, and data that is retained can only be used for certain law enforcement purposes. The Working Party lost many points in the debate, most importantly the fact that countries can require data retention for up to two years. But the presence of the Working Party substantially altered the course of the European debate.

Since the passage of the privacy directive, the EU has constructed a detailed regime for the protection of privacy. Additional legislation has been adopted for the use of personal information in the telecommunications sector, the area of electronic commerce, and the institutions of the EU itself. As part of the Treaty of Amsterdam, the EU agreed to create a European Data Privacy Supervisor who oversees data privacy issues in the supranational institutions and has the authority to consult on third pillar questions dealing with police and judicial cooperation.[27] With the passage of proposed legislation covering the third pillar, Europe will have finalized the last piece in the most comprehensive privacy protection regime in the world.

While data privacy legislation in Europe has substantially shaped both the development of European economies and security systems, it does not create an absolute right to privacy. The regime balances individual interests against those of business and government. Privacy disputes, therefore, are not eliminated by the regime. The emergence of biometric data and satellite positioning information typifies just a few of the new threats to privacy on the horizon. Data privacy regulations will not be able to resolve these challenges in isolation. Rather, government regulations work in concert with (and at times in opposition to) technological solutions, private actor self-regulation, and societal norms (Bennett and Raab

---

[27] See *The Directive concerning the processing of personal data and the protection of privacy in the telecommunications sector*, Council of the European Union and the Parliament 97/66/EC, 1997 OJ (L24)1; *The Directive concerning the processing of personal data and the protection of privacy in the electronic communications sector*, Council of the European Union and the Parliament 2002/58/EC, 2002 OJ (L202)37; *The Regulation on the protection of individuals with regard to the processing of personal data by the Community institutions and bodies and on the free movement of such data*, Council of the European Union and Parliament 2001/45/EC, 2001 OJ (L)1.

2006). Data privacy authorities—the product of administrative feedbacks—will no doubt play a significant role in mediating the various policy problems as the regime evolves.

Conclusion

Since their creation in the 1970s, data privacy agencies have worked individually and as part of a cooperative network to shape regional privacy policy. Relying on their legal expertise and their ability to control the transfer of information across Europe, they were able to construct a European agenda and influence the preferences of the Commission and important member states. Few national governments could have imagined at their conception, that data privacy authorities would become part of the European policy landscape. At the same time, if market integration had progressed prior to the institutionalization of data privacy authorities, it is unlikely that Europe would have moved forward with such a comprehensive privacy strategy. The origins of the European data privacy regime are fundamentally tied to national decisions made in the 1970s to create new political institutions.

In conclusion, it is important to stress two theoretical implications of the argument developed in this chapter. First, the chapter builds on existing historical institutional work to isolate the relationship between policy change and administrative feedbacks. While past literature has identified the role policy plays in the future capacity of a state to take (or not take) certain actions, the administrative feedback argument posits that policy reconfigures the state, creating new political actors. As governments delegate authority to agencies, these agencies can develop independent interests from their government principals. Based on their professional training, ideological beliefs, or desire for expanded authority, agencies will promote their political ends in the policy process. They will use the resources at their disposal to achieve these ends including their technical expertise to define a regulatory agenda and power to sanction non-compliance.

Independent agencies are best positioned to exercise their autonomy when they are buffered from political control by government officials. Two factors are critical: institutional design and reputation. Agencies that have a guaranteed funding mechanism, non-political appointments, and organizational independence enjoy a greater deal of autonomy than agencies that were not created with such institutional features. That being said, organizational experience matters as well. Agencies that are effective, respected by the public, and have productive relationships with their regulatory constituents are able to use their reputation to assert their interests. Governments that attempt to overturn popular agency initiatives will face the considerable political costs of doing so.

Second, the case of data privacy exemplifies a political transformation under-way in Europe. Since the 1970s, European governments and the EC have worked to liberalize their economies. Shifting from Keynesian demand management and direct market intervention to arms-length governance structures, Europe has developed in a rather short period a complex regulatory state (Majone 1996a; Majone 2001). Governments have, for example, gone out of the business of running companies and focus instead on setting the rules by which companies compete. In constructing a regulatory state, governments have created a host of new institutions to oversee these markets—regulatory agencies, administrative courts, and ombudsmen. These new political institutions naturally serve important governance functions which have been identified in the existing literature (Majone 1997; Thatcher 2002). But the chapter contends that in addition to sharing infor-mation or promoting regulatory harmonization, the process of re-regulation has created a host of new actors in Europe. The rise of the regulatory state, then, has the potential to transform the political landscape within regional politics.

8

Financial Transformation in the European Union

ELLIOT POSNER[1]

The introduction of the euro has attracted a great deal of scholarly attention. Meanwhile, the transformation of financial regulations and institutions in Europe has been largely neglected. Yet harmonized rules, mutual recognition of foreign national laws, new regulation-making procedures, and coordinated implementation and supervision could have a more fundamental impact on European societies and the global political economy than the single currency. This regional development is exceptional even for the world of international finance, where markets and regulatory regimes have been in constant flux since the breakdown of the Bretton Woods system. Around the globe, changes in EU financial arrangements are creating new expectations among transnational firms and enhancing the positions of European national and EU officials in international forums (Posner 2005*a*). Inside Europe, the financial transformation is propelling the region toward a single financial market. It is likely to generate far-reaching economic, social, and political repercussions by accelerating the posteuro improvement in the ability of households, companies, and governments to access capital at rates and in amounts comparable to the USA. Large and small companies, as well as the owners and managers of mobile capital, are already able to meet their financing and investment needs in Europe to a much greater extent than in the past when New York was frequently the only option (Burgess and Postelnicu 2005; Authers and Gangahar 2006; Blackwell 2006; Wighton 2006).

The sudden acceleration of EU financial integration is a puzzling turn after years of seemingly modest progress and disagreement. Financial markets are institutions that are highly resistant to change, reflect accepted political bargains and often seem like a natural part of social life (Zysman 1983; McNamara 1998; Fligstein 2001; Posner 2005*b*; Jabko 2006). In the era following the SEA, finance emerged as among the most sensitive areas, and intergovernmental cooperation

[1] The author thanks Tim Büthe, Roy Ginsberg, Harold James, Kathryn Lavelle, Kathleen McNamara, Sophie Meunier, Abraham Newman, Nicolas Véron, Amy Verdun, James Wallar, Steven Weber, Gillian Weiss, and John Zysman for helpful comments. He is grateful for the financial support of the American Consortium of EU Studies (ACES) and the Institute for European, Russian and Eurasian Studies (IERES) at George Washington University's Elliott School of International Affairs.

lagged behind other sectors. Then, in the late 1990s and early 2000s, a broad consensus to leap ahead with financial integration crystallized. This chapter examines and explains this empirical pattern of abrupt change.

EU financial transformation also poses theoretical challenges for scholars interested in how history contributes to understanding institutional change. There is a strong tendency to attribute abrupt change to abrupt causes such as exogenous shocks (Pierson 2004: 96–102). In the case of the end-of-the-millennium transformation in Europe, the temptation is to look for explanations in the euro's introduction or the American economic challenge. Recent research, however, drawing attention to 'slow moving' causal processes (Pierson 2004; Thelen 2004; Posner 2005*b*) prompts the central theoretical questions of this chapter: to what extent and by what mechanisms are small integrationist actions that cumulate over time responsible for the EU's financial transformation? In more general terms, can incremental processes cause sudden bursts of change?

This chapter thus addresses core themes of the volume. In particular, it explores the impact of path dependence and shocks on an important EU outcome (see the editors' introduction to this volume). My findings offer an interesting twist to HI efforts to explain institutional innovation. They suggest that path-dependent (i.e. self-reinforcing) processes are more complex than commonly portrayed. Small incremental changes may generate a parallel process: they accumulate over time in ways that make existing arrangements vulnerable to policy entrepreneurs when a potentially transformative exogenous event occurs. In EU finance, powerful interests vested in the status quo ensured for decades that financial change would proceed slowly and in small stages. But the formidable obstacles to change did not lock institutional arrangements in place. Instead, a buildup of seemingly unremarkable actions produced conditions that by the late 1990s made EU finance ripe for rapid change. For certain, the euro's advent and the rise in US competitiveness are important. However, their impact was contingent on a quarter-century of actions, largely by Brussels civil servants but also by governments, transnational firms and other interested parties. In the remaining sections, I demonstrate that any explanation that does not take these slow-moving cumulative effects into account will be inadequate.

EU Financial Transformation: A Puzzle

What is an integrated or single financial market and what do I mean when I refer to recent developments as a financial transformation? An integrated financial market would allow capital and financial services (such as those provided by banks, brokerage houses, stock exchanges, asset managers, and insurance companies) to flow freely throughout the region. Advocates of increased integration argue that the absence of a single large financial market has had profound economic effects (Lamfalussy 2001: 9–10). On the micro side, they point to the higher costs of financing because of an inefficient match between the supply of capital from savings and its demand from businesses and to limited and poor consumer choices of investment and pension funds, mortgages, and insurance policies. On the macro side, they highlight the losses to potential gains in productivity, economic growth, and job creation. Detractors of financial integration are concerned about the effects on domestic financial services industries (especially the centralization of financial activity in London), the autonomy of national governments to carry out an independent economic agenda, and the welfare state's ability to act as a buffer against the extremes and risks that accompany financing via capital markets.

I use financial transformation to refer to recent substantive and procedural reforms that have moved the EU significantly closer to an integrated financial market. Even though the development of such a market was among the earliest EU aims, strongly reinforced in the single market program, until the late 1990s progress had been modest. An agreement to liberalize capital accounts (Council Directive 88/361/EEC) proved only an initial step, and a series of directives, applying the principle of mutual recognition to banking, insurance, and investment services, was generally too weak to overcome differences in national regulations, legal systems, and cultures. In addition, the financial integration project was plagued by inconsistent implementation of regional legislation as well as old-fashioned national protectionism (Story and Walter 1997: 314–15).

The European Council's March 2000 endorsement of the Financial Services Action Plan or FSAP, a list of forty-two proposed EU laws aimed to remove the above-mentioned obstacles, marks a turning point (Commission 1999). In contrast to other parts of the Lisbon agenda, EU policymakers met the original timetable set by the European Commission for adopting 98 percent of the new legislation and have now entered the consolidation stage focused on consistent implementation and enforcement and correcting poorly performing legislation (Dombey 2004; FT 2004; Commission 2006c). This outbreak of legal activity contrasts sharply with the post-SEA legislative processes in two ways.

First, the recent acceleration of legal integration differs both in its magnitude (i.e. the number of new laws and the breadth of issues addressed) and quality (i.e. the degree to which EU legislators employed the principles of harmonization and convergence). Second, unlike the earlier period, it was accompanied by an agreement, known as the Lamfalussy Process, that alters financial rule-making procedures and bolsters coordination mechanisms for transposition, implementation, and enforcement (Lamfalussy 2001; Bergström et al. 2004; Alford forthcoming; Quaglia forthcoming). The Lamfalussy Process introduced two innovations in the formal legislative procedures. It distinguished between broad framework legislation produced through normal codecision procedures and detailed rules created through committees of experts, national regulators, and European Commission officials (i.e. through a comitology procedure); and it introduced a more transparent process involving public hearings and opportunities for outside commentary. The Lamfalussy Process also spawned an elaborate informal network of new and reformed committees that links national finance ministries and supervisors, the European Commission, the EP, and private sector experts. As a whole, these changes contrast sharply with decades of slow, intermittent and uneven change and ineffectual agreements. They amount to a giant shift of financial regulation from the national to the supranational level and put in place many of the institutional and political foundations necessary for integrated financial markets.

The transformation in finance is particularly surprising because of the remarkable degree of consensus and willingness to compromise among European policymakers in an area traditionally plagued by sovereignty concerns. In the words of a European Commission official, 'No one wanted to be seen to be blocking it'.[2] The financial revolution is all the more mysterious because it began and picked up momentum at a moment when other major EU projects were faltering. In fact, finance, at the time of writing—when member governments seem to be losing their appetite for future enlargements as well as challenging core EU principles—may very well be the site where the integration project is proceeding most intensively.

Existing Explanations for Financial Reform

For the most part, scholars analyzing finance did not interpret European-level developments as important enough to merit investigation. Empirical and theoretical work instead centered on the degree to which global factors or previous national financial arrangements shaped *domestic* institutional change (see Moran 1991; Vogel 1996; Deeg 1999). An important exception is Jonathan Story and Ingo Walter, who maintained in *Political Economy of Financial Integration in Europe* (1997) that the post-SEA Europe-wide laws created a European Financial Area, producing some overall, albeit modest, benefits.[3] They argued that finance lagged behind other parts of the single market program because governments considered it an extension of national sovereignty. Government preferences derived from distinct and largely incompatible financial systems, creating what Story and Walter call a 'battle of the systems'. They thus put forth a two-stage model for accounting for EU financial developments that included a HI derivation of national preferences and an intergovernmentalist bargaining analysis of outcomes. Writing in 1997, they predicted national regimes would 'continue to evolve within their own logic' in the face of global forces and were skeptical of the view that

[2] Author's interview with European Commission official with DG Internal Market in Brussels (June 9, 2004).
[3] Jabko (2006), a welcome addition to the EU focused approach, was released too late to be engaged directly in this chapter. Underhill (1997) and Moloney (2002) are also important contributions.

a future EMU would swiftly bring about benefits and sweep away major national conflicts over the design of a future EU financial system (Story and Walter 1997: 314–15). Their analysis explains well the general resistance to and slow pace of change until the mid-1990s. However, by placing emphasis on national regimes, it fails to capture the potential for transformation inherent in the integration process itself.

Story and Walter were not alone in expecting continued nationally based fragmentation in the euro's aftermath. The projections of most academic and policy-oriented economists who specifically considered EMU's potential effects on financial integration mirrored some of Story and Walter's conclusions: rapid integration of some wholesale markets (e.g. government bonds and the interbank market) but continued fragmentation of a host of others as well as all retail markets (e.g. banking and brokerage services and insurance products) (Gros 1998; Dermine and Hillion 1999).

One difference, however, is that most of these authors maintained an underlying theme of automaticity, whereby a single currency would eventually lead to an integrated financial market (Gros 1998; Dermine 1999). In this sense, several analysts implicitly assumed that the euro's introduction would produce wide-ranging effects, including regulatory reform necessary for intensified market integration. Yet nowhere does one find in this work theoretically derived mechanisms or conditions for explaining why, when and how the elimination of currency risk and transaction costs might shift policymakers' preferences toward the kind of consensus necessary for transformational regulatory change.[4] In fact, recent research, showing that EU countries both inside and outside the euro-zone are experiencing similar EMU effects, raises serious doubts about the direct causal linkages between the single currency, financial markets, and regulatory systems (Askari and Chatterjee 2005).[5] Thus, the research investigating the euro's impact leaves us without an account for why, when, and how EMU might prompt decision-makers and firms to alter their positions toward financial integration.

Gradual Causes, Abrupt Change

Even though the new currency's introduction has received most of the attention, it was not the only major event that may have had an impact on the EU's financial transformation. International developments, especially the acceleration of US economic growth in the late 1990s, were also important. The challenge,

---

[4] For a compelling discussion of the relationship between monetary union and political development, see McNamara (2003).

[5] Even a cursory understanding of the US experience, where postdepression laws ensured fragmentation of a range of financial markets along state lines for decades, might have raised these doubts.

then, is to understand in what sense and to what extent such external events cause institutional change and, specifically, preference convergence in turn-of-the-millennium Europe.

One way scholars have begun to tackle such problems is to think about causes and effects in temporal terms (Büthe 2002; Pierson 2004; Thelen 2004). In the most prevalent approach, researchers envision institutional change in terms of sudden causes and abrupt leaps forward (Pierson 2004: 96–102). The shock-and-shift approach lends itself to parsimonious models because one can assume a static institutional context and fixed interests, capabilities and authorities without stretching the imagination. If the lion's share of institutional change occurs at discrete moments in time, then small reforms taking place in between critical junctures can be ignored for the sake of theorizing. For students of the EU, the underlying causal story is a familiar one. Actors with fixed interests shift policy preferences in reaction to stimuli—whether these derive from the international system or previous acts of EU integration. Actors interpret such changes in the external environment with little difficulty, know what they want and adjust their policy preferences unproblematically and quickly. European Commission officials, for example, would be expected to take advantage of the euro's advent by leading a crusade to reap the benefits of the currency through a dramatic advancement in financial regulatory integration.[6] Finally, the shock approach is well suited for generating falsifiable hypotheses. If it accounts for the EU's financial transformation, we should find evidence showing a correlation between the timing of preference change and political action, on the one hand, and the stimuli, on the other.

My skepticism towards such an explanation for financial transformation is not rooted in doubts about finding supportive evidence. As I show below, substantial evidence ties the timing of the euro and the US economic rise to EU institutional change. In particular, the empirical record demonstrates that the European Commission and some finance ministries of large member states, especially France (though also multinational firms to a lesser extent), responded to the new currency and the US challenge, generated broad support and otherwise led the process of change. My concern is that this type of analysis mistakes catalyst for cause.[7]

The problem lies not in what the shock-as-cause models contain, but in what is missing. The gradual thickening of the EU polity, the process preceding the shocks, is excluded as a plausible causal force. This makes little sense. To a significant extent, landmark institutional change must by necessity be the result

---

[6] Arguing that the European Commission acts as a policy entrepreneur, taking advantage of political opportunity structures, is standard across multiple approaches to European integration. See Sandholtz and Zysman (1989), Garrett and Weingast (1993), Fligstein and Mara-Drita (1996), see also Büthe (in this volume).

[7] This phrase is a modification of Jonah Levi's (1999: 55).

of incremental processes, and any persuasive explanation will weigh the impact of these background processes against the effects of shocks and investigate their interaction. The logic here is based on the complexity of major institutional change. Consider what the EU financial transformation entails. Below the surface of new legislation and procedures lies a foundation of necessary building blocks. An incomplete list includes, first, a general set of ideas for interpreting problems and developing solutions; second, a practical program of specific legislative measures; third, a frame that resonates broadly among firms, governments, national and supranational officials, and the EP; and finally, a supportive coalition of actors. Creating any one of the four would have posed formidable challenges. None could easily have been constructed from scratch in the six years between the FSAP proposal and completion. At least some of them were products of the past, of small steps that went largely unnoticed.

Thus, a second type of temporal analysis, focusing on the development of conditions over time that enable shocks to hasten history, is necessary for understanding major episodes of change. Such an approach pushes historical institutionalism in new directions. In the classic version, as Meunier and McNamara highlight in the opening chapter of this volume, a major theme is that existing arrangements often generate increasing returns to empowered interests, who then seek to maintain the status quo. This insight allows scholars to develop powerful logics for understanding slow-moving causes and effects, but fails to provide tools for generating a priori arguments to explain sudden episodes of institutional innovation. By building on an overlooked aspect of such path-dependent arguments, my approach contributes to efforts to overcome this shortcoming (Pierson 2004).

The key point is that mechanisms that reinforce the status quo rarely lock existing arrangements in place. They slow the pace of change by ensuring that it occurs in increments but do not typically halt its progression altogether. What then happens to these by-products of path-dependent processes? What is the effect of these incremental changes over time? I argue that their accumulation lays conditions that make existing arrangements vulnerable to sudden events. Absent external shocks, slow-moving cumulative causal processes are unlikely to produce rapid transformation and are less deterministic than other slow-moving processes, such as those following threshold or causal chain logics (Pierson 2004: 82–90).[8] Yet the relationship between cumulative effects and shocks is clear: the latter serve more as catalysts than causes.

In the EU, as in all polities, multiple actors contribute to forging such conditions. Companies, government officials, supranational civil servants and judges, and other interested parties fill the workday with small acts that contribute to

---

[8] Note that my conceptualization of threshold effects differs slightly from Pierson's. See Pierson (2004: 82–7).

the construction of the regional polity.[9] They support or produce studies, reports, conferences, legal interpretations and proposals, all of which in turn generate discourses and frames, political contests and debates, new networks and actors, and rules that add to the fabric of the regional project. Over many years actions like these add up, producing cumulative effects. At any given moment in time, opportunistic policy entrepreneurs may draw on these preformed coalitions, studies, and political frames to advance their agendas. Gradualist actions thus refashion the political landscape in ways that contribute to incremental institutional change and simultaneously create the conditions for external stimuli to produce rapid transformation.

The emphasis on the accumulated impact of incremental interventions takes us quite far from shock-and-shift approaches that merely stress opportunistic behavior during externally induced crises and helps us understand why some shocks generate immediate and transformational change while others do not. If such an approach is useful for explaining the EU's financial transformation, we would find that *before* the euro's advent and the late 1990s US economic acceleration, interested parties would have already: (*a*) developed general ideas about how a single financial market could be achieved and what problems it would solve (Fligstein and Mara-Drita 1996; McNamara 1998); (*b*) interpreted a need for specific pieces of legislation that could be included in a broad list of financial integration initiatives; (*c*) experimented with effective frames to harness support for financial integration (Posner 2005*b*; Jabko 2006); and (*d*) constructed new political voices and networks of financial sector firms and other nongovernmental bodies inclined toward financial integration (Heritier 2001; Mazey and Richardson 2001; Posner 2005*b*).

Weighing the Effects of Causes with Different Tempos

This section uses three particular outcomes to illustrate the balance and interaction between shocks and background processes in producing sudden institutional innovation.[10] The first and longest example is the emergence of *general* support for a single EU financial market, which coalesced around the FSAP. Observers of past EU efforts to integrate finance might easily have dismissed the Council's March 2000 endorsement of the FSAP as little more than lip service, if this consensus for dramatic change had not also yielded dozens of laws and a new set of procedures for expediting decision-making and improving transposition,

---

[9] These ideas build on recent research about bureaucratization and bureaucratic action. See Fligstein (1997), Carpenter (2001), Heritier (2001), Mazy and Richardson (2001), Barnett and Finnemore (2004) and Posner (2005*b*).

[10] I build a historical record from interviews with participants, official documents, the financial press, and secondary sources by other scholars.

implementation, and enforcement. Thus, the second case is the passage of a major piece of legislation, the regulation mandating convergence of national accounting standards, which exemplifies how the general consensus translated into specific laws. The third is the adoption of the Lamfalussy procedural reforms.

Building a Consensus for Change: Twin Shocks and the FSAP

How much of the *general* support for regulatory change can be attributed to major events taking place in the late 1990s and how much to cumulative effects of incremental actions? What outcomes did the confluence of the two produce?

The timing of the euro's 1999 introduction and America's end-of-century economic acceleration certainly suggests that there was a link between these 'shocks' and the consensus that emerged in favor of the FSAP. The European Commission's leaders, notably Commissioner Mario Monti, and finance ministers recognized that the euro's introduction and the US challenge presented a unique opportunity for advancing financial integration. The new currency made possible an argument that opportunistic Brussels officials, firms, and governments correctly perceived would resonate broadly and could not be countered easily:[11] the US economy was catapulting ahead of Europe's, and the EU could not reap the full benefits of the single currency until the obstacles to an integrated financial market were removed.[12] This framing quickly became a focal point for rallying support. No one wanted to be seen as opposing financial reform.

Of course, other factors also contributed to the timing of the new consensus. The expansion of domestic capital markets in the late 1990s, for example, imbued both Frankfurt and Paris with a considerable degree of hubris about their prospects for competing with London as the future seat of EU finance. The French Trèsor adopted an offensive strategy, believing that the exportation of French-like regulations would support Paris's role as a future financial center (Lalone 2005). The arrival to the UK Treasury of Gordon Brown in May 1997, moreover, reinvigorated financial reform at home and brought new zeal to the sometimes lukewarm British support for EU financial integration.[13] Brown is not the first Chancellor of the Exchequer to see advantage in a single European market (SEM)—at least in principle. In the late 1990s, however, he found eager French and German counterparts, who having agreed to the new currency could not easily counter a legislative program claiming to deliver the euro's benefits. In addition, Brown had allies in the EP, such as Chris Huhne and Theresa Villiers,

---

[11] Author's interviews with Delegation of the European Commission official in Washington, DC (May 4, 2004) and European Parliament official with the Committee on Economic and Monetary Affairs in Brussels (June 8, 2004).

[12] One of the earliest articulations can be found in Commission (1998*a*: 5).

[13] Author's interview with former UK Treasury official in Washington, DC (November 4, 2005).

who could fight effectively for City interests while being part of a surprisingly broad profinancial integration coalition that included social democratic Chair of the Committee of Economic and Monetary Affairs, Christa Randzio-Plath.[14]

Finally, financial services firms across the various subsectors, while not initiators of the reinvigorated financial integration project,[15] were easily won over by the Commission's logic. They had watched American financial services companies benefit from a giant home market, develop pan-European businesses and rise to the top of the financial league tables in Europe. Without enhanced integration, the major US banks were likely to be the biggest beneficiaries of the new currency. Not only did the initiative for renewed financial integration prompt existing business lobbies to develop policy positions, it also prompted the creation of new pan-European political voices. The European Financial Services Round Table, composed of the leaders of Europe's major banks and insurance companies, was formed in 2001 and began to produce research and publish their positions in 2002.[16] Eurofi, representing Continental Europe's retail-oriented financial services companies, was launched in 2000 with the stated goal of creating a single capital market in Europe.

Building a Consensus for Change: Cumulative Effects and the FSAP

The above section shows that there is substantial evidence tying major events of the late 1990s to the general consensus for financial change. But persuasive explanations of institutional change must weigh the effects of exogenous shocks against the impact of preexisting conditions and clearly specify how one is related to the other. Were there background conditions, built gradually over time, that were necessary for preference convergence to occur? The following five pieces of evidence suggest there were.

First, the successful framing of the problem and solution was in large part a product of trial-and-error. Brussels officials, in particular, had been experimenting with arguments for selling financial integration since the late 1970s (Posner 2005*b*; Jabko 2006). By giving a euro twist to slogans about job creation and international competitiveness used only six months before the FSAP proposal (Commission 1998*b*), Brussels officials were adding to a gradual evolution of frame experimentation.

Second, the European Commission parlayed a renewed interest in integration among finance and treasury ministers into a massive legislative program. This maneuver required political skills and expertise of how the EU polity works. Neither was instantaneously produced in the EMU's aftermath. The impetus for

---

[14] Huhne's writings on the subject are available at http://chrishuhne.org.uk/.

[15] Others also find that firms often react to, rather than lead, reform in the EU. E.g., see McNamara (1998: 43–71).

[16] See www.efr.be/index.asp.

the FSAP came from a modest European Council invitation 'to table a framework for action . . . to improve the single market in financial services, in particular examining the effectiveness of implementation of current legislation and identifying weaknesses which may require amending legislation' (European Council 1998: 9). It is not at all clear that the ministers, individually or as a group, envisioned their invitation resulting in a regulatory overhaul. Officials inside DG Market downplayed the ambition of their program, arguing that passage and implementation of nearly four dozen pieces of legislation would 'not require radical surgery' (Commission 1998*a*: 2). They also went to great lengths to make it seem as though the member governments and firms were always in the lead and to appear to be fulfilling a mandate. They achieved this, in part, through a leadership committee, the Financial Services Policy Group (FSPG), whose creation they recommended (Commission 1998*a*: 3). Mario Monti and his successors, Fritz Bolkestein and Charlie McCreevy, later used the committee's chairpersonship to push their agendas.[17]

Third, member government preferences were not merely products of a new framing campaign or other factors related to the events of the late 1990s. They also reflected the particular evolution of regional cooperation over financial regulation. By the time the Commission submitted the FSAP, the preferences of finance ministries were already in the process of changing. It is difficult to imagine French and German support for the financial program in 2000, for example, if the 1993 Investment Services Directive or ISD (Council Directive 93/22/EEC) had not helped to thwart London's dominance of continental equities trading. Provisions and ambiguities in that law protected exchanges against competition, giving the Frankfurt and Paris bourses time to re-organize and modernize (Story and Walter 1997: 21–2, 266–9; Steil 1998: 40–3).[18] This legacy of previous legislation contributed to a sense in France and Germany that domestic banks could prosper in a Europeanized regulatory system. It also helps to explain why the French continued to support the regionalization of regulation, even when core pieces of new legislation had a decidedly British flavor (Lalone 2005). Firm preferences were in flux before the Commission's campaign as well. In many cases, company preferences evolved as technological innovation combined with deficiencies in existing EU directives to create new problems. Internalization (i.e. in-house trading between clients of a single firm) and electronic trading networks, for example, led to new demands for an updated ISD.[19]

Fourth, European Commission officials tend publicly to depict the specific program of legislation contained in the FSAP as the outcome of intense consultation

---

[17] Author's interview with Delegation of the European Commission official in Washington, DC (May 4, 2004).

[18] Article 15.5 is the main source of ambiguity concerning stock exchange competition.

[19] 'Synthesis of Responses' to COM (2000) 729 at http://ec.europa.eu/internal_market/securities/isd/index_en.htm.

with vested parties following the June 1998 Cardiff Council (Commission 1998*a*: 2). Brussels civil servants did indeed consult broadly and embedded US-style openness in the new decision-making processes (see below). At the same time, however, the FSAP's legislative program was very much a product of history, pulling together legislative ideas that had been circulating for decades.[20] A previous relaunch of financial integration began with the Commission's April 1983 'Financial Integration', the main proposals of which made their way into Lord Cockfield's white book, 'Completing the Internal Market' of June 1985 (Commission 1983, 1985*a*). In the late 1990s, Commission officials did not simply dust off old proposals that had been sitting in drawers. In fact, many of the original ideas for integrating finance changed significantly over three decades, reflecting the constant state of change in financial sectors and the various constellations of interests among governments and firms.[21] The substantive focus of legislation, however, was remarkably consistent. More than a fourth of the proposed legislation comprised actual revisions of previous laws.

Finally, the general support for financial transformation was also due to the ability of Brussels officials to incorporate the views, preferences, and concerns of Europe's financial services companies. The civil servants were able to do so because of their central position in a policy network of Brussels-based European-level business lobbies (Posner 2005*b*; Jabko 2006). While some active pressure groups emerged in response to the FSAP, many others had been in operation for years, had symbiotic relationships with European Commission officials and often owed their existence to them. FESE (the Federation of European Securities Exchanges) is a good example. Commission officials had a hand in its origins, provided funding for various initiatives, and generally worked closely with its leadership for decades.[22] In putting together the FSAP, the officials trusted FESE to produce quality recommendations in sync with their own visions. Not only were many of its recommendations adopted, but at times they were indistinguishable from the Commission's, evidence of the close relationship developed over the years.[23]

The Passage of Major Legislation: The 2002 Accounting Standards Regulation

The broad support for financial transformation did not end with a long list of proposed legislation; it led to the passage of forty-one of the original forty-two by the 2005 agreed deadline as well as other measures not included in the

[20] Author's interview with European Commission official working for the Delegation of the European Commission, (May 5, 2004), Washington, DC.

[21] See, e.g., the discussions about a top-down single stock exchange in Commission (1980) and Schmidt (1977).

[22] Author's interview with FESE secretary-general in Brussels (June 9, 2004).

[23] Compare the recommendations on institutionalizing cooperation among securities regulators in FESE (2000), Commission (1998a), and Lamfalussy (2001).

initial package (Commission 2006c). The introduction of an EU law (Regulation [EC] No. 1606/2002 of the EP and the Council), mandating that publicly traded companies issue their consolidated accounts in accordance with new international financial reporting (accounting) standards,[24] illustrates well how years of incremental change built a foundation for rapid enactment of new legislation in the euro's wake. This example suggests that without decades of a slow-moving process, the FSAP's promoters would have achieved much less.

The 2002 accounting regulation is important because of the centrality of disclosure rules to capital markets. Accounting standards specify what information companies must reveal about their internal finances and operations and serve as a means of communication for determining value. Long-standing differences among accounting standards pose significant barriers to cross-border economic integration and contribute to continued fragmentation along national lines.

The law's passage represents a distinctive turn away from previous opposition by large member states to further accounting harmonization. The objective of two previous EU accounting laws (the Fourth [1978] and Seventh [1983] Company Law Directives) was minimal harmonization, and the resulting directives left a wide range of choices for national governments (Dewing and Russell 2004). In fact, by the end of the 1980s, the UK and Germany had all but abandoned the goal of further regional harmonization. Even though they had succeeded in imposing a core British principle[25] into the EU directives, UK negotiators found European legislative efforts too constraining (van Hulle 2004). In Germany resistance to increased disclosure came especially from smaller companies.

Part of the explanation for accounting standardization lies in the consensus built around financial reform and the opportunities it created for European Commission activism. From this perspective, the sense of urgency coalesced into agreement among Brussels officials, European finance ministers and the EP for convergence. Indeed, the City of London, the UK Treasury, and the French Trésor were all strong proponents. Everyone, moreover, seemed to agree that convergence of accounting standards would be central to a regional financial market. In June 2000, just two months after the approval of the FSAP, the European Commission announced its plan to propose mandatory standardization. In February 2001, it rolled out the official proposal, which gained approval from the EP and member state governments the following June.

While this momentum opened the door for a more activist role by European Commission officials, the passage of the new law can only be fully grasped by taking into account a series of small political compromises and bureaucratic steps,

[24] International accounting standards produced by the International Accounting Standards Board and its predecessor, the International Accounting Standards Committee, are now commonly referred to as International Financial Reporting Standards or IFRS. In the past, they were known as International Accounting Standards (IAS).

[25] The 'true and fair view' principle. See Dewing and Russell (2004).

beginning in the 1970s, that set the groundwork for future convergence (van Hulle 2004). The turning point was the adoption of US standards in the early 1990s by some high-profile European multinational firms (Ball 2004). This prompted European policymakers to revisit the issue. The firms, responding to market forces, chose US standards to reduce the cost of raising capital in US financial markets. From the perspective of EU decision-makers, however, the problem was more political than economic.

They chose international standards, rather than building directly on existing EU legislation, creating new European standards or adopting US standards (Commission 1995). The US option was eliminated because no one wanted to cede power to the US standard setter. One reason for the plausibility of adopting international standards was that EU company law already shared a common principle. Although unintended, the compromise that led to the adoption of the British principle in 1978 and 1983 facilitated convergence to international standards in 2002. Another reason was the already close ties between the European Commission and the international body that produced the international standards. This was a deliberate tactic on the part of Brussels civil servants, who recognized that these close interactions promised less painful adjustments in later harmonization efforts. For several years the two parties, through a symbiotic relationship, shared concepts in developing laws and standards (Knorr and Ebbers 2001).

Overcoming Procedural Obstacles: The Lamfalussy Process

Compared to decades of sporadic and piecemeal agreements, the comprehensive package of turn-of-the-millennium financial services legislation would alone represent a regulatory revolution. But the EU's financial transformation also includes metamorphic change in the procedures for producing new laws and rules, implementing them and supervising their application. The 2002 adoption of the Lamfalussy Process[26] is all the more striking because it marks a breakthrough in long-standing interinstitutional impasses (Pollack 2003*a*: 140–4; Bergström et al. 2004). Member governments (wary to delegate powers to the European Commission in a highly sensitive domain) and the EP (concerned about unequal oversight powers vis-à-vis governments) had resisted the extension of 'comitology' to the area of financial market regulation.

Again the widespread consensus is remarkable. Despite the significant interests at stake, nobody wanted to be seen as blocking procedural reforms that promised to enhance the prospects of the legislative program and to expedite the creation of a single financial market. German Finance Minister Hans Eichel, for example, accepted an ambiguous commitment from the European Commission not to override a simple majority (a promise that appears to have changed nothing) in order

[26] The Lamfalussy Process was first applied only to the securities sector. In 2004, it was extended to banking and insurance/occupational pension (Alford, forthcoming).

to clear the way for his government's approval of the Lamfalussy Process (Pollack 2003*a*: 143). French Finance Minister Laurent Fabius's support for overall financial transformation was so strong that he backed the final report of Alexandre Lamfalussy's Committee of Wise Men, even though it rejected his pet proposal for a centralized EU Securities and Exchange Commission (*The Economist* 2001). The EP, too, was affected by the momentum for sweeping financial change. In 2002, while it was still holding up procedural reform for reasons related to the interinstitutional division of powers, the legislature made several public statements making clear its support for the Lamfalussy report and a single financial market (Bergström, Almer, and Varone 2004: 14–15).

What accounts for this wave of support for overcoming the obstacles to procedural changes? How much of the explanation lies in shocks and how much in the accumulation of prior actions? At one level, the Lamfalussy Process can be interpreted as a direct and immediate spillover of the more general financial integration project. The Lamfalussy Committee explicitly used the argument that procedural reform was necessary to expedite the legislative program and ensure that regulatory structures did not undermine the potential benefits of an integrated financial market (Lamfalussy 2001: 7–8). It even borrowed some of the same framing that invokes both the euro and the US challenge: 'If [the EU] does not succeed, economic growth, employment and prosperity will be lower, and competitive advantage will be lost to those outside the EU. And the opportunity to complement and strengthen the role of the euro and to deepen European integration will be lost' (Lamfalussy 2001: 8).

At a deeper level, however, the Lamfalussy report appealed broadly and was perceived as a plausible reform package because its main provisions represented incremental changes. Indeed, the entire set of reforms is predicated on its practicality. Rather than opt for ideal regulatory structures like the risky proposal for a European SEC that would have had to be created from scratch, the committee built organically on what already existed. Thus, the attraction of the Lamfalussy Process is as much rooted in the small steps of the past as in the momentum sparked by the euro or the FSAP.

The creation of two new committees and the reliance on two levels of legislation and transparent and open consultation are the most important parts of the Lamfalussy reforms. All are adaptations of previous entities or ideas. The new Committee of European Securities Regulators or CESR, for example, is the formalization of the Forum of European Securities Commissions or FESCO, created five years before the adoption of Lamfalussy (*The Economist* 2001). The creation of a regulatory committee composed of high-level representatives of national finance ministries can also be traced to prior actions and ideas. The Commission's 1989 proposal for a directive on investment services recommended the creation of a European Securities Committee or ESC to monitor the implementation process (Bergström et al. 2004: 7–10). Although finance ministers rejected the proposal, the Commission kept the ESC idea alive throughout the 1990s. When the ministers finally agreed to an ESC, the EP, exercising its new powers under codecision in financial matters, blocked the extension of comitology to securities regulation until the interinstitutional deadlock could be resolved. Thus, the ESC met for the first time in 2001, but policymakers did not create the idea for the new committee *de novo*.

Likewise, the procedures that distinguish between framework laws and detailed rules and formalize open consultation were also not innovations of the Lamfalussy Committee. This approach to EU law-making evolved gradually from the introduction of comitology procedures (Sabel and Zeitlin 2006), made its way into the Commission's 1998 'Financial Services' document (Commission 1998a), and reflected the Prodi Commission's approach to EU governance in general (Almer and Rotkirch 2004), rather than a special solution to euro-era EU securities regulation. Indeed, the Lamfalussy Process synthesizes many generic forms that embody EU governance in the post-SEA era (Sabel and Zeitlin 2006).

Conclusion

This chapter concludes that the gradual accumulation of previous actions creates conditions for a seemingly exogenous event to quicken the pace of institutional change. The result in this case was profound financial transformation in Europe. The empirical evidence suggests that the euro and the US economic challenge were catalysts, largely responsible for the timing of change. They sparked a general consensus for broad reform, the passage of major pieces of legislation and the adoption of new legislative and supervisory procedures. The causes of the transformation, however, are more deeply rooted in a slow-moving cumulative process. Years of effort generated frames, political skills, proposals, legislation, and networks that enabled policy entrepreneurs to translate shocks into a consensus for financial regulatory change. Previous cooperation in Europe and years of close interaction between an international standard-setting body and EU officials, moreover, made later passage of an extraordinary accounting standard law possible. Finally, various components of the Lamfalussy Process are rooted in predecessors and innovations made years before, sometimes in different contexts. Without the gradual build-up of these conditions, the euro and US economic acceleration might have spurred some reform, but institutional and regulatory change would not likely have been as expansive nor would it have occurred as rapidly.

The empirical record, by revealing the importance of slow-moving background processes in shaping the effects of shocks, gives important support for HI insights about the constraining effects of the past. Yet a focus on the small acts produced by path-dependent processes—but, importantly, off the main policy path—also advances our understanding of rapid instances of institutional change. These increments accumulate over time to create conditions that open possibilities for institutional innovation.

Finally, the EU financial transformation moves Europeans closer to one of their early goals: a single financial market (Commission 2005*a*). Ironically, the passage of a US law opened the world's eyes to the remarkable progress already achieved. By inadvertently increasing the cost of raising capital in New York, the 2002 Sarbanes-Oxley Act prompted global investors and companies to search for alternative financial centers (GAO 2006). With stable political systems, liquid and well-regulated capital markets, and a menu of assets that increasingly match the range of securities offered in the USA, the EU emerged as an obvious choice (Burgess and Postelnicu 2005; Authers and Gangahar 2006; Blackwell 2006; Wighton 2006). Predictions should always be proffered with caution. Yet it is now plausible to imagine that another external shock would consolidate the EU's role as an alternative to the American financial system, by driving petrol dollars and other financial flows and activity from the USA to Europe. Could such shocks include geopolitical strife and anti-Americanism? US deficits, a weakening dollar and global current account imbalances? Potential triggers are not in short supply, and time will tell how the foundations of the European project may translate them into further transformation at the EU level.

9

The European Company Statute and the Governance Dilemma

ORFEO FIORETOS[1]

Introduction

The central institutional dilemma of the European Union (EU) has remained how to create a common economic space without barriers to exchange in ways that do not undermine national designs held dear by individual member states. Already in the negotiations surrounding the Treaty of Rome, this governance dilemma shaped debates among member states over what powers and competencies should be given to Community institutions and what should be the structure of common European-wide rules. Similar debates took place during deliberations over the internal market in the 1980s, economic and monetary union in the 1990s, and most recently during the Constitutional convention that ended in 2005. With the EU's enlargement to twenty-five members, national economic designs today are more heterogeneous than ever, and the governance dilemma persists. What can the history of integration teach us about how member states have resolved the governance dilemma?

This essay examines how member states resolved the governance dilemma in the context of company law, and specifically how they managed the dilemma in the protracted negotiations surrounding the European Company Statute (ECS). Because company law has historically been entrenched in national institutions and is closely linked to multiple parts of the modern economy, member states are often reluctant to embrace community-wide instruments for fear that they will undermine designs that have proven important in achieving national economic and social objectives. One of the best illustrations of how the governance dilemma shaped debates over company law is the protracted history of the ECS, an initiative that emerged in the wake of the Rome Treaty but that took more than four decades to become European law.

[1] Thanks to Steve Casper, Maria Green Cowles, Harold James, Sophie Meunier, and Kate McNamara for comments on earlier drafts. My gratitude also to Timo Weishaupt and Pooja Shah for research assistance.

The European Company Statute is a novel legal instrument that gives companies the opportunity to eschew national law in favor of transnational legislation governing major areas of the modern firm, including its terms of incorporation, board structure, and reporting system. The Statute offers public limited liability companies operating in more than one member state the option of being incorporated as a single European company. Rather than being subject to different national laws in each member state where a subsidiary is located, a company can choose to operate under one set of EU rules with unified management and reporting systems throughout the entire Union. Companies opting to incorporate under the ECS will have the letters SE precede or follow their name (for *Societas Europaea*, Latin for 'European Company'). Among the many notable aspects of the ECS is the fact that it represents the very first instance in the history of capitalism where firms can choose to be legally transnational.[2]

Debate on establishing a European legal identity for firms began shortly after the Rome Treaty, but agreement on a statute proved elusive despite repeated attempts by key member states and the Commission to broker a compromise. Arguments in favor of the ECS have remained consistent over time and invoke the benefits both to European firms from rationalizing their administrative structures and to the European economy from a single legal code (Sanders 1960; Bolkestein 2002). The ECS allows companies to avoid the cost of setting-up and administering networks of subsidiaries throughout Europe and enables them more easily to move activities across national boundaries.[3] A frequently cited figure during a third round of ECS negotiations in the 1990s suggests that the ECS would deliver *annual* savings of €30 billion (CAG 1995).

Despite this very substantial sum, considerable progress in other areas of European company law and the perceived lack of competitiveness in Europe's entrepreneurial sector, agreement on the ECS eluded member states for a longer period of time than any other legislative initiative in EU history. The central reason member states could not agree was their concern over how a European statute would impact on their ability to retain valued national designs, above all those governing employee representation. In each of three phases of negotiation, a new solution to solving the governance dilemma was introduced. In the early stages, a harmonization strategy was favored; in a second round of negotiations, the principle of mutual recognition was thought to be a viable solution; and in

----

[2] Recall that descriptions of multinational companies (MNCs) as 'stateless' or 'transnational' are erroneous in the sense that all MNCs have one national domicile for each of their subsidiaries. As management scholars often note, MNCs are, therefore, more appropriately thought of as 'multidomestic' companies. In contrast, companies incorporating under ECS provisions would be genuinely transnational in their legal status.

[3] If a corporation with multiple subsidiaries in several countries wishes to transfer its main offices from country A to country B, it must first close its offices in A *before* opening its new offices in B. The ECS allows a company to avoid this cumbersome process, and thus offers distinctly lower costs of mobility.

the end a novel resolution was brokered that introduced a layered arrangement including both a regulation and a directive.[4] This dual solution, which lawyers describe as 'a very complex amalgam of EC and member state law' (Mendelssohn and Oliphant 2004: 3) and the European Council (2001*b*: 6) likes to think of as an 'indissoluble whole', was far less ambitious than earlier proposals. Key provisions were left aside in the final draft, diverse national rules governing employee representation on company boards were left intact, the type of company that could make use of the statute was circumscribed, and no major tax incentives were created to entice companies to make use of the statute. But the most striking part of the outcome was that member states elected to replace the instrument of harmonization—which has been the one favored in most areas of company law as a means to reducing complexity and promoting the internal market—with a solution that had two components. One, the solution entailed a regulation that constructed a separate legal architecture for SEs, and secondly, it introduced a directive that served to consolidate the historic diversity of national regimes. The history of how and why member states arrived at this layered arrangement offers valuable lessons for how the governance dilemma can be resolved in other areas where member states are caught between having to adapt collectively to new market realities and not wanting fully to jettison historic institutions at home.

This essay explains why the ECS has the unusual distinction of having the longest dossier period of EU legislative proposals, what consequences different solutions to the governance dilemma had on the bargaining process, and why the statute took its final form. In the following section, I discuss the insights from distinct theoretical traditions in accounting for the ECS case. I suggest that historical institutionalism (HI) supplemented with insights from the literature on varieties of capitalism offers a particularly good foundation on which to explain the finer dimensions of the ECS process. The subsequent section breaks down the history of the ECS into its distinct periods and examines the political battles that dominated negotiations, namely disagreements over the nature of employee representation in firms, the universe of companies that would be able to avail of the statute, and matters of taxation. Finally, the concluding section explores what lessons the ECS holds for the study of the EU, as well as for how the EU may reconcile institutional diversity among its member states without jeopardizing a course of greater integration.

---

[4] Regulations and directives are distinct legal instruments in the EU. While both are binding on member states, the former requires members to transpose the same rules into national law, while the latter only requires compliance with the goals enshrined in common rules. In other words, in the case of directives, member states can use different national rules and solutions to meet the objectives of EU prescriptions.

Company Law and Institutional Development

Company law can be defined as the rules governing the incorporation and operation of firms. Issues such as who can establish a company, how a company is dissolved, the rights of shareholders, the responsibilities of directors and managers, and whether employees should be represented in management boards are all matters for company law. However, because the formal rules and regulations that govern enterprises emerged at different moments in different economies, and because countries often have tailored company law to enable distinct national economic traditions, there are great discrepancies across countries (Andenas and Woolridge 2005). Recognizing that this diversity would be an obstacle to a well-functioning common market, member states gave the community competence in company law in the Treaty of Rome. It was argued that without greater harmonization in national rules governing companies, member states may employ national legislation to obstruct the free market of goods and services and fail to promote a dynamic European market (Buxbaum and Hopt 1988).

The scope of the Community's competence in company law grew substantially after the Rome Treaty. From having been limited to ensuring that companies incorporated in one member state would be recognized in all other states and harmonizing standards for safeguarding shareholders and creditors, the Community gained competence in other areas, including matters concerning accounting, corporate governance, and cross-border information-sharing. By the fiftieth anniversary of the Treaty of Rome, more than a dozen company law directives emphasizing harmonization of national laws had been introduced.[5] While progress in the specific case of the Company Statute proved elusive, it would not be an exaggeration to say that company law in general represents one of the most active areas of legislative activity by the Community, and that the Commission has generally been successful in pushing forward its harmonization agenda as a means to promoting the internal market.

What explains the relative success of the Community in expanding the scope of European company law? There is a voluminous literature exploring this issue, and much of it owes a great deal to the neofunctionalist interpretation of European integration (e.g. Burley and Mattli 1993). A neofunctionalist explanation for the expansion of European legislative initiatives and the considerable degree of harmonization that has taken place in company law stresses the importance of the European Commission in steering the process, the role of interest groups in pushing for greater integration as a consequence of their preference for a single Community-wide legal code, and the role of functional interdependencies across

---

[5] Of the thirteen company law directives developed by the Commission, only two (the fifth and the tenth directives) were shelved after significant opposition for reasons similar to those preventing agreement on the ECS.

economic and legal domains (Haas 1958; Sandholtz and Zysman 1989). While the neofunctionalist interpretation captures several important aspects of the expansion of company law, it has difficulties explaining why the history of negotiations surrounding the ECS differed so extensively from other areas of company law.

For example, neofunctionalist analysis may have predicted that the ECS would be among the first areas of a European-wide agreement. It is a case where economic groups across member states could have been expected to transfer their loyalty to the European level both as a means to reducing administrative and transaction costs, as well as to enhancing their prospects to form larger more competitive companies for the global market. Yet firms were not particularly enthusiastic about the ECS in the early, or indeed later stages. Particularly puzzling from a neofunctionalist angle, large companies in Europe were the ones expressing the least interest in the ECS, and they often sought to protect their access to national legal instruments rather than jettison them in favor of a single European code.

I identify these difficulties of neofunctionalism not to reject this theory, which does as good a job as any general theory of institutional development in explaining the path of European integration. Rather, I point out these difficulties to illustrate that the most prolific theory of legal integration underestimates the importance of historical legacies and variations in national economic systems in shaping member states' views on the ECS over forty years. The theoretical traditions of historical institutionalism and varieties of capitalism offer tools to redress these matters and help give a nuanced understanding of what shapes the process of integration.

Historical Legacies and Varieties of Capitalism

Historical institutionalism is a theoretical tradition that straddles multiple disciplines and emphasizes the role of historical contingency and path dependence in shaping social groups' preferences over change and continuity in institutional designs (Thelen and Steinmo 1992; Thelen 1999; Pierson and Skocpol 2002, see also the editors' discussion in Chapter 1). Among other matters, this tradition argues that groups' preferences over institutional alternatives are a function of the setting in which they are embedded, and that historic investments in national designs often cause groups to reject alternatives that may be considered more efficient by some global standard (Pierson 2004; Thelen 2004). Historical institutionalism also informs other traditions in the social sciences, including a large part of the varieties of capitalism approach to political economy (Hall and Soskice 2001). The latter approach distinguishes between different types of market economies and extends the former approach's claims about historical legacies. In particular, the varieties of capitalism approach suggests that because national economic systems are composed of multiple interacting domains (such as the financial, corporate governance, and industrial relations systems), nationally embedded groups are often reluctant to radically alter the structure of a single domain for fear that this may undermine the complementarities that are produced by the interaction of domains. Thus, for example, scholars drawing on the varieties of capitalism approach have shown that despite the pressures of economic globalization, states often follow strategies of incremental change over radically altering national designs because nationally embedded firms favor relative stability in national designs in which they have major investments over a transformative strategy that entails uncertain benefits (Hall and Soskice 2001; Hall and Thelen 2005).

Together, historical institutionalism and varieties of capitalism offer a compelling lens through which to understand the evolution of the ECS. More specifically, they help address three central questions: why states' preferences over what to include and exclude from the ECS varied along distinct lines, why states were reluctant to accept harmonization and mutual recognition as a way of reaching a compromise, and why member states adopted an arrangement that added a new layer of institutions rather than an arrangement that lessened the number of diverse national instruments governing company law.

State Preferences

The structure of member states' preferences and the decision-rules used to broker agreements are central in determining when agreements are reached within the EU. When national preferences show a great deal of uniformity, agreements are typically brokered quickly and implementation tends to be swift. Conversely, the farther apart members' preferences are, the more difficult it is to broker agreements. The varieties of capitalism approach gives nuance to why member states' institutional preferences have varied in significant areas of cooperation within the EU and thus why agreements sometimes are difficult to reach. It explains variations in both the structure *and* intensity of member states' preferences with reference to differences in national economic systems and the effects that domestic actors anticipate common rules will have on the institutional advantages and disadvantages associated with those national systems (Fioretos 2001).

The varieties of capitalism approach distinguishes between two types of economies, the liberal and coordinated market economies, depending on the structure of institutions used to resolve contractual dilemmas between economic groups. In liberal market economies such as the UK and Ireland, there is a heavy reliance on arm's-length negotiations in the major areas impacting the product market strategies and core competencies of firms. Whether it be in the area of industrial relations, corporate governance, finance, or interfirm cooperation, coordination between firms and other economic groups takes place primarily in competitive market settings. This institutional setup gives firms in liberal market economies significant advantages in product markets characterized by cost competition and radical innovation but presents problems in sectors that benefit from specific skills, patient capital, and patterns of incremental innovation (Soskice 1999).

The situation in coordinated market economies is quite different. Nonmarket coordination is an important feature in all major domains of such economies. Through high levels of coordination within the business community and a legal architecture that promotes extensive involvement of economic and social groups in the formation and sustainability of systems of employee representation, finance and corporate governance, coordinated market economies bring advantages to firms that require higher levels of specific skills, long-term capital, and wage moderation (Casper 2001; Hall and Soskice 2001).

The role of the systemic differences in the two models of capitalism is evident in areas directly implicated in the ECS, especially the issue of employee representation. While in liberal market economies, employee representation at the board level constitutes a threat to the institutional advantages of that model (namely, its flexibility and the way it places downward pressures on wages), such representation is viewed as an asset by many firms in coordinated market economies. However, for the latter, structures of employee representation are not assets that function in isolation from other domains of the economy—they are part of the larger matrix that produces institutional complementarities between domains of the economy. Phrased somewhat differently, while some companies may consider alternatives to codetermination more attractive, radical changes could cause a reduction in the returns that firms receive from other domains of the economy. Moreover, since codetermination enjoys strong support within the worker movement, attempts to lower provisions that guard the interests of employees ensure strong opposition from large sections of the electorate. For these reasons, coordinated market economies are expected to raise significant opposition to an ECS that would undermine their ability to sustain and reform national systems of employee representation.

Basing our understanding of what informs states' preferences over the specifics of EU legislative initiatives in historical institutionalism and varieties of capitalism leads us to expect that the key cleavage over the ECS would be one between liberal and coordinated market economies. It also predicts that the intensity of states' preferences will increase over time and that opposition to a statute that would undermine national institutions would grow among coordinated market economies since domestic groups' investments in extant designs become more deeply entrenched over time. Similarly, the intensity of opposition from liberal market economies is expected to decline over time if provisions are made to exclude rules that would negatively impact core domains of the liberal model. Finally, given the centrality of labor market institutions in each model of capitalism, the varieties of capitalism approach expects the ECS to be a case where states

will be particularly keen to ensure that deliberations within the Union be governed
by articles requiring unanimity in the Council rather than a qualified majority.

Costs of Uniformity

The basic reasoning behind the original ECS proposal was that a common European code would help companies compete more effectively with non-European
companies by not having to take multiple national rules into account. A European
statute was also thought to have significant psychological benefits and potentially
to help attract greater levels of foreign investment. To achieve these goals, the
Commission preferred a strategy of harmonizing national company law. However,
for member states with investments in their particular mix of national economic
and legal institutions, attempts to bring about a singular model represented a
potential *cost* in terms of lost access to valued domestic designs. For this reason,
Commission proposals promoting harmonization in national company law led
either to opposition from liberal market economies when the standard of harmonization was along the lines of coordinated market economies, or the opposite if
a liberal model was under discussion.

From a varieties of capitalism approach, the same reasoning that led states
to reject harmonization should inform their view on applying the principle of
mutual recognition as a means to reaching an agreement. The principle of mutual
recognition gained credibility in the context of the Community's renaissance
in the 1980s when it was the foundation for the successful agreement on the
internal market. In short, mutual recognition is the principle by which any product
produced legally in one member state must be allowed access to all other member
states. Following a decision by the ECJ in 1979, the Commission embraced mutual
recognition as an alternative to regulatory harmonization. It also came to be used
in the context of legislative initiatives, where mutual recognition stood for the
idea that rather than forcing states to converge on a solution agreed on in the
Council, member states would simply accept that practices that were permissive
in one national context would be permitted elsewhere. Thus, in the context of
the ECS, mutual recognition represented the idea that member states could retain
their diverse traditions and that each European Company could choose to observe
whichever standard they saw fit.

But the use of mutual recognition as a way of resolving the governance
dilemma also entailed potential costs to member states. Specifically, what a
mutual recognition solution fails to take into account are situations where the area
under consideration is closely related to the core domains of national systems of
governance. While an effective mechanism in resolving differences in areas with
little consequence for the overall functioning of a system of governance, states
will be reluctant to accept the potential risks that come with mutual recognition
when it is applied in sensitive areas defining market economies (e.g. employee

representation or corporate governance). In countries where standards are high, opposition is expected to be particularly strong since groups with investments in existing designs will fear that mutual recognition will engender a race to the bottom.

Benefits of Institutional Layering

Historical institutionalists have shown that in cases where the costs to transforming an existing institution are high to actors with stakes in existing designs, and where it is difficult to gain political support for transformation, actors will opt not to change existing structures but rather place new institutions on top of existing ones (Shickler 2001; Pierson 2004: ch. 5; Thelen 2004). Known as *institutional layering*, this process is one in which actors can avoid jettisoning investments in extant designs while also making use of new institutions to adapt to new circumstances. The attractiveness of employing this strategy of institutional development rises if successful adaptation to new realities is deemed paramount and if success is also thought to be dependent on retaining existing structures of governance. Applied to the EU context, institutional layering can be expected to be a particularly prominent feature in those cases, like the ECS, where states hold strong and divergent preferences over the structure of multilateralism but nevertheless agree that some common rule is necessary to facilitate adaptation to new realities.

Historical institutionalism and varieties of capitalism are not traditions that were developed to explain broad patterns of interstate negotiations and the construction of international rules. Yet, by shedding light on how domestic groups evaluate the consequences of international institutions for their investments in domestic designs, they offer insights into processes that are rarely explicated in general theories of regional integration. They also introduce an important temporal element by suggesting that the willingness of states to support one or another supranational solution will evolve over time depending on changes they undertake domestically. Thus, in the context of the ECS, since early attempts to broker a compromise were unsuccessful, states devised alternative national solutions to facilitate greater cooperation among firms across borders. As a consequence, one may expect that the interest among firms for the ECS may actually have declined over time despite the fact that it fits well with an increasingly borderless economic environment. If this prediction is correct, one would also expect that the depth of any compromise would need to grow over time for an agreement to be reached.

The next section explores the evolution of the ECS through the lens of historical institutionalism and varieties of capitalism pointing out that the costs states perceived from institutional uniformity and the benefits they saw from adding a new layer of governance that helped entrench historic national designs played significant roles in shaping the evolution of the ECS.

The European Company Statute

The history of the ECS can be divided into three distinct phases: one that roughly coincided with the consolidation of the EEC (1965–82), a second that overlapped with the implementation of the internal market program (1985–96), and a final phase that includes the Constitutional process (1997–2004). Across these periods, three issues took center stage in negotiations over the ECS. Chief among these was the issue of employee representation on company boards. While several member states grant employees seats on company boards (e.g. Germany, Austria, the Netherlands, and Sweden), other members make no such provisions (e.g. Britain, Ireland). Finding an agreement in which the rights of employees in the former category would not be diluted, and where companies in the latter category would not be forced to accept the higher standards of the former proved to be the source of the most protracted disagreement (see Hopt 1994; Blanpain 2002; Keller 2002).

A second source of disagreement concerned what type of companies would be able to make use of the ECS. In particular, debate centered around whether existing companies could opt to exchange their existing national foundation of incorporation in favor of a European one. If a company could simply convert its national legal existence into a transnational one, it could potentially choose any location for incorporation while maintaining its productive activities in its existing place. This would be similar to a flag-of-convenience arrangement, and was strongly opposed by member states with higher regulatory and tax burdens.

The third major source of contention revolved around taxation, including whether there would be a single tax for all SEs, whether losses in one country could be counted against gains in another country, or whether SEs should be taxed in each country in which they operate. In each of these three areas, the dynamics highlighted by varieties of capitalism and by historical institutionalism—including the role of groups' investments in historic structures and their rationale for giving new layers of governance-specific designs—played major roles in shaping the evolution of national positions and the nature of the EU's rules governing the Company Statute.

First Phase, 1965–82

The first proposal for a 'European stock company' was presented by the French government in 1965. The proposal was reflective of French strategies of modernization after World War II and stressed the benefits of establishing large-scale, European-wide industrial companies. The French argued that such a vehicle would enable scale and scope economies in European companies, as well as help companies develop next-generation technologies. The proposal argued for enacting a uniform statute in all member states but favored a solution in which jurisdiction would be vested with national authorities. The Commission published a memorandum a year later supporting the basic idea of the French proposal, but favored an arrangement where jurisdiction would lie with supranational institutions, including European courts. The Commission convened a group of experts to study the feasibility of establishing a European Company and asked a prominent lawyer to formulate a proposal for further deliberation (see Sanders 1969).

These early initiatives did not generate much enthusiasm among member states. Given their overall strong economic performance in the early postwar decades, member states focused on the potential costs that a common statute may have on their national legislative agendas during a period of economic expansion. To renew debate, the Commission presented its first formal proposal in 1970 (European Commission 1970). In response to discussions over how to deal with the diverse national systems of interest representation, the Commission suggested that SEs have a mandatory two-tier structure that included executive and supervisory boards. This mirrored the German model, and the Commission suggested that employees would select a third of board members and that two-thirds be chosen by shareholders. It also suggested that European Works Councils with co-determination rights be established, and that collective agreements on working conditions be negotiated between SEs and unions. Following a generally favorable reception in the Economic and Social Committee (1972) and the European Parliament (1974), a revised proposal for a Regulation was presented five years after the original one (European Commission 1975*a*). To allay concerns in member states with weak or no systems of employee representation, the new Commission proposal suggested greater parity in terms of board appointments. However, the same disagreements that existed before reemerged and countries were again divided along lines of their national systems of interest representation. After repeated attempts by the Commission to find room for compromise, the revised proposal was shelved in 1982.

In addition to disagreements over the structure of worker participation, extensive criticism was levied in the early stages against the complexity of Commission proposals.[6] Support was also muted in the 1970s because of a general economic downturn which led many governments to reason that greater benefits would be had from national industrial policies aimed at economic modernization than from a European-level initiative that may reduce national control over key legislative acts. While there were many reasons for why an agreement could not be reached, the issues highlighted by the HI and varieties of capitalism traditions—especially the role of groups' investments in historic designs and structural variations in national economic systems—were the key factors that prevented an early agreement on common European rules governing transnational companies.

---

[6] Unlike the 21 page final proposal that was adopted in 2001, the Commission proposal from 1970 was over 700 pages long.

Second Phase, 1985–96

In the mid-1980s, the EC relaunched efforts to create a single market for goods, services, and labor. Interest in the ECS re-emerged, and was identified in the Commission White Paper on the internal market as an 'essential component' to ensuring that firms would gain the full benefits from an integrated market (European Commission 1985*a*). In 1989, the Commission thus prepared a second proposal for the ECS (European Commission 1989*a*, 1989*b*).

As a means to breaking the historic impasse, the new proposal entailed a novel solution to the governance dilemma. The Commission suggested that terms of company incorporation be dealt with in a regulation that would be binding on all member states, and that a separate directive be devoted to the employee representation issue. The directive, which the Commission characterized as an 'indissociable complement' to the regulation, spelled out several optional systems of worker participation that member states could choose from. Based on the Commission's decision to abandon the goal of harmonization in favor of mutual recognition, the Commission reasoned that the strategy of separating the regulation and the directive would isolate the contentious worker participation issue from the technicalities of how SEs would be formed, and that the optional nature of the directive would calm fears in member states with weak forms of worker representation.[7] After consultations with interested parties, the Commission presented a revision to its second proposal (European Commission 1991*a*, 1991*b*).

The second Commission proposal stressed the benefits from a single supranational framework for businesses, the advantages of the ECS over the complexity of existing merger arrangements, as well as significant tax advantages. Member states responded to the proposal along familiar lines. States with extensive systems for worker participation such as Germany, the Netherlands, Denmark, and Luxembourg expressed support for the proposal. Countries with liberal market economies—Ireland and the UK—were vociferous opponents. Their opposition was anchored in worries that the ECS would bring 'through the back door' solutions antithetical to liberal designs and erode their competitive advantage.[8]

Despite the Commission's innovation of a separate regulation and directive and a watered down proposal that made several concessions to the UK, an agreement could not be reached over several years of negotiations. In essence, agreement failed because both Britain and Germany expressed fear that the new ECS proposal would undermine central components of their respective corporate systems. While the British feared that the ECS would force 'a continental model' on their

---

[7] In practice, the directive allowed member states to choose between several different systems of worker participation ranging from extensive board representation to solutions giving workers only limited information and consultation rights.

[8] Countries such as France and Italy that had less extensive arrangements for worker participations than Germany, but more than Britain, expressed support for the Commission proposal.

companies, Germany raised concerns that companies would set up fictitious SE headquarters in places with laxer rules while continuing their operations at home. Thus, while there was support in both camps for a regulation establishing a common statute, the content of the directive was a source of concern for both sides since its menu-driven approach was seen as a threat to the institutional integrity of national economic systems on *both* sides of the historic ECS cleavage. Even strong pressure from business and the impending completion of the internal market failed to convince governments to accept the new proposal. Instead, because of the potential threat of the ECS to the institutional integrity of their national economic systems, governments opted to keep the ECS outside the large legislative package that constituted the internal market program.

The reasons that agreement could not be reached during the second phase were similar to those in the first period and again reveal how important the factors stressed by the varieties of capitalism and HI traditions were in shaping states' reluctance to accept the new ECS proposal. Member states on both sides of the historic cleavage attached a great deal of importance to sustaining those institutions that are integral to achieving the comparative institutional advantages of their respective type of market economy. And while the Commission's innovation of adding a new layer of governance that included a separate regulation and directive were welcomed and designed to break the impasse, it was ultimately rejected on both sides because of fears that the new layer could undermine institutions in both coordinated and liberal market economies.

Third Phase, 1997–2004

In 1997 the Commission convened a high-level expert group to find a solution to the ECS impasse. Named after its chair, Etienne Davignon, the Group argued that member states' systems of worker participation were too diverse and that attempts to foster uniformity in the structure of SEs would never succeed. Its main solution to the employee representation issue was that the management of each SE negotiate with its employees and jointly agree on what system of representation should govern their company (Davignon Group 1997). In cases where management and employees failed to reach an agreement, the Davignon Group recommended that a set of default rules apply.

While the Group's report received a favorable reception, member states disagreed over the inclusion of the 'zero-option' that would allow managers and workers to agree *not* to have any formalized system of representation. With the British and Portuguese strongly favoring the zero-option, and Germany, Austria, Denmark, Finland, Sweden, Luxembourg, and the Netherlands opposed, no compromise could be reached. Moreover, disagreement emerged on whether existing companies should be allowed to transform themselves into an SE. Germany and the others opposed such an arrangement for reasons they had long cited: they maintained that easy conversions would be a Trojan horse that would allow established companies to circumvent national laws by merely registering elsewhere.

Renewed negotiations followed and compromise was finally reached in December 2000 at the Intergovernmental Conference in Nice. The agreement maintained the separation of the regulation and the directive. But changes in the latter gave member states the option of whether to transpose a fallback reference provision into national law that would apply if agreements between management and employee representations could not be reached.

The final agreement, then, was one that served to entrench significant and diverse elements of national company law, while also excluding provisions that would encourage greater institutional competition across national borders. The former dimension is most apparent in the directive's rules on worker participation, which eliminated the zero-option and gave companies in coordinated market economies incentives to maintain models with significant worker representation. The latter part is evident in the exclusion of tax incentives when forming the ECS, the limited type of companies that can become SEs, and in leaving it to individual member states to determine whether to transpose a fallback reference provision.[9] The very final adoption of the agreement, reached at a meeting of Social Affairs Ministers following negotiations with the EP, took place on October 8, 2001 (European Council 2001*b*, 2001*c*). Three years later, the ECS became a reality after more than four decades of deliberation. The same month, Elcoteq, a small electronics company with its domicile in Finland, became the first *Societas Europaea*.

The ECS agreement illustrates how much importance member states attach to maintaining the integrity of institutions that are central to sustaining the institutional advantages of their respective type of market economy. Unlike in the two earlier phases, an agreement was possible in the third phase because the risk that uniform rules would undermine valued national designs was significantly reduced by amending the Directive in ways that gave individual states greater autonomy in deciding what to transpose into national law and by excluding tax incentives and provisions that would enable easy conversions by existing companies. Thus, as expected from a HI analysis of negotiations over core economic institutions,

---

[9] The tax issue concerned whether companies would be able to choose a single location of taxation (presumably where it would be lowest) and thus avoid the historic arrangement where each subsidiary pays taxes in its respective locale. SEs are taxed in the same ways as are MNCs; that is, taxes are levied through national fiscal provisions on companies or branches operating within national borders. The final agreement excluded the option for existing companies to transform themselves into SEs. The Statute allows companies to form an SE in one of four ways: (*a*) through the merger of two or more existing companies based in at least two member states, (*b*) through the creation of a holding company that is formed by public or private companies from at least two member states, (*c*) through the creation of a subsidiary company from at least two member states, and (*d*) through the transformation of an existing public company that for at least two years has had a subsidiary in another member state.

the new supranational layer of company law was designed by member states to help them retain historic national designs that were highly valued while also giving companies new opportunities, albeit somewhat circumscribed, to form new transnational entities without threatening historic practice at home.

Conclusion

'Swiss cheese' is how one legal scholar describes the ECS in its final form (Teichmann 2003: 310). The implication is that the many compromises that were made to reach an agreement after decades of negotiations led to an outcome with so many holes as to make it ineffective in achieving its original goals. Compromises between member states are nothing new in the EU. Nor is it unusual that long-standing national traditions shape states' preferences over common European legislation. Yet the ECS case offers a particularly clear window through which we can expand our understanding of what shapes the process of integration, including how the Union may resolve the governance dilemma in other areas.

What the ECS case makes most apparent is the role of variations in national economic designs in shaping the process of integration. Of the thousands of rules that have been adopted in the area of company law, the ECS is one of a handful of cases that member states insisted should be governed by unanimity decision-making. The issue was not whether member states thought a European statute would be a welcome addition to existing rules, but rather what consequences it would have for historic designs at home. In particular, as this most protracted of negotiations in EU legislative history illustrates, historic differences in national models of capitalism were key in shaping the process of negotiations and the final form that the statute took.

In addition to showing the value of anchoring our understanding of what informs states' institutional preferences over EU rules in the literature on varieties of capitalism, the ECS case shows the value of employing central propositions from the HI tradition. Scholars in this tradition have argued that actors with stakes in existing designs often ensure continuity in valued structures by promoting new layers of governance rather than accepting the transformation of existing ones. The ECS captures this logic particularly well: economic groups stood to lose substantial investments in national designs if early ECS proposals had been adopted, and the introduction of a new layer of governance allowed these groups to ensure that the national designs they valued remained structurally intact while also enabling companies to take advantage of the Statute.

The case also underscores the importance of historical contingency in shaping national approaches to EU reform. Consider for a moment a counterfactual: would coordinated market economies such as Germany and the Netherlands have objected to the ECS proposals pushed by Britain in the 1990s if they had not yet established their extensive systems of worker representation? The answer would most likely be no; liberal designs offered several advantages in terms of greater flexibility for firms. Had the worker participation models that are so integral to the coordinated market economies not existed, Germany and other coordinated market economies would have been more likely to accept British proposals. It is also likely that an agreement would have been found much earlier and that the outcomes would have had less resemblance to Swiss cheese.

One of the most striking features of the final outcome was that it only emerged after the Commission and member states failed to reconcile differences through the traditional means by which the governance dilemma has been resolved. Early suggestions by the French government that a strong community instrument be introduced that would replace national company law with a single supranational code were quickly dismissed because it was thought to limit states' ability to implement national programs of industrial specialization. Harmonization, which was used to great effect in most areas of company law, was also rejected because of its potentially negative consequences for the integrity of national economic institutions. Attempts to resolve this conflict by enshrining the principle of mutual recognition, which was the cornerstone of the internal market program, also failed to reconcile the diverse preferences held by the disparate coalitions of coordinated and liberal market economies. Only when a solution emerged that eliminated the costs from uniformity and added a new layer that protected historic national structures were member states able to reach agreement.

The ECS case offers some lessons for how the EU as an organization of disparate market economies may go about resolving the governance dilemma in the future. First, the case shows that formal rules matter a great deal to states and suggest that a process stressing informal rules may have reached a resolution earlier. In recent years, the EU has devoted increasing attention to using more informal rules to handle the governance dilemma. New modes of governance (like the OMC) point to solutions to the governance dilemma based in informal, peer-oriented processes based in soft law. These aim to foster a process of gradual change within states by means of consistent peer comparisons and loosely designed guidelines. While informal rules may not always have as far-reaching consequences as more formal ones, they may be a more efficient way of moving forward the process of determining whether a common instrument is desirable and of allaying fears that common designs threaten valued national structures. It is hard not to think that an earlier agreement, perhaps one with less holes in it, would have been possible had the process by which member states sought to reconcile their differences been organized along informal rules stressing partial solutions rather than by attempts to find total solutions through the use of uniform formal rules.

The second lesson we can draw from the protracted nature of the ECS negoti- ations and how a resolution was found to the governance dilemma concerns how to understand the trade-off between common EU instruments and the protection of valued national designs. Frequently, EU-wide instruments and national rules are seen as being in a zero-sum relation; an expansion in the former is thought necessarily to entail a decrease in the effectiveness of the latter. As the ECS case shows, this does not have to be the case. It is possible to adopt common EU-wide regulations and to give states great discretion in what they transpose domestically by employing flexible directives. Indeed, from having been envisaged for many decades as a vehicle that would bring about opportunities from uniformity, the final statute is now viewed as one bringing 'opportunity in diversity' (Bolkestein 2002). How significant these opportunities are is not yet clear. But if the number of companies availing of the ECS continues to expand and to include major firms, the Statute may come to represent a powerful example of how the governance dilemma can be resolved in ways that both promote integration and protect designs that member states hold dear.

10

The Politics of Competition and Institutional Change in European Union: The First Fifty Years

TIM BÜTHE[1]

Competition causes suppliers of goods and services to lower prices, raise quality, and innovate. It is crucial for maximizing social welfare in a market economy. Ironically, however, the market by itself does not guarantee competition, unless one makes heroic assumptions about the costlessness of market entry (North 1981; Neumann 2001: 5ff.). As Adam Smith famously warned, 'people of the same trade seldom meet together...but the conversation ends in a conspiracy against the public, or in some contrivance to raise prices'. Yet it is not just monopolies, cartels, and mergers that can inhibit competition. Government subsidies and special privileges may also distort the market—within a country and even abroad through trade. Competition thus is an inherently political issue, as well as an economic one.

Safeguarding competition, whose economic importance is explicitly acknowledged in Article 3(1)g of the Treaty of Rome, is one of the most prominent governance functions of the European Commission for the EU Common Market. The Commission exercises real, supranational power in this realm.[2] In sometimes dramatic 'dawn raids', the antitrust experts of the Directorate-General Competition (DG Comp) have discovered and broken up illegal market-sharing, price-fixing, and other competition-impeding agreements from sugar and steel pipes to vitamins, video game consoles, and cars. When Volkswagen, for instance, was

[1] I thank Barbara Haskel, Lee McGowan, Kate McNamara, Sophie Meunier, Mark Pollack, Elliot Posner, Mitchell Smith, Milada Vachudova, and Stephen Wilks for comments on earlier drafts, Duke University's Graduate School of Arts & Sciences for financial support, and Mark Dubois, Julia Torti, and Seema Parkash for research assistance.
[2] Title VI of the Treaty of Rome (as amended), which contains the Rules on Competition, still applies only to the EC portion of the EU, but in keeping with the series title, I speak of the EU throughout this chapter. For simplicity, I also refer to specific articles as renumbered in the Amsterdam revision of the Treaty and use 'DG Comp' even for the period prior to 1999, when it was called 'DG IV'. DG Comp's remit is similar to the shared remit of the Department of Justice's Antitrust Division and the Federal Trade Commission's Bureau of Competition in the USA, though EU law establishes an administrative process rather than a judicial one, and DG Comp's authority extends to government subsidies and other 'state aids', over which the US competition agencies have no say.

found in 1998 to have banned its Italian dealers from selling to German and Austrian customers (in whose home markets VW was selling the same cars at a notably higher price), the EU forced them to end the practice and fined VW 90 million euros for violating EU competition rules. Similarly, DG Comp's Merger Task Force has blocked or forced changes in the terms of merger agreements that they considered a threat to competition in the European market.[3] The merger of petroleum products giants TotalFina and Elf Aquitaine in 2000, for instance, was allowed only on the condition that the companies sold off a large number of motorway service stations in France, of which they otherwise would have controlled 60 percent. The merger of Pfizer and Pharmacia in 2003 was allowed only conditional on the sale and/or licensing of some of their pharmaceutical patents for products for which competition would otherwise have been severely reduced.

Commission powers in the realm of competition policy extend even to firms headquartered outside of the EU, as evidenced not only by the ongoing EU antitrust action against Microsoft but also by EU intervention in the proposed mergers between General Electric and Honeywell, which was blocked when GE rejected the Commission's conditions for approval. Moreover, the Commission's power is clearly supranational, as most evident in the realm of subsidies ('state aid(s)'). Here, the EU has, for instance, forced the governments of Germany, Austria, and France to stop giving competition-distorting loan guarantees to public banks; it has also made companies like SCI Systems repay subsidies that the Commission found had been paid to them by the Dutch government, in violation of EU rules, for the building of a computer assembly plant.

While some of its decisions are quite controversial and virtually all of them involve fierce conflicts of interest (Ross 1994: 132ff., 176ff.), DG Comp is generally highly respected. Inside the EU, 'the competition portfolio has become one of the most powerful and prized positions in the Commission' (Hix 2005: 244), and its civil service positions are among the most prestigious in Brussels. DG Comp not only enjoys the highest degree of discretion of any DG (Pollack, 2003a: 94f.), it is also very respected among the general public and outside competition policy experts. An international survey of public and private sector specialists in the summer of 2006 identified DG Comp as the most trusted and admired among thirty-eight competition watchdogs (Cavendish 2006). In the realm of state aid, it 'has managed to elicit an unusually high degree of compliance', which exceeds compliance with comparable competition authorities at the national level (Wolf 2004: 88).

It has not always been that way: The DG Comp started out in the early years after the Treaty of Rome as 'a sleepy, ineffectual backwater of Community

---

[3] The Merger Task Force was a separate unit within DG Comp until 2004. Its functions have now been taken over by merger specialists within DG Comp's industry-specific Directorates B through E.

administration' (Wilks with McGowan 1996: 225). It had only 'a handful of "A" grade officials' (Goyder 2003: 531), and 'little prestige' was attached to working there (Cini and McGowan 1998: 24; see also Cini 1996: esp. 461ff.). European-level competition authority thus has experienced a striking and largely unantici-pated institutional evolution over the past fifty years. How might we explain such institutional change?

Büthe and Swank (2006) have recently shown that a modified neofunc-tionalism—understood explicitly as a HI theory of institutional change—provides a compelling explanation for the evolution of merger control authority in the EU. Such a neofunctionalist theory recognizes that institutional change may arise out of intergovernmental bargaining. The critical insight, however, is that insti-tutional change can occur even when the member states oppose it, provided that *subnational actors*, using the political opportunity structures of the supranational institutions, act jointly with supranational actors in pushing for change, each *pur-suing their own, selfish interests*. As a HI theory, this modified neofunctionalism also leads us to pay close attention to the sequence of events in the process of European integration (Büthe 2002), such as when intergovernmental bargaining over institutional change followed rather than preceded the change. This chapter extends Büthe and Swank's analysis of the evolution of supranational merger control authority to the other issue areas of EU competition policy: antitrust enforcement and state aid (subsidies). I first discuss the theoretical argument, focusing on the hypothesized causal mechanisms. I then sketch the institutional evolution of EU competition authority in the three areas of competition policy from the provisions of the Treaty of Paris through the most recent developments. As I show, the theory helps explain why competition policy has so decisively shifted to the EU level, as well as when those shifts have occurred. The finding that neofunctionalism explains institutional change over time as well as the variation across issue areas also refutes the common assertion that it cannot predict or explain variation in the evolution of the EU (e.g. Moravcsik 1993: 477).

Competing over Competition? Explaining Institutional Change

Neofunctionalism has its origins in Ernst Haas's first theoretical account of the process of European integration (Haas [1958] 2004; see also esp. Schmitter 2004; Börzel et al. 2005). It is in essence a HI theory of institutional evolution and change. Neofunctionalism combines what are essentially rational choice assumptions of traditional liberal IR theory—that individuals pursue their self-interest in instrumental ways and that there is a multitude of subnational groups that can become political actors both domestically and transnationally—with an assumption usually associated with social constructivism—that self-interest is a function of identities and loyalties, which are highly persistent in the short run

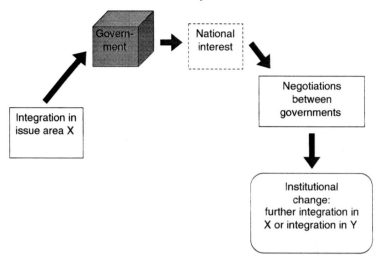

FIGURE 10.1.   Government-driven institutional change in neofunctionalism

but malleable over the course of time (Büthe and Swank 2006). Based on these assumptions, neofunctionalism identifies three paths toward greater integration, recognizing that any shift of political authority from the national to the supranational level will engender opposition, as well as support.[4]

First, neofunctionalism predicts greater integration in a partially integrated issue area, or some integration in an issue area that was previously not integrated, when governments see it as being in the aggregate economic interest of the country. Here neofunctionalism differs little from Realist intergovernmentalism, except that it specifies one particular reason for why governments might decide to pool decision-making in a particular issue area at the supranational level: to achieve agreed objectives in *another* issue area. This of course is the famous spillover mechanism (Figure 10.1).

The second path to institutional change starts from the assumption that the observed or imagined experience with supranational authority in *some* issue areas leads a subset of subnational actors (i.e. groups with distinct interests within a country, including possibly within the government) to expect that further integration would be to their benefit. If these conditions hold, neofunctionalism expects those subnational actors to seek institutional change, shifting decision-making to the supranational level. Each subnational actor may do so by trying to influence its national government's preferences through the normal course of domestic politics

---

[4] This section is largely based on my own close reading of the foundational work by Haas (1958), though I go beyond his work to incorporate key insights from the more recent historical institutionalist literature (see Meunier and McNamara (in this volume) and Büthe and Swank (2006)), which are entirely consistent with Haas's assumptions and logic, but not spelled out in his works.

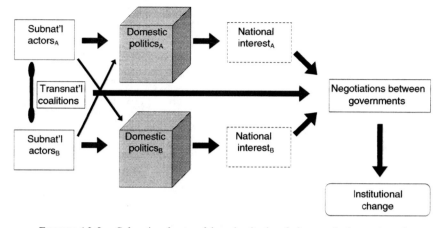

FIGURE 10.2. Subnational actor-driven institutional change via domestic and transnational politics

(thick short arrows in Figure 10.2), which may result in institutional change subject to intergovernmental negotiations.[5]

If this were all, the second causal mechanism would differ little from liberal intergovernmentalism. But unlike liberal intergovernmentalism, neofunctionalism does not treat domestic politics as a hermetically sealed system. Based on its assumptions, neofunctionalism expects subnational actors not just to lobby their respective national governments but also to form transnational coalitions and to engage in transnational politics to advance their interests (thin, diagonal arrows in Figure 10.2). This strategy should be particularly attractive to those who cannot build the political coalitions at the domestic level to achieve their desired policies but see a chance of forming a majority at the EU level. Accordingly, neofunctionalism expects such subnational actors (or their transnational coalitions) also to pursue their interests directly at the inter-/supranational level by lobbying the Council collectively, especially in issue areas where the Council decides by majority.

The third and most distinctive causal mechanism starts from the observation that, in many issue areas, the European Commission and the ECJ also provide political opportunity structures, which neofunctionalism expects subnational actors to use if doing so promises to advance their interests. It is this push for increased integration by subnational actors that gives the Commission and/or the ECJ the chance to bring about institutional change. Based again on the assumption of self-interestedness, neofunctionalism would expect the representatives of these supranational institutions generally to favor greater integration—at least

---

[5] Neofunctionalism lacks a theory of domestic politics, but its basic liberal IR theory assumptions suggest that subnational actors are more likely to succeed in redefining the national interest the more economically powerful and numerous they are, and the more concentrated their interests.

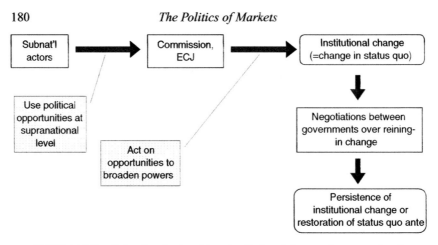

FIGURE 10.3.   Subnational actor-driven institutional change via supranational
institutions

within the constraints of identity and loyalty (Hooghe 2005): Greater integration enhances their power and ensures them of more interesting, more substantively important work. Consequently, the Commission and the ECJ are generally
expected to act on such opportunities to broaden their powers. *This can lead to
institutional change without any prior bargaining among the member states* (top
portion of Figure 10.3).

Member state governments might then of course undo any such changes—
but their negotiations start in this case from a new status quo. This changes the
political dynamic: The *status quo ante* cannot be restored if a single member state
or a blocking minority of states favors the new arrangements over the old ones
(see also Stone Sweet and Caporaso 1998: 127f.). In other words, those who favor
the change can ensure that it persists, even though they could not have brought it
about through intergovernmental negotiations.

In sum, neofunctionalism emphasizes subnational actors and transnational
coalitions pursuing their own material or ideological interests. These subnational
actors and transnational groups are expected to act in concert with supranational
actors and to make use of the political opportunity structures provided by existing
national and European institutions. They will push for a shift of authority from
the national to the supranational level *if such a shift allows them to achieve their
goals more efficiently or if they expect to be able to form a winning coalition at
the European level while they cannot do so domestically.* Note that institutional
change for neofunctionalism is not expected to occur automatically. Quite to
the contrary, it is expected to arise out of political conflict. Supranational actors
might of course foster groups that see further integration as being in their interest
(Burley and Mattli 1993; Alter 2001), but institutional change is expected to
occur only if and when such groups exist and take the initiative. The alternative
route—supranational actors, especially the Commission, attempting to extend

their own powers vis-à-vis member states through overtly political proposals for institutional change—is expected to fail since such overtly political attempts will stimulate opposition, whereas incremental change with the support of (and at least in seeming response to demands from) subnational actors will likely succeed (Haas [1958] 2004: xxxiv, 26, 106ff.).

The next three sections provide brief analytical accounts of the institutional evolution of the EU in the three issue areas of competition policy, from the law and practice under the ECSC and the provisions in the Treaty of Rome to the latest changes of 2003–04. As stipulated by the analytical framework above, these narratives pay close attention to sequence. They also illustrate the importance of substate actors engaged in transnational politics for explaining specific unanticipated consequences of the initial institutional arrangements, as well as the broader process of institutional change in the EU.

Antitrust Enforcement: Restrictive Practices and Abuse of Market-Dominating Position

The competition provisions of the Treaty of Paris, the founding treaty of the ECSC, were 'the lengthiest and most detailed in the entire document' (Gillingham 1991: 283). After months of bitter opposition from cartel-operating industries, which was overcome only thanks to American prodding (Gillingham 1991: 254–83; see also Berghahn 1985: 285f.)—and despite persistent concerns about creating a 'dictatorship of experts' (Rittberger 2001: 695, quoting the Dutch chief negotiator)—the six prospective member states agreed on strong antitrust enforcement authority for the supranational High Authority (HA), the ECSC's version of the Commission. Articles 65 and 66 prohibited all 'agreements' and 'concerted practices' that would 'prevent, restrict, or distort the normal operation of competition within the common market' for coal and steel and authorized the HA to enforce these rules, grant exceptions under specified conditions, and act against abuses of economic power (Gerber 1998: 339, 341). But although Monnet (quoted in Gillingham 1991: 313) interpreted these provisions as 'a mandate to dissolve cartels, ban restrictive practices, and prevent any concentration of economic power', the HA of the ECSC exercised these powers in the realm of antitrust only starting in 1956 and even then only with great restraint (Diebold 1959: 350ff.; McLachlan and Swann 1967: 117ff.; Haas [1958] 2004: 76ff.).

Notwithstanding this restraint in the early years of ECSC, the inclusion of similar language against cartels and monopolies in the Treaty of Rome was hotly contested, partly due to cross-nationally different visions of competition policy (see Gerber 1998: 346f.; Motta 2004: 17–24), but also due to conflicts of interest *within* the prospective member states of the EEC. That relatively powerful antitrust provisions were included in the Treaty of Rome in the end was due to a coalition in the late stages of the 'Messina' negotiations between the governments of the Netherlands and Belgium and some ordo-liberal officials from the internally divided German government, who sought at the European level the strong competition and antitrust rules that they had been unable to get through at the domestic level (Milward 1992: 217f.; Groeben 2002: 17, 66–71; Hentschel 2002: 279).[6]

Specifically, Article 81 established that agreements among two or more 'undertakings' (i.e. firms or other economic entities), 'which may affect trade between Member States and...have as their *object or effect* the prevention, restriction, or distortion of competition' are prohibited (emphasis added). Contractual provisions to this effect are not enforceable.[7] Somewhat more vaguely, Article 82 established the principle that the EU could and would intervene against 'any abuse...of a dominant position', including distortion of supply, dumping in order to bankrupt competitors, etc. The Commission (represented by DG Comp) was to act as the executive, with the power to enforce these provisions (Gerber 1998: 349ff.).

Legal provisions, however, do not make practice. The Commission's power of antitrust enforcement was subject to implementing regulation that was to be passed by the Council within the first three years. When it was finally passed in March 1962 as 'Regulation 17', it nominally gave the Commission truly supranational powers in antitrust enforcement (including supremacy over national courts and regulators), though 'it is almost certain that the politicians in the Council at the time had little conception of the potential for independent action latent in Regulation 17' (Wilks with Bartle 2002: 164). In fact, to many it seemed that EC competition policy was just an exercise in declamatory politics, where regulatory governance is delegated to an agency to give the appearance of addressing an issue that is important to a certain constituency, while ensuring that little or nothing would be done by the understaffed, under-resourced regulator (Mitnick 1980: 335f.).

Yet DG Comp tried to make the most of what it got. It built institutional capacity in the early years and slowly began to test its supranational powers, focusing at first primarily on Article 81 violations (Cini and McGowan 1998: 21ff.). The case against 'restrictive practices' that became the first one to solicit ECJ involvement, *Établissements Consten and Grundig* v. *Commission* (56 and 58/64 [1966] ECR 299) is exemplary of DG Comp's work in the early years: Grundig

---

[6] Ordo-liberalism is a philosophical school of thought—motivated in part by the experience with cartels and trusts in Weimar and Nazi Germany—that rejects government intervention when it seeks to direct economic activity but sees the state as having a necessary 'ordering' function in the economy to safeguard individuals against any concentration of political *and economic* power that would threaten their freedom and equality of opportunity.

[7] Exemptions could be granted in the interest of technological advancements or economic 'progress' if the agreements did not substantially impede market competition.

(a German electric and electronic goods manufacturer) had made Consten its exclusive distributor in France, ensuring relatively high prices for Grundig products in France. After the removal of quotas for electronic goods within the EEC in 1961, UNEF, a competitor to Consten, had started parallel importing of Grundig products into France. Grundig gained an injunction against UNEF in French courts, but UNEF lodged a complaint with the Commission, which declared the agreement between Grundig and Consten void. When Consten and Grundig challenged the Commission's decision (as well as its authority on the matter), the Court upheld much of the Commission's decision and, more importantly, affirmed Commission authority as a matter of principle, against the firms— and against the governments of Germany and Italy, which had joined the case in support of the firms' position. As predicted by the neofunctionalist argument above, it was private, subnational actors pursuing their economic self-interest who provided the Commission with an opportunity to move from nominal to actual antitrust enforcement authority under Article 81 when one of them (UNEF) pushed for expanded supranational authority. This institutional change took place despite continued differences among the member states about its desirability. The private actors also provided the ECJ with an opportunity to develop an expansive competition law doctrine. The success of UNEF showed others that they could advance their interests with the help of the Commission. This led in turn to further complaints against restrictive agreements by competitors or customers, as well as quiet tip-offs about cartel agreements, such as the famous price-fixing agreement that covered 80 percent of the European market for dyestuffs (busted in 1969, with fines imposed for the first time on firms headquartered outside the then member states).

The provisions of Article 82, against abuse of a market-dominant position, gained 'teeth' only in the late 1960s and early 1970s. This is consistent with the neofunctionalist argument emphasizing subnational actors: Conflicts of interests among private parties involving an (alleged) dominant position in the European market could only arise after the completion of the customs union in 1968. Here, the ECJ became involved initially when economic competitors invoked Article 82 in domestic courts and those courts asked the ECJ for advisory opinions, beginning in the late 1960s and early 1970s. Those early ECJ decisions, 'indicat[ing] a willingness to support attempts by the Commission to find abuse in cases of high prices by dominant firms' (Gerber 1998: 357), helped establish the Commission's authority in this realm as well.

DG Comp continued to gain stature in antitrust and greatly expanded its case load in the 1980s and 1990s. It achieved notable successes in taking on companies like IBM for abuse of its dominant position in the computer market (1980–84), numerous industries for market-sharing agreements (e.g. insulated pipes, 1998; airline services, 2001), price-fixing (e.g. amino acids, 2000; ferry services, 1996,

1998), exclusive purchasing (e.g. musical instruments, 2003; ice cream, 1992), and exclusive/selective distribution agreements (car manufacturers, ongoing).[8] As the ECJ has repeatedly confirmed, the Commission has truly supranational authority on these matters, including the power to conduct invasive investigations, level substantial fines (to the tune of €2 billion for cartels in 2001 alone, Nugent 2003: 142), and force changes in corporate structures or practices on firms found to be in violation of EU competition law.

DG Comp's increasing prestige led to a virtuous circle in attracting high quality EU staff, helped further by the leadership of high-profile and able Commissioners Sutherland (1985–8), Brittan (1989–93), van Miert (1993–9), and Monti (1999–2004). Its prominence was surely also aided by the increasing neoliberal economic consensus in Europe (McNamara 1998). But sequence matters here: the key institutional change, the acquisition of real supranational power in antitrust by the Commission, largely preceded these developments. It has exercised these powers increasingly and very visibly in the course of the 1990s and in several prominent instances against the express preferences of the largest member states; yet taking away or seriously curbing the Commission's antitrust enforcement authority has not even been seriously discussed anymore in any of the treaty revisions since (and including) the SEA.

Two more recent developments warrant mention. The Court of First Instance (CFI), created in the wake of the SEA, attained responsibility for competition (antitrust and merger) cases starting in November 1989. This institutional change followed largely the second path outlined above in that the CFI was created by agreement among the member states, at the suggestion of the ECJ as the case load of the ECJ rapidly increased and private interests (esp. firms) called for faster judicial decisions (e.g. Cini and McGowan 1998). Starting with the *Italian Flat Glass* decision (T-68, 77 & 78/89, [1990] 4 CMLR 535), the CFI has asserted the power to review the facts of competition cases *de novo*. Moreover, in a number of cases the CFI overturned DG Comp decisions for DG Comp's failure to provide a thorough economic analysis—which is especially difficult for abuse of dominance cases (e.g. Motta 2004: 411). These CFI decisions have led to the hiring of numerous economists at a DG so far dominated mostly by lawyers. Yet, as Harding and Joshua point out, the common perception of a Court that is now restricting the Commission's authority in competition matters is quite mistaken. They find that appeals to the CFI have increased simply with the number of decisions taken by DG Comp (see also Guersent 2003: 50f.) and 'a large number of such claims brought . . . are rejected by the Court' (Harding and Joshua 2003: 179). Moreover, CFI decisions to overturn were limited to a few

---

[8] See *Report on Competition* XXVIII 1998 Sec.(99)743 Final: 36, 140f.; XXXI 2001 Sec.(2002)462 Final: 19, 31; XXX 2000 Sec.(2001)694: 36f.; XXVI 1996: paragraph 97; XXVIII 1998 Sec.(99)743 Final: 36, 140; XXXIII 2003 Sec.(2004)658 Final; *Official Journal* 1993 L183:1–37; and http://ec.europa.eu/comm/competition/car_sector/ (last visited 6/10/2006).

cases where DG Comp had made clear errors, and for much of the 1990s, 'the Court of First Instance spent its time in cartel cases confirming the Commission's fact finding and approving the manner of its exercise of power' (2003: 179). At the same time, the CFI cases illustrate the seriousness of the underlying conflicts of interest. Consistent with the theoretical assumptions above, they show that private parties might also use the political opportunity structures at the supranational level to challenge the Commission's competition authority if doing so can help them overturn Commission decisions that are detrimental to their interests.

Finally, the implementation of EU antitrust policy was reformed by Council Regulation 1/2003 (OJ January 4, 2003:L1/1-25), which replaced Regulation 17 and came into effect on May 1, 2004. These reforms provide for a larger role for national competition authorities and national courts (for details, see Wilks 2005: 131ff.). Some have warned that these reforms constitute a renationalization of competition policy and thus an anti-integration institutional change (e.g. Mestmäcker 1999). A close examination of the changes and the proposals leading up to Regulation 1/2003 shows, however, that these changes were long sought by DG Comp itself (see e.g. Cini and McGowan 1998: 179ff.). Regulation 1/2003 includes several safeguards against the inconsistent application of EC antitrust law in different national jurisdictions and reserves for DG Comp the power to take over any particular case (Riley 2003a, 2003b). In effect, the changes amount to a farming out of the vast majority of minor, routine cases to national agencies that have been to a large extent trained and socialized by DG Comp, to which they remain tied in an exemplary transgovernmental network, the European Competition Network (Slaughter 2004: 21, 36).[9] The changes thus allow DG Comp to focus its limited resources on crucial big cases and should make DG Comp more efficient as well as politically stronger as the hub of the ECN, in line with the demands by firms and transnational business lobbies in Europe for a faster 'one-stop' decision-making process.

Merger Review[10]

Article 66 of the Treaty of Paris gave the ECSC HA the power to block mergers if they created firms with the power 'to influence prices, control or restrain

---

[9] See http://ec.europa.eu/comm/competition/antitrust/ecn/ecn_home.html. As recently as 1997, more than half of the member states were judged as lacking national competition authorities with the capacity to apply Articles 81 and 82, see Cini and McGowan (1998: 193); today all member states have such authorities, including (with some variance, see Hölscher and Stephan 2004: esp. 335ff.) the new member states, where extensive training and 'socialization' for the often newly created competition authorities has been part of the transition assistance provided by the EU.

[10] This section draws largely on Büthe and Swank (2006), where more detailed references can be found. Following the EU's practice, I use mergers here in a broad sense to include acquisitions and equity investments. In EU law, they are collectively referred to as 'concentrations'.

production and marketing, or to impair the maintenance of effective competition in a substantial part of the market for such products'. All mergers involving firms in the industries regulated by the ECSC had to receive prior authorization from the HA, though this requirement was not intended to impose a tight constraint. In fact, Article 66 makes authorization the default *unless* the merger predictably has the above effects. In practice, this was understood to make mergers generally permissible unless they created an enterprise with a monopolistic position in its market (Gerber 1998: 340f.; Haas [1958] 2004: 81), and the HA did not begin to impose conditions (or block mergers) until 1958 (McLachlan and Swann 1967: 197ff.).

The Treaty of Rome was a further step back for supranational merger review— mergers are not even mentioned. By most accounts, this omission was not accidental: Mergers were generally considered desirable by European governments in the 1950s. This view was tied to an industrial policy seeking economies of scale in a world where 'European corporations were . . . smaller in size than their American (and Japanese) counterparts' (Dumez and Jeunemaître 1996: 232). Therefore, European companies were still 'frequently encouraged [to] merge' through most of the 1960s 'even when the effect would clearly have been to hinder competition' (1996: 232). Even in the 1970s and 1980s 'several [member state governments] did not want to cede any authority [over mergers] to the Commission' (Schwartz 1993: 624). Yet the Commission acquired authority over European mergers all the same. How could this happen?

Based on the general provisions for competition policy (Articles 81 and 82), the Commission started to claim in the early 1970s that it already had authority over (some) mergers. It exercised this power for the first time in December 1971, when it prohibited the acquisition of a Dutch company, TDV, by its German competitor, SLW, for exacerbating SLW's already dominant position in the market for certain packaging materials. SLW's American parent, Continental Can Company, appealed this decision to the ECJ in February 1972, arguing *inter alia* that the Commission had no authority to apply Article 82 to mergers. In its 1973 decision (ECJ case 6/72, 1973 ECR 215), the Court decided against the Commission on the facts and let the merger go ahead. However, it held that the overarching intentions of the Treaty, especially Article 3(1)g, and the provisions in Articles 81 and 82, logically required that Article 82 should also be applicable to mergers in which a company increased its dominant position in a market (Goyder 2003: esp. 336f.).

Having been given the opportunity by the actions of the Commission and by the actions of private actors from several member states, which were pursuing their interests by shifting political activity to the supranational level, the ECJ thus advanced the cause of integration. However, while supporting the view that merger review and antitrust were linked and that the Commission had some authority over them, the court did not specify how far that power extended nor how it was to be exercised. The Commission therefore proceeded to propose to the Council a clarification of scope and process through a merger regulation that would formally grant merger control authority (for details, see Allen 1977; Pollack 2003*a*: 287ff.). These overt political proposals for institutional change in 1973, 1981–82, 1984, and 1986 were rebuffed by the Council every time.

Subnational actors, however, began to make use of the political opportunities offered by the ECJ decision in the *Continental Can* case. In particular, firms demanded that DG Comp review and block certain mergers of their competitors. These actions of subnational actors led to further institutional change when in 1981 Philip Morris sought to acquire a large stake in one of its major competitors in the European cigarette market, Rothmans, from the South African conglomerate Rembrandt. Three other competitors thereupon submitted complaints to the Commission, asserting that the merger violated Articles 81 and 82, triggering an investigation by DG Comp. Philip Morris and Rembrandt satisfied the Commission's initial objections through a revision of their agreement, and the Commission then cleared the merger and rejected the competitors' request to block the equity investment altogether, prompting two of the competitors to take the Commission to court. In its 1987 decision in *British American Tobacco Company Ltd* v. *Commission* (142/84) and *R. J. Reynolds Industries* v. *Commission* (156/84), the ECJ upheld the Commission's decision on the facts, but used the opportunity to confirm the Commission's authority over mergers in much more general terms than in *Continental Can*. The resulting dynamic is well summarized by Bulmer (1994: 432): 'The corporate uncertainty that was created, in part orchestrated by the Commission, resulted in ... an unstoppable alliance of the Commission, ECJ jurisprudence, corporate actors and their interest groups ... for the establishment of a clear set of supranational rules.' Multinational firms began to notify the Commission of any merger intention and asked for advance clearance. They also formed transnational coalitions to lobby national governments as well as the member states' representatives jointly in the Council for the swift adoption of a merger regulation that would establish specific thresholds for EC jurisdiction and criteria for allowing mergers.

The resulting Merger Regulation (4064/89), which was adopted by the Council with unanimity in December 1989, was important in that it increased legal certainty for economic actors and resources for DG Comp. It also arguably went beyond Articles 81 and 82 (Partan 1993: 286). But again sequence is crucial to understanding institutional change: the regulation just formally assigned to the Commission powers that it had largely already acquired informally.

In the later 1990s, the Commission then blocked a number of mergers and imposed strict conditions on others, thus acting repeatedly against the express wishes of the largest member states. Yet, as in the realm of antitrust, the changes brought by the revision of the Commission's mandate in Council Regulation

139/2004 (OJ 16 December 2003: L24/1) primarily seem to strengthen the Commission further. They allow it to defer merger reviews to national competition authorities while retaining supremacy over those authorities. It constitutes 'decentralization without renationalization', while the threshold for mergers with a 'Community dimension' remains unchanged (and thus effectively has been lowered). Also as in antitrust, recent decisions of the CFI have demanded more thorough economic analysis, but court insiders deny that the CFI has raised the standards of evidence for a negative (blocking) merger review decision, and the judgments do not appear to be indicative of a general weakening of DG Comp's authority (Vesterdorf 2005).

In sum, DG Comp's attainment and exercise of merger review authority constitutes a series of even more striking institutional changes than its attainment of antitrust authority. These changes are well explained by the modified neofunctionalist theory of institutional change developed above.

State Aid(s): Subsidies, Tax Breaks, and Special Provisions/Guarantees

Article 4(c) of the Treaty of Paris stated categorically that 'subsidies or aids granted by States, or special charges imposed by States, in any form whatsoever' were considered 'incompatible with the common market for coal and steel and shall accordingly be abolished and prohibited within the Community'. Other provisions in the Treaty, however, tempered the strict prohibition of what became known in the EU as 'state aids', allowing in particular for governments' funds to help with adjustment to economic openness (see Ruggie 1983). In practice, the HA pushed member states toward a significant reduction in subsidies, but also allowed long transition periods (e.g. McLachlan and Swann 1967: 42ff.).

In the Treaty of Rome, state aids are addressed in Articles 87–89 (originally 92–94). Article 87 (1) contains a general prohibition of 'any aid [i] granted by a Member State or through State resources in any form whatsoever [ii] which distorts or threatens to distort competition [iii] by favoring certain undertakings or the production of certain goods … [iv] insofar as it affects trade between Member States' (each of the four elements has been subject to extensive debate, see Plender 2004). It is followed by criteria for statutory and discretionary exemptions. Article 88 requires member states to notify the Commission of all planned state aid, which within two months has either to clear the aid—based on Article 87 (2) or (3)—or initiate a full 'contentious' review, at the end of which it may conclude that the member state must 'abolish or alter' the aid if it is found to violate Article 87. The power to review state aid prospectively or *ex post* and to grant exemptions is delegated exclusively to the Commission, except in that Article 88 (2) para. 3 allows for the Council unanimously to grant an exemption in 'exceptional circumstances'. Article 89, finally, allows for the Council to pass implementing Regulations.[11]

Notwithstanding these treaty provisions, which in many ways resemble those for antitrust, state aid has long been considered the competition area where Commission authority has been the weakest and where the shift toward unambiguously supranational authority has been the most recent (and subject to repeated litigation). In part this might be explained by inherent differences. Since it involves external review of the policy decisions of member state governments, state aid policy is inherently supranational with no direct counterpart at the national level save in federal systems (Cini and McGowan 1998; Thielemann 1999; Wolf 2004). Any decision to restrict or prohibit state aid pits the Commission directly against one or more of the member states. While some economic liberals within governments might quietly welcome EU pressure to reduce subsidies as a counterweight against the clamoring for subsidies from domestic groups, more often member state governments seek to retain their autonomy. A direct challenge to the decision-making autonomy of the state is bound to be politically sensitive. Moreover, state aid need not just distort or reduce competition, as cartels do. Rather, state aid may at the same time help in achieving important EU objectives outside market integration and efficiency, such as reduced economic disparities within the EU or adjustment assistance to the losers of liberalization. Subsidies have also long been a key instrument of industrial policy and a potential substitute for trade policy (Nicolaïdis and Vernon 1997: esp. 292 ff.). The Treaty accordingly exempts, as a matter of principle, aid to individual consumers based on social criteria (from housing subsidies for the poor to progressive taxation) and disaster relief aid (87(2)); it also *allows* the Commission to consider as 'compatible with the common market' aid to underdeveloped regions within the EU, aid to facilitate economic adjustment, and (since Maastricht) aid to promote culture (87(3)). These inherent characteristics of state aid, however, cannot explain why DG Comp's state aid control has acquired 'teeth' in recent years.

In the early years, the Commission appeared to limit itself to defining 'state aid', which was at best vaguely defined in the Treaty. State aid thus came to be understood to include subsidies, tax breaks, state guarantees, and any other special treatments that give a particular firm or industry a competitive advantage. Proposals by the Commission for a detailed implementing regulation went nowhere in

---

[11] The provision allowing for the Council to exempt a particular case distinguishes state aid from the other issue areas of competition policy, restricting Commission discretion (Pollack 2003: 99f.). The rarely used provision does not, however, amount to an opportunity for the Council to overrule the Commission *ex post*, as the ECJ held in *Commission* v. *Council* (C-110/02 [2004] ECR I-0633). For various reasons, state aid in four industries/economic sectors is governed by a different set of procedures and/or in different DGs: transport, coal, fisheries, and agriculture.

the Council, and after 1972 the Commission stopped submitting further proposals (Cini 2001: 197)—until the late 1990s, when it felt that its authority in this realm was sufficiently well established to ensure that the Council would not use such a regulation to roll back the Commission's powers (Wolf 2004: 89). To be sure, the lack of an implementing regulation did not keep the Commission from gathering information about state aid, conducting the reviews that it was asked to do in Article 88(1), or acting against national export promotion programs. But through most of the 1970s, the Commission still rarely challenged sectoral, regional, and other forms of state aid that member states considered an integral part of their industrial policies. This restraint was surely due in part to DG Comp's realization that it would be wise to gain experience and power in less controversial issue areas such as antitrust before challenging the member states directly. But it also appears to have been a function of savvy political calculation consistent with the theoretical argument above: Those benefiting from state aid generally have concentrated interests and tend to be well organized whereas the costs tend to be diffuse, which makes it very difficult to put together a self-sustaining coalition in favor of reducing state aid, as long as markets are mostly national and subsidies are available to an entire industry. Only after the full integration of the European product markets, especially the removal of a multitude of nontariff barriers through the Single Market program (1986–92), could the Commission hope to find and foster political allies among substate actors who would have concentrated interests in genuinely supranational (aid-reducing) authority over state aid to counteract the political opposition from state aid recipients.

Even though member states are required to notify the Commission of all planned aid prior to giving it, compliance with the notification requirement has been far from perfect. For some time, the Commission has therefore relied on complaints from competing firms (or other governments) to make them aware of possibly illegal, unnotified state aids (Cini and McGowan 1998: 139). In the late 1980s, then, in an apparent case of learning from its own earlier successes in fostering constituencies for its authority in other areas of competition policy, the Commission adopted an explicit policy of encouraging complaints about state aid by European businesses (Smith 1998: 63). To be sure, the political sensitivity of publicly lodging a complaint against the government of one's own country or a major trading partner has meant that competitors of aid-receiving firms have sometimes preferred quietly 'tipping off' the Commission to unnotified aid rather than having any public involvement with DG Comp (e.g. Peterson and Bomberg 1999: 70f.). But as the Commission's review of state aid became better known as offering a political opportunity structure, firms increasingly made use of the opportunity (Smith 1998: 98). As in antitrust and merger review, many of those complaints in the 1990s have come from competitors of a subsidized firm or nationally subsidized industry. They have taken the form of complaints against the Commission for failure to review the aid program formally under Article 88(2) or failure to prohibit it (Cini 2001: 203). In other words, they were demands for more supranational governance.

As in the other issue areas of competition policy, the Commission thus incrementally gained authority in response to demands from substate actors pursuing their own selfish interests, often with help or *ex post* confirmation from the Court. Most important here was the power to impose repayment of aid (from the aid-receiving entities to the aid-granting state) as a penalty in cases where the Commission established *ex post* that illegal aid had been given. 'Recovery of illegal state aid' was not provided for in the Treaty, and many member states opposed it. Yet the ECJ noted as early as *Commission* v. *Germany* (70/72 [1973] ECR 813) that it had to be an available remedy in order to retain the incentive for governments to notify the Commission *ex ante*. And the Court explicitly confirmed the power of the Commission to impose such penalties when the Commission's authority was challenged in *France* v. *Commission* (301/87 [1990] ECR 307) after the Commission started to impose such penalties in the mid-1980s (Priess 1996).

Yet do these institutional changes matter? Is the Commission actually exercising influence? Studies of state aid tend to show that the total amount of aid has barely declined and only recently has it declined consistently. Only about 1 percent of state aid notifications to the Commission result in a rejection. As Mitchell Smith points out, however, those might be the wrong numbers to focus on (1996: 564 f.). Informal communication between governments and DG Comp ensures that many aid proposals are revised in ways that make them less market-distorting, before they are even initially submitted or well before the Commission might otherwise open an Article 88(2) investigation. The very informality of this practice makes it hard to establish how common and substantial such revisions are, but the very existence of the practice suggests that the Commission has real power in this realm and Smith concludes: 'The evidence suggests that Member States over time increasingly have had to adapt their industrial policies in significant ways to take account of DG IV's state aid policies' (Smith 1998: 57). Moreover, compliance of member states with EU state aid rules has in recent years been notably better than compliance of the federal states of Germany with similar rules at the national level or compliance with rules against subsidies in GATT/WTO (Wolf 2004). All of this comes in the context of apparently improved compliance with the notification requirement. As reported in the Commission's biannual *State Aid Scoreboard*, the percentage of 'registered aid cases' known to the Commission but not notified by the government in question has declined from 15 to 11 percent from the early 2000s to 2005 alone, despite increased incentives for competitors and taxpayers to notify the Commission of state aid that governments might have failed to notify.

Some recent developments should be briefly noted: After the CFI gained jurisdiction over state aid cases by private plaintiffs in 1994, resulting in an increase in state aid-related court cases brought by substate actors, the court began to demand more extensive economic analysis in critical cases (as in the other issue areas). The resulting demand on DG Comp's resources contributed to the Commission's decision to seek, after all, Council regulations on state aid. Council Regulation 994/98 (OJ 1998 L142/1) authorized the Commission to exempt entire categories of aid from the notification requirement, akin to the 'block exemptions' in antitrust (thus freeing up DG Comp resources previously needed to conduct the initial two-months review of aid proposals) and 659/99 (OJ 1999 L83/1) largely codified DG Comp's review procedures. Since 2001, aid to small and medium-sized companies and training aid is categorically exempted, as is aid below a certain threshold (*de minimis* rule), while private parties can take complaints directly to national courts (thanks to direct effect of EU law) if they feel that a government is abusing a block exemption (Sinnaeve 2001; Rehbinder 2004). Finally, the EU has increasingly sought to externalize its state aid policy vis-à-vis its trade partners, for example via the EEA and association agreements (see e.g. Cremona 2003; Rydelski 2004).

Alternative Explanations

While a proper discussion of alternative explanations of the developments sketched above is beyond the scope of this chapter, I want to address some of the most promising alternatives briefly. First, principal–agent theory has become a popular framework for the analysis of politics in the EU and has yielded important insights into variation in member states' ability to control the EU institutions (e.g. Pollack 2003*a*: here esp. 281–99; Tallberg 2000). As currently formulated, however, this approach to the delegation of authority leads one to overlook actors outside the principal–agent relationship such as the subnational actors that I have found to have played a crucial role in all three issue areas and which neofunctionalism (as refined here) emphasizes as central to institutional change.

Second, ideational or constructivist explanations have illuminated important episodes in the process of European integration (e.g. McNamara 1998; Parsons 2003) and might contribute to a more complete explanation of the developments in EU competition policy. As noted above, the ascent of neo-liberal economic thought in the 1980s and 1990s surely contributed to the increased prestige of DG Comp. By itself, however, this ideational shift cannot explain the variation in the timing of changes across the issue areas of competition policy.

Intergovernmentalism, finally, allows for significant changes only as a function of agreements among the member states; it therefore cannot account for the many incremental but cumulatively substantial changes described above. Where (some) change did come about through an intergovernmental bargain (as in the passage of the 1989 Merger Regulation), neofunctionalism provides an endo-genous explanation for the underlying change in government preferences, which remains exogenous for intergovernmentalism (see e.g. Schwartz 1993).

Neofunctionalism—as a HI theory in the broad sense espoused by Meunier and McNamara (this volume)—can account for these observations and is heuristically more useful: It leads us to pay close attention to sequence and to discover that Council Regulations in the realms of merger and state aid codified rather than created Commission authority. It also leads us to see (possible) actors and actions at the sub- and transnational levels that are beyond the purview of other theoretical approaches. In a Lakatosian sense, then, it is most promising as a theory of institutional change in the EU.

Conclusion

In this chapter, I have sketched the major developments in the key areas of EU competition policy over the 'first fifty years' since the Treaty of Rome. I have sought to provide an overview of one of the economically and politically most important and interesting issue areas, on which political science scholarship is still scarce. I have focused on the key dynamics of the institutional evolution in EU competition policy, namely how DG Comp came to attain real supranational power at different times in the different issue areas of competition policy, some-times against the express preferences of the member states. I also have tried to show that we can understand and explain these dynamics by adopting a modified neofunctionalist theoretical perspective. The key theoretical contributions here are to clarify the centrality for neofunctionalism of substate actors engaging in transnational politics and to integrate key insights from historical institutionalism. This theoretical perspective yields, I have suggested, a superior explanation for the evolution of the politics of competition in the EU over the last fifty years. Its analytical usefulness across several issue areas suggests that Haas's foundational neofunctionalist work deserves a second, close reading and that the theory can and should be fruitfully developed further.

Given my findings, a key question for the future of competition policy is: When might subnational actors be expected to push for further integration? In the realm of competition policy, the existence of concentrated interests that can benefit from the shift of authority to the supranational level in a given issue area of competition policy appears to be a prerequisite. Yet it does not make a push for institutional change automatic. Numerous factors enter into a firm's (or potentially consumer group's) decision to raise a concern with DG Comp or bring a case at the CFI or ECJ. Indeed, it may be an inherent weakness of HI theorizing that the appreciation for context and contingencies makes it difficult to generate precise *ex ante* predictions, even as it yields better explanations.

11

A Historical Institutionalist Analysis of the Road to Economic and Monetary Union: A Journey with Many Crossroads

AMY VERDUN

Introduction

Today, EMU is a key policy area in Europe, even though it was not even mentioned in the 1957 Treaty of Rome. Indeed, what is remarkable about the historical trajectory of EMU are its dramatic turnarounds: absent at the outset, EMU made considerable progress in the 1960s, failed in the 1970s despite being adopted by the Council as an objective in 1971, only to re-emerge onto the agenda in full force in the Maastricht Treaty in 1992. Created in 1999, and with euro banknotes and coins circulating in twelve member states since 2002, EMU can without doubt be seen as one of the greatest achievements of European integration. Yet, few could have predicted fifty years ago, at the signing of the Treaty of Rome, that it would ever come into being.

Also remarkable is the striking similarity between the concept of EMU in 1971 and that of 1992. There is a case to be made for path dependence (Pierson 1996) in what is considered to be the core concept of EMU. This concept of EMU envisaged not only a single currency and a transfer of sovereignty over monetary policy from the national level to the European level (to a new supranational institution). The concept of EMU was also similar in that it aimed at finding a compromise solution for dealing with the more tricky aspect of budgetary policy coordination. Both in 1971 and in 1992, the founding fathers of EMU were aware that some degree of coordination on budgetary and fiscal policies was necessary but that political will was lacking to make a significant transfer of sovereignty over budgetary and fiscal policies to the supranational level. In the 1970s the ambition to transfer sovereignty in this area was more pronounced and was stated as an aim up front. In the 1990s by contrast it was not incorporated into the institutional structure from the outset, but many thought that it would somehow follow in the early years of EMU. As a result of these difficulties in the domain of budgetary and fiscal governance of EMU some would say EMU is still incomplete although it features a European Central Bank (a supranational monetary authority) it lacks the 'parallel' supranational authority, that is, some sort of economic government. As the chapter shows, transfer of sovereignty over budgetary and fiscal policies to a supranational institution has been considered politically undesirable during the entire period of the history of EMU (and in fact still is to this day). As a result, budgetary and fiscal policies remain subject to coordination and final responsibility over these policies lies with member state governments. This asymmetrical EMU (Verdun 1996), where monetary union exists without economic union, is different from the model of integrated monetary and broader economic governance that was conceived to be underlying EMU by prominent early thinkers of EMU. Yet it has been the preferred choice of heads of state and government at the important crossroads.

This chapter traces the origins of EMU and follows the progress of European monetary integration over the past fifty years. In analyzing this process, the chapter adopts a HI analysis (Steinmo, Thelen, and Longstreth 1992; Hall and Taylor 1996; Fligstein, Sandholtz, and Stone Sweet 2001; Pierson 2004) and asks a number of questions: what was the concept of EMU at important historical crossroads? Who were the main actors pushing and resisting EMU at those important junctures, and what type of EMU did they envisage? What interests did these actors have, what were they most concerned about, and what power resources did they have at their disposal? What was the anticipated next step that EMU was to take? Did it happen or not? If not, why not? In making this assessment the chapter focuses on the role of the concept of EMU: the actors that played an important role, the institutional context, the effect of exogenous shocks, and the type of EMU chosen at that time. The chapter adopts a HI framework to show the connection between what was conceptualized at an earlier stage and how that idea influenced the next stages. We concentrate on the concept of EMU and see how this concept changes or not over time as we move from one time period to the next. We also analyze who were the actors prominent at that time period. Furthermore, in line with the HI analysis we examine the general institutional context to see how it influences the choices made by the actors at the time. The chapter examines seven important crossroads:

1. The 1957 Treaty of Rome,
2. The run-up to the Werner Report of 1970,
3. The European Monetary System created in 1979,
4. The Delors Report (1989) and the 1992 Maastricht Treaty,
5. The Stability and Growth Pact,
6. Creation of EMU 1999 and introduction of banknotes and coins 2002, and,
7. Post-EMU difficulties with the implementation of the Stability and Growth Pact.

The chapter discusses each of these crossroads and finally draws some conclusions. The chapter finds that that EMU was constructed asymmetrically as transfer over monetary policy was acceptable, but there was no consensus about transferring budgetary and fiscal policies. At each of the crossroads the question was how much integration was desirable. In practical terms it meant determining how much sovereignty (over what policy area) to transfer and when to transfer it. The problem remained that member state governments were not ready for a parallel development in the budgetary and fiscal domain.

The 1957 Treaty of Rome

The 1957 Treaty of Rome does not mention EMU. The concept of EMU in these early years consists of only economic and monetary policy coordination; nothing more. At this point in time, the interests of the actors include moving toward closer integration in some areas, such as agriculture, but not in the area of exchange rates. The actors pushing for macroeconomic policy coordination in this period are the government representatives of the six member states, in particular heads of state or government and ministers of economics and finance. An important explanatory factor for the lack of focus on a European Exchange Rate Mechanism (ERM) or even the move toward a single currency can be found in the institutional context. In the late 1950s the Bretton Woods arrangement enables fixed exchange rates among most of the advanced industrialized societies. The implications for Western Europe are that exchange rates are already stable. Thus, European exchange rate collaboration is not seen to be a problem—much less so one that would merit dealing with through the institutions of the EEC. Furthermore, although the Rome Treaty is already very ambitious in a number of areas (such as a customs union and a CAP), these are the very early days of the EEC. It is therefore not at all surprising that the aim of EMU is not mentioned in the Treaty. What is worth pointing to is that at this time a set of new institutional governance structures are set up which consist of member state representatives. Examples of these are the monetary committee or MC (central bank and ministry of finance representatives) and the committee of governors (consisting of the central bank presidents) (Verdun 2000*b*). If one is to categorize these early crossroads, one finds a type of economic and monetary cooperation that does not aim at moving toward full EMU. Nevertheless, these early pressures for coordination and the creation of two important committees (MC and committee of governors) do provide a first step toward EMU. A considerable amount of socialization, learning and opportunity to discuss further steps in the future, is facilitated through the creation and frequent meetings of these committees (cf. Rosenthal 1975).

The 1970 Werner Report

Economic and Monetary Union comes onto the agenda for the first time in the late 1960s. It is a direct response to the circumstances of the day: with the completion of the customs union in 1968 (eighteen months ahead of the deadline) and the success of the CAP at a time when the Bretton Woods system of fixed exchange rates is showing signs of stress, EMU looks to be a useful goal to consider. At this time the concept of EMU is economic and monetary policy integration in stages. In these years following the signing of the Treaty of Rome, a number of important scholarly books have come out that are influencing the thinking surrounding EMU. Authors, such as Balassa (1961), Scitovsky (1958), and Tinbergen (1965), spell out that economic integration is conceptualized as moving through stages. Further economic and monetary integration—according to these thinkers—would imply a transfer of sovereignty of monetary policy as well as economic policy (budgetary and fiscal policies) to a supranational European level. Other scholarly works that influence some of the debates are the contributions by Mundell (1961) and McKinnon (1963) on optimal currency areas. Those contributions are not so much about creating EMU in stages but rather the importance of having convergence between countries be present before one can move on to currency cooperation or integration.

When EMU comes onto the agenda in the 1960s, the actors pushing for it are in particular the Commission (which already in 1965 adopts the introduction of a common EEC currency as one of the major strategic objectives, Tsoukalis 1977: 60). Others instrumental in the process are those sitting on the various EC committees that deal with economic and monetary affairs. The Commission gradually obtains support from leaders of the six member states (heads of state or government and economics and finance ministers). The French government is particularly keen to push forward the idea of EMU as functionally desirable to secure the CAP (although it is nervous about transferring sovereignty). It becomes clear that with exchange rates becoming more volatile, the so-called 'green currencies' (a system of pricing at the heart of the CAP) are increasingly difficult to maintain.

Two people in particular make important contributions to the plan for the development of EMU in stages: Raymond Barre, the EC Commissioner for economic and financial affairs, and Pierre Werner, prime minister and finance minister of Luxembourg. During the period of drafting a blueprint for EMU, it becomes apparent that a difference of opinion exists regarding the mechanism that will lead to a successful EMU (the so-called 'economists' vs. the 'monetarists' debate, see Tsoukalis 1977; Kruse 1980; Verdun 2000*a*; Maes and Verdun 2005). 'Economists' (Germany and the Netherlands) are keen to have far-reaching economic policy coordination (budgetary, fiscal policy, and perhaps even incomes policy) before introducing a common monetary policy (Rosenthal 1975: 107–8). By contrast, monetarists (France, Belgium, and Luxembourg) figure that a common monetary policy could precede, and in so doing, generate, economic policy coordination. This dichotomy proves to be a fundamental point of contention. It boils down to asking the question, to what extent should one already have converging economies and perhaps even a larger role for economic policy at the Community level before locking exchange rates and transferring sovereignty over monetary policy to a new supranational central bank? Note that at this time this supranational institution was conceptualized as a 'Eurofed'—the analogy was made to the US federal reserve system. The difference between the two camps was large. The members of the Werner Group (representing these differences among themselves) had the difficult task of coming up with a compromise solution that carefully balanced the focus on both 'economic' and 'monetary' policies as being part of the first steps (Werner Report 1970). They introduced 'parallelism' that seeks to do both at once, but really does not settle the question of what should precede what. Their proposal is to create EMU in three stages, with the first stage lasting three years, the second stage undetermined in length, and the third stage being completed by 1980 by which time EMU would be a fact.

The institutional context of this time holds an important key to understanding why EMU comes onto the agenda. The early signs of the breakdown of the Bretton Woods system, the dollar crisis, and the so-called 'Triffin Dilemma'[1] all play a role in bringing about awareness that the international system of fixed exchange rates is on its return as well as success in European integration with completion of the customs union and the success of the CAP were other reasons for heads of state and government to make the next step toward economic and monetary integration. The immediate aftermath of the publication of the Werner Report (1970) is extremely troubled. In August 1971 the Bretton Woods ERM effectively is abolished when US President Richard Nixon announces the suspension of the convertibility of the dollar into gold. The member states' response to the crisis is to seek to reproduce stable exchange rates within the context of the EC. They develop a system whereby European currencies stay within small (±2.25 percent) fluctuation parities (the 'snake') and that that system as a whole does not fluctuate much (again ±2.25 percent) against the dollar (the so-called 'tunnel'). However, this exchange rate system does not work well during the 1970s. Again, part of the explanation can be found in the changing context and a few exogenous shocks,

---

[1] In 1960, Robert Triffin pointed out that a fundamental contradiction exists between the mechanism of producing dollars for the world market and international confidence in the system. Triffin proposed to create a European fund to reduce instability in the system. His proposals lay at the heart of Jean Monnet's 1962 Action Committee for the United States of Europe (Commission of the EC 1962) (see for further discussion Verdun 2000a: 52).

in particular the 1973 oil crisis and the diverging national responses to it. These factors play an important role in explaining why the EMU plan fails in the 1970s.

What is truly remarkable about this period, and what makes these crossroads interesting for tracing the creation of EMU, is that the type of EMU conceptualized at this stage is in a number of ways remarkably similar to what would be reinvented in the late 1980s. One can almost say that the circumstances were not yet right, but the plan itself was starting to materialize. The type of EMU envisaged has a far-reaching form of EMU which includes a new supranational monetary institution. The one major difference, and thus still subject to considerable discussion today, is the matter of what role there was to be played by a supranational body in economic policy (budgetary and fiscal policies). Let us explore that issue a little.

The Werner Report suggests the creation of a 'Centre of Decision of Economic Policy' which is to have a number of tasks. The CDEP will oversee the coordination of economic policies, by carrying out at least three annual surveys of the economic situation in the Community, which in turn will enable the adoption of common guidelines. Regarding budgetary policies, the CDEP will adopt quantitative guidelines on budgetary expenditures and receipts, and the distribution of the latter between investment and consumption and the directions and amount of the balances. On the fiscal side the Werner Report calls for progressive harmonization of indirect taxes as well as taxes on interest payments on fixed-interest securities and dividends (Verdun 2000*a*: 60). A Community budget is called for, although it will be modest and fall short of the usual size of a federal budget. Even though the Werner Group is quite vocal in its call for these far-reaching elements in the area of supranational economic governance, the differences among member states are too big. The Dutch and the Germans are keen to have the supranational provisions in place, whereas the French, in particular, are unwilling to go that far. The consequence is that these provisions are watered down in the Commission memoranda and subsequently the type of EMU the Council eventually adopts in March 1971. Furthermore, the irreversible elements (i.e. transfer of sovereignty), that the Werner Report calls for to start immediately, are postponed for three years (to occur in stage two). In other words, the Werner Group has a concept of EMU in mind that follows some of the thinking of the 1960s path to currency union, drawing on the insights of Balassa, Scitovsky, and Tinbergen, but the member states' differences in opinion about transferring sovereignty lead to a messy compromise that pushes sensitive issues to the future.

With the benefit of hindsight one can say that those three years that follow the 1971 Council decision were full of external shocks to which member states responded differently, which in turn led them away from a joint view on EMU. The rest of the 1970s and early 1980s did not provide any real opportunities for EMU to materialize further.

The 1979 European Monetary System

In the 1970s the plans for EMU do not take off. Plan after plan is made to change, revise, relaunch EMU, but the time is never right. An example of such a failed plan is a report by the Marjolin Group (Marjolin 1975). The Group was asked by the Commission to analyze the problems raised by EMU and to find appropriate solutions. The recommendations made by this Group included transferring both monetary and economic policymaking to a Community institution. This was not the message the member state governments wanted to hear, so nothing came of it. Another example of a failed attempt to restart EMU was made by nine well-known economists in the so-called 'All Saints' Day Manifesto' of November 1, 1975 (*The Economist* 1975). They analyzed the situation as one in which the Werner Group had underestimated the reluctance on the part of member state governments to transfer sovereignty. Thus they pleaded for a more gradual process but at the same time also monetary reform. This Manifesto also did not attract the attention of member state governments that it would have needed to boost the development of EMU. Another report that is ambitious in tone, and that could have brought new life into the integration process, was the Tindemans Report (1976) that sought to create a EU. Its vision for EMU was that—if need be—it should allow for a two-speed Community. According to this plan some member states should be entitled to go ahead sooner than others. Again, we see a plan that does not connect up with the priorities of the member state governments of the day. Another example of a plan that could have revived the EMU initiative was the MacDougall Report (1977) on EC public finance. This report recommends that the EC should seek to secure a larger EC budget and use the funds for redistribution within the EC. It would also be a way to have a larger EC budget that could be used, once the time was right, for further budgetary and fiscal integration. Yet this report is too ambitious in its scope and thus does not generate the enthusiasm needed to consider seriously its far-reaching recommendations.

As a result, when a next step in economic and monetary integration is made in the late 1970s, namely to create the European Monetary System (EMS), the concept of EMU is narrowed down. It now only focuses on exchange rates (phase one); a second phase is foreseen but will never be implemented (Ludlow 1982). It probably is safe to say that the interest of actors in the late 1970s is to deal with the lack of success in securing an EC ERM (and perhaps also, though much less so, an awareness that EMU has not materialized or moved forward in the 1970s). The so-called 'snake' fails to work with all member states (notably the French franc joins and leaves the snake three times during the 1970s). Actors initiating and pushing for this type of integration are the heads of state and government, in particular the French and West German leaders, and the new Commission President Roy Jenkins.

The institutional context also plays an important role. The EC has witnessed its first enlargement in 1973. So by 1978 the EC consists already for a few years of nine member states including the more skeptical UK, Denmark, and Ireland (the latter with particularly close linkages to the UK). Another important factor is that, not only does the snake fail to incorporate all EC member states, it also increasingly seems to work as a large Deutschmark zone (and will become even more so during the 1980s). More generally, enthusiasm for European integration is at an all time low at a low at this time ('eurosclerosis'). This period is characterized by another major exogenous shock: the second oil crisis. The result is that overall economic conditions deteriorate. What also happens at the turn of the decade is a change in leadership and paradigm in a number of prominent countries (see Henning 1994). Monetarism starts to attract considerable support in some countries, and influential leaders sympathetic to monetarist views rise to powerful positions—Margaret Thatcher becomes prime minister in the UK; Paul Volcker is appointed to be the chairman of the US Federal Reserve Bank; and Ronald Reagan moves into the White House (on the turn to monetarism as an important factor in the creation of EMU, see Marcussen 1998; McNamara 1998). Overall the response to all these challenges is diverging policies in the leading European countries (cf. West Germany and the UK vs. France and Italy). The type of EMU that is envisaged at this point is a very watered-down version (one can hardly speak of EMU at all). The EMS and its ERM call for a small system of institutions. The hope of European monetary integration enthusiasts is that with sufficient political support it will push the economic and monetary integration project to the next level in due course. It is worth noting, however, that EMU was not so much abandoned as an idea, but rather seems to be a very distant future at these crossroads. Yet the effect of the operation of EMS in the 1980s is that EMU comes closer to being a reality. But from the point of view of the early 1980s, it would have been a far cry to consider that EMU would take off so rapidly and effectively in the late 1980s.

The 1989 Delors Report and the 1992 Maastricht Treaty

Developments in the 1980s are crucial for understanding why EMU comes onto the agenda again, and why it takes the shape it does. The concept of EMU at these crossroads is an ambitious three steps to full EMU (albeit with a supranational monetary union, and mostly macroeconomic coordination on budgetary and fiscal policy rather than an 'economic government'). Here we see the original Werner Plan updated so as to include the developments of the current time (the SEA and the plan to complete the Internal Market, the liberalization of the capital market, and so on). The actors pushing for integration are heads of state and government and finance ministers of member states, the Commission, and expert committees (mainly central bank governments) (on the Commission see Jabko 1999). Heads of state and government at the European Council meeting in Hanover in 1988 ask the central bank governors of the twelve EC member states plus a few others to draft a blueprint of EMU. The first step the central bankers take is to look at the Werner Report and how they can salvage some of it, and which part needs to be changed (see the background papers attached to the Delors Report 1989). They take a lot from it as their three-stage plan is in fact remarkably similar to the Werner Report, except that it reflects the realities of the day (so no transfer of sovereignty to a CDEP, and no central budget for the EU to accompany EMU) (Verdun 1999). The Delors Report was used as a basis for the Maastricht Treaty and many of its elements were taken on board in the final text of the treaty. Much has been written about these precise crossroads and the roles played by various actors (Garrett 1993; Martin 1993; Dyson 1994; Grieco 1995; McNamara 1998; Moravcsik 1998; Dyson and Featherstone 1999; Verdun 2000*a*, to name just a few), and the picture painted is that EMU is supported by Jacques Delors (as Commission president), is endorsed by the governments of a number of member states (in particular, those of France and Germany) and that central bank presidents endorse an EMU that will be focused on price stability and bring into existence a European Central Bank modeled after the German Central Bank. The institutional context since the early and mid-1980s—the enlarged EC, now twelve member states—is confronted with a reasonably successful EMS, renewed optimism following the success of the SEA, and the prospect of 'completing the single market'. Enthusiasm is high. Some EC countries have made policy changes so as to be in a better position to support a new regime.

In 1989 (after the Delors Report is already published—it came out in April) the international context changes importantly, in fact it witnesses another exogenous shock, with the fall of the wall and with German reunification. Given the crucial role played by Germany in European monetary cooperation, it further strengthens the felt need to deal with EMU. The type of EMU envisaged is a far-reaching form of integration which includes the creation of a new European Central Bank. EMU is built on the experience of more or less successful exchange rate cooperation in the 1980s. Because the creation of a new supranational institution requires a treaty change, the idea of treaty reform subsequently pushes integration forward in other areas.

The 1997 Stability and Growth Pact

In the course of the 1990s when member states are preparing for entry into stage three of EMU, voices in Germany are heard that are concerned about some member states being allowed into EMU from the outset (Heipertz and Verdun 2004). These voices are found throughout Germany: in the Bundesbank (the

German central bank), in the German federal government, in think tanks, in opposition circles, and elsewhere. The concern is that if countries with less stellar performance on inflation and on other indicators (such as budgetary deficits and public debt) were to join EMU right away from the outset, that EMU as a whole would not be as credible compared to if EMU were to start with a smaller group of countries that were better prepared (i.e. had a stronger track record). Of course the so-called 'convergence criteria' included in the Maastricht Treaty had been inserted to ensure that all member states that wanted to join needed to meet criteria that dealt with these very factors. But by the mid-1990s the Germans are concerned that EMU might take off with too many 'weaker countries'. The result is that there is a good feeding ground in Germany to discuss possible further strengthening of EMU after countries will have joined.

In the fall of 1995 Finance Minister Theo Waigel proposes an idea for a Stability Pact that aims at ensuring that countries will keep on performing well once in EMU. Interestingly Waigel's initial proposal contains an element that one could trace back to being more in the tradition of an 'economic government', namely it called for a 'stability council' to look into the performance in the area of budgetary deficits (Heipertz and Verdun 2004). (Of course it is also in line with the views of the 'economists' who put emphasis on the need to have economic coordination.) Shortly after announcing it to the German parliament, Waigel's proposal is discussed in the context of the Ecofin Council. A few weeks later a plan is prepared in the MC. Most of the actual drafting and crafting of the text is done in the MC (today's Economic and Financial Committee) that eventually sends the proposal to the Council for final approval as per the normal proced-ures. The eventual SGP contains rules concerning deficits, and a set of steps—ultimately sanctions—against those member states who, for a continued period, would run excessive deficits. The SGP further strengthens the framework set out in the Maastricht Treaty.

The concept of EMU envisaged at this time still builds firmly on the concept of EMU underlying the Maastricht Treaty. What has triggered the SGP is the concern that member states with a weaker historical performance could be joining EMU and that there are insufficiently clear checks and balances to deal with poor performance after exchange rates have been locked (i.e. post-stage three). The other point that is worth observing is that Waigel's proposal at first included a Stability Council that could have been a step toward further integration (supra-national governance) of economic policies. However, he withdrew that part of the proposal when it became clear to him that the French might think that this aspect of the plan could lead to their notion of a *Gouvernement économique* (Howarth 2000). The Germans were concerned that the French concept of *Gouvernement économique* could include the notion of restricting the independence of the ECB. The other observation is that the SGP was set up to deal with rules in the post-EMU period that had been kept vague in the Treaty. Again, originally the Germans were considering setting up a Stability Pact outside the framework of the Treaty. However, the Commission services quickly clarified that it would be impossible to set up an institutional structure related to economic and monetary governance, and ultimately rules regarding the governance of EMU, outside the Treaty. Thus the arrangements were set up within that context. So we see the Commission using path dependence very actively in the context of framing the SGP within the EU legal framework, and in so doing discouraging the German initiative to move outside the EU legal framework.

Though there is little doubt that the SGP was inspired by domestic concerns in Germany, carried by the then finance minister, and brought to the attention of Ecofin and thus to the other member states, the main actors who crafted the final details of the Stability and Growth Pact are the MC and the Commission (Heipertz and Verdun 2005). They play the most important role in shaping the Pact. The Commission makes sure the SGP stays firmly embedded within the context of the Maastricht Treaty, whereas the MC (representing high officials of Ministries of Finance and Economics of the member states) discuss the various options of how to come up with a workable SGP that signals the right things (need to keep debt and deficits low) yet making the rule sufficiently simple and straightforward for national governments to work with. It is for this reason that they end up focusing on deficits (rather than debt—even though that would make more sense if one is concerned about the effect of high debt on interest rates, risk of debt defaulting and thus the risk that a national government might one day need to be bailed out). The idea is that deficits are more or less controllable by national governments, whereas the public debt is an accumulation over time, over which a sitting government has only very limited control.

The institutional context in this period is one in which Germany can still set the rules of EMU as it was clear that if Germany were to have second thoughts about EMU, that it might be difficult for EMU to come into effect. Thus as long as the proposals are in line with 'sound policies' following from German monetary practices and concerns, and based on the Maastricht Treaty (not needing an amendment of the Treaty) the SGP could be created without too much difficulty. The other factors that play a role in this regard are the fact that the EU at this time is gradually preparing for enlargement, and that it is hoped that EMU will be 'ready' before enlargement takes center-stage on the EU agenda. The other important aspect in this regard is that the SGP eventually is discussed at the same summit at which the Amsterdam Treaty is being discussed. Because of the SGP arrangement some felt it to be important that other elements be included in the Treaty, such as the employment provisions, and a stronger role for an informal group to discuss policy coordination in the area of EMU. Against this context the Eurogroup was conceived (Puetter 2006). Thus, while not strictly speaking directly included in SGP, the creation of the SGP was a trigger to have the creation of the Eurogroup be included in the Amsterdam Treaty.

Again, at these crossroads the type of EMU was still very much the one conceived of at Maastricht, with a supranational ECB and only *coordination* of budgetary and fiscal policies. Yet the SGP (and the creation of the Eurogroup) sought to facilitate further coordination and cooperation in this policymaking area without needing to go the full route of transferring sovereignty to a new EU supranational institution.

Creation of EMU in 1999 and Introduction of Banknotes and Coins in 2002

The period between signing the Treaty on EU in 1992 and the actual start of full EMU is worthwhile reviewing as it is fascinating to see how the integration mood, as well as confidence in whether EMU was going to happen, swings back and forth like a pendulum. In the end, by 1998 EMU is considered feasible to all those that meet the convergence criteria set out in the Maastricht Treaty which are to be judged fairly liberally. The concept of EMU that eventually is created in 1999 is one of full monetary union and coordinated budgetary and fiscal policies (in other words the Maastricht Treaty plus the so-called 'Stability and Growth Pact' that was accepted in 1997). It is a clear political choice to include in EMU as many countries as deemed politically possible without violating the treaty rules (but again, interpreted in a flexible fashion).

The actors pushing for a large EMU (i.e. with many participating member states from the outset) include all the heads of state or government and finance ministers of member states that are concerned they may be left out of such an initial round (i.e. Greece, Italy, Portugal, and Spain). By contrast, those that are more skeptical at first of having the Southern European member states join EMU from the outset and hence would be perfectly happy with a small EMU, include countries such as Germany and the Netherlands. But as time goes by, it becomes clear that even countries such as Germany and France are at risk of not completely meeting the convergence criteria, which causes these countries to drop their objection against a large EMU. The EU institutions (European Commission, European Monetary Institute) accept the desire to have numerous countries join, and thus one could say they 'buy in' to that outcome.

The institutional context at this time consists of renewed optimism in the late 1990s (following considerable pessimism in the mid-1990s). In the late 1990s there is economic growth albeit that it is turning to recession in the early years of the twenty-first century. In this period the EU has gone through major changes both in its governance, its size (now fifteen member states), scope of EU policies, and it has the knowledge that it will be enlarging further in the near future. The fact that the rules for entry are interpreted somewhat flexibly so as to allow the largest possible number of member states to join in the first wave should be placed in the context of the planning for the upcoming enlargement of the EU with Central and Eastern European countries. One could argue that the EU member states want EMU to be 'completed' before turning to the Eastern enlargement. The type of EMU envisaged is still the one set out in the Treaty on EU but interpreted in a political fashion (i.e. which countries to accept was interpreted reasonably 'liberally') so as to include a large number of member states from the outset.

A Post-EMU Crisis?

A review of the period following the introduction of banknotes and coins sheds important light on a number of important governance and external factors. At this time the concept of EMU is still the same as before but the focus is more on the lack of effective macroeconomic policy coordination, in particular on keeping budgetary deficits below the agreed ceiling of 3 percent of gross domestic product (GDP). Thus, given that there is no 'economic government' to enforce coordination or to determine these policies, the EU relies on 'rules' set out in the Maastricht Treaty and further clarified in the Stability and Growth Pact. These rules are envisaged to ensure coordination in this field.

At this time the actors pushing for enforcement of the rules as part of the vision of economic and monetary integration are the Commission, the heads of state or government and finance ministers of small member states, and the European Central Bank (on small member states, see Jones, Friedman, and Torres 1998). The institutional context again is crucial. At this time there is overall pessimism about the state of the economy and an awareness of the need for structural reforms. Yet elected governments find themselves in a difficult position to carry through deep reforms, seeing that their electoral mandate is short, the costs of reforms high, and the positive effect of reforms only likely to be felt in the longer run. Other factors play an important role. The process of enlargement focuses attention away from EMU. An exogenous shock hit the EU on September 11, 2001 when terrorist attacks and their aftermath changed the role of Justice and Home Affairs policies and, to a lesser extent, the European Security and Defence Policy and, thus, the focus of the EU as a whole. Following the Laeken Declaration of 2001 renewed optimism emerges around the discussions in the Convention on the future of the EU and subsequently some enthusiasm is generated around the draft Treaty establishing a Constitution, though it signals renewed optimism about where the EU might be going but also starts to bring to the surface the latent conflict between small and large member states. The authors of the *Treaty Establishing a Constitution for Europe* do not change the fundamentals of EMU in the Treaty as no one wishes to touch the delicate balance contained therein. This is also a time in which the application of the SGP rules are being tried out. In addition, considerable criticism from the scholarly community is voiced, whether the specific rules of the SGP are really needed to sustain EMU. At this time, Germany and France (formerly the motors of integration) end up seeking ways to refrain from having to meet the rules, which ends dramatically in an Ecofin Council decision on November 25, 2003 in which the SGP is temporarily suspended for those two countries. The type of EMU at these crossroads: completion of the plan set out in the Treaty on EU and in the SGP. During this time there is a gradual changing of the content of the SGP to accommodate flexibility and the needs of large member states. There is no structural change in type of EMU (no economic government or attempt to build one), and thus the changes take the form of revised regulations (as opposed to treaty changes). Whether the actual implementation of the SGP post its reform of March 2005 will mean the demise of the SGP is as yet unclear.

Conclusion

To understand better the development toward EMU in the EU, this chapter has suggested using insights from historical institutionalism. I offered an analysis of seven major crossroads in European economic and monetary integration from 1957 to the present day. While EMU was not even mentioned in the 1957 Treaty of Rome, and had a checkered history between 1957 and 1991, it still became integrated into the 1992 Treaty on EU and eventually materialized as one of the most prominent examples of 'successful' European integration. EMU's history is characterized by dramatic turnarounds, missed opportunities, sudden successes, and yet continuity in its institutional setup.

A historical-institutionalist analysis allows us to examine a number of important points: the concept of EMU, the actors who are pushing (or unwilling to move toward) EMU, the institutional context, exogenous shocks and their mediation through institutional structures. What the chapter shows is that there is a remarkable continuity in the basic concept of EMU. The concept implies a transfer of sovereignty in the area of monetary policy but not so in the area of budgetary and fiscal policies. The result is that the concept of EMU adopted by heads of state or government of member states is different from that conceptualized by economic theorists of the 1950s and 1960s who saw EMU as a next step in integration, and hence expected there to be more supranational governance in the area of budgetary and fiscal policies.

The actors that have been influential at the crossroads have typically been EU institutions (the Commission and the various EC economic and monetary committees). Yet when examining these important crossroads one finds that support is needed from heads of state or government of EU member states. At the times when EMU stalled it was often that government leaders were unwilling to make the next step in transfer of sovereignty. Yet the content of the proposals has been surprisingly coherent over time, particularly if one considers large changes in thought about economic and financial government over the fifty year period. The path dependence of the content of the Werner Plan and later the Delors Report is noteworthy.

The institutional context and exogenous shocks also played a crucial role. At each of the crossroads these two factors were an important determinant in whether EMU plans managed to come onto the agenda, and whether member states were willing to accept the next transfer in sovereignty. Without listing them all again, major changes in the institutional context and exogenous shocks affected what Community institutions and member state leaders perceived as being the main problem and what a solution to the problem might be. The type of EMU chosen at each of the crossroads reflected the concept of EMU, the actors pushing for it, the institutional context and any exogenous shocks.

Today's problems with EMU can be traced back to the fundamental ambivalence among EU leaders about what integration is all about and what the end goal is. They have accepted the transfer of monetary sovereignty to the EU level. They see the use of it, and realize that the mileage a government can get out of having its own independent monetary policy is limited. However, the step to a more supranational budgetary and fiscal policy signals that next important step toward further federalization. It is a step that not many governments feel comfortable taking. Without there being a serious problem that needs addressing (i.e. a problem which would require as a possible solution the transfer of sovereignty over budgetary and fiscal policies to an EU-level institution), member state governments have remained reluctant to transfer this sovereignty. In today's world this asymmetrical EMU (Verdun, 1996) (supranational monetary policy, national budgetary and fiscal policies) seems still to offer an acceptable half-way house between national sovereignty and European supranational sovereignty over economic and monetary matters. As time goes by, one should be prepared to encounter another crossroads whereby EU institutions and EU member state leaders will find themselves once again reflecting on the road ahead. Perhaps when EMU is in serious jeopardy will the leaders consider transferring sovereignty over budgetary and fiscal policies to a supranational institution. For now it seems they are assuming they can live in this half-way house without too much difficulty.

III

Law and Society

12

The Constitutionalization of the European Union: Explaining the Parliamentarization and Institutionalization of Human Rights

BERTHOLD RITTBERGER AND
FRANK SCHIMMELFENNIG

When It All Began: Constitutionalization and the Treaties of Rome

Constitutionalization has become one of the buzzwords in the study of the EU. Past years have seen a constant increase of references to constitutionalization in the academic literature and in political commentary. In the EU literature, constitutionalization has traditionally been employed to denote the process of European legal integration which has led to a remarkable transformation of the EU replacing the traditional notion of a state-centered international organization with 'a vertically integrated legal regime conferring judicially enforceable rights and obligations on all legal persons and entities, public and private, within the sphere of application of EC law' (Haltern 2002: 2).[1] Hitherto, the political science and legal literatures have dedicated volumes to the question of constitutionalization *qua* legal integration by taking recourse to and refining theories of European integration, most notably intergovernmentalism and supranationalism/neofunctionalism (see e.g. Garrett 1995 vs. Burley and Mattli 1993; Stone Sweet 2000). However, constitutionalization is more than legal integration. The constitutions of liberal democratic polities encompass a set of core principles such as fundamental rights, the separation of powers, and democracy. From this perspective, the constitutionalization of the EU relates to all those processes through which these core principles are becoming embedded in the EU's legal order. This chapter analyzes precisely two constitutionalization processes: the development of a representative parliamentary institution and the codification of fundamental rights at the EU level.

Looking back half a century, the Treaties of Rome featured little with regard to parliamentary powers or human rights provisions. The embryonic EP's first and foremost role was still—akin to the Treaty of the ECSC—the supervision of the

---

[1] See e.g. the pioneering works by Stein (1981) and Weiler (1981).

Communities' supranational 'executive': the Commission. After the double failure of the European Defense Community and the European Political Community in the mid-1950s and their respective attempts to promote constitutionalization, strong supranational or federal-style institutions were all but *en vogue* by the time the Treaties of Rome were negotiated. Against this background, the six founding states of the EEC and Euratom endowed the EP merely with a supervisory role vis-à-vis the Commission and refused to grant the assembly budgetary or legislative competencies. Regarding the former, it was not until the Treaty of Luxembourg in 1970 that the EP was assigned more than a consultative role in the budgetary procedure. Concerning its legislative function, the Treaties of Rome envisaged a consultation procedure which obliged the member states to consult the EP in certain policy areas, yet it took another thirty years—until the adoption of the SEA— until the so-called 'cooperation procedure' provided the EP with 'real' legislative powers. How about the institutionalization of human rights? The Treaties of Rome did not contain any general human rights provisions—let alone a 'bill of human rights'—nor did they accord the supranational organs any competencies in this area. It was through the ECJ that fundamental rights were evoked in its jurisprudence since the late sixties (Stone Sweet 2000). The recent past has seen the codification of fundamental rights in the Charter of Fundamental Rights and, most recently, in the Treaty establishing a Constitution for Europe.

Fifty years after the signing of the Treaties of Rome, both processes of constitutionalization—parliamentarization and the institutionalization of human rights—have thus progressed remarkably. Today, the EP has 'significant legislative and executive investiture or removal powers and all the trappings of a democratic parliament' (Hix, Raunio, and Scully 2003: 191–2). Furthermore, human rights are firmly embedded in the EU's legal order. Existing theories of International Relations, such as rational choice institutionalism and sociological institutionalism, have failed to offer explanations for these two striking developments (see Rittberger 2005; Rittberger and Schimmelfennig 2006). In the ensuing sections, we present our theory and hypotheses to explain these constitutionalization processes. We then demonstrate the plausibility of our theory by offering a set of illustrations from the empowerment of the EP and the institutionalization of human rights (see Rittberger and Schimmelfennig 2006 for a more complete and detailed analysis).

Liberal Community, Rhetorical Action, and Normative Spillover

Neofunctionalist Expectations

In spite of the scant or almost invisible powers of the embryonic EP as well as the nonexistent human rights provisions in the Treaties of Rome, neofunctionalism offered a possible explanation as to how constitutionalization could progress. Neofunctionalists, most notably Ernst Haas, pointed at the potential held by political elites in the new supranational institutions, such as the Commission's forerunner—the High Authority (HA) of the ECSC—or the political parties in the Common Assembly to promote the European integration project by triggering political spillover processes. Haas argued that the new supranational political elites possessed the ability to persuade national political elites 'to shift their loyalties, expectations and political activities' (1958: 16) toward the new central institutions: 'If permitted to operate for any length of time, the national groups now compelled to funnel their aspirations through federal institutions may also be constrained to work within the ideological framework of those organs.' (1958: 19). For Haas, the political parties in the Common Assembly carried the potential to become 'crucial carriers of political integration' (1958: 437; see also Scalingi 1980). Given their sense of intraparty discipline and the prior commitment of most parliamentarians to further political integration, the perspectives and expectations of the vast majority of the Assembly's members would 'outgrow the boundaries of the national state as the referents of legislative action' (Haas 1958: 438). In due course, Haas expected the main impetus of the Common Assembly for political integration to consist in the promotion of 'political spillover', the process whereby formerly national actors form transnational coalitions to generate new problem-solving perspectives which may even result in a shift of loyalties toward the new center.

According to neofunctionalism, supranational constitutionalization would thus be explained as the result of political spillover of functional integration. The socialization of individuals acting in the new supranational organizations, the increasing political activities of the Community, and its supposedly superior problem-solving capacity would induce elites to shift their political loyalties away from the nation-state and increasingly to provide the new center with the characteristics of constitutional statehood. Following Schmitter's politicization hypothesis, one might also imagine this process as a conflictive one (1969: 166). As the functional scope of European policies and the centralization of decision-making increase, supranational integration would become more controversial and involve interest groups and parties opposing each other on European issues. Politicization would in turn result in a more assertive stance of the EP and in an increase of its power, and it would generate demands for the protection of human rights at the European level.

As we know today, these expectations did not match with the realities of the integration process for decades to come. Empirical tests of the expectation of significant socialization proved disappointing (Pollack 1998). Whereas studies on actor socialization generally found evidence of cognitive change—individuals involved in integrated decision-making structures and processes became more interested in and knowledgeable about international organizations—they detected little in the way of positive affective change, especially if factors like self-selection, national and party affiliation had been controlled for. Recent studies of socialization in EU organizations also come to skeptical conclusions in this regard (Beyers 2005; Hooghe 2005; Scully 2005). Whereas the adoption of and support for supranational norms may indeed be strong, this cannot be explained by supranational socialization but is conditioned by domestic factors. What is more, EU-related identities and constitutional ideas of member state governments and parties are not only rooted in divergent national traditions but have also changed little over the course of European integration and continue to shape their constitutional preferences to this day (see Marcussen et al. 1999; Jachtenfuchs 2002; Scholl 2005).

Finally, the historical record contradicts the expectation of constitutionalization as a result of politicization. The main steps toward the increase of parliamentary powers and the institutionalization of human rights have been undertaken in the absence of public debate, societal mobilization, and interest group pressure. There was conflict, indeed, but it was largely confined to governments interacting at intergovernmental conferences and organizations such as the ECJ and national constitutional courts.

We therefore present an alternative explanation. While our explanation also draws on the basic neofunctionalist mechanism of spillover, it theorizes the process in a different way. In a nutshell, we argue that functional supra-national integration has regularly undermined existing democratic and human rights institutions at the national level and thereby created a democratic legit-imacy deficit of European integration. This legitimacy deficit triggered argu-ments, in which interested or committed actors drew on the shared liberal-democratic community norms in order to create normative pressure in favor of the constitutionalization of the EU. We propose to term this process 'normative spillover'.

Rhetorical Action in a Liberal International Community

Any theoretical solution to the puzzle of EU constitutionalization needs to explain why and how the EU has made progress toward parliamentarization and the institutionalization of human rights in spite of stable divergent member state attitudes and in the absence of socialization effects conducive to constitutional-ization. The solution we propose is 'strategic action in a community environment' (Schimmelfennig 2003*b*: 159–63).

Like neofunctionalism (and liberal intergovernmentalism) we start from the assumption that supranational integration begins with functional integration in areas of high interdependence and common interests. It is designed as an instru-ment to solve common problems and to realize gains from international cooper-ation. Supranational organizations are established to help governments maximize these gains, reduce the transaction costs of international negotiations, and prevent them from defecting from cooperative agreements.

In addition, however, European integration is embedded in an international community. A community is most fundamentally based on a common ethos. The ethos refers to the constitutive values and norms that define the collective identity of the community—who 'we' are, what 'we' stand for, and how 'we' differ from other communities. From the beginning, the member states of the European Communities have been part of the Western international community. The members of this community share a commitment to fundamental liberal-democratic values and norms: respect for individual liberties and civil rights, the rule of law, democracy, private property, and a market-based economy.

Such a community environment affects interaction and collective outcomes in the following ways:

1. It triggers arguments about the legitimacy of preferences and policies. Actors are able—and forced—to justify their preferences on the basis of the community ethos. They engage in 'rhetorical action', the strategic use of the community ethos. They choose ethos-based arguments to strengthen the legitimacy of their own goals against the claims and arguments of their opponents.
2. The community ethos is both a source of support and a constraint that imposes costs on illegitimate actions. It adds legitimacy to and thus strengthens the bargaining power of those actors that pursue goals in line with the community ethos.
3. Community actors are concerned about their image. Their image does not only depend on how they are perceived to conform to the community ethos but also on whether they are perceived to argue credibly. Credibility is the single most important resource in arguing and depends on both impartiality and consistency (Elster 1992: 18–19). If inconsistency and partiality are publicly exposed, and actors are caught using the ethos opportunistically, their credibility suffers. Thus, community members who diverge from the community ethos can be shamed into conformity with the community's fundamental norms and their prior argumentative commitments by supporters of further constitutionalization—even if these contradict their current policy preferences.

These theoretical ideas imply that the outcomes of functional integration will regularly come under normative scrutiny with regard to the community ethos. If functional integration undermines liberal-democratic standards such as parliamentary power and human rights protection, a legitimacy deficit arises. Under this condition, actors interested in changing the distribution of power or committed to democratic and human rights norms are able to draw on the liberal-democratic norms of the community to argue in favor of constitutionalization and to put effective pressure on reticent community members to accommodate these normative concerns. Thus, even though parliamentarization and institutionalization of human rights at the EU level may not be functionally required or 'useful', and may not reflect the interest of the dominant community actors, their collective identity as democratic states and governments and as members of a liberal international community obliges them in principle to conform to basic norms of liberal democracy.

These community effects vary according to several context conditions. Salience is an essential condition (see Rittberger 2005). Constitutionalization becomes salient if a proposed or implemented step of functional integration is perceived to curb the competencies of national parliaments and to undermine national or other international human rights provisions. As we have shown elsewhere in a comparative study of EU constitutional decisions, salience reliably triggers demands for constitutional change and, with a few exceptions, it has reliably resulted in a progress of constitutionalization as well. By contrast, without salience, demands for the strengthening of the EP or EU human rights protection have either been absent or unsuccessful (Schimmelfennig et al. 2006).

In addition, coherence is a helpful condition. Coherence denotes that demands based on precedent exert an additional compliance pull. We distinguish between two types of coherence, internal and external. Internal coherence refers to earlier treaty provisions, common member state declarations, or informal practices, while external coherence—especially in the case of human rights—refers to the international codification of community norms elsewhere in the Western community. Historical institutionalism and supranationalist integration theory stress the role of institutional or legal precedent in systematically structuring future decisions thereby producing institutional path-dependencies (see Pierson 1998) or argumentation frameworks (Shapiro and Stone Sweet 2002: 113–35). Accordingly, coherence has proven more important in the more recent process of European integration than during its early phases (Schimmelfennig et al. 2006).

We speak of normative spillover in the sense that steps of functional supranational integration in the Community have regularly undermined national parliamentary competencies and the protection of human rights by either national institutions (constitutional courts) or international organizations (such as the Council of Europe), and the resulting legitimacy deficit has regularly triggered successful demands to enhance parliamentary competencies and human rights protection at the EU level. This normative spillover, however, has not been the result of elite socialization at the top or political mobilization from below, but of normative argument among member state governments and organizations of the EU multilevel system. To illustrate these processes in detail, we will now turn to two cases of constitutionalization.

Extending the Legislative Powers of the EP

Under the so-called consultation procedure which was introduced in 1957 with the Treaty establishing the EEC, the EP merely played a consultative role in the legislative decision-making process which was dominated by member state governments in the Council of Ministers who decided upon a Commission proposal. Even though the application of QMV in the Council was envisaged after a transition period following the entry into force of the Rome Treaties, the 'empty chair crisis' and the subsequent 'Luxembourg Compromise' stalled the de facto application of QMV for a long time to come. This also had a sustained effect on the legislative powers of the EP. It took until the signing of the SEA for the so-called 'cooperation procedure' to be adopted which, in turn, led to a remarkable increase in the powers of the EP, making it more difficult for the Council to overturn parliamentary amendments than to accept them (see Tsebelis 1994). How can we explain this increase in the legislative powers of the EP?

The introduction of QMV in the Council and its application to virtually all matters relating to the creation of an internal market was one of the quintessential features of the SEA. All national governments came to the conclusion that this large extent of pooling sovereignty was acceptable or even desirable given the objective to pass almost 300 pieces of Community legislation until the end of 1992, the target date for the completion of the internal market. In the run up to the IGC and during the negotiations, several member state governments responded to the introduction of QMV by voicing concerns about the increasing marginalization of national parliaments in their capacity to exercise control and influence over EU decision-making. With the introduction of QMV, so our argument goes, evermore policy decisions would be taken at the EU level through bypassing national parliaments, thereby triggering a democratic legitimacy deficit. At the same time, the member-state governments were well aware of the possibility that the legislative empowerment of the EP—in order to compensate for this legitimacy deficit—would run to the detriment of their own decision-making influence in the Council. Not only the British and French governments but also the German government were not enthused by this prospect. Yet, even though the governments of the 'Big Three' were privately not committed to push strongly for the legislative empowerment of the EP, the proconstitutionalization camp, represented most notably by small member states—such as the Netherlands—or medium-sized ones—such as Italy, prevailed.

Many national governments, members of national parliaments, and European parliamentarians have, throughout the 1980s, consistently complained that the Community suffered from a 'democratic deficit' (see Corbett 1998). However, it was the potential impact of the introduction of QMV and the ensuing prospect for a reform of the EEC Treaty, which made the prospect of an empowerment of the EP in the legislative domain increasingly likely. There is ample evidence that political elites perceived parliamentarization to be salient. For example, at the European Council summit meeting in Fontainebleau in June 1984, an *Ad Hoc Committee* composed of personalities appointed by the governments of the member states was created to discuss the pressing issues of deeper cooperation and institutional reform (the so-called 'Dooge Committee'). In its final report to the Brussels European Council in late March 1985, the Dooge Committee advocated, *inter alia*, the creation of a 'fully integrated internal market' and simultaneous institutional reform in order to achieve the policy goals set out by the report. A plea was made for the provision of more 'efficient' but also more 'democratic' institutions. A majority of member state representatives wanted the EP to play a more prominent role in the Community legislative process once the member states opted for QMV.[2]

Parliamentary debates and resolutions in many of the national parliaments equally reflected the awareness that the introduction of QMV would exacerbate the democratic legitimacy deficit.[3] In France, for example, Charles Josselin, a Socialist MP said before the Assemblée Nationale that 'the process embarked upon will lead ... to a considerable reduction of the competences of national parliaments in almost all domains',[4] and in a similar vein, the center-right politician Adrien Zeller emphasized that 'the only means to re-establish democratic control of such decisions [which evade national parliamentary control] is to endow the EP with the means not just to *influence* Community decisions but also to *legitimize* them by its votes.'[5] In Germany, the governing Christian Democrats (CDU/CSU) and Liberals (FDP) as well as the opposition Social Democrats (SPD) were very explicit about the challenge the introduction of QMV posed for *procedural* legitimacy. For example, the chair of the EC Committee, Renate Hellwig (CDU), criticized the executive dominance of Community decision-making and concluded that to reduce the 'legitimacy deficit' the legislative powers of the EP had to be increased.[6]

The argumentative link which was established between the introduction of QMV and the demand to enhance the EP's legislative powers also informed subsequent Treaty reforms. Following the SEA, further rounds of integration produced extensions of the application of QMV to new policy areas. Proponents of parliamentarization thus employed the argument which linked the extension

[2] See *Agence Europe* (March 16, 1985). The report reflects a 'majority opinion' and reveals that the Danish, Greek and UK representatives entered reservations to the report, *inter alia* with respect to the democratization of Community decision-making.

[3] See Corbett (1998: 185–94) for an analysis of the debates in national parliaments prior to the SEA.

[4] Journal Officiel, Assemblée Nationale, debate of June 11, 1985: 1599–600 (author's translation).

[5] Journal Officiel, Assemblée Nationale, debate of June 11, 1985: 1613 (author's translation, emphasis added).

[6] Deutscher Bundestag, debate of June 27, 1985: 11111.

of QMV to parliamentary powers as precedent (*internal coherence*). This simple formula became a guiding principle for future instances of Treaty reform since the extension of QMV to new policy areas was always an issue which was placed on the agendas of subsequent intergovernmental conferences. In the period preceding the adoption of the Maastricht Treaty, government representatives and major political parties voiced the demand that any further extension of QMV must be accompanied by granting the EP legislative powers (see e.g. Corbett 1992; Rittberger 2005). Following Maastricht, the intergovernmental conferences leading to the adoption of the Amsterdam and Nice treaties also invoked the 'Council QMV equals EP participation'-formula. During the Amsterdam inter-governmental conference, the Benelux governments issued a memorandum in which they explicitly acknowledged the link between the application of QMV and legislative codecision for the EP (see European Parliament 1996: 20). Similarly, a Spanish government document foresaw that 'there will be considerable scope for progress through an extension of the field of application of the codecision procedure; this concept should . . . logically be viewed in close relation to majority decision-making' (European Parliament 1996: 47). During the Nice intergovern-mental conference, the question of parliamentary involvement in QMV-based legislative decision-making procedures (codecision) was a lesser concern. The Treaty provided for six new cases of codecision. Yet, among the new cases under QMV, three legislative ones remained outside the codecision procedure: financial regulations, internal measures for the implementation of cooperation agreements, as well as the Structural Funds and the Cohesion Fund. Since some member states consider these policies to be particularly 'sensitive' on account of their major budgetary implications, the call for codecision in these areas was resisted, and the EP bemoaned that 'in refusing even to consider switching matters already subject to QMV to the codecision procedure, the [intergovernmental conference] was rejecting a basic institutional principle on which significant progress had been made at Amsterdam: as a general rule, codecision should accompany QMV in matters of a legislative nature' (European Parliament 2001: 28). Following the European Council meeting at Laeken and the establishment of the European Convention, a working group on 'Simplification' was instituted facing the twin objectives of making the European system of governance more transparent and more comprehensible.[7] The report issued by the working group stipulated that the legislative codecision procedure should 'become the general rule for the adoption of legislative acts'.[8] The Draft Treaty establishing a Constitution for Europe (DTC) and the ensuing intergovernmental conference which resulted in the sign-ing of the Treaty establishing a Constitution for Europe (TCE) implemented the working group's recommendation: Article I-34(1) TCE stipulates that what was

[7] See European Convention, CONV 424/02.
[8] See European Convention, CONV 424/02: 15.

hitherto known as the codecision procedure becomes the 'ordinary legislative procedure'. The logic inherent in the 'Council QMV equals EP participation'- formula had thus not only gained broad acceptance in the post-SEA era. Some commentators have even gone so far as to label this formula a *technical* formula. This label strips the formula of its potential political and normative character and gives credence to the interpretation that the link between Council decision- making by QMV and legislative participation by the EP is a 'natural' one and hence not (or not any more) politically or normatively contested (see Norman 2003: 102).

We have shown in the previous paragraphs that political actors supporting further constitutionalization have made ample use of salience- and coherence- based arguments. Were these arguments effective in making recalcitrant political actors comply with proposals to further constitutionalization? One central indica- tor for the normative strength of the salience argument is the fact that none of the governments openly launched an argumentative attack against the participation of the EP in the legislative process. Arguments that appealed to political self-interest ('keeping the power in the Council') were not voiced publicly.

The only argument that was presented to fend off attempts to endow the EP with legislative powers pointed to the potential efficiency-harming effects of legislative empowering. Since all governments had subscribed to create the internal market by improving and speeding up Community decision-making through the use of QMV, it was evident to all that a more influential Parliament would certainly not improve the efficiency of the legislative decision-making process. The fiercest opponents of constitutionalization, the British and Danish governments, had pur- sued a line of argumentation stressing that the main criterion for institutional reform was the *efficiency* of any new decision-making procedure[9] and insisted that an increase of the legislative powers of the EP would run the risk of com- plicating or even paralyzing the legislative decision-making process and would thus counteract the overarching objective of creating the internal market (De Ruyt 1989: 75).

This line of reasoning, however, left a door open to the proconstitutionalization camp or 'creative maximalist draughtsmen' (Budden 1994: 327). As long as the recalcitrant member state governments could be presented with a proposal that did not compound the efficiency of the new decision-making procedure and assured that the member states kept the 'last word', proposals to empower the EP would have a chance of success. Under pressure from domestic MPs and MEPs, a German proposal which foresaw a conciliation committee between Council and EP[10] was hailed by opponents of constitutionalization to fail the 'efficiency test' and was scrapped quickly. However, as Budden (1994: 333) put it, the British government's strategy to play the efficiency card 'left the Government potentially

---

[9] *Agence Europe*, June 19, 1985.			[10] *Agence Europe*, September 27, 1985.

exposed to discovery of a ... procedure which met the [efficiency] criterion'. And so it came. 'The introduction of a Council "common position" and second EP reading marked a breakthrough ... Drawing on French ideas to link the Council's decision-making rule to the EP's vote, the Presidency introduced a formal procedure offering considerable influence to the EP, while protecting ... Council prerogatives' (Budden 1994: 338).

Having fallen into the efficiency rhetoric trap, the British delegation lived grudgingly with the proposal of the so-called cooperation procedure which effectively gave the EP a substantial role in the legislative process: At second reading stage, Parliament could pass amendments which (if accepted by the Commission) could be adopted by the member state governments by QMV (but amended only by unanimity). In the interstate arena, the British government was thus effectively silenced and refrained from advancing new proposals to counteract parliamentary involvement. To the domestic audience, the British government attempted to sell the cooperation procedure as being both power-neutral as well as efficiency-neutral, claiming that the Council kept the 'last word'. In his address to the House of Commons, Foreign and Commonwealth Secretary Geoffrey Howe— deliberately or unknowingly—misrepresented the implications of the new co-operation procedure for the Council's capacity to affect legislative outcomes. He claimed that 'the [European] Parliament can in certain circumstances change the Council's voting provisions back from qualified majority to unanimity. In no circumstances can it change them the other way'.[11] Howe thus talked into existence a 'protective' mechanism for the member states which, in fact, did not exist. The exact opposite was the case. Unanimity, as employed by Howe, meant that the Council could only *reject* or *change* amendments tabled by the EP unanimously, whereas the Council 'only' needed QMV to *accept* them. This 'illusion' of unanimity thus worked to the detriment of the Council and not to its advantage. And it was a crucial step to a parliamentary Europe.

The Institutionalization of Human Rights[12]

The initial steps of institutionalizing human rights in the Community were taken by the ECJ in its case law from the late 1960s onward. It was only in the Preamble of the SEA of 1986 that human rights featured in an intergovernmental treaty of the Community for the first time and in a purely declaratory manner.

The ECJ did not start as a champion of European-level human rights protection. In its *Stork* judgment (1959), the Court refused explicitly to 'rule on provisions of national law' and maintained that the HA was 'not empowered to examine

---

[11] Hansard, House of Commons, (April 23, 1986): 322.
[12] This section draws on Schimmelfennig (2006).

a ground of complaint which maintains that, when it adopted its decision, it infringed principles of national constitutional law'.[13] In the *Geitling* case (1960), it reiterated that 'it is not the function of the Court to ensure respect for national law in force in a member state, and this is true even of constitutional laws'.[14] The ECJ only changed its stance in its *Stauder* and *Internationale Handelsgesellschaft* decisions when its claim for the supremacy of Community law was challenged by German courts.

In its two landmark decisions *Van Gend en Loos* (1963) and *Costa* (1964), the ECJ had claimed the direct effect and supremacy of EC law. According to the ECJ, the EC would not be able to attain its central goal of creating a common market otherwise. The claim for supremacy was thus clearly based on *efficiency*. Supremacy not only applied to ordinary domestic law but also to national constitutional law and the individual rights and freedoms protected under it. National constitutional review was effectively suspended for issues regulated by EC law. At the same time, there was no EC system of human rights protection. As a result, direct effect and supremacy threatened to reduce the level of human rights protection in the Community (*salience*). This legitimacy gap could be used by national courts to challenge the supremacy of EC law and ECJ jurisdiction.

This challenge came in the *Stauder* case, when the Stuttgart Administrative Court asked the ECJ about the compatibility 'with the general principles of community law in force' of a decision by the European Commission that required recipients of surplus butter under welfare schemes to reveal their identity to the seller. In its judgment of November 12, 1969, the ECJ offered a liberal interpretation of the Commission decision and concluded that 'interpreted in this way the provision at issue contains nothing capable of prejudicing the fundamental human rights enshrined in the general principles of community law and protected by the Court'.[15] In other words, the ECJ used this preliminary ruling to assert two things: that human rights were indeed, however implicitly, part of the EC legal system and that they were judicially protected within this system. *Stauder* thus marked the Court's first attempt to establish itself as a rights-protecting constitutional court on par with national constitutional courts. It thereby sought to counter the salience arguments of national courts, protect the autonomy of the Community legal system, and add legitimacy to the efficiency-based justification for the supremacy of EC law.

In subsequent judgments, the ECJ pursued this argumentative strategy further and refined the doctrine. The *Internationale Handelsgesellschaft* case had its roots in another referral to the ECJ by a German administrative court. The *Verwaltungsgericht* Frankfurt argued the case for salience much more strongly than the

[13] ECJ, *Stork v. High Authority*, Case 1/58.
[14] ECJ, *Präsident, Geitling, Mausegatt, and Nold v. High Authority*, Joined Cases 36–38/59 and 40/59.
[15] ECJ, *Stauder v. City of Ulm*, Case 29/69.

Stuttgart court by putting forward that EC provisions were 'contrary to certain structural principles of national constitutional law which must be protected within the framework of community law, with the result that the primacy of supranational law must yield before the principles of the German Basic Law'.[16]

In its decision of December 17, 1970, the Court conceded that such community measures needed to be subject to constitutional human rights review in principle (thus paying tribute to the community's standard of legitimacy). However, it rejected the argument for national constitutional review and insisted that this review must be conducted within the legal system of the Community:

[A]n examination should be made as to whether or not any analogous guarantee inherent in community law has been disregarded. In fact, respect for fundamental rights forms an integral part of the general principles of law protected by the Court of Justice. The protection of such rights, whilst inspired by the constitutional traditions common to the member states, must be ensured within the framework of the structure and objectives of the community.[17]

In this ruling, for the first time, the ECJ introduced the 'constitutional traditions common to the member states', a general *resonance* argument, as a second legal basis besides the 'general principles of community law' invoked in *Stauder*. This was another attempt by the ECJ to silence national courts by showing that it used their standards of human rights protection and that there was no salient human rights deficit. At the same time, the ECJ was cautious enough not to tie itself formally to any national human rights catalog or system of human rights protection. It only declared to be '*inspired* by the constitutional *traditions*'. This wording allowed the ECJ to remain autonomous in its interpretation and application of national constitutional rules and rights.

The Frankfurt administrative court did not accept this preliminary ruling and referred the case to the German Federal Constitutional Court (FCC). In the meantime, the ECJ added another 'source of inspiration' to its human rights jurisdiction in its *Nold* decision (1974). The Nold company asserted that trading rules authorized by the Commission constituted an infringement of its fundamental right to property 'as well as its right to the free pursuit of business activity, as protected by the Grundgesetz of the Federal Republic of Germany and by the constitutions of the other member states and various international treaties', including the European Convention on Human Rights (ECHR).[18] The ECJ countered this move by including 'international treaties for the protection of human rights' among the 'guidelines' which it would follow 'within the framework of community law,'[19] thereby establishing *external coherence* for its human rights

---

[16] ECJ, *Internationale Handelsgesellschaft* v. *Einfuhr- und Vorratsstelle für Getreide- und Futtermittel*, Case 11/70.
[17] Ibid.   [18] ECJ, *Nold* v. *Commission*, Case 4/73.
[19] Ibid.

protection. The general strategy of the ECJ was to argue that all human rights otherwise observed by the member states and enforced by national and international systems of human rights protection would also be protected in the EC legal system.

For the time being, however, the FCC did not accept this conclusion. Two weeks after *Nold*, on May 29, 1974, it issued its ruling on the referral of the *Internationale Handelsgesellschaft* case by the Frankfurt administrative court. Although it found no violation of German constitutional rights in this particular case, it used the occasion to make the general statement that, 'as long as the integration process has not progressed so far that Community law also contains an explicit catalog of fundamental rights, passed by a Parliament, valid and equivalent to the catalog of fundamental rights of the Basic Law', national courts would have the right and, indeed, the obligation to refer the case to the FCC for constitutional review if they deemed the preliminary ruling of the ECJ to collide with fundamental rights as protected by the Basic Law.[20] The FCC rejected the 'supremacy' of EC law as a general principle and limited the direct effect of EC law to those provisions that did not encroach upon essential elements of constitutional structure—in particular the Basic Law's catalog of fundamental rights.

Yet the FCC's claim of supremacy for national constitutional rights and review was conditional, not categorical. Its reservations were based on the provisional state of the integration process at the time. In the opinion of the FCC, the 'admittedly rights-friendly jurisdiction' of the ECJ was insufficient but an institutionalization of human rights and democracy similar to that at the national level would eliminate the Court's reservations. The FCC thus remained within the ethos-based argumentative framework and its decision effectively transformed the competition for supremacy into a competition for the legalization of human rights. This gave the supranational institutionalization of human rights further impetus. It was clear that if the Community was to strengthen the status of its legal order, it would have to progress further toward the institutionalization of human rights.

First of all, the ECJ persisted on its path of defending the supremacy of Community law. Its judgments neither referred to the FCC's decision directly, nor did they change in its aftermath. Starting with *Nold*, the ECJ also made increasingly detailed use of the European Convention to imbue its case law with legitimacy. In the absence of any internal EC norms it could draw upon, it had to opt for external coherence. External coherence with the ECHR had two strategic advantages for the ECJ. First, it was a single human rights catalog that was signed and ratified by all member states of the EC.[21] It was thus not only highly legitimate but also easier to use than the constitutional traditions of the member states, which required

---

[20] *Bundesverfassungsgericht, Solange I*, BVerfGE 37, 271, author's translation.
[21] France was the last member state to ratify the Convention in May 1974.

a comparative analysis of national constitutional provisions. In addition, it was beyond the purview of national constitutional courts. However, the Court could not do anything on its own to meet the other thresholds of legitimacy claimed by the FCC in 1974. For that, it required the assistance of other Community actors.

On April 5, 1977, the EP, the Council, and the Commission published a joint declaration 'concerning the protection of fundamental rights', in which they 'stress the prime importance they attach to the protection of fundamental rights, as derived in particular from the constitutions of the member states and the European Convention for the Protection of Human Rights and Fundamental Freedoms' and vowed to respect these rights 'in the exercise of their power and in pursuance of the aims of the European Communities'. In the preamble to this declaration, the three Community organs explicitly mentioned the Court's recognition that the law of the Community 'comprises, over and above the rules embodied in the treaties and secondary Community legislation, the general principles of law and in particular the fundamental rights, principles and rights on which the constitutional law of the Member States is based'.[22] In their 1978 'Declaration on Democracy', the heads of state and government joined in the European Council aligned themselves with the interinstitutional declaration. In the preamble to the SEA, the member states then proclaimed their determination 'to work together to promote democracy on the basis of the fundamental rights recognized in the constitutions and laws of the member states, in the Convention for the Protection of Human Rights and Fundamental Freedoms and the European Social Charter, notably freedom, equality and social justice'.[23] The transfer of case law to treaty law via political declarations added further legitimacy to the ECJ's rulings.

How did the FCC react to these developments? In its *Solange II* decision of October 22, 1986, the FCC ruled that 'as long as the European Communities, in particular the jurisdiction of the Court of Justice of the Communities, generally guarantee an effective protection of fundamental rights ... which is equivalent in principle to the protection of fundamental rights required as indispensable by the Basic Law ... the Federal Constitutional Court will cease to exercise its jurisdiction on the applicability of secondary Community law ... and to review the compatibility of this law with the fundamental rights of the Basic Law'.[24] This decision was still far from an unconditional acceptance of the ECJ's supremacy but, for all practical purposes, the FCC gave up its claim that ECJ decisions needed to be reviewed for their compatibility with the national constitution.

In the explanation of its decision, the FCC accepted the ECJ's functional, efficiency-based reasoning that, for the common market to work, the ECJ's interpretation of Community law had to be binding for national law and national

---

[22] Official Journal C103, April 27, 1977.   [23] Official Journal L169, June 29, 1987.
[24] *Bundesverfassungsgericht, Solange II*, BVerfGE 73, 339, author's translation.

courts. However, it reiterated its position that Community law must not undermine the constitutive structures of the national constitutional order including
the fundamental rights it guarantees. Yet in contrast with its 1974 decision, it
came to the conclusion that 'in the meantime, there has emerged a degree of
fundamental rights protection in the jurisdiction of the European Communities
that is, in principle, equivalent to the fundamental rights standard of the Basic Law
with regard to its conception, content, and effectiveness'. According to the FCC,
'all major organs of the Community . . . have committed themselves in a legally
relevant way to the respect for human rights in the exercise of their competences
and in the pursuit of the goals of the Community'. In addition to a detailed
analysis of the ECJ's jurisdiction over the past fifteen years, the Court referred to
the 1977 and 1978 declarations as evidence. There were 'no relevant indications
that the achieved Community standard of fundamental rights was not sufficiently
consolidated or of merely provisional nature'.[25]

The interaction can be plausibly reconstructed as the competition of two courts
claiming adequate (ECJ) and inadequate (FCC) human rights protection in the
EC in order to support their respective claims of supremacy. Whereas the ECJ
was entrapped in its human rights rhetoric by the need to legitimate its claim for
supremacy, the FCC was entrapped to accept ECJ supremacy once human rights
had been institutionalized in the EC. Without the rights-based challenge of the
German administrative and constitutional courts, the ECJ would not have been
pressed to introduce, and increasingly strengthen its commitment to, human rights
review.

Implications for European Integration Theory: Constitutionalization and Normative Spillover

Our case studies provide evidence that constitutionalization progresses through
a novel type of spillover mechanism: normative spillover. Normative spillover
arises when steps of functional supranational integration undermine the fundamental liberal-democratic norms of the Western international community, and
when the resulting legitimacy deficit triggers demands to redress the situation.
These demands generate a process of arguing, in which committed or interested
actors draw on the community ethos to make the case for constitutionalization
and put normative pressure on their reticent opponents. As a consequence of
normative spillover, parliamentary competencies and human rights protection at
the EU level have thus been regularly enhanced. We have also argued and shown
that normative spillover works neither top-down (as a result of elite socialization
at the top) nor bottom-up (as a result of political mobilization from below), but

---

[25] Ibid.

through the exchange of normative arguments among member state governments and organizations of the EU multilevel system.

Over time, the effects of normative spillover on constitutionalization are likely to be enhanced as a result of the increasing normative force of precedent-based arguments. The Historical Institutionalists (HIs) stress the role of institutional or legal precedent in systematically structuring future constitutional decisions thereby producing institutional path dependencies or argumentation frameworks. As a result, coherence adds force to normative spillover in the more recent process of European integration.

Has EU constitutionalization reached equilibrium? According to our analysis, this would be the case if the EU's legitimacy gap was closed. Then, salience would disappear and the normative spillover mechanism would cease to operate. With regard to the cases we analyzed in this chapter, this might indeed happen if a European constitution made codecision the general rule, included a binding human rights catalog, and provided for the accession of the EC to the ECHR. However, the Constitutional Treaty, which would have gone a large step in that direction, has been rejected. And if it had been adopted, it would probably not have marked the end-point in European integration. We thus expect that as long as functional European integration continues and the EU is invested with new competencies, it will create new legitimacy gaps and new normative spillover.

13

The Evolution of EU Citizenship[1]

WILLEM MAAS

Introduction

Although the formal category of EU citizenship was introduced with the Maastricht Treaty (1993), the extent to which the term reflects reality is unclear. In its most common definition, citizenship is composed of rights, which usually evolve through a process of contestation among individuals, groups, and institutions, shaped by and in turn transforming the political culture. European citizenship emerged out of a series of critical political junctures that span the entire history of European integration, coupled with an ongoing institutional and political commitment to safeguarding and promoting the development of European rights. Initially, the freer trade of the 1950s and 1960s created demands for freer movement of labor. Political commitment transformed this demand for mobile labor into individual mobility rights for workers. This altered the political environment and produced pressures to extend the scope and expand the content of those rights. Because of continued political commitment on the part of national political leaders, supported by the supranational institutions they or their predecessors had created, this process of extension and expansion of rights resulted in a common European citizenship in the Maastricht Treaty. But as long as the resulting supranational citizenship continues to be based on a political bargain among member states rather than deep popular support, the process that created the supranational citizenship and the rights that comprise it are not irreversible. EU citizenship thus remains contingent on sustained political support from the member states and their populations.

The development of EU citizenship differs from the evolution of citizenship in most nation-states in one key respect: Union citizenship emerged as a result of a series of bargains among leaders of putatively sovereign states, whereas

[1] This chapter condenses and extends arguments presented in more depth in Maas (2007), for which I gratefully acknowledge the support of a Social Sciences and Humanities Research Council of Canada doctoral fellowship and Federalism and the Federation supplement, the Mackenzie King Travelling Fellowship, and various sources at Yale University, Universiteit Leiden, University of Oxford, and the European Commission. I also thank Kate McNamara and Sophie Meunier for their useful suggestions.

citizenship in most states grew gradually as a result of popular pressure. Historical institutionalism illuminates this distinction because it highlights the contingent nature of European rights: the changing way in which the Council reached decisions, the evolving nature of Commission pressure, and the growing influence of the Parliament all impacted on the timing and nature of European rights. Furthermore, the case of citizenship illustrates well the crucial role of 'context and configurations' in explaining change. Quite simply, both the rights of EU citizenship and the measures selected to implement those rights reflect the particular circumstances at each stage of their development. Indeed, since EU citizenship—as distinct from the free movement provisions that are its most notable component and that, in the minds of EU citizens, represent what the EU means for them—remains largely a project of European elites, it is unclear how it will develop in the future. Is EU citizenship indeed a reflection of the genuine European political community that some early proponents envisioned, or will it remain a simple supplement to national citizenship—providing a thin veneer of common European rights over the thick national identities that underlie those rights? To what extent will the introduction of common European rights cause individual citizens to identify with the Union? What lessons does the evolution of EU citizenship provide for the development of supranational rights more generally? The next section considers the meaning of citizenship and outlines how EU citizenship fits with the general pattern of European integration. The bulk of the chapter then analyzes the political development of European citizenship, providing the historical background to the theoretical claims. The final section concludes.

The Meaning of Citizenship

Rights evolve through political contestation involving actors, institutions, and political culture. To make this claim is to distinguish legal rights from the natural or divine rights which long shaped European political thought about the relationship between individuals and political authority. Starting in the seventeenth century, political theorists rejected divine law as the source of rights, identifying states as the sole foundation of law, rights, and citizenship (Maas 2001). Along with sovereignty and exclusive territoriality, citizenship defines the modern state, and only states can confer citizenship (Sassen 2002). Yet EU citizenship is super-imposed onto populations that already possess national citizenships. Although historical comparisons are possible—such as the formation of federal states or the unification of Germany or Italy from formerly independent states—there are no other recent examples of citizenship aggregation at the supranational level: indeed there are many recent examples of citizenship *disaggregation*, such as the citizenships of the USSR, Czechoslovakia, and Yugoslavia. Even the reunification of Germany should be viewed not as the creation of a new political community but rather as the return to a previously existing one. (Indeed, the Federal Republic of Germany never recognized a separate East German citizenship and had declared in 1957 that East Germans should be considered FRG citizens under Community law.) In a crucial distinction, EU member states remain responsible for determining admission to citizenship, while for example Tuscany, Connecticut, or Bavaria long ago lost that power.

Sovereignty, citizenship, and nationalism tend to be connected phenomena (Giddens 1985), and modern nation-states are expected 'to incorporate their people as individual citizens, to educate and mobilize them around economic and social developmental goals, and to promote welfare through public programs and the expansion of citizenship rights' (McNeely 1995: 11). Scholars of nationalism have long argued that processes of state-building were linked with the rise of a national consciousness, for which easing restrictions on free movement within state territories was a critical prerequisite. Just as a key development in the EU is the reduction or elimination of internal boundaries, so too the removal of internal borders was a crucial condition for the successful rise of states a century or more earlier. One of the modern state's most notable functions is to facilitate the free movement of people within its boundaries, and the essence of full-fledged state citizenship, as distinct from earlier local citizenships, is its uniform applicability throughout the state's domain (Wiebe 2002).

EU citizenship significantly alters intergovernmental bargaining because new actors (European citizens) have been created who can invoke rights and act autonomously, thus changing the dynamic of the integration process and the nature of the resulting structure in ways not predicted by intergovernmentalist theory. Neofunctionalist explanations are also on unsteady ground because there is no self-evident market or functional need for European rights and because the development of European rights has not been a stable trend over time. In this light, some might argue that states are bound to be resolutely against any increase in European citizenship, because such a citizenship threatens to introduce supranational welfare rights, thereby putatively weakening the domestic legitimacy of the member states (Streeck 1995). Yet the political development of EU citizenship demonstrates that many government leaders have actively pursued European rights in ways contrary to both intergovernmentalist and neofunctionalist explanations. Rather, the process of EU citzenship's development lends itself to an interpretation emphasizing critical junctures (the bargains among member state leaders), without unintended consequences (leaders decide what European rights to introduce, and revise or renegotiate them when desired, or secure opt-outs such as the special provisions for Denmark after the failed Maastricht referendum). There is limited path dependence (because rights are more difficult to reverse than simple policies), some institutional interaction (the Parliament's increased power helps explain why the member states could afford to ignore its Draft Treaty establishing the European Union (DTEU) recommendations before the SEA but largely accepted them in before Maastricht), and perhaps limited feedback (mobile European citizens may play a role in pushing for greater rights, though the evidence for this is mixed). Though different member state citizenship traditions will continue to exist for the foreseeable future, the political development of EU citizenship is the best way to understand the evolution of European rights more generally: its growth mirrors the changing nature of the European political community (perhaps 'united in its diversity'—as the draft constitutional treaty proposes) superimposed on established national political communities that, however well-established they appear, also remain open to change and contestation.

Political Development of European Citizenship

The political development of European citizenship has been far from smooth or uniform. Rather, it has been marked by false starts, unexpected advances, and some setbacks as national leaders renegotiated the meaning of European rights. Nonetheless, we can frame the history in terms of six critical junctures that have decisively shaped the outcome of supranational citizenship rights today. Early on, the Treaty of Paris introduced free movement for coal and steel workers. Subsequently, the Treaty of Rome expanded this right to most workers and their families. The Community's first enlargement in 1973 counterbalanced the support for common citizenship in most of the original six member states to opposition from the new ones, particularly Denmark and the UK, delaying the further growth of European rights. The subsequent Mediterranean enlargements brought on board Greece, Spain, and Portugal—three states supportive of common citizenship, perhaps because they all had significant numbers of expatriates residing elsewhere in the EU. More recently, the Maastricht Treaty finally achieved what some had hoped for as early as the immediate postwar period, and the 2004 enlargement added so significantly to the Union's diversity that further development of EU citizenship appears unlikely in the short and medium terms. Below, these historical junctures are each explored in detail.

The first critical juncture for European citizenship was the Italian insistence that free movement of labor be included in the 1951 treaty establishing the ECSC, the Treaty of Paris. Free movement of workers was of minor importance in the ECSC negotiations, except for Italian negotiators: millions of Italians had for decades been emigrating to find work elsewhere in Europe, and the promise of free movement for workers was a key reason for Italian participation in the ECSC.[2] The negotiations proceeded with the Italians pushing for a better deal on migration by raising the specter of a HA (the future European Commission) authorized to set and enforce wage levels across the Community and the Dutch

---

[2] Maas (2005*a*) develops the arguments of this paragraph and the next.

and Germans determined to keep HA powers to an absolute minimum so that it could not overturn domestic political compromises. Since the Netherlands and Germany in the early 1950s were labor exporting countries, they too favored easing restrictions on worker mobility (Vignes 1956). Opposition might have come from the only potential member states with significant numbers of foreign coal workers: Belgium and France. There were over 70,000 foreign coal workers in Belgium, just under 57,000 in France, less than 4,000 each in the Netherlands and Germany, few in Luxembourg and almost none in Italy (ECSC 1953). In Belgium, two of every five coal workers were non-Belgian, primarily Italian. In France, one of every five coal workers was foreign, mostly Polish and thus unaffected by any potential ECSC treaty provisions. Bolstered by strong public support for the Schuman Plan, and intent on forging a deal, the French delegation led by Jean Monnet was willing to grant concessions. The Belgians were more concerned with the fate of their ailing coal and steel industries than the prospect of more worker immigration: if coal mines were to close, it seemed likely that foreign workers would return to their countries of origin (Dumoulin 1988; Milward 1988). The Italians succeeded in enshrining free movement rights for workers in the ECSC Treaty, which announced that 'Member States undertake to remove any restriction based on nationality upon the employment in the coal and steel industries of workers who are nationals of Member States and have recognized qualifications in a coalmining or steelmaking occupation, subject to the limitations imposed by the basic requirements of health and public policy.'

Sluggishness in implementing free movement proved a constant irritant to the Italians: most of the speeches by Italian members of the Common Assembly (the future Parliament) concerned the delay (Mason 1955). Indeed, the Common Assembly included the issue in its constitutional proposals concerning the Treaty of Rome negotiations: free movement was the *only* policy issue to appear in a document otherwise entirely about constitutional issues. Dissatisfied with the slow implementation of free movement, the Common Assembly wanted the HA to establish common definitions of skilled trades and qualifications, propose immigration rules, ensure that social security arrangements did not inhibit labor mobility, and address disparities between labor supply and demand (Kreyssig 1958).

The second critical juncture was the expansion of free movement to all workers and its enshrinement as an individual right in the 1957 treaty establishing the EEC, the Treaty of Rome. In contrast with the restrictiveness of the Treaty of Paris, the Treaty of Rome expanded the scope of free movement to all workers, with the exception of those employed in the public service. The Treaty of Rome gave workers the right to accept offers of employment, to move freely among the member states for this purpose, to reside in any member state if employed there, and to stay in any member state if formerly employed there. The difficult experience of enacting the ECSC provisions demonstrated the need to simplify decision-making about the EEC ones (Romero 1991; Maas 2005*a*). In a key difference with the ECSC Treaty, which had left the member states responsible for drafting and implementing free movement provisions, the EEC Treaty empowered the Commission to do so, and free movement for workers was fully achieved by 1968 (European Council 1968*a*, 1968*b*).

Walter Hallstein, the first president of the European Commission, called free movement for workers one of 'the most spectacular points in the program which is to lead to the integration of Europe'. He continued: 'On the basis of this success alone, the Community could claim the right to call itself the "European Economic and Social Community". The consequences in terms of constitutional policy are incalculable. Do they point to the beginning of a common European "citizenship"?' (Hallstein 1972: 173–4). Hallstein echoed his vice president, the Italian socialist Lionello Levi Sandri, who had earlier maintained that free movement of persons 'represents something more important and more exacting than the free movement of a factor of production. It represents rather an incipient form—still embryonic and imperfect—of European citizenship' (Levi Sandri 1968: 9).

The third critical juncture was the Community's first enlargement on January 1, 1973 as the six founding member states were joined by the UK, Ireland, and Denmark. At the first joint summit with the government leaders of the new member states, in October 1972, the Belgian and Italian prime ministers suggested granting all Community citizens the right to vote and be elected in local elections (European Commission 1975). Commission President Sicco Mansholt concurred, urging that 'checks at the Community's internal frontiers should be done away with, and nationals of Member States progressively integrated into the social, administrative and political fabric of their host countries, with the aim of gradually conferring upon them "European civic rights"' (*Bull. EC* 11-1972: 58–59). German Chancellor Willy Brandt observed at the summit that if 'we can put social policy into a European perspective, then many of our citizens will find it easier to identify themselves with the Community' (*Bull. EC* 11-1972: 30). Two years later, the member states established working groups to examine the conditions under which citizens of member states 'could be given special rights as members of the Community' and study 'the possibility of establishing a passport union' which would necessitate a 'stage-by-stage harmonization of legislation affecting aliens and for the abolition of passport control within the Community' (*Bull. EC* 12-1974: point 1104). The Italian delegation proposed to study 'under what conditions and according to what timetable European citizenship could be granted to the citizens of the nine Member States' (European Commission 1975: 28).

The Commission's 1975 report *Towards European Citizenship* examined the idea of a passport union and extending to citizens of other member states the right to vote and run for office, seen as 'the logical goal of the principle of national treatment and integration into the host country' (*Bull. EC* 7/8-1975: point 1303). It argued that 'complete assimilation with nationals as regards political rights is desirable in the long term from the point of view of a European Union' (European Commission 1975: 28). Another 1975 report, written by a committee chaired by Belgian Prime Minister Leo Tindemans, included a chapter on 'People's Europe', promoted the values of the European Social Charter—freedom, equality, and social justice—and argued that an 'unfinished structure does not weather well: it must be completed, otherwise it collapses' (Tindemans 1976). Since 'Europe must be close to its citizens', and since common European rights constituted a goal of a 'people's Europe', it was necessary to make continual progress toward common rights.

Meanwhile, the Commission proposed more policies for the protection of migrant workers, the Economic and Social Committee concluded that Europeans 'aspire to the abolition of frontiers', and Parliament issued a resolution supporting European citizenship (*Bull. EC* supplement 5/75: 21; *Bull. EC* supplement 9/75: 26). Germany favored gradually granting further rights, but the Council as a whole did not agree to grant citizens of other member states the right to vote in local elections.[3] In July 1979, the Commission finally published a draft Directive on a general right of residence for European citizens, proposing to abolish all remaining restrictions on movement and residence for nationals of member states, but specifying that member states might require citizens not covered by other legislation—anyone other than workers, the self-employed, and those who wished to stay after retirement—to 'provide proof of sufficient resources to provide for their own needs and the dependent members of their family' (European Commission 1979: 14).

Although Parliament supported the proposed Directive, the Council's positive attitude soured, due to the increased immigration of third country nationals into the Community and the election in May 1979 of the stridently Euroskeptic Margaret Thatcher as British prime minister: although the draft Directive did not cover third country nationals, Council discussions broke down (Taschner 1993). The next few years were punctuated by debates in the deadlocked Council about requiring applicants to possess sufficient resources and medical insurance and about whether this was a matter of Community competence at all (O'Leary 1999). As Greece joined the Community in 1981 and as accession negotiations were underway with Portugal and Spain, Europe was experiencing low economic growth coupled with high unemployment and inflation, hardly propitious to granting new rights to 'foreigners' from other member states, particularly given the large Greek, Spanish, and Portuguese communities within the Community. Yet Parliament's DTEU announced that 'citizens of the Member States shall *ipso facto* be citizens of the Union. Citizenship of the Union shall be dependent upon citizenship of a Member State; it may not be independently acquired or forfeited.

---

[3] See K. von Dohnanyi, German foreign minister during its presidency, in European Parliament (1979) and European Commission (1994).

Citizens of the Union shall take part in the political life of the Union in the forms laid down by the Treaty, enjoy the rights granted to them by the legal system of the Union and be subject to its laws' (European Parliament 1984).

In June 1985, the Commission issued a White Paper on Completing the Internal Market. A section on free movement, subtitled 'a new initiative in favor of Community citizens', argued that it was 'crucial that the obstacles which still exist within the Community to free movement for the self-employed and employees be removed by 1992' (European Commission 1985). Citing the preliminary findings of the People's Europe report, it continued that 'measures to ensure the free movement of individuals must not be restricted to the workforce only' (European Commission 1985). The White Paper's aim of ensuring general free movement rights would form the core of European citizenship. Also in 1985, in the Luxembourg town of Schengen, Germany, France, Belgium, Luxembourg, and the Netherlands signed an agreement to eliminate border controls. The Belgian secretary of state for European affairs affirmed that the agreement's ultimate goal was 'to abolish completely the physical borders between our countries' (Maas 2005*b*). For Luxembourg's minister of foreign affairs, the agreement marked 'a major step forward on the road toward European unity', directly benefiting the nationals of the signatory states and 'moving them a step closer to what is sometimes referred to as "European citizenship"' (Maas 2005*b*).

The final decisions on the text that would become the SEA were left to the Luxembourg meetings of December 1985, where the internal market was the dominant issue. Parliament called for specific deadlines for free movement: the treaties of Paris and Rome had prioritized the free movement of goods over that of persons, but Parliament gave equal importance to goods and persons (two year proposed deadline for implementation), ahead of services (five years) and capital (ten years) (European Parliament 1984). Meanwhile, the Commission proposed a single deadline of December 31, 1992 (the end of term of the next Commission) for establishing an area without borders, in which persons, goods, services and capital would move freely. It also proposed that free movement issues should be decided by QMV instead of unanimity, and that the Commission's implementing measures should be adopted unless the Council unanimously adopted its own (Corbett 1998). In the final stages of SEA negotiations, despite extensive parliamentary lobbying, the DTEU's citizenship proposals and the idea of including a treaty article on fundamental rights were scuttled (Schmuck 1987; Corbett 1998).

In keeping with the relaunched integration heralded by the SEA, the Commission's Directorate-General (DG) for Social Affairs undertook a series of initiatives to facilitate mobility and promote the 'social dimension of the internal market' (European Commission 1988). Spain and Portugal had joined the Community in 1986 with special provisions phasing in free movement rights, provisions that parallel the later transition arrangements for workers from the 2004 enlargement countries, but fears of massive migration of Spanish and Portuguese workers proved unfounded (Maas 2006).

The perceived injustice of the transition period helps explain the subsequent support of Greece, Spain, and Portugal for EU citizenship. The old member states did not much change their positions between the SEA and Maastricht negotiations, but the addition of new member states that had not had the right to vote on the SEA altered the outcome of the Maastricht negotiations: Spain and, to a lesser extent, Portugal were key actors promoting the notion of European citizenship. The European Council summits at The Hague in June 1986, London in December 1986, and Hanover in June 1988 had all concluded that a general right of residence should be extended to all European citizens in order to create a citizens' Europe, but they failed to approve the Commission's proposed general right of residence—now many times amended from the original 1979 version. Some member states were concerned that extending residence rights to all citizens would prove costly to states with generous welfare rights. Thus Denmark argued that the treaty provided only for the free movement of workers and the self-employed, meaning that a treaty change rather than normal legislation was needed to extend residence rights beyond workers and the self-employed (O'Leary 1996). The UK also remained wary of extending the right of residence beyond workers and the self-employed, arguing that 'students, pensioners, and the self-supporting should not become a burden on the host state's social security or health services' (United Kingdom 1990). In 1989, the Commission finally changed its approach, proposing three separate Directives, for students, retired persons, and nonworking citizens (European Commission 1989; Taschner 1993).

The fall of the Berlin Wall prompted intense efforts to advance European integration, culminating in the Maastricht Treaty. In the changed geopolitical context, a key concern was to use European citizenship to shape future political union. The government leaders asked how the new Treaty would 'include and extend the notion of Community citizenship carrying with it specific rights (human, political, social, the right of complete free movement and residence, etc.)' (European Council 1990: 15–16). This concern grew out of earlier work, such as a 1988 report which argued that though the SEA had encouraged developing the Community, it did not allow adequate action in a range of fields, including citizenship (European Parliament 1988). On the basis of the report, Parliament asked the member states to hold an IGC not simply on EMU but also on incorporating fundamental rights into the treaties, increasing social and environmental provisions, and reforming Community institutions.

The Italian parliament passed a resolution supporting the European Parliament's resolution, while the Italian delegation to the IGC argued that 'a European citizen is developing even before actions by States shape Europe' and that a 'legal framework [must] be provided to this new situation' (Wiener 1998: 253). Meanwhile, Belgium suggested remedying the democratic deficit by empowering

Parliament and expanding citizens' rights by removing border controls, writing human rights into the Treaty, joining the ECHR, and allowing Europeans residing outside their state of citizenship to vote in local and EP elections (Laursen and Vanhoonacker 1992; Magnette 1999). Greece favored including European citizenship and basic human rights in the Treaty, extending the right to vote in local and EP elections to citizens living in other member states, and simplifying citizens' access to the Court. The point of these reforms was to remedy the democratic deficit and engender constitutional patriotism: the Community should 'strengthen its citizens' feelings of belonging to one legal community' (Memorandum of May 15, 1990). German Chancellor Helmut Kohl and French President François Mitterand agreed, urging extending the notion of Community citizenship in favor of citizens of the Union (Corbett 1998).

With France and Germany urging the introduction of European citizenship, the other member states could not ignore the issue, although the British delegation immediately voiced reservations (Mazzucelli 1997). At the Dublin summit of April 28, 1990, the government leaders asked their foreign ministers to decide whether a second IGC parallel to the one on EMU would be necessary. The British government was opposed, but other governments convened a second IGC on Political Union and European Citizenship. In a letter of May 4, 1990, Spanish Prime Minister Felipé Gonzalez urged the other governments to address European citizenship, arguing that it should be based on the legal framework of Schengen and the free movement of persons (SEC(90) 1084; SEC(90) 1015/2). At the end of September 1990, Spain sought to define the proposed European citizenship in a memorandum entitled *Towards a European Citizenship*, which argued that the idea of EU required creating an integrated space in which the European citizen plays a central and fundamental role.[4] Reaching firm policy positions was difficult, because where the EMU IGC dealt with one subject, the political union and European citizenship IGC comprised many more issues. Following the Commission's report on European Citizenship, the Luxembourg presidency prepared a 'non-paper' or comprehensive draft on political union, narrowing the content of European citizenship from the earlier proposals made by Parliament and some of the national delegations. By May, three issues on which government leaders' personal representatives were unable to agree—citizenship, social policy, and economic policy—were discussed by their ministers. The citizenship discussions focused on whether it should have direct effect: Denmark and, to a lesser extent, the UK opposed creating a European citizenship that would entitle individuals to force member states to respect their rights as EU citizens (Mazzucelli 1997). Meanwhile, Parliament passed a resolution in June stipulating

---

[4] Council Document SN 3940/90 of September 24, 1990. The Spanish government proposed 'a qualitative jump which allows an area of essentially economic character to be transformed into an integrated area which would be at the direct service of the citizen'. Europe Documents 1653, October 2, 1990. (Solbes Mira 1991). For a detailed account, see (Handoll 1995).

that EU citizenship should be additional to national citizenship, that it should be placed within the framework of human rights contained in the ECHR, and that third-country nationals should also enjoy rights (European Parliament 1991*a*). Parliament submitted another report on European citizenship on 6 November, proposing a system of European social rights within the framework of European citizenship (European Parliament 1991*b*).

In the Maastricht negotiations of 9 and 10 December 1991, 'France and Germany focused on foreign policy and security, Spain on citizenship and cohesion, Italy and Belgium on the powers of the Parliament and majority voting, Denmark on the environment' (Corbett 1998: 314). Consistent with their traditional role as the 'motors of integration', support from the French and German delegations was key to passing the citizenship provisions. The proposed right of EU citizens to vote in municipal and European elections in their state of residence rather than state of origin posed constitutional problems and would become a major focus of the French ratification debate, but President Mitterrand had a strong political stake in supporting it. Although Mitterrand realized that the citizenship provisions would require amending the French constitution, he also wanted to divide the opposition parties, which would 'be caught between a desire to preserve national sovereignty and yet not appear anti-European'.[5] Dividing his political opponents was a powerful reason for Mitterand to support European citizenship. But doing so also furthered what Mitterand called his *grand projet*, to 'turn the whole of Europe into one space' (Tiersky 2003: 115). Maastricht represented not only a process of supranational institution building and integration but also the national politics of the member states and the intergovernmental conflicts and bargaining among those states (Cameron 1992). Amending the Treaty of Rome, the Maastricht Treaty granted all EU citizens four sets of rights: free movement rights, political rights, the right to common diplomatic protection, and the right to petition Parliament and appeal to the ombudsman.

While Robert Schuman had claimed that European integration would not eliminate ethnic or political borders, Helmut Kohl and Jacques Chirac in 1995 proposed to 'put the finishing touches to the formation in Europe of a homogeneous space, where freedom of movement will be guaranteed by a common approach (Declaration to the President of the European Council 1995). By contrast, in March 1996, the UK government of John Major issued a White Paper entitled *A Partnership of Nations*, rejecting new rights by arguing that fundamental rights were already sufficiently protected in Europe and that extending European rights might ultimately transform the EU into a state (United Kingdom 1996*c*). Many other member states proposed to extend citizenship rights, but these were not adopted in the final treaty. Ultimately, the Amsterdam Treaty postponed the

---

[5] 'La citoyenneté divise les Douze', *Libération*, May 15, 1991: 32. (Guigou 1994; Mazzucelli 1997).

hardest decisions on institutional enlargement, including citizenship, instead focusing mostly on EMU. Indeed, the member states excluded half the bargaining issues in order to secure a smooth ratification (Hug and König 2002). In terms of citizenship issues, Amsterdam accomplished little more than granting citizens the right to communicate with Union institutions in any of the Treaty languages, which resulted from a last-minute Belgian proposal presented at the summit rather than earlier in the IGC. Although many expected that citizenship would become a key element of Amsterdam, it did not. The shadow of the Danish rejection of Maastricht had made states wary, lest strengthening Union citizenship be interpreted as weakening national citizenship (Halligan 1997). In order to ease fears that citizenship would be used to transform the EU into a sovereign state, the member states agreed to add a new clause to the citizenship provisions: 'Citizenship of the Union shall complement and not replace national citizenship' (Article 8A: paragraph 2). This clause went well beyond the declaration attached to the Maastricht Treaty, which simply stated that the question whether an individual possesses the nationality of a member state would be settled solely by reference to the national law of the member state concerned. In the end, British and Danish intransigence blocked the wider conception of citizenship rights supported by the other member states.[6]

The next major negotiations, at Nice in December 2000, likewise made only incremental changes to EU citizenship. The Nice summit 'was not the European Union's finest hour. Nor, however, was it an unmitigated disaster' (Ludlow 2004: 47). Most of the negotiations concerned the way in which decisions would be made after enlargement, and the resulting changes were 'technical' and 'limited' (European Commission 2001). In terms of citizenship rights, however, Nice extended QMV to free movement: henceforth, decisions about the right to move and reside freely within EU territory would no longer require the unanimous support of all member states. The member states did exempt passports, identity cards, residence permits, social security, and social protection from QMV. Provisions in those areas would continue to require unanimity, but decisions about free movement provisions could now be made more easily.

The Laeken summit of December 2001 focused on the need to increase the EU's democratic legitimacy. In the Laeken Declaration, the government leaders of the member states affirmed that, within 'the Union, the European institutions must be brought closer to its citizens. Citizens undoubtedly support the Union's broad aims, but they do not always see a connection between those goals and the Union's everyday action' (European Council 2001). What was needed was more democracy, more transparency, and more efficiency. If European citizenship is

---

[6] Luxembourg—which at Maastricht had obtained the phase-in period for voting rights— opposed introducing QMV on a range of issues, including citizenship. But it also pushed with Belgium and the Netherlands for a greater EU role in free movement of persons (Kerremans 2002).

as inconsequential as some believe, then democratic legitimacy would not pose a problem. In this view, the Union remains above all an intergovernmental organization in which EU policies are subordinated to the scrutiny and control of national governments which, unlike supranational institutions such as the Parliament and Commission, are by definition legitimate (Moravcsik 2002). But if Europeans are Union citizens, and their Union citizenship reflects a similar relationship with the Union as they have with the member state of which they are also citizens, then the absence of democratic legitimacy is serious. At Laeken, Europe's political leaders determined that European citizens wanted better democratic scrutiny at *all* levels of government (European Council 2001).

The Laeken summit established a constitutional Convention, whose work ultimately resulted in a draft constitutional treaty. For the Commission, a key task of the Constitution was 'to give European citizenship...its full meaning' (European Convention 2002*a*: 15). Representatives of the Committee of the Regions agreed, writing that the Constitution should 'flesh out European citizenship. The incorporation of the Charter of Fundamental Rights into the future constitutional text...will play a vital role in achieving this. The Charter will enable every national of an EU Member State to recognize European citizenship as a source of new rights and the expression of belonging to a new community' (European Convention 2002*b*). Responding to such demands, the first comprehensive draft of the constitution specified that each EU citizen 'enjoys dual citizenship, national citizenship and European citizenship; and is free to use either, as he or she chooses; with the rights and duties attaching to each' (European Convention 2002*c*). The wording suggested that the EU would come to resemble a federal state, in which residence determines local affiliation. Opponents of a federal Europe were quick to charge that the reference to dual citizenship would accomplish exactly that. Danish Euroskeptic MEP Jens-Peter Bonde argued that dual citizenship was designed so that 'EU citizenship can grow. National citizenship can be removed to the museums'.[7] Reacting to such criticism, the Convention returned to the language of the Amsterdam Treaty: rather than mentioning dual citizenship, the constitutional draft specified again that 'Citizenship of the Union shall be additional to national citizenship; it shall not replace it'. The mention of dual citizenship was removed from the final draft because of the opposition of a number of the larger member states; in order to assure passage, it was necessary to satisfy those most critical of a stronger EU citizenship, although Convention members were confident that dual citizenship would be introduced in the future.[8]

---

[7] J.-P. Bonde, 'Nation states get same status as Bavaria!', *EU Observer*, November 5, 2002. Bonde had been an MEP since 1979. From 1999, he chaired the Parliament's Euroskeptic group EDD (Europe of Democracies and Diversities). After the 2004 election, the EDD merged into the IND/DEM (Independence and Democracy) group, with Bonde remaining chair.

[8] Interview with Jan Kavan, Czech member of the Convention, March 5, 2004.

Because the draft constitution does not introduce any new citizenship rights, the perspective of former Spanish Foreign Minister—and Convention member—Ana Palacio may be overly optimistic. Palacio has argued that 'Until now, Europe was mainly associated with a common market. Now Europe will be more and more a place of citizenship' (Quoted in 'Seeking Unity, Europe Drafts a Constitution', *New York Times*, June 12, 2003). Yet perhaps it is unnecessary to expect new rights in order to proclaim that the constitution represents a step forward. Given the political sensitivities of the looming enlargement, it was not realistic to expect many new rights. But the constitution does consolidate the existing rights of European citizenship. And it is significant that the coordination of social security provisions for migrant workers will move from unanimity to majority voting, since progress on coordination has often been hampered by the resistance of one or a small number of states. This change will simplify reaching decisions— perhaps with opt-outs for various member states, similar to the way in which the Schengen system started with five member states before gradually growing— and contribute to the mobility of workers. Yet the addition of ten new member states—likely to be followed by more states—makes the further deepening of EU citizenship unlikely. As Sophie Meunier and Kathleen McNamara noted in the introductory chapter, the 2004 and 2007 enlargements and the projected future ones, including the question of admitting Turkey, highlight the uncertain future of European identity. Since a shared citizenship has always depended to some extent on a shared political identity, however thin, the inability of some Europeans to consider the new member states to be 'us' rather than 'them' throws the future development of EU citizenship into doubt. Given the deeply divisive nature of the debates surrounding the extension of free movement to citizens from the enlargement states, free movement, and other European rights for those who move within Europe will continue to dominate the political agenda for years to come.

Conclusion

The core right of EU citizenship is freedom of movement, which was introduced to enable the mobility of labor and then justified as a measure to complete the single market. Yet there is no self-evident market or functional need for European rights: the economic need for labor could be met with bilateral or multilateral agreements between states, rather than individual rights that make markets less free as governments must regulate markets in order to satisfy rights (Streeck 1995). Instead, this chapter has detailed how the drive for European rights was the product of national bargaining based on a variety of national preferences rather than simply an economic calculation that a common market requires free movement of labor. Establishing European rights altered the political and institutional environment and generated demands for extending and expanding the content of the original free movement rights. This process contributes to the fragmentation of the system, and creates a situation in which policies develop beyond the control of any single member state. Introducing citizenship reduces the power of member states if citizenship rights are both substantially important and cannot easily be revoked. This is because new actors (European citizens) have been created who can invoke rights and act autonomously, thus changing the dynamic of the integration process away from one controlled exclusively by states. In this sense, 'it could be said that the status of "Community citizen" had been officially recognized from the moment when the Treaties granted rights to individuals and the opportunity of enforcing them by recourse to a national or Community court'.[9]

Yet the development of European citizenship rights has also not been a stable trend over time, against what neofunctionalists might predict. The Community's first enlargement delayed a common citizenship as the UK and Denmark objected, and the eventual adoption of EU citizenship resulted not from Commission pressure but rather from bargaining among member states—including the new members, Greece, Spain, and Portugal—and between member states and the EP. With the SEA in 1987, Parliament had gained the power of codecision, which helps explain why the member states could afford to ignore the Parliament's citizenship proposals in the run-up to the SEA but accepted them in the discussions preceding Maastricht. The EP described EU citizenship as 'a dynamic institution, a key to the process of European integration, and expected gradually to supplement and extend the rights conferred by nationality of a Member State' (European Parliament 1998). This may be true, but member states continue to control the introduction of new rights, deciding whether and when to supplement or extend rights of European citizenship.

---

[9] European Commissioner (later Commission vice-president from 1981–5) Viscount Étienne Davignon in (European Parliament 1979).

14

EU Social Policy, or, How Far Up Do You Like Your Safety Net?

Social issues figured prominently during the debate surrounding the European constitution, and claims that the EU is not sufficiently concerned with social policy contributed to its collapse. The French 'no' vote in May 2005 was in part spurred by concerns about high rates of national unemployment and fears that increased integration would contribute to further job losses and lower social standards. The French media symbolized this fear in the mythical 'Polish plumber', a specter of cheap Eastern European labor come to rob the French, and perhaps all of western and northern Europe, of their well-paid and high-benefit jobs. And yet this backlash about the weakness of the EU's role in social policy came at a time when EU governance of social policy had never been greater. How do we explain this? Was it that the EU had done too little, too late, or was it that the EU was not doing the right kinds of social policy? Or, perhaps, did citizens simply not know what the EU was doing in the social policy field?

This chapter first lays out a framework for analyzing current debates, putting forth three hypotheses based on historical institutionalism in order to explain the evolution of EU social policy over time. Next I examine several critical junctures in which institutional change and public interest combined to change the decision-making structure around social policy development, as well as policy outputs. In the conclusion I explore the predictive power of historical institutionalism to explain the likely trajectory of European social policy. The resulting analysis will be this chapter's contribution to the broader questions posed in the introductory chapter of this volume, namely whether there is a stable institutional structure and equilibrium in the EU, or whether current debates and failed referenda indicate a threat to institutional stability and efficacy (McNamara and Meunier 2006).

[1] The author would like to thank Sophie Meunier, Kate McNamara, Mark Pollack, and the other participants of a workshop held at Princeton University in September 2005 for their comments on earlier drafts of this chapter.

A Framework for Analyzing Current Debates

The EU social project found itself the subject of intense debate and criticism, from all sides of the political spectrum, during the constitutional debates. This is surprising when one considers the expansion of EU involvement in this area over the past two decades. At its root, the 'European Social Model' aims to advance both open and competitive markets and solidarity among citizens. The backbone of this model is at both the national level, where the regulation of the labor market and the promotion of social cohesion is a key function of law and the welfare state, and the EU level as embodied in the EC Treaty, in particular the Social Chapter and Employment Title and EU labor law. By 2005, EU social policy had expanded from an originally narrow Treaty basis focused on labor mobility and gender equality to include workplace health and safety and the regulation of the employment contract and working time.

The role of the ECJ was critical in this expansion as was Treaty reform that consolidated and legitimized new policies and decision-making structures. Social Dialogue between employers and employees had been established as a means of creating new legislation and, after a bumpy start, new legislation had resulted. The Lisbon Strategy introduced a focus on employment policies to encourage 'more and better jobs' and a competitive EU labor market, and had created a new method of cooperation at the EU level—the OMC—which had been added to the Treaties and adapted to cooperation on issues such as social inclusion. Even if its tools and outputs were modest in comparison to national welfare states in Western Europe, EU social policy had certainly not produced a leveling downward in social conditions or working conditions (Johnson 2005). The evolution of these forms of social policy is all the more interesting as they expanded in a relatively short period, given that QMV was only introduced in the SEA. Subsequent Treaty revisions over the next fifteen years at Maastricht, Amsterdam and Nice have each resulted in the expansion of EU competence in the social policy field.

In order to answer why public debates about EU social policy were intensifying despite the increased activity in this area, this chapter examines several critical junctures in the evolution of the EU social policy, during which decision-making structures and outcomes changed. Dates of enlargement are such junctures, as are times of Treaty reform and moments of new policy implementation.

Alongside the examination of critical junctures in social policy development at the EU level, national preferences for EU-level cooperation in the social policy field are vital to explaining the political dynamic. Social policy has a long history of being at the heart of ideological differences between the left and right in the EU, and great tensions continue to exist between political parties about the proper role of the EU in creating an effective and cohesive labor market. Political ideology is not sufficient to explain variations in national preferences regarding EU social policy, however. The diverse national welfare state histories of member states are also critical to explaining why specific member states have emerged as leaders in this field, while others have remained guarded partners no matter what the political stripe of their head of government.

To help frame this examination of EU social policy, several hypotheses drawn from the central preoccupations of HI theory will be useful (Scharpf 1997; Armstrong and Bulmer 1998; Bulmer 1998; Pierson 1998; Aspinwall and Schneider 2001; Pierson 2004). The first hypothesis draws on the basic assumptions in Leibfried and Pierson's original work on HI and EU social policy in which they argued that the EU is 'not under the firm control of member states' and that both the 'autonomous activity of EU organizations' such as the Commission and the 'impact of previous policy commitments . . . lock member states into initiatives that they otherwise might not choose' (Leibfried and Pierson 1995). This hypothesis suggests that even if there is a lack of consensus among EU member states about the positive benefits of EU-level social policy we should still see, over time, the development of formal rules governing social policy in ever-expanding areas of competence as autonomous EU-level institutions ratchet up the level of cooperation in ways that cannot be explained simply by bargaining among autonomous, self-interested member states. These formal rules should set a path that will influence the future development of social policy, which may be deepened by events and innovations not initially anticipated by the contracting parties. Alternatively, we would see social policy reach a stasis or point of nil or little policy growth. This hypothesis speaks to the *process* of the development of EU social policy.

The second hypothesis is that if the existence of EU-level institutions has been successful in exerting influence over cooperation among EU member states in the social policy field, then we should see policy outputs that are more than just the lowest common denominator reflecting 'the views of the least ambitious participants in a minimum winning coalition' (Leibfried and Pierson 1995). Alternatively, EU-level social policy would reflect the lowest standard that exists among the member states. This hypothesis speaks to the *outcomes* of EU social policy.

The third hypothesis is that if institutions are effective in encouraging cooperation among member states, then we should see examples of policy learning that lead to a greater consensus among member states regarding the social policy goals of the EU. Although unintended consequences are a key element in the HI explanation of how cooperation evolves, especially when there is spillover to new initiatives (Leibfried and Pierson 1995), policy learning should lead to the diminishing importance of unanticipated consequences over time; as actors come to understand in more detail the arena in which they are cooperating, they are better able to control how policy evolves and shut down possible deviations from their choices, in effect ring-fencing policy. Alternatively, if institutions do not foster learning in ways anticipated by HI we should see a breakdown in the ability of member states to cooperate effectively in areas where there is common interest, or very disparate pockets of social policy with little common reasoning to connect them. This hypothesis speaks to the evolving *understanding and refinement* of EU social policy.

Keeping these three hypotheses in mind as we enter into a brief examination of EU social policy will allow us to weigh HI explanations of the development of EU social policy against an explanation that emphasizes national preferences and member state interests as the determining factor of the course of EU social policy development (Moravcsik 1998). Table 14.1 outlines the key periods and events in the evolution of EU social policy that will be examined in the subsequent sections.

Early Regional Social Policy: Regulation and Court Activism

Social policy cooperation in the Treaty of Paris was centered around the coal and steel industry, and included a voluntary and cooperative approach to health and safety standards, as well as the housing and payment of workers (Collins 1975: 87). Interestingly, while focused on just one sector, the European-level institutions were able to involve themselves in issues such as pay and housing conditions, but along with the expansion of the European project in the Treaty of Rome to economy-wide regulation came a focus on the free movement of workers, equal pay for men and women, and the improvement of working conditions as the six original member states settled upon a limited vision of social policy at the regional level. Despite calls from Belgium and France for the harmonization of working time, benefits, and holiday periods in order to export many of their own welfare state policies, the Treaty did not include these more activist provisions. Even among the original six member states there was an inability to agree on common EU standards due to different wage and productivity levels and the administrative and fiscal challenges of harmonization (ILO 1956). Instead, the most activist elements of the EEC relating to social cohesion were in fact reserved for the agriculture sector where, in the 1950s, more than 20 percent of the workforce was still located.

Cooperation relating to workplace health and safety proceeded slowly, while most of the national and regional political energy of the time was devoted to the initial steps toward an internal market, a common external tariff and the CAP. The first Community Social Action Programme on safety and health at work did not began until 1978 with a series of Directives proposed under ex Article 100 (now Article 94), that focused on legislative harmonization in the area of product safety standards (Commission 1978). The aim of legislative harmonization, however, met with 'resistance from employers and the majority of the member states' which, under unanimity voting, led to 'a fairly rapid whittling down of the pro- posed action areas' (Vogel 1993: 67–8). Legislation in the 1970–85 period—on safety signs, lead, asbestos, noise, and chemical, physical, and biological agents— was thus largely due to Commission activism rather than member state interest, and was concentrated in highly specific areas of activity. Additional EU-level

TABLE 14.1. *The evolution of EU governance in social policy, 1957–2006*

	1957–1971: Declaratory Politics	1972–1993: Gradual breakthrough	1993–2006: Substantive but Limited Politics
Treaty provisions and major initiatives	Preamble Article 3: free movement Title III Art. 48–51 free mov't of workers Art. 51 social security provisions Part III Social Policy Art. 117–128	1972 Paris Summit Declaration 1974 Social Action Plan 1986 SEA: Art. 118a QMV on Health and Safety Art. 118b concept of Social Dialogue introduced 1989: Social Charter	1993 Maastricht Protocol on Social Policy, Social Dialogue as new form of governance (now Art. 139) 1999 Amsterdam Title VIII Employment 2002 Nice, included OMC as a working method for social exclusion and other issues 2003–05 Draft constitution includes previous provisions; Part I Art. 3 'social market economy'; Part II Charter of Fundamental Rights incl. core labour standards
Voting rules in Council	Unanimity	1986 SEA: start of QMV in Health and Safety legislation (Art. 118A)	Governance by law: QMV is extended in each treaty revision; Governance by Social Dialogue: Council approves Framework Agreement according to voting rules of Article 137; Governance by coordination (OMC): Council helps develop guidelines, approves NAPs, approves Commission recommendations, writes joint Employment Report.
Activism of the Commission in the social policy field	Low (constrained by Council)	Medium 1972–1984 High 1985–1990 (Delors)	High 1993 (Delors) Medium 1993–2006
Role of the European Parliament in social policy making	Consultative role. EP not directly elected.	EP directly elected from 1979. 1986 SEA introduced cooperation procedure under QMV; consultation when unanimity voting in Council	Governance by law: Co-operation or codecision for QMV. Consultation for unanimity voting Governance by Social Dialogue: Governance by Coordination (OMC): consultation
Enforcement mechanisms	ECJ	Governance by law: ECJ can sanction member states with fines, and back-date application of legislation.	Governance by law and Social Dialogue: ECJ Governance by coordination: Naming and shaming.
Role of the social partners	Consultative, through European Social Committee (ESC)	Consultative, through European Social Committee and through Article 118b on social dialogue	Governance by law: consultative Governance by Social Dialogue: Legislative role through EU-level collective bargaining Governance by Coordination (OMC): consultative, may also propose new guidelines
Relation of social policy to economic policies	Creation of customs union: Limited social policy harmonization to export largely French preferences for gender equality, holidays. Creation of ESF	SEM: QMV in social policy only extended to health and safety policies. Cohesion funding to aid adjustment of least developed Member States	EMU project: Social Dialogue promoted by Commission. Employment Title promoted at Amsterdam by non-EMU states. Increasing relation between Broad Economic Policy Guidelines (BEPG) and European Employment Strategy (EES).
Other important EU-level initiatives	1961 Social Charter at Turin 1966 Veldkamp Memorandum Gender equality legislation	1974 Social Action Plan; 1977 77/187/EEC on worker consultation; 1985 Val Duchesse Dialogue	1989 health and safety framework directive; 1994 Cohesion Funds; 1995 first social partner agreement

Based on a chart from Johnson (2005).

regulation on subjects, such as electrical equipment, tractors and agricultural machinery, lifting devices, and protective equipment, was slow in development, however, and was quickly outpaced by technological change (Pelkmans 1987).

In order to address the need for more reactive and timely law-making in health and safety, and to aid in the completion of the internal market, the 'New Approach to Technical Harmonization and Standardization' was introduced in 1985 (Council 1985). It was based on mutual recognition and delegation to private standardization bodies (Eichener 1992:19). This reorientation to mutual recognition in order to overcome the problems besetting approaches based on product standard harmonization is 'perhaps the best example of policy learning taking place at both the national and European levels' (Majone 1996*b*: 268), and yet when introduced, the Treaty basis for policymaking in the social field was still highly circumscribed.

Alongside policy-making, gaps in the understanding and application of EU social policy were being closed by the ECJ, in cases largely centered on ensuring equality of treatment for female employees and workplace mobility rights. The series of landmark cases involving Gabrielle Defrenne, an employee of the Belgian airline Sabena who complained of working time policies that discriminated against women, is one of the best examples of the importance of the ECJ to the implementation and reinforcement of EU social policy (ECJ cases *Defrenne I, II, III*; also *J.P. Jenkins* v. *Kingsgate Clothing Productions Ltd*), as is case law related to the free movement of workers (including *Levin* v. *Staatssecretaris van Justitie* and *R.* v. *Immigration Appeal Tribunal, ex parte Antonissen*) that 'suggested a wider scope for ex Article 48 (now Article 39) than the words of the Article themselves convey' (Craig and de Burca 2003).

Thus, the early period of EU social policy was characterized by a limited Treaty basis for cooperation determined by member states, and by Commission and ECJ activism in those limited areas of EU competence.

The First Major Treaty Reform: Qualified Majority Voting and Governance by Law

Unanimity in decision-making in social policy was the norm until QMV was introduced in a very limited area of social policy, Article 137 (ex 118a) on health and safety, in the SEA. The story of the extension of QMV in the SEA is long and complex, and not without different viewpoints (Budden 1994; Corbett 1998; Moravcsik 1998; Sandholtz and Stone Sweet 1998). What is clear is that the SEM was the fundamental driver and that social policy had few champions at the IGCs. Most surprisingly, Socialist France had abandoned the ideas it presented in 1981 to reduce the workweek and fight unemployment, highlighting the inconsistency between President Mitterrand's rhetoric on this subject and French inaction. Although specific interests in member states, such as trade unions in Denmark and Germany, expressed fears about the negative effects economic integration would have on social policies, member states did not push for widely expanded EU competence in the social policy field during the SEA negotiations. Most governments of the time were of the right and center-right and did not have the expansion of EU social policy as a goal in bargaining, despite the coming Southern enlargement to poorer member states with weaker social regulation and lower levels of social benefits.

It was the Delors Commission which, beginning in 1985, started an agenda of extending QMV and enhancing EEC social powers. The Commission presented a package linking the SEM with three flanking policies: monetary cooperation, technology policy, and 'communautaire' policies that were in essence economic and social cohesion (Commission 1985*b*: 10). The accompaniment of economic and political union by a European form of *solidarité*—in this case through cohesion funding for less developed member states—was a constant leitmotif of Delors's presidency of the EU.

The Danes—initially resistant to an expansion of EU competencies and under a Conservative government—picked up on the Commission ideas and proposed an expansion of QMV to Article 118 to help set minimum standards and permit member states with higher standards to retain them (Baldwin and Daintith 1992: 11). Only the UK explicitly opposed the Danish proposal, but ultimately agreed to QMV in health and safety because it wanted agreement on its primary objective of the SEM. An intergovernmental analysis of the SEA negotiations can correctly identify and explain the most resistant member states on the issue of QMV—namely Greece, because of its relative poverty, and the UK because of its Conservative government. However, it cannot identify the policy leader, Denmark, which had a government of the Right yet consistently pushed for an extension of QMV to health and safety policy because of its domestic policy history and the need to create national consensus on the SEA. Only an explanation of preferences that emphasizes the particular features of the policy area under consideration, in this case national welfare state history and national preferences regarding social policy, does a good job of identifying the leader in this case of Treaty reform.

The implications of Article 118a were not anticipated by the UK, as described in a memorandum of the UK during a later Treaty revision process:

The UK's intention in agreeing to the incorporation of Article 118a into the Treaty was to allow the adoption, by QMV, of minimum requirements specifically related to the health and safety of workers.... The ECJ has ruled...that the scope of Article 118a is much broader than the UK envisaged when the article was originally agreed.

(United Kingdom 1996*a*)

Over successive treaty revisions, QMV has been extended to other social policy areas, including working conditions and the information and consultation of workers. Further, in a constantly enlarging EU it has become impossible for a single large member state (UK, Germany, France, Italy, or Poland) to block an undesired policy.

As for policy outputs, the Commission was 'a key actor' in the process of creating health and safety legislation at a high standard throughout the 1980s and early 1990s (Eichener 1992: 1). The Commission, as the manager of the governance process established at the EU level, created a 'dominant position' in the various consultative arenas that create policy proposals and the committees that debated the proposals (Eichener 1992: 56). The development of health and safety Directives in EU committees—first the tripartite Advisory Committee on Safety, Hygiene and Health at Work and in later stages in the Social Affairs committee composed of national officials—means that the influence of resistant member states is countered by constant Commission entrepreneurship and leadership by high standard member states. Passivity on the part of low standard Southern member states (Greece, Portugal, and Spain), as expressed by the low number of their interventions during legislative development (Eichener 1992; Johnson 2005), permitted agreement at a higher level than would be expected on the basis of relative bargaining power, or by a social dumping hypothesis. Overall, standards adopted in health and safety regulation have been similar to Sweden, Denmark, and the Netherlands, and higher than that of Germany (Eichener 1992: 6–8). The standards supplied in the Framework Directive are thus 'capable of being constructed as affording protection at a very high level, certainly not a minimum one' (Baldwin and Daintith 1992: 11).

The Second Major Treaty Reform: Governance by Social Dialogue

In addition to the introduction of QMV in the SEA, the Commission had proposed a 'new Article 118(b) providing for a social dialogue with the possibility for contractual relationships, at European level' (Corbett 1998: 238). The preferences of member states alone cannot explain the evolution of Social Dialogue from an informal process and subsection in the SEA to an alternative to the Community Method of regulation. Three institutional factors are a vital part of the explanation.

The first is Commission entrepreneurship. Without the activism of the Commission in creating opportunities for social partner involvement in EU institutions, and the entrepreneurship of Jacques Delors as Commission president in suggesting a new form of governance based on EU-level collective bargaining, Social Dialogue would not have been introduced at the EU level. The belief in the superiority of negotiated settlements between capital and labor over technocratic rule setting was at the heart of Delors's personal political philosophy (Ross 1995a: 45). Delors made the enhancement of Social Dialogue 'one of his own personal projects' (Gold 1998: 112). Delors's overall vision was that as the SEM progressed, the Community needed a social policy to demonstrate a balanced approach to integration and solidarity as expressed by the Structural

Funds. Further, by supporting the development of EU-level confederations of the social partners, most notably the ETUC, the Commission helped to create the very interests that would participate in, and eventually call for an enhancement of the Social Dialogue (Dolvik and Visser 2001). The Commission thus acted as a kind of 'policy incubator', keeping the idea of a Social Dialogue alive and building up support for it throughout the 1980s and early 1990s despite conflicting interests among member states. In particular, active opposition came from the UK under the leadership of Margaret Thatcher and then John Major, which at the national level pursued policies to weaken the role of unions in wage agreements and economic policy.

The second institutional factor is the failure of unanimity voting to permit agreement on social policy in the EU. Given blockages in Council, member states in favor of cooperation looked to extend QMV and were disposed to consider new regulatory paths. By the 1980s, there was a 'considerable backlog of draft legislation', even with the limited introduction of QMV in then-Article 118(a) (now Article 137) (Addison and Siebert 1997: 12) and 'considerable dissatisfaction with the lack of progress on social policy' (Deakin 1997: 124). Legislation that could not be passed by the Council included various drafts of the 'Vredeling initiative', the draft Fifth Directive on company law, the ECS, working time, 1982 and 1983 proposals on atypical work, 1982 proposals on temporary employment agencies, and failed attempts to propose parental leave provisions. The Social Action Program, launched after the 1989 Social Charter, created a 'small ad hoc group' that met to discuss training and labor market issues but the Commission was stymied by the Union of Industrial and Employers' Confederations of Europe's (UNICE's) refusal to participate in discussions (Ross 1995*b*: 377).

Social Charter initiatives were also blocked in Council by the UK, and in specific instances by Portugal (European Works Council, posting of workers), Italy (pregnant workers, young workers), Greece (young workers), and Spain (young workers). An enhanced EU-level Social Dialogue could, therefore 'circumvent or break social policy stalemates in the Council' (Falkner 1998: 72). Breaking such stalemates took on a greater sense of urgency for high standard states in light of the completion of the Internal Market, which highlighted the differences in national labor market regulation. Such differences were also amplified in the EU by the post-SEA enlargement to Spain and Portugal, who, along with Greece, were low-wage countries.

Gerda Falkner has noted the role of the posted workers case (the *Rush Portuguesa* case of 1989), and the relocation of multinationals such as Renault and Hoover, in highlighting the differences in labor market regulation in Europe around the time of the completion of '1992' (2002: 105–6). Notably, however, it was not member states but Jacques Delors who, as Commission President, consistently pushed the Social Dialogue 'as a solution to the stalemate in Council over social policy' (Addison and Siebert 1997: 14).

The third institutional factor is learning effects. As a result of multiple instances of cooperation over time, actors involved in social policy—governments, unions, and employers—learned that the Commission would continue to propose social policy regulation at a high level. Commission-proposed legislation would have the opportunity to pass in Council if QMV was extended. As a result, even those governments and employer organizations that would have been expected to reject the Social Dialogue on the basis of national preferences supported the Social Dialogue as a 'second best' solution (the 'first best' being no regulation at all), with the knowledge that the Commission would continue to propose social regulation that might be approved if QMV was extended to new areas. Support for the Social Dialogue is thus also explicable in the case of those who wanted to circumvent, and even prevent, policy regulation led by the European Commission. As the secretary-general of UNICE explained:

Experience so far in EC social legislation is that the legislator is getting it wrong. The legislator is being too detailed, too prescriptive, is trying to do everything from Brussels. . . . We felt we would be better custodians of subsidiary than the legislator. We were also convinced that the unions would be too. The reason is that our members and theirs will be breathing down our necks because they do not want to lose national sovereignty. That is very healthy. They will also allow us to go along with broad framework type agreements rather than the prescriptive and detailed type of legislation that we are getting from the Commission.

(Dolvik 1997: 211)

Ultimately, member states were surprisingly passive regarding the evolution of the Social Dialogue. Notably, the Commission continued to exert leadership in this field in the context of the IGC that would lead to the Maastricht Treaty. Backed by Belgium, and acting on the basis of a text proposed by the social partners, the Commission was the key advocate for the enhancement of Article 118b during the negotiations. Negotiations looked poised to fail altogether when the UK government of John Major had rejected all proposed versions of a social policy agreement including QMV. The Commission's intervention then proved crucial. Delors proposed a Social Protocol that would allow eleven member states to move forward in limited areas using QMV, and including an enhanced Social Dialogue. While the UK, as predicted, opted out of the Social Protocol in its entirety, Helmut Kohl advanced the Commission proposal to the heads of government, and it was adopted (Ross 1995*b*: 380; Pierson 1998: 55).

Thus, the agreement on the Social Protocol at Maastricht, that moved eleven member states along a cooperative path while excluding the UK, was an awkward compromise between policy leaders and the most resistant member state brokered by an entrepreneurial Commission. Even an intergovernmental analysis of the Maastricht negotiations concedes that 'it is fair to say that Delors intervention moved the resulting policy slightly in the direction of a more active social policy' (Moravcsik 1998: 454).

In the final agreement, Article 2 of the Social Agreement extended QMV to a host of new issue areas, such as working conditions, the information and consultation of workers, gender equality in the labor market, and the integration of persons excluded from the labor market. As Paul Pierson has succinctly explained: 'member state governments, which had exploited Britain's expected position to engage in cheap talk, suddenly found themselves exposed' (1998: 55) and locked-in to agreement.

In terms of creating policy outputs, the Social Dialogue has had mixed results, but importantly has permitted legislation in areas where traditional law-making had failed previously. Examples include the Framework Agreement on parental leave and the Framework Agreement on part-time work. The parental leave Directive (Directive 96/34/EC) provided a 'low' standard 'if compared to what the more advanced member states already had before, but constituted significant progress . . . for Ireland, and advances in detail for several other countries' (Falkner 1999: 93). However, the details of the Agreement required adjustment even in high regulation states, such as Sweden, where the new EU rules allowed parents to take time off before the birth of their child (Johnson 2005).

Legislation reached via the Social Dialogue on Part-Time Work has had a mixed impact on member states. While the German DGB union confederation viewed the Agreement as being too weak (avoiding the issue of equality of treatment between full time and part-time workers in social security provisions), part-time work legislation has 'far-reaching implications' for the UK 'because of the absence of current labor law protection for most part-time workers' and because the Agreement brings the national social partners into discussion on the implementation of the Directive (Dolvik 1997: 341). The most significant backdrop to the Social Dialogue remains, however, the Commission's ability to propose legislation if dialogue fails.

The Third Major Treaty Reform: The European Employment Strategy and the Open Method of Coordination

The development of the European Employment Strategy (EES) also repeats the features of Commission entrepreneurship, policy learning, and outcomes ultimately at levels higher than theories of inter-state bargaining would predict. In 1993, Padraig Flynn, the commissioner of DG V, first proposed a 'framework for actions' at all levels within the Community in relation to employment. The *Community-Wide Framework for Employment* committed the Community institutions and the member states to a 'structured, cooperative and systematic, process of analysis of policy reflection on possible solutions to the employment problem with a view to concerted policy action' over an eighteen-month period (Commission 1993: 7).

Commission activism was further empowered by the Danish presidency, who gave the Commission a mandate to develop a White Paper, *Growth, Competitiveness and Employment*. The White Paper was presented in December 1993 under the Belgian presidency, known by Delors to be sympathetic to a more activist EU social policy (Ross 1995*b*). In essence, the White Paper used the field of employment policy to address issues about Europe's global competitiveness and economic modernization while maintaining social solidarity. George Ross has called this period 'another basic decision point' similar to the decision to launch European and Monetary Union, but in this case the decision was about preserving the basic tenets of the 'European social model', and in particular collective bargaining and the role of unions in wage setting (1995*b*). On one hand, the Germany wage-setting and benefits system represented the archetype, with other member states such as Belgium, Denmark, Ireland, and Italy having variations. On the other hand, the Conservative UK government and many of the national and pan-EU employers' confederations wanted a more 'open' labor market based not only on competitive wages, but also employment terms that allowed greater flexibility for the hiring and firing of workers. The White Paper aimed to find a way through this ideological minefield, using negotiated settlements between the social partners and more active intervention to ensure the training of workers to try and preserve the solidarity elements of the social model while answering the concerns of those who felt the single market had left rigid labor markets relatively untouched.

From these origins, subsequent European Councils identified the 'fight against unemployment and equality of opportunity for men and women' as 'the paramount tasks of the EU and its member states' (Council 1994). Labor and Social Affairs Councils, ECOFIN, and the Commission were charged with monitoring employment trends and the policies of the member states and were to report annually to the European Council starting in December 1995, and subsequent European Council meetings affirmed the creation of an 'employment strategy' and a 'framework' for the development of member states' employment policies on a 'multi-annual' basis (Council 1995: Annex 2).

Employment policy at the EU level from 1989 to 1995 was thus the result of Commission entrepreneurship, supported by successive presidencies and validated by European Councils. In this period the process was not explicitly designed to become an annual one, but it gradually evolved as the Council replied to Commission Communications and reports, and as successive Councils tried to put their own stamp on the employment discussion. Thus, even in its informal stages, cooperation on employment policy had led to the unanticipated result of a multi-annual process of reporting on national employment policies at the EU level on the basis of commonly articulated guidelines.

The 1995 enlargement to Austria, Finland, and Sweden cemented the 'middle way' through the labor market debate, as these states have long-standing traditions of tripartite or bipartite bargaining and intense involvement of labor unions in national politics. Sweden, in particular, devoted considerable energy to promoting the adoption of active labor market policies (ALMPs), not least to sway a Euroskeptic public and promote its own 'Nordic' brand of labor market policies to other member states. In the Amsterdam Treaty negotiations, Sweden, with Commission support, championed the informal employment process as a separate employment title, and was backed by Belgium, the Netherlands, Luxembourg, Sweden, Denmark, Finland Greece, Spain, Italy, and Portugal. Absent in this coalition in favor of an employment title was the Franco-German axis. Germany was concerned about the evolution of EU competencies in employment policy, and the risk of being drawn in to transfer payments based on employment levels that could expand the budget (Algieri and Janning 1996: 5). In addition, no French leadership on the Employment Title was forthcoming because of concerns that an EES would take attention and resources away from the launch of EMU (Cohen-Tanugi 1996: 28; Parliament 1996). The UK opposed any development of the EU's powers in the field of employment and would not give up its opt-out of the Social Protocol (United Kingdom 1996*b*).

The UK eventually agreed to the Employment Title only after the election of the Blair Labour government in 1997. It was Germany that was the final hold out. A clear statement of the retention of competence by the member states, a consultative voice for the Committee of the Regions, and no new budgetary provisions were necessary in order to secure German agreement. This 'fear of financing' was an element of the German reluctance to agree to the Employment Title that may be described as an example of institutional learning—after repeated experiences of policy implementation over time Germany was well aware that unexpected financial consequences could result from the creation of new policies at the EU level, such as the Cohesion Funds that had accompanied the agreement to proceed with EMU (Johnson 2005).

Importantly, the Commission laid the groundwork for an ongoing process of cooperation in the employment field even before the Treaty negotiations. Thus, while employment policy was elevated to a formal process at Amsterdam, it is clear that EU-level action would have persisted even if the Employment Title had not been agreed to.

Less expected was the creation of a new system of EU policymaking, which follows the EES model of reports and national action plans, but that may or may not include Commission recommendations. The method of national coordination and inter-institutional cooperation developed by the EES was 'baptized' the OMC at the Lisbon summit in March 2000 (Larsson 2002). The OMC takes the specific features of the EES—Commission proposed and Council approved guidelines, national reporting, a Joint Commission–Council report, and, finally, recommendations made by the Commission—and identifies them as a mode of governance that may be used in other areas. The Lisbon summit conclusions of March 23–4, 2000 endorsed the OMC as the key method to guide various policies on employment, social exclusion, and including such issues as poverty, long-term unemployment, social protection, and pensions (Council 2000).

The Treaty of Nice, negotiated under the French presidency in late 2000, incorporated the OMC into Article 137 for the areas of social exclusion and the modernization of social protection systems (EU, 2000, Article 137 (1) (j & k) and Article 137 (2) (a)). Thus, soft law, involving information sharing, the setting of common objectives and guidelines, the diffusion of best practice, and the naming of good and bad policy performers have been elevated to a formal regulatory system in social policy by the inclusion of the OMC in the Treaty of Nice (Bruun 2001).

Member states have been varyingly affected by the EES depending on their own national policy history. This observation was noted in the five-year review of the EES by the Commission, which noted that 'while a few member states were already implementing policies largely in line with [Commission 1997] ... clear convergence can be noted for other member states—albeit at different paces' Commission 2002: 10. In particular, convergence toward the use of ALMPs, gender equality policies, and social inclusion was noted across member states. Greece, for example, has implemented employment policies for the inclusion of women and minorities in the labor market that would not have been implemented had it not been for the EES guidelines (Johnson 2005). Learning among member states with previous experience in ALMPs has been more limited, in particular in France and Germany where national debates have proven more robust in influencing employment policy than the EES (Casey and Gold 2005).

One of the most significant changes may be the structural shift in perception in the EU from 'managing unemployment, toward managing employment growth', with the attendant shift of focus on labor market participation, training, life-long learning, and the reduction of taxes on labor (Commission 2002). The synchronization of the employment guidelines with the Broad Economic Policy Guidelines begun in 2003 was also encouraging in structural terms. EMU, and the Broad Economic Policy Guidelines that underpin monetary union and fiscal convergence, provide a macroeconomic framework within which the EES guidelines can be more effectively translated into specific labor market outputs, such as wage restraint, worker training, and an increase in availability of flexible forms of employment. As of 2005, the EES has been further revamped to focus more clearly on the synergy between improving productivity and growth through microeconomic policies centered on training, life-long learning, and flexible employment opportunities. The coordination of policies and dissemination of best practices is the value-added of the EU level, while national governments are charged with implementing national reform programs that address the specific challenges of their labor market (Commission 2005b). Interestingly, it was a method of discussion, information sharing, and coordination in order to prevent market distortion that Balassa recommended in the case of social policy in his seminal work on economic integration (Balassa 1961: 229). The parallels with the OMC of today are striking.

The Most Recent Debates

The last two years have been a particularly intense period of attention and examination regarding EU social policy. Despite the recent development of new forms of EU governance in social policy, the 2005 enlargement called into question the strength of EU policies to address the growing public concerns about employment security and national social systems in a larger European labor market.

Most member states had already determined prior to 2005 that there would be derogations on the free movement of workers from eight of the ten new member states (Malta and Cyprus were not included in the transitional arrangement) (Commission 2004). Sweden, the UK, and Ireland were the only three member states *not* to issue derogations on the free movement of workers from the date of enlargement. In the case of the UK and Ireland, this reflects not only their position on the far West of the EU (where, some may argue, they are more sheltered from illegal immigration from the East), but also their ideological commitment to the 'free market' principles UK governments have long advocated should be the motivating spirit for EU cooperation. For the rest of the EU member states, a fundamental principle of the European project at the core of social and employment issues—the freedom of movement—which was laid down in the EU's founding Treaty, was compromised at the very moment of the greatest expansion of the EU project ever witnessed. This calls into question the commitment of these member states to a broader form of regional solidarity based on access to labor markets, although an intergovernmental analysis would be quick to point out that in the context of high national unemployment rates, Germany and France were acting in their perceived national political self-interest in seeking derogations from the free movement of workers from Eastern Europe.

There were also extensive debates during both the drafting of the EU Charter of Fundamental Rights and Freedoms and during the drafting of the EU Constitution over the scope and legal status of social rights. On one hand, while social and economic rights were expanded upon alongside traditional civil and political rights in the Charter, there was resistance by some member states to give it legally binding status. Also, during the Constitutional Convention, despite the active involvement of several Social MEPs who promoted the Constitution as an opportunity for the expansion of EU social policy, there was an unwillingness to expand the areas of social policy subject to QMV. Even the chair of the working group on Social Europe admitted that the achievements of the group were modest (Norman 2005).

The debate has continued over the EU Services Directive (Commission 2006*a*). A majority of MEPs in early 2006 rejected that service providers would be governed by the rules of their 'country of origin' (or home country) and instead would be governed by their host country. Services of 'general interest', including health care, transport, postal services, and temporary work agencies, were excluded from the Directive. Those in favor of liberalization, such as the UK's largest employers' organization, the CBI, condemned the MEP's decision as having delivered 'an emasculated version of a Directive that had promised a single, open European market for services'. Those in favor of restrictions on service providers were pleased that the Directive removed the 'country of origin' principle that they feared could have resulted in fewer jobs, lower wages, and 'an influx of rogue companies' ('MEPS Unveil Free Market in Services' 2006). Still others saw the resulting Directive as a 'necessary compromise' whereby local rules apply but may, over time, increasingly come to recognize the rules of other member states to the extent that mutual compatibility of societal norms and inter-state negotiation allows (Nicolaïdis 2006).

There are three critical features to note in the recent debates about social policy. The first is that the proliferation of activity at the EU level has required the Commission to concentrate on maintaining the current cycle of programs rather than on finding new innovations—keeping the (ever-growing) bicycle going rather than being able to devote time to developing new components. New forms of cooperation such as OMC also place increased responsibility for the development of policies in the hands of member states. The second is that the diversity of national policies and the challenges of harmonization are further highlighted, leading members of *both* the left and the right of the political spectrum to question the real influence and efficacy of EU policy in creating EU standards. The third feature is that 'the coalition of the interested' in EU social policy varies greatly depending on the issue at hand; when more activist EU employment policies are discussed it is mostly governments of the left and unions who promote EU-level cooperation (although not at the expense of national bargaining traditions), while on the EU services Directive it was employers, business, and governments of the right that argued the importance of a pan-European labor market in the services sector. Cleavages along political and interest-based lines, depending on the specific issue, continue to create difficulties in assessing and communicating the success of EU social policy to date, and creating a vision for the future.

Conclusion

As Pierson has explained, the key claim to be derived from historical institutionalism is 'that actors may be in a strong initial position, seek to maximize their interests, and nevertheless carry out institutional and policy reforms that fundamentally transform their own positions...in ways that are unanticipated and/or undesired' (1998: 30). A broad review of the history of EU social policy, framed by our three hypotheses about the *process, outcomes,* and *understanding* of EU social policy reveals the following:

1. On process, we will continue to see EU competencies in social policy expand—in particular in areas linked to equality and labor market regulation issues such as social inclusion, policies to increase female participation in the labor force (including issues around child care), and regulation of new forms of work. However, binding social standards will continue to be flanked by soft forms of cooperation centered around the OMC designed *not* to create additional harmonized requirements on member states, but rather to reinforce policy sharing and dialogue.

2. On outcomes, the lowest common denominator is not the output of EU social policy, but neither have outputs been dominated by legislation representing the highest standards present in member states. It is predicted that in an EU of twenty-five or more member states it will be harder for the Commission to build the effective coalitions it requires to support legislation at a high standard, and the need for active coalitions of member states and interventionist presidencies will be at a premium in the development of social legislation.

3. On learning effects and the consolidation of an understanding of what EU social policy should mean, member states have clearly agreed to cooperate in an expanding range of social policy but have shifted to less demanding forms of cooperation. Learning effects have also improved the ability of member states to ring-fence the Commission that has led to the reduction of unanticipated consequences generated by factors endogenous to the EU institutions. However, ring-fencing has its problems, as witnessed by the reluctance of member states to provide a robust articulation of the EU's social values and policies in the constitution, with ultimately devastating results when put to the public.

In returning to one of the central themes of this volume—whether EU policies have reached an equilibrium—the lessons of fifty years of policymaking indicate that we should be careful in asserting that there is a 'stable agreement' among member states that EU should only apply to a very limited extent in social policy, as Andrew Moravcsik has stated recently (Moravcsik 2005c). Such plateaus in EU governance have been witnessed in the past and have been surpassed. Indeed, more than ten years ago Leibfried and Pierson described a trend 'toward immobility' in social policy, and yet the last ten years have seen significant legislation and innovations in specific areas of social cooperation (1995a). For example, in answer to concerns that the EU needs to do more to address the concerns of dislocation and job insecurity brought about by global competition and to reinvigorate the European Social Model, President Barroso has proposed a *Globalization Fund* to come into effect as of January 1, 2007 of up to €500 million each year for job search assistance and training to individual workers who are 'adjusting to the consequences of globalization, acting as a sign of solidarity from those who benefit from open trade to those who face the sudden shock of losing their jobs' (Commission 2006*b*). Member states must demonstrate the link between 'job losses and significant structural changes in global trade patterns' in order to secure this funding.

The demands of maintaining public support for the common market and common EU macroeconomic policies will require that the EU becomes more, not less, involved in social policy. The overarching logic of the 'European Social Model'—to guarantee a high standard of living and economic security to EU citizens—still stands despite criticisms from neoliberal critics of the right and the declining union density in most EU member states. Both the Commission and member states must innovate in the coming years to stay relevant to current labor market and social policy challenges, and if the height of the regional social safety net is to be perceived by the public as approaching their level.

IV

The EU as a Sovereign State in World Politics

15

Understanding the European Union as a Global Political Actor: Theory, Practice, and Impact

ROY H. GINSBERG AND MICHAEL E. SMITH

The EU today is one of the most unusual and widest-ranging political actors in the international system. Since the 1950s, this capacity has gradually expanded to encompass foreign policy initiatives toward nearly every corner of the globe, using a range of foreign policy tools: diplomatic, economic, and now limited military operations. This capacity, however, was neither included in the original Treaty of Rome, nor was it expected by many knowledgeable observers of European integration. On both sides of the functional-intergovernmental spectrum we find skepticism about the EU's prospects as a global actor: Ernst Haas (1961) explicitly excluded foreign and security policy from his neofunctional logic of regional integration, which stresses spillover processes in socioeconomic affairs, while Stanley Hoffmann (2000) argued that political cooperation in the EU would remain very difficult owing to concerns over national sovereignty. Even after the cold war, when the EU continued to expand its foreign policy cooperation, many observers (particularly those influenced by realism) made somewhat outlandish predictions that Germany would attempt to acquire nuclear weapons, that the EU (and even NATO) would deteriorate, and that the EU would never be able to organize its own security/defense cooperation (Mearsheimer 1991; Waltz 1993; Art 1996; Gordon 1997–98). Others with little or no experience with European integration studies, such as Robert Kagan (2003), argued that the EU has secured its own corner of the world through economic integration and it can now simply enjoy the fruits of its efforts while the USA continues to play the tough role of world policeman.

Whether ignoring or belittling the EU as a global actor, these predictions turned out to be incorrect. While the EU certainly has had its share of difficulties, setbacks, and failures in the area of foreign policy, the same holds true of any other global actor, including the USA. And in the face of such skepticism the EU has engaged in a continual process of institutional growth in this domain, produced regular foreign policy 'outputs', and positively influenced various global problems. The EU's shift in terminology from 'external relations' to 'foreign/security policy' since the 1990s also speaks volumes about the change in the EU members' own understanding of, and preference for, the EU's role in the world. Usage of the term 'European foreign policy' (EFP), which is now becoming commonplace, denotes all of the global behaviors of the EU: the foreign economic policy and diplomacy of pillar one (the EC); the CFSP and ESDP of pillar two, and the police cooperation and anticrime/antiterror work of Justice and Home Affairs (JHA) in pillar three.

This chapter analyzes EFP to understand better why the EU defied the predictions of many skeptics and grew into a true *global political actor* rather than remaining a regional economic power. Specifically, it examines two related strands of research into this topic: first, the gradual emergence of the EU's institutional capacities in this realm despite their conspicuous absence in the Treaty of Rome; and second, the extent to which the EU actually influences non-member states and other actors, thus helping to narrow the so-called 'capability-expectations gap' in EFP posited by Christopher Hill (1993). We are particularly interested in how HI theory sheds light on the growth of EFP as a process of increasingly coherent and centralized—though not necessarily supranational—international cooperation, involving both EU member states and EU institutional actors (chiefly the Commission). Institutional theory is also helpful in illuminating why and how EU member states have exploited economics and politics of scale in the conduct of their foreign/security policies under conditions of regional interdependence, globalization, and transatlantic competition.

Overall, we argue that the EU's status as a global actor cannot be fully understood by orthodox theories of international relations (whether realist or liberal), as the EU's wide-ranging activities are not merely a response to either the stimuli of power/threats or the more instrumental prerogatives of either functional regime theory or supranational integration theory. However, nor is the EU wholly *sui generis* in possessing this capacity: its institutions and policies may yield useful lessons for other troubled areas of the globe. In fact, the EU's deliberate efforts to 'export' its novel techniques of political cooperation, global governance, and regional integration comprise one of its most important foreign policies. A more complete understanding of these dynamics may offer useful lessons about alternative ways to maintain regional and global order.

Theorizing the EU as a Global Actor

While the EU's pursuit of a global political role inspires a number of interesting research questions (for overviews see Smith 2003; Hill and Smith 2005), this subject is most usefully divided into two essential areas: the internal dimensions of EFP (including institution-building, policymaking, and the influence of EFP on EU member states) and the external dimensions of EFP (particularly its impact on specific problems outside the EU itself). One major mistake made by EFP skeptics is their tendency to focus almost exclusively on the latter issue without appreciating fully the former. Indeed, it can be argued that EFP primarily serves internal functions, particularly if one includes the enlargement process in the analysis. At a minimum, these include:

1. Confidence-building among EU member states,
2. Defining EFP as a distinct multilateral issue area (rather than as a unilateral right) related to the pursuit of European integration,
3. Creating common viewpoints and analyses, or the so-called '*communauté de vue*' posited by de Schoutheete de Tervarent (1980), as a frame of reference on key issues, and
4. Preventing disputes over foreign policy from adversely affecting other areas of European integration (the damage-limitation function).

These processes help explain the EU's persistent pursuit of, and desire for, foreign/security cooperation despite its supposed failures in certain cases.

For those who are primarily concerned with the EU's external impact, a second major problem of analysis involves the difficulty of choosing an appropriate frame of reference for evaluating EFP. Observers often fall into analytical traps along two dimensions: how to define the EU itself as a global actor, and whether to compare the EU to other powerful actors in world politics. Regarding the former dimension of EFP, it is unproductive to define the EU solely as a functional regime, an international organization, an alliance, a collective security arrangement, or as a 'supranational state'. Although the EU shares some attributes of all of these political entities, in the realm of foreign/security policy it is best appreciated as a *highly institutionalized multilateral forum* for encouraging regular international cooperation on foreign policy issues among independent states. This is where both functionalists and intergovernmentalists err in their interpretations: EFP is not a distinct issue area amenable to functional spillover processes, so it operates according to different logics of both intergovernmental and transgovernmental integration. Specifically, formal EFP institutional reforms are often codified through intergovernmental conferences (IGCs), yet many of those innovations are in fact a result of intensive communication, socialization, and learning-by-doing among lower-level diplomats who make EFP on a daily basis.

However, intergovernmentalists make the additional mistake of underestimating the highly institutionalized nature of EFP, not only in terms of managing common external problems through a 'politics of scale' (Ginsberg 1989) but, more importantly, also in terms of helping to influence national preference formation to make such international cooperation more likely (Smith 2004*a*; Smith 2004*b*). This latter tendency is a direct result of the internal functions of EFP noted above. And regarding whether to measure the EU's influence only by reference to the roles of other important actors (particularly the USA but also NATO and even individual EU member states), EFP skeptics make the mistake of assuming that global influence is a zero-sum game: US influence will 'crowd out' any possible independent role for the EU. It is also important to note that a 'common' foreign and security policy does not mean a *single* foreign policy like that of a state. European foreign policy activities constitute the foreign policy framework or *acquis politique* of the EU, but EFP can never be as complete as that of a state; it lacks the legal sovereignty claimed by states and the EU, unlike states, is not responsible to a single electorate.

A third mistake observers of EFP sometimes make is to conceptualize power quite narrowly in terms of the primacy of military force. Most realists argue that the EU will not 'matter' as a global actor until it possesses such an independent force and makes use of it to achieve certain aims. Even with such a force, the EU is then measured against other military actors (namely the USA and NATO). Without neglecting the utility of military force in certain situations, a more complete understanding of the EU as a global actor would recognize: first, the virtues of alternative forms of power, including both economic power and so-called 'soft', 'civilian', 'ethical', or 'normative' power (Manners 2002, 2006; Meunier and Nicolaïdis 2006; Sjursen 2006); and second, the limits of military power in handling complex security problems. The EU does possess a strong power of attraction and does attempt to lead by example rather than force its values on others through threats of military force (see e.g. Mary Farrell's chapter on regionalism in this volume). However, unlike the case just a few years ago, the EU now has recourse to military means, as a last resort, to defend its values and principles in the conduct of its foreign policies and in the service of humanitarian, peacekeeping, and other defensive security operations. In doing so, EFP deliberately attempts to create synergies between the traditional economic diplomacy and foreign aid policies of the EC and its growing competencies in the forms of the CFSP (since 1993) and the ESDP (since 1999). Although problems of cohesion still exist, they are not terribly different from similar problems confronting other complex international actors (including the USA, which has multiple sources of foreign policy). Moreover, the EU is mitigating these problems through both institutional reforms and common strategic plans. The EU Security Strategy document of 2003 and related initiatives (such as the ENP; see Weber, Smith, and Baun, forthcoming) have clearly started to crystallize EFP strategically in terms of the EU's appropriate global political role, one often in opposition to that of the USA.

A fourth mistake evidenced in much conventional wisdom about the EU involves the too-narrow definition of political impact, which often follows from the use of a too-narrow definition of power resources above. Measuring impact only or primarily in terms of a response to threats of violence greatly underestimates the EU's external power. Adopting a wider range of measures allows one to appreciate both direct and indirect types of impact, the general roles played by the EU at the global level (Allen and Smith 1996; Elgström and Smith 2006), and the EU's impact on specific issues/problems (Ginsberg 2001). One might also consider the use of counterfactuals to judge the EU's actual impact: how might the absence of EU involvement with a certain global problem have influenced the outcome? We return to this question of EU impact later in the chapter.

Process: The Institutional Dimension of EFP

To address some of these analytical problems, and to understand the EU's actual status as a global power better, we offer an institutional argument. Indeed, the criticisms made by EFP skeptics can often be attributed to an underappreciation of institutional processes relative to other factors, such as material power. As suggested above, the EU's tendency to strike a balance between intergovernmental and supranational approaches to EFP was much less a conscious decision than a result of various factors that gradually led EU member states to break a deadlock between these competing visions. Although EFP initially centered on a weak inter-governmental forum in the form of European Political Cooperation (EPC) in the 1970s, over time it became far more institutionalized and more closely attached to other aspects of European integration, both functional and institutional. The institutionalization of EFP involved both informal and formal rules, and most often took place outside the high-level IGCs (i.e. treaty negotiations) that attract so much attention by intergovernmental theorists. In other words, socialization processes and learning-by-doing by lower-level officials were more responsible for EFP institutional changes than high-level bargains among heads of state or government.

Thus, as EFP involves a wide variety of institutional elements to realize its ambitions, ranging from intergovernmental bargaining to transgovernmental rela-tions to supranational implementation, we must be aware of multiple sources of institutional growth. Such growth directly affects policy cooperation, even in sensitive domains such as foreign policy. This cooperation in turn increases the EU's overall political impact/influence in world politics in conjunction with other factors often outside the EU's control. Finally, feedback mechanisms lead back to debates over institutional reforms in the EU, most recently in the form of the Convention on the Future of Europe. Although the Constitutional Treaty is currently stalled, we argue that the EU is in fact operationalizing some of its foreign policy provisions in order to maintain some momentum of reform. The Constitution would have instituted key improvements in EFP making and imple-mentation, but some of these improvements merely codified existing practices while others will likely be instituted by actions on the ground in the absence of a new Treaty. We also note that despite the French and Dutch rejections of the Treaty, European public opinion overall still exhibits strong support for both the CFSP and the ESDP, both of which would have been strengthened by the Treaty.

In terms of institutional growth, EFP has evolved over four general phases of development following the collapse of EDC in 1954. In phase one (1958–70), the EC began using its economic and diplomatic instruments to project its foreign commercial and political interests. In phase two (1970–93), the member states introduced and developed EPC as a weak intergovernmental forum for foreign policy coordination outside the Treaty framework in order better to address external demands on the EC and to help harmonize the foreign policies of its member states. The SEA linked EPC to the EC Treaty framework and added international security to the EPC's remit in 1987. In phase three (1993–9), EPC was superseded by CFSP, and although established as an intergovernmental pillar of the new three-pillar EU, informal reforms to CFSP through the 1990s helped it deal with the aftermath of diplomatic defeats in former Yugoslavia. In phase four (1999–present), the EU is executing its ESDP component to strengthen the CFSP, deploying military and civilian personnel abroad in support of peacekeeping and other security operations, and slowly narrowing the gap between the rhetoric of international security action and shortfalls in the member states' capabilities to deploy force abroad. In 1999 the EU declared a Headline Goal to develop the capability to deploy up to 60,000 troops for the so-called Petersburg Tasks (humanitarian and rescue tasks, peacekeeping, and tasks of combat forces in crisis management, including peace enforcement). This nascent 'Eurocorps' was later retooled into a Rapid Response Force with contributions from nearly all EU member states. The EU also appointed Javier Solana as the new CFSP High Representative to give a voice and face to its foreign policy.

Between 2000 and 2004, a wide range of ESDP support institutions were created within the EU (including a Political and Security Committee, a Military Committee and Staff, a Planning Unit, a Situation Center for ESDP, and a European Defense Agency), while arrangements for cooperation were created with NATO. A new Headline Goal committed the member states to introduce thirteen EU battlegroups by 2010; eighteen are currently scheduled, thus exceeding that goal. A battlegroup is a form of rapid response: a combined-arms, battalion-sized, high-readiness force package of 1,500 troops reinforced with combat support elements, including relevant air and naval capabilities, which can be launched on the ground within ten days after the EU decides to act. All of these arrangements, including the EU's de facto 'absorption' of the Western European Union and now meetings of EU defense ministers, were practically unthinkable less than a decade ago, for both Euroskeptics and EU officials.

In light of these major changes, the CFSP High Representative Solana released the EU's first ever *European Security Strategy Paper* in December 2003. This paper identified the major threats to EU security (terrorism, WMD proliferation, regional conflict, state failure, and organized crime); emphasized that European security must first be enhanced in its own neighborhood by stabilizing the Balkans and extending cooperation and security to the east and south, with a focus on resolving the Israeli–Palestinian conflict; and articulated the principle of 'effective multilateralism' as the cornerstone of EU foreign policy. Following release of the EU Security Strategy document, the EU has extended the range of its crisis management activities to include joint disarmament operations, financial/technical support for nonmember states engaged in counterterrorism, and security sector reform (see below). With the Madrid bombing in 2004, the EU now includes anticrime/antiterrorism in the work of the ESDP and has appointed a counter-terrorism 'tsar' to assist such cooperation among EU member states. These activities build on long-standing EU security initiatives regarding issues such as nonproliferation, controls on dual-use technologies, organized crime, and antipersonnel landmines. Morever, all of these efforts are increasingly linked to internal 'soft security' EU policies, particularly those involving JHA (such border security, immigration/asylum policy, and anticrime efforts), a trend that makes it even more difficult to treat CFSP/ESDP as purely intergovernmental in practice and external in orientation (Occhipinti 2003; 2005).

Outcomes: The Impact Dimension of EFP

As an international political actor, the EU is too often dismissed by scholars who assume a group of states cannot have common foreign/security policies or these policies cannot be effective. In truth, the EU engages in a full range of foreign policy activities that cannot be easily distinguished from similar state behaviors. We argue that processes of institutional development directly result in greater foreign/security policy cooperation among EU member states, and therefore contribute to the EU's impact on important global problems. The connection between the gradual expansion of both institutional mechanisms and EU foreign policy actions since the 1960s has been well documented in the literature (Ginsberg 1989; Smith 2003) and we need not examine it here in great detail. It need only be mentioned that EU foreign policy actions today cover virtually all major areas of the globe, and deal with a much wider range of topics than was the case during the formative years of EPC. Similarly, the EU has expanded the range of policy tools it can bring to bear on these issues, most recently in the form of crisis management teams involving a military component. These new tools are increasingly linked to other EU policy domains, making the entire EFP enterprise far more complex, even while the EU (mainly in the form of the Commission) attempts to improve the coherence of these activities through the creation of comprehensive strategy plans and tools (such as the European Security Strategy and the ENP), a unique activity for a regional international organization.

The question of impact is far more complicated. Here we focus on external political impact across security issues and regions and countries, as this question receives most of the attention by EFP skeptics. The EU's influence on global economic issues, such as WTO negotiations or on antitrust questions, is uncontested, as is its commitment to humanitarian assistance, environmental cooperation, and development aid (the EU with its member states is the world's largest aid donor). And the EU's ability to influence the foreign policy practices and preferences of its own member states (and potential member states) in line with the argument made above has also been demonstrated in the literature on EFP (Hill 1996; Manners and Whitman 2000; Smith 2004*a*, 2004*b*). In continuing to institutionalize EFP, the EU still attempts to assert and defend a value set that is uniquely and indigenously European: conflict prevention and resolution, interstate political reconciliation and regional problem-solving through economic integration, the protection of human and minority rights, environmental and social protection, and respect for the rule of law. In this sense EFP is a mirror reflection of the intense multilateral cooperation that occurs among the EU member states themselves.

Still, a dose of sobriety is needed when examining foreign and security policy. There are instances (such as Rwanda, Bosnia-Hercegovina, and Kosovo in the 1990s, and Iraq more recently) when the EU was unable to act abroad given divergent interests of the member governments. EFP can work only when EU member states agree to discuss matters *before* forming distinct national positions of their own, and this basic rule of the system is not always respected (though it is respected far more today than in the 1970s). These shortcomings notwithstanding, if one were to focus only on when the EU failed to act when it might have, an incorrect generalization about the EU as an ineffective international political actor is perpetrated. In truth, there are many more instances, as shown below, when the EU does execute CFSPs that reflect its own unique collective interest. Overall, we argue that the EU has shown more influence toward non-member states than realists predict but possibly less than one might expect based on its total economic weight and combined military capabilities. However, rather than reduce expectations in light of its limitations in world politics, the EU in fact consistently raises them while also attempting to expand its range of capabilities.

The dramatic expansion of the EU's direct involvement in security affairs in recent years is a case in point. This activity provides some of the most compelling evidence in response to the realist dismissal of EFP. Here the rapid growth of the ESDP framework is quite surprising considering the taboo against this capacity felt by many EU member states. When it acts in international security the EU has multiple impacts: on the states who request EU security assistance, on the EU itself in terms of confidence-building, on other international security organizations when the EU cooperates with them or replaces their forces with EU forces and personnel (NATO, UN), and on non-EU members who participate in EU security actions because of complementary interests and values. All of these impacts can be seen where the EU endeavors to act across the range of the so-called Petersburg Tasks, namely the sixteen ESDP actions deployed between 2003 and 2006. These actions involve three new types of EFP initiatives: military crisis management, police actions, and rule of law/border monitoring missions. In the rest of this section we focus on these EFP 'trouble spots' and necessarily exclude the EU's possible impact on more friendly countries, such as the USA, Canada, Australia, New Zealand, Japan, and many countries in Central and South America.

Military Crisis Management

Since 2003 the EU has taken three military crisis management operations: Operations Concordia (Macedonia), Artemis (Democratic Republic of Congo), and Althea (Bosnia-Hercegovina, or BiH). In Macedonia, Skopje asked the EU to deploy an EU military force to help oversee implementation of the Ohrid Framework Agreement (a ceasefire accord between the government and rebel forces cosponsored by NATO and the EU in 2001) and to succeed NATO's Operation Allied Harmony in 2003. Concordia was an operation of twenty-six countries which offered 350 lightly armed personnel under EU command to patrol ethnic Albanian regions on Macedonia's frontiers. Concordia also engaged in surveillance, reconnaissance, and other security tasks. The security situation in the country has stabilized and the EU has agreed to open up negotiations with Skopje for membership in the EU. Whereas in the past the EU had recourse only to its civilian power to assist a country in transition, the EU now has a clear capacity for security assistance. Therefore, the EU has been a more effective and influential actor in Macedonia. The EU had an impact on its own level of confidence in its first-ever military operation, and on non-EU states who participated in the operation under the command of the EU. Concordia also was important to the EU–NATO relationship because it tested the 'Berlin Plus' arrangements by which the EU used NATO logistical and planning assets for an ESDP operation; and to NATO as a litmus test of the EU's ability to take action effectively that would free up NATO forces to redeploy elsewhere. On the basis of the success of Operation Concordia, the EU launched a new police mission to Macedonia (see below).

Further afield, from June–September 2003 the EU led a military force (Operation Artemis) of 2,000 troops to the unstable Ituri region of the Democratic Republic of Congo (DRC) at the request of the UN. The objective of the mission was to provide security and improve the humanitarian situation in Bunia. EU troops worked to help displaced persons return to their homes, reopen markets, protect refugee camps, secure the airport, and ensure the safety of both civilians and UN and humanitarian aid workers. Artemis, like Concordia, had multiple impacts. It helped stabilize the region while the UN redeployed peacekeepers and thus aided the humanitarian effort in Bunia and the UN organization itself. It had a major impact on NATO and the USA, demonstrating the willingness of the EU to take an action completely autonomously of NATO and its planning/logistics. This willingness was in direct opposition to America's somewhat unrealistic desire to have all ESDP missions vetted by NATO (i.e. the USA). Artemis also was very important to internal EU confidence-building as the EU's first military action outside Europe as well as one in a dangerous environment. Finally, the operation had impact on other countries who joined the EU mission (e.g. Brazil, South Africa, and Canada) because it gave them an opportunity to work with and expand cooperation with the EU.

The EU Force in BiH, Operation Althea, deploys nearly 7,000 troops from twenty-two EU and non-EU member states under EU command since late 2004. It succeeded the NATO force there and is responsible for security throughout the country. The purpose of Althea is to ensure compliance with the Dayton–Paris Peace Accords, maintain a secure and safe environment in BiH, combat organized crime in support of local authorities, provide support for the ICTFY, contribute to defense reform, and support the UN/EU High Representative. British and Finnish officers command EUFOR with costs to the EU in 2005 amounting to approximately €70 million. Althea is the third and largest EU military operation to date and it too has had impact on the EU and the players involved. It demonstrates the EU's capability to take over from NATO a major security operation under the Berlin Plus agreement. Althea is important to NATO because it freed up NATO forces to redeploy in Afghanistan. The mission is important for the EU in terms of bringing together in one country the range of EU civilian and military policy instruments as it has done in Macedonia. Typically, the EU is the largest provider of economic and humanitarian aid in the country and is working with authorities toward negotiating a future SAA that would codify institutional relations between Sarajevo and the EU. Since Althea is the result of a UN Security Council mandate, the UN system has much at stake in how well the EU conducts a military operation on its behalf. Non-EU members (Albania, Argentina, Bulgaria, Chile, Morocco, New Zealand, Norway, Romania, Switzerland, and Turkey) participating in the mission also gain experience working with the EU. And most importantly, Althea is critical to the security and safety of BiH. Also in the region, the EU is tentatively planning to deploy an ESDP operation to Kosovo in 2007, a clear expansion of its commitment to the security of that province.

Police Actions

To date the EU has deployed four police missions abroad: BiH (2003), Macedonia (2003), DRC (2005), and the Palestinian Authority (PA) (2006). Police actions draw on a history and tradition of gendarmerie in Europe and the desire of the EU to fill a niche in international security not handled by the USA. The EU Police Mission (EUPM) in BiH which began in 2003 succeeded the UN International Police Task Force. The purpose of the EUPM is to maintain local stability in BiH by providing assistance to establish an effective police force, fight organized crime and corruption, strengthen police administration, monitor performance, and support a wide variety of police training, border patrol, and criminal justice support programs. Five hundred police officers from over thirty states comprise the EUPM. Clearly this mission, which complements Althea and the EU's civilian efforts to build peace, is a critical litmus test for the EU effectively to bring to fruit in BiH the panoply of its instruments as a foreign and security policy player. The EUPM was the first civilian crisis management mission to operate under the ESDP. The mission was critical to confidence-building among the EU members and institutions. EUPM had impact on UN interests because by replacing the UN police mission there it allowed its personnel to deploy elsewhere. EUPM had impact on non-EU members who participated, including eighty officers from non-EU member states.

The EU also deployed a police mission, Operation Proxima, to Macedonia at the request of Skopje as a follow-up to Concordia. Its objectives are to monitor, mentor, advise, and reform the police, help fight organized crime, promote sound policing standards, promote border management and the creation of a border police, and support a political environment conducive to facilitating the Ohrid Framework Agreement. Like other police and military missions, Proxima is important to the EU because it helps strengthen the external borders of the EU in terms of anticrime and antiterrorism measures; and it is important to Macedonia as a measure of continued support for the country's peaceful transition and closer relationship with the EU. And regarding the Balkans in general, the EU has demonstrated a very high degree of learning-by-doing since the difficult years of the 1990s, and today it is able to use a full range of foreign/security policy instruments, the lack of which so hindered its efforts a decade ago.

Two new police missions were deployed since 2005: EUPOL-KINSHASA in the DRC and EUPOL-COPPS (Coordination Office for Palestinian Police Support) in the Palestinian Territories. EUPOL-KINSHASA aims to assist the Transnational Government in the DRC to establish an effective police program. This helped to pave the way for future democratic elections in the country, which the EU will help monitor. EUPOL-COPPS, launched to help the PA establish an effective, modern, civilian police force through advising, mentoring, and training police and judicial officials, consists of thirty-three unarmed personnel seconded from the EU member states with an annual budget of €6.1 million. Non-EU member states also have been invited to participate in the operation. In addition, as the world's largest donor of aid to the PA and to Palestinian refugees through the UN, the EU not only underwrites the PA institutions, but contributes substantially to the operating budget of the PA. Without institutions of civil society taking root in the PA the Palestinians will not be in a position to negotiate with Israel for a final settlement. The EU also supports the monitoring of the Gaza–Egyptian border (see below) and is financing Israeli–Palestinian projects aimed at raising the level of tolerance among Israelis and Palestinians through education, human rights and democracy, media, and other joint projects.

These EU police actions demonstrate a global commitment to assisting countries to establish an indigenous rule of law and therefore importantly influence national and international security. The growing demand for EUPM from foreign governments reflects the impact the EU is having and is likely to have in the near future. European gendarmerie are willing and able to lend their expertise abroad. There is also a need for EUPMs not only to address what most interests the EU—anticrime cooperation and border control—but what most interests average citizens of the recipient states: street crime. That said, the EU has an important niche to fill in international security in ways complementary to the UN, NATO, and the USA among other international security providers (Penska 2006).

Rule of Law and Border Patrol/Monitoring Missions

The EU has deployed two rule of law missions, one to the Republic of Georgia in 2004 (EURJUST Themis) and one for Iraq (EUJUST LEX) in 2005. A rule of law mission is designed to provide EU assistance to third countries in transition that require assistance in establishing independent judicial systems. The Georgia mission is designed to assist the government to reform and improve the criminal justice and law enforcement systems. The EU is currently training Iraqi judges, senior police, and prison officers in managing the criminal justice system. The mission comprises 520 judges from the EU and other states and had a 2005 budget of €10 million.

In 2005 and 2006 the EU deployed four border or monitoring missions and one mission in support of African peacekeepers in Darfur, Sudan. In the Aceh Monitoring Mission (AMM) the EU monitors the ceasefire in Banda Aceh between the Free Aceh Movement and the Indonesian government. Since 2005, the EU has been supporting a ceasefire in Banda Aceh, Indonesia, following the recent tsunami devastation in the region. The goals of the AMM are to monitor the implementation of the peace agreement signed between the Indonesian government and the Free Aceh Movement in 2005 in Helsinki. It includes 219 personnel from the EU, Switzerland, Norway, and five ASEAN countries (Thailand, Malaysia, Brunei, the Philippines, and Singapore). In the EU Border Assistance Mission, the EU provides police and customs officials on the border between Moldova and Ukraine to help prevent smuggling, trafficking, and customs fraud. The EU also agreed, in response to invitations from Israel and the PA, to dispatch a monitoring mission at the Rafah border crossing between Gaza and Egypt (EU Border Assistance Mission for the Rafah Crossing Point—EU BAM Rafah). The opening of the Rafah border crossing is an important step toward Palestinian statehood and to the MEPP. The EU mission here provides a third party presence at Rafah to monitor the PA, improve Palestinian border control and customs authorities, and contribute to the liaison between the PA, Israeli, and Egyptian authorities. The seventy staff members of the mission are mostly seconded from the EU member states, and their efforts help to assuage Israel's legitimate security concerns about the openness of the Gaza–Egypt border-crossing. Finally, since 2004 the EU has been providing a wide range of financial, technical, and logistical support and personnel and equipment for the peacekeeping troops of the African Union (AU) in Sudan, which are in the region to oversee a ceasefire between government and rebel forces. EU military personnel also participate in the AU ceasefire commission, and the EU provided €2.1 billion in assistance to the AU in 2005.

Beyond these specific ESDP missions, the EU also has provided significant financial and political support for the post-Taliban Afghan government and the country's postwar reconstruction. Twenty-three EU member states account for nearly two-thirds of the total deployment of NATO troops stationed in Afghanistan as part of the International Stabilization Force in Afghanistan (ISAF). In 2004, the five-nation Eurocorps assumed command of ISAF, and the EU and its member states are the world's largest donors to Afghan reconstruction. To bolster the Afghan government and coordinate EU aid, the EU in 2002 opened a Commission Delegation and an EC Humanitarian Office in Kabul; in 2004 it sent an EU Special Representative to Afghanistan. In 2002, the EU expended €800 million and in 2003 €900 million in overall aid to the country. Total EU aid for reconstruction pledged for the 2004–6 period amounts to €2.2 billion, and the EU and Afghanistan envisage a formal trade and cooperation agreement once the Kabul government is able to extend its authority over more areas of the country.

Finally, although EFP in Asia is still underdeveloped, the EU is using its considerable diplomacy, development aid, and tariff preferences in pursuit of political objectives. In the mid-1990s, the EU joined the Korean Development Organization (KEDO), a group of the USA, South Korea, and Japan committed to assisting Pyongyang to secure energy supplies in exchange for agreement not to pursue a nuclear energy program. The EU not only has granted extensive food aid but has tied that aid to agricultural market reforms. When the EU extended diplomatic recognition to North Korea in 2001, it used the occasion to engage the North Koreans in how to advance human rights and market economics in the country. And the AMM noted above demonstrates the EU's ability to move beyond mere economic engagement to facilitate security-related cooperation with the Asian region.

In sum, even this brief overview demonstrates the breadth of EFP activities across continents and functions. Today EFP covers the gamut of multilateral functional issues and bilateral relationships; increasingly couples or intermingles civilian and military aspects of crisis management; draws direction from the European Security Strategy Paper of 2003; and thus challenges realist assumptions that foreign policy belongs only to nation-states. Moreover, the ESDP in particular has been applied effectively across the gamut of Petersburg tasks and extended from EU's own backyard to Africa, the Middle East, and now Asia. The ESDP allows the EU to act with both civilian and military instruments, which is what most distinguishes EU foreign policy in the early twenty-first century from its late twentieth century origins. These early ESDP actions were designed to enhance internal EU confidence in ways similar to the early CFSP actions in the 1990s. The EU has thus demonstrated that it can deploy force under limited circumstances, against the expectations of most EFP skeptics. While the EU still has major capabilities shortfalls in the areas such as sustainability, reconnaissance, surveillance, and intelligence, the EU is fully aware of these problems and is taking steps to address them while also gaining valuable operational experience (i.e. learning-by-doing). The more the EU gains such experience in handling lower-level and soft international security tasks the more it will gain the confidence to take on more dangerous tasks. And although it is too soon to measure the long-term impact the EU has had in the countries where it has conducted ESDP actions, we do know that the demand for new ESDP actions is growing by the number of states who request EU action and is expanding geographically from Europe to Africa, the Middle East, and Asia, and that in countries such as Macedonia and BiH the security situation has improved.

Conclusion: The Future of EFP

The empirical record clearly demonstrates steady growth in EFP activity and impact since the 1970s, even though skeptics continue to belittle the EU as a global political actor. In fact, our review has only scratched the surface of European diplomatic efforts, especially since we have largely excluded the EU's traditional role in economic affairs. We have also directly linked this expansion of activity to the process of institutional growth in the EU in general and the EFP domain in particular. Although numerous endogenous and exogenous factors help explain individual EFP actions, their cumulative growth over time in terms of raw numbers, geographic/functional scope, and complexity is a result of the two-way relationship between institutional processes and cooperative behaviors on the ground.

We do not argue, however, that this process is always unidirectional or even efficient in terms of improving EFP behaviors. EFP as an institution is subject to stress like any other institution, and numerous factors (i.e. the Constitutional Treaty debate, enlargement, the Iraq war, and terrorism) have certainly stressed the system. And there is no doubt that decision-making is becoming more cumbersome with twenty-five or more member states. However, it is also true that the EU is unlikely to abandon its efforts in light of the foreign policy issues discussed in this chapter, as the EU is directly exposed to a wide range of problematic issues and countries, even wider perhaps than the USA. We also suggest the EU might be better than the USA at managing certain problems of regional interdependence and globalization given its location, history, and institutional experience. The EU is almost certainly more effective at long-term state-building and real policing than the USA, which may be more effective at traditional methods of war-making. Even more interesting is that the EU, rather than other institutions (OSCE, Council of Europe, and NATO), has become the primary means for resolving certain global problems, first through enlargement and the single market, more recently through the CFSP/ESDP and related policies. And while elites have built the EU's institutional architecture in this area, EU citizens themselves demonstrate consistently strong support for a greater European political role, more so even than in other core areas of European integration such as the single currency.

Regarding the future of EFP, we therefore explicitly, though cautiously, predict a steady expansion of EU influence and institutional growth. The EU will manage to address the EFP reforms provided in the Constitutional Treaty, though perhaps informally rather than constitutionally. This includes the possibility of an EU foreign minister and diplomatic service, as well as an implicit security guarantee for EU member states. Moreover, we also expect the EU to continue its deliberate efforts to export its mechanisms of cooperation—largely involving institutional factors and other types of soft power—through foreign policies such as the European Neighborhood Program, as detailed in Mary Farrell's chapter in this volume. While success here will vary as always, these efforts will often directly challenge America's own policies toward certain countries and problems, and may therefore increase rather than undermine the EU's status and influence. Whether these efforts should be framed as explicit EU 'soft balancing' against the USA is an open question (Pape 2005; Paul 2005), but certainly individual EU states will be tempted increasingly to challenge the USA and its emphasis on unilateral military intervention. The question of a 'European' army with offensive capabilities will be a sensitive one in the next few years, and may create as many problems of collective action as it solves (not least in terms of its relationship to American leadership). However, the EU has confounded its skeptics many times before, and it may do so again even in the high stakes world of foreign and security policy.

16

Trade and Transatlantic Relations: Old Dogs and New Tricks

JOHN PETERSON AND ALASDAIR R. YOUNG[1]

Transatlantic relations, it is widely alleged, have fallen on hard times. For every analysis that concludes that the relationship between Europe and America is 'broadly healthy and, in some areas, thriving' (European Commission 2005d: 3),[2] there are more that portray the transatlantic allies as being 'at war' (Gordon and Shapiro 2004), 'at odds' (Mowle 2004), or 'under stress' (Andrews 2005). In the circumstances, it is easy to forget how much western Europe and the USA invested in institutionalizing their relationship after 1945, to the point where it became common to refer to a 'transatlantic security community' (see Risse 2003b).[3] This community was built largely on mutual security guarantees and the NATO, but one of its primary foundations was an economic relationship that became a source of enormous prosperity.

In fact, much of what we associate with globalization is very largely the result of expanding economic exchange between Europe and America over the past twenty-five years. Today, it remains the case that 'no other commercial artery in the world is as integrated or fused together' as the transatlantic one (European Commission 2005d: 13). One consequence is that Washington's main institutional interlocutor in its relationship with Europe is less frequently NATO Europe, and more often the EU.

This chapter focuses on the institutionalization of transatlantic relations, especially since the agreement in 1995 of the New Transatlantic Agenda (NTA). The NTA is an overarching system of bilateral institutions designed to manage the USA–EU dialogue. In an era when the lack of capacity for 'global governance'

---

[1] An earlier draft of this chapter was presented at the International Studies Association conference in San Diego in March 2006. We are grateful to colleagues who commented on it then as well as to Matthew Baldwin, Elizabeth Bomberg, and the editors for helpful suggestions.

[2] In the interest of full disclosure, one of us was the lead author of the study referenced here, and the other was a leading contributor.

[3] This term does not appear to have been made obsolete by recent transatlantic troubles. See the speech given by incoming NATO Secretary-General, Jaap de Hoop Scheffer, on November 17, 2004 entitled 'The Future of the Transatlantic Security Community'. Available at: www.nato.int/docu/speech/2004/s041117d.htm

is much remarked upon (see Waltz 1999; Keohane 2002; Nicolaïdis and Howse 2002; Moore 2003; Lamy 2004; Möttölä 2006), recent attempts by the USA and EU to engage in economic policy cooperation via new bilateral institutions offer an interesting analytical case. Whether such cooperation can effectively 'govern' transatlantic economic exchange is an important question for any student of international political economy.

We also confront questions that link directly to the general themes of this volume. In particular, how and how much are transatlantic economic relations mediated by the institutional setting(s) in which they take place? What light does historical institutionalism shed on their character and prospects for change?[4]

While the transatlantic economic relationship is broadly robust and healthy, we argue that the political institutions framing it are ill-suited to fostering further transatlantic economic integration. More specifically, we find that economic relations are increasingly dominated by a 'deep trade' agenda, which features strong pressures from economic actors on both sides to go beyond traditional trade diplomacy and agree disciplines on domestic economic rule-making (see Young and Peterson 2006). For over a decade, considerable efforts to manage the deep trade agenda have taken place within the framework of the NTA. However, its institutions are weak and rest on domestic policy systems that were designed for a far 'shallower' trade agenda focused on tariffs. As such, each side soldiers on with traditional trade policy institutions that are products of a bygone age and entirely unequipped to tackle regulatory differences.

The USA and EU will thus fail to tackle the most important remaining real obstacles to transatlantic economic exchange in the absence of dramatic reform of domestic economic policy institutions. The old dogs of postwar trade wars need to learn new tricks if they wish to use the economic bedrock of their relationship as a foundation for anything more ambitious in the globalized era in which they find themselves. Moreover, we have considerable reservations about the desirability of more ambitious transatlantic institutions. Yet we find ourselves skeptical about the ability of the USA and EU to address these challenges. We doubt that the transatlantic deep trade agenda is likely to result in an expansion and upgrading of domestic and international trade institutions anytime soon.

It is worth noting that this chapter differs from those in the rest of the volume in that the EU itself is only part of our story: we also focus on institutionalized co-operation between the Union and the USA, as well as the development of US trade policy institutions. We begin by surveying (briefly) the literature linking economic interdependence and institutionalization. We then examine the development of the transatlantic economic relationship, before focusing on the shortcomings of

---

[4] We are unable, in such a short contribution, to answer a more primordial question: is the economic relationship enough to preserve a transatlantic 'alliance'? However, we hope our analysis might help others to do so.

transatlantic institutions. We draw on historical institutionalism to help explain these shortcomings, highlighting in particular the path dependence of domestic trade policy institutions on both sides of the Atlantic. We conclude by reflecting on how historical institutionalism makes sense of much about our case that other theoretical accounts find mysterious.

Theorizing Institutional Change: The Case of Transatlantic Relations

Most theories of international cooperation assume that economic interdependence 'pushes' international institutionalization (see Goldstein et al. 2000; Keohane and Nye 2001). This is especially the case with general work on regional integration (see Mattli 1999). This assumption also underpins disparate theoretical accounts of European integration. The link between interdependence and institutionalization is fundamental to 'transactionalist' approaches to EU politics, which argue that the integration of political structures occurs where there is the most demand for it from economic actors (see Sandholtz and Stone Sweet 1988; Stone Sweet, Fligstein, and Sandholtz 2001). It also appears in liberal intergovernmentalism, according to which governments pursue institutionalized cooperation as a response to the impact of economic interdependence on domestic economic actors (Moravcsik 1998).

Moreover, the nature of transatlantic economic interdependence creates particular incentives for institutionalization. Domestic rules have emerged as the key barriers to trade in the transatlantic relationship in part because of the importance of FDI—investment by businesses on one side in assets located in the other's market—and trade in services in the economic relationship (see the next section). Successive rounds of multilateral trade negotiations have dramatically reduced tariffs affecting transatlantic trade in goods (OECD 2000; USTR 2001), which makes regulatory barriers more evident. These developments have given rise to political constituencies that advocate international cooperation in order to mitigate the adverse consequences for international economic exchange of differences in domestic rules (Dymond and Hart 2000; Hocking 2004). Given the difficulties of agreeing such rules in multilateral fora, there are strong incentives for the world's two largest economies, for which these issues matter most, to pursue bilateral cooperation.

The extent and nature of transatlantic economic interdependence, therefore, contribute to expectations of closer cooperation and greater institutionalization in the transatlantic relationship (Fogarty 2004). More than a decade after the NTA was signed, however, transatlantic institutions remain underdeveloped. The rest of this chapter contrasts the health of the economic relationship with the weakness of the institutional relationship, and seeks to explain the disparity.

The Historical Trajectory of the Transatlantic Economy

Two observations about the evolution of the transatlantic economy are particularly important for our purposes. First, three key measures of economic interdependence—trade, FDI, and affiliate income (garnered from sales by firms headquartered on one side but who produce and/or sell on the other) are interrelated and tend to rise and fall together. As such, USA–EU trade relations are now very broad-based and reflect a deep trade agenda featuring a far wider array of economic actors that are highly sensitive to 'behind the border' policies, especially regulation. Second, transatlantic economic relations reflect the powerful agglomeration effects of economic geography: that is, the tendency for a critical mass of economic activity in a given sector to attract more firms in the same sector to regions where the activity takes place (see below). The result is a powerful, economic form of path dependence, which underpins the transatlantic economy even in the absence of strong political institutions.

The postwar history of USA–European economic relations is often presented as a narrative dominated by trade rounds and disputes. Since the Kennedy Round (1964–7) progress in multilateral trade rounds has depended on the USA and EU overcoming their differences and cooperating intensively (Sally 2004). Until the mid-1990s, such cooperation was aided by a generally balanced trading relationship, in that neither side incurred large bilateral deficits with the other for very long (Peterson 1996). Of course, the relationship has always been complicated by disputes, particularly over agriculture, which have arguably become more threatening since the mid-1990s as they have involved deep trade issues, such as the regulation of beef hormones and genetically modified crops, and the tax treatment of exports (Baldwin, Peterson, and Stokes 2003: 39–43). But the wider point is that the narrative of transatlantic economic relations has been dominated by trade traditionally defined: imports and exports of goods and, to a lesser extent, services.

Trade remains an important barometer of transatlantic economic interdependence (see Graphs 16.1 and 16.2). The total value of trade between Europe and America continues to outstrip FDI flows and affiliate income. Yet because of the intense economic interpenetration that results from these latter two types of economic activity, between one-quarter and one-third of USA–EU trade now takes place within firms with investments in both markets.

The USA now runs a chronic trade deficit with the EU, although it is dwarfed in size (and political importance) by a much larger one with China. Yet, more fundamentally, 'trade' per se is now, in important respects, only the third most important measure of transatlantic economic interdependence. Joseph Quinlan (2006: 200) calls trade 'a shallow, underdeveloped form of integration' compared to FDI— 'the deepest form of cross-border integration'—and 'the activities of foreign

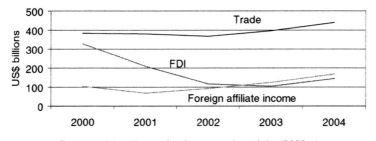

GRAPH 16.1.   Transatlantic economic activity, 2000–4.
Source: European Commission (2005*d*: 12).

affiliates', which form 'the backbone of transatlantic commercial activity'. Thus, it is plausible to argue that globalization, as a strictly economic phenomenon, is still largely a product of Europe's intensive economic engagement with the USA (and vice versa). Of course, US investment in China and India is expanding rapidly: in both cases, volumes were twice as high in 2000–4 as in the second half of the 1990s. But US investment in the EU is still far greater. US investment flows to France in 2004—at the peak of the diplomatic flak over Iraq—were around 45 percent higher than the total American investment in China. About four times more US investment flowed to Italy than to India in the same year. Europe attracted 56 percent of all American FDI during the first half of the 2000s. Corporate Europe accounted for a whopping 75 percent of all foreign investment

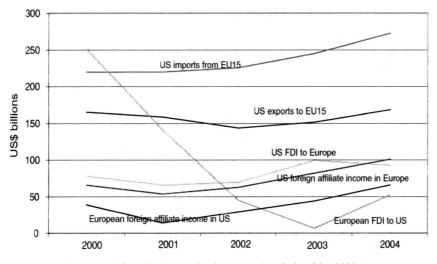

GRAPH 16.2.   The Transatlantic economic relationship, 2000–4.
Source: European Commission (2005*d*: 13).

that flowed to the USA. Quinlan (2006: 101) insists that the defining feature of globalization is 'the increasing integration and cohesion of the transatlantic economy'.

The powerful path dependence we find in transatlantic investment patterns may seem surprising. But it is entirely predictable from the point of historical institutionalism (see Meunier and McNamara in this volume) and given what we know from economic research on increasing returns in the spatial location of production. Physical proximity still generates powerful 'agglomeration effects' that matter far more in economic life than we might expect in our globalized age. A critical mass of firms attract suppliers, skilled workers, specialized business service providers and may even promote infrastructure development, all of which can act as a magnet that attracts similar firms to locate production in the same place (Pierson 2004: 25).

The importance of such increasing returns leads us to expect especially powerful path dependence in patterns of exchange within knowledge-intensive sectors that dominate transatlantic economic exchange. It also explains the higher share of international trade that is 'North–North', when comparative advantage based on 'natural' features of different countries would predict more North–South exchange of manufactured goods for raw materials. Krugman (1991: 80) claims that 'if there is one single area of economics in which path dependence is unmistakable, it is in *economic geography*—the location of production in space' (emphasis in original).

For their part, Suzanne Berger and others at MIT (2006: 44) have recently argued that firms make business decisions mostly on the basis of 'dynamic legacies', or their 'reservoir, or legacy, of resources that have been shaped by the past'. In what is very much an HI approach to globalization, Berger et al. (2006: 44) contend that a firm is a product of the 'institutions and values in the country where the company was born'. Intuitively, we might conclude that both institutions and values are likely to be far more alike in the USA and any European country than when either is paired with China, India, or most other countries. Moreover, Berger et al. (2006: 46) contend that previous successes and failures and long-term relationships with suppliers and customers are crucial. Thus agglomeration effects, comparable institutions and values, and accumulated experience of each other's market combine to create a powerful path dependency that underpins the transatlantic economic relationship.

Nevertheless, there is recent evidence to suggest that economic gains achievable by eliminating remaining barriers to transatlantic economic exchange, especially regulatory barriers, are considerable. According to the Organization for Economic Cooperation and Development (OECD 2005), a 'deep but not a broad cut in regulations' could boost European GDP per capita by 2 to 3.5 percent, and US GDP by 1 to 3 percent. It was to address such barriers and realize such gains that the NTA was launched in 1995.

The Historical Trajectory of the Transatlantic Institutions

The construction of a series of USA–EU institutions began with the Transatlantic Declaration in 1990 and accelerated after the NTA was unveiled in 1995. In a sense, these agreements signaled that the USA and EU were moving on from old-style trade issues to a new, more modern agenda of seeking to iron out differences in domestic regulation that often make it difficult for firms to produce economically for both the USA and EU markets. When first proposed, the NTA looked like a potentially major institutional innovation given its ambitions to create (after 1998) a 'Transatlantic Economic Partnership' by building on (then) rapidly expanding efforts toward transatlantic regulatory cooperation (Pollack and Shaffer 2001; Pollack 2005*a*).

As a caveat, the primary inspiration behind the NTA was not economic as much as political: the recognition by Washington of the EU's new geopolitical magnetism in post-cold war Europe together with fears that the end of the common security threat with the collapse of the Soviet Union would unravel the transatlantic relationship. The Clinton administration also viewed a more institutionalized link with the EU (as opposed to NATO Europe) as a useful step toward ending the transatlantic nightmare of the Balkans, but more broadly as a means to hasten reform in the regions to the EU's east and south. Still, economic ambitions ('the expansion of world trade and closer economic relations') were important enough to constitute one of the NTA's four main chapters, alongside ones dedicated to 'promoting peace and stability', 'responding to global challenges' (terrorism, environmental degradation, and so on), and 'building people-to-people bridges across the Atlantic'.

Institutionally, the NTA created a series of new bilateral channels for political and policy dialogue. They extended from bilateral summits at the highest political levels to an 'NTA Task Force' at the operational level of policy-specialized officials. A Senior Level Group, at the US Undersecretary of State and EU Commission Director-General levels, would oversee implementation. Existing exchanges between MEPs and the US House of Representatives would be recast (eventually) as a Transatlantic Legislators Dialogue (see European Commission 2005*d*: 10–11).

Ten years after the NTA was agreed, Pollack's verdict (2005*a*: 900) was that the USA and EU had created 'a new and novel institutional architecture'. The NTA represented 'the most systematic effort at genuine bilateral governance in the history of the transatlantic partnership'. One might go even further and consider that, leaving aside the EU itself and the WTO, the NTA was perhaps the most ambitious attempt *ever* to institutionalize cross-border economic policy cooperation between sovereign entities.

Yet the NTA's balance sheet has been very mixed. USA–EU cooperation has exploded since 1990 to the point that in 2005 there were some thirty-three

bilateral, sectoral agreements and forty-nine separate dialogue structures at official and political levels (European Commission 2005*d*: 10). By 1998, a bilateral
Mutual Recognition Agreement (MRA), covering product certification in six
sectors and estimated to save firms something like $1 billion annually, was in
place, although negotiations on the agreement were advanced by the time the
NTA was agreed. It was easier to credit the new USA–EU dialog with achieving
a 'veterinary equivalence agreement' on the treatment of live animals and animal
products. Its boosters claimed it would lower barriers worth up to $3 billion in
two-way trade.

The NTA, however, was never sturdy enough to prevent subsequent back-
sliding even on these agreements (see Nicolaïdis and Steffenson 2005). Economic diplomacy between the USA and EU generally has remained ad hoc and
unsystematic. Many of the most effective examples of cooperation—such as
those on Borders and Transport Security or Financial Markets Regulation—have
been achieved essentially independently of the NTA's institutional framework.
Informal exchanges between the USA and EU regulators, particularly competition
authorities and financial services regulators, have produced tangible results in
the form of successful management of potentially damaging economic disputes
(Devuyst 2000; Devuyst 2001; Mehta 2003), but without much (if any) credit to
the NTA. Trade negotiations, such as on the Doha Round, or the management of
trade (and even many regulatory) disputes are not matters for officials engaged
in NTA exchanges. Neither are exchange rate management or monitoring or
(crucially) most investment issues. The NTA never gets near defense issues,
including defense industry issues, or even the regulation of aviation or agriculture
(European Commission 2005*d*: 32–3). When major, politicized problems arise—
such as over Iraq, Boeing/Airbus, or the breakdown of the Doha Round—there is
no expectation that they will be addressed in the NTA dialogue.

Perhaps we should not be surprised. The NTA framework is highly technocratic,
operating primarily at official level and with diplomats (not regulators) from
the US State Department and European Commission (and its DG for External
Relations) in the lead. The types of issues that present problems in transatlantic
trade are rooted in domestic regulatory and legislative processes. The rules in
question address public policy objectives that cannot simply be waved away. What
the NTA reveals about the transatlantic economic relationship, above all, is that
even given the similarities of their markets, there remains considerable 'system
friction' between the two regulatory systems (Kahler 1995; Vogel 1997). US regulatory agencies often enjoy, and guard, their autonomy with considerable vigor.
In Europe, the regulation of risk—especially associated with biotechnology—is
now highly politicized after numerous food-safety scandals produced a collapse in
consumer confidence (see Vogel 1997, 2003; Pollack and Shaffer 2005). Specific
regulatory disputes over beef hormones, airplane 'hush kits', and genetically modified foods have been seen on both sides to 'call for policy responses distinct from

those best suited to the prevention and settlement of traditional trade disputes' (Pollack 2003*b*: 595).

Regulatory cooperation has been further hampered by pronounced differences in procedures and administrative law (Egan 2001*b*; Nicolaïdis and Egan 2001; Shaffer 2003; Nicolaïdis and Steffenson 2005; Steffenson 2005). Thus, the transatlantic institutions created for exchanges between the USA and EU on regulatory cooperation have little traction over regulators and legislators who are focused on their domestic responsibilities and who often, particularly on the US side, actively oppose new, further, cooperative agreements.

As a consequence, transatlantic regulatory disputes tend to be extremely protracted. Few are resolved bilaterally and even fewer are taken to the WTO (although those that are tend to take on a very high profile). There seems to be no clear antidote to transatlantic system friction besides patient dialogue between regulators and low-key measures such as encouraging specific commitments on the part of regulators to earmark personnel and budgets for international cooperation.

Despite the limited success of the NTA to date, some policymakers and private actors see these various transatlantic exchanges as replicable in enough other economic sectors to sustain a vision of a 'Transatlantic Marketplace by 2015'.[5] For others, the main lesson to be drawn from the past ten years of USA–EU regulatory cooperation and disputes is that such a vision is unrealizable in the absence of very ambitious (and barely imaginable) steps, such as creating binding systems for regulatory harmonization or mutual recognition, with some kind of Transatlantic Court to adjudicate disputes (see Pollack 2003*b*: 600–1). Short of such ambitions, the USA and EU have little choice but to rely on mostly informal, imperfect, existing institutions, which are often not clearly or directly linked to NTA exchanges (see European Commission 2005*d*: 41–51), to keep regulatory dialogue open and to manage disputes.

The Historical Trajectory of Domestic Trade Institutions

Even if the task of removing regulatory barriers to transatlantic trade were less daunting, transatlantic institutions would be ill-equipped to deal with a deep trade agenda. Although the NTA and the TEP in particular are intended to do just that, they rest upon domestic institutions designed for an earlier, and simpler, type of trade. On both sides of the Atlantic, trade policy institutions have remained remarkably unchanged since their inception. Of particular import for the NTA, regulatory policy remains mostly divorced from trade policy. Moreover, there is

---

[5] This idea has significant support within the European Parliament. See 'EU–US Forum: "A Transatlantic Marketplace by 2015" ', Brussels: Centre for European Policy Studies (February 2, 2006). Available at http://www.ceps.be/Article.php?article_id=291

little appetite in either the USA or EU for radically strengthening transatlantic institutions (see European Commission 2005*d*). On both sides there are strong reservations about accepting further constraints on regulatory autonomy, which reinforce ebbing support for liberalization.

The following sections document the (lack of) development of trade policy institutions on both sides. They highlight the disconnect between trade policy and domestic policy. They seek to explain the lack of appetite for much more ambitious cooperation.

US Trade Policy: The '1934 System'

US trade policy institutions have their roots in the Roosevelt era 'Reciprocal Trade Agreements Act' 1934. It delegated much of Congress' power to regulate foreign trade to the US executive, specifically (since the 1960s) to the US Trade Representative (USTR).[6] The resulting system has always depended on time-limited grants of authority by Congress to the executive to negotiate trade agreements, which are then subject to up or down (with no amendments) Congressional votes: a system now known as 'trade promotion authority' (TPA), or 'fast track' before 2002. Until the late 1990s, in Destler's memorable prose (2005: 9), the system survived: 'It eroded. It bent. But despite the fears of many, it did not break'. In many respects, its ultimate achievements came just as it became evident that globalization was becoming irreversible: that is, with the creation of the North American Free Trade Agreement and WTO in the early 1990s.

The system has recently shown signs of serious dysfunction. Trade doubled as a share of total US output of goods after 1985, and thus 'trade policy became too important to be left to the trade specialists' (Destler 2005: 254). In addition, the increasing importance of FDI in economic diplomacy and the rise of 'trade and [other policy issues previously distinct from trade] . . . ' debates, fusing trade with environmental, labor, consumer, and development concerns, meant that what was once a low profile, technocratic area about which few cared beyond a small group of trade policy wonks became the focus for a large movement of disparate groups with diverse concerns and priorities.

Meanwhile, the USTR's narrow competence over traditional, cross-border trade leaves it far short of anything close to unchallenged leadership in economic diplomacy. Thus, bureaucratic competition to be the main institutional guardian of economic relations with Europe has increased over time, particularly as the agenda

[6] Article I of the US Constitution grants Congress exclusive power to 'regulate commerce with foreign nations'. It gives the executive (President) no trade-specific authority at all. All powers that the USTR wields are thus delegated to it by Congress, and 'in no sphere of government policy can the primacy of the legislative branch be clearer' (Destler 2005: 14).

has broadened beyond narrow trade concerns. Again, the State Department is formally the lead US department under the NTA. It and the US Treasury compete for control over the investment agenda. The Commerce Department has become more assertive on a range of regulatory issues under the Bush administration. Its International Trade Administration (ITA) continues to shoulder responsibility for administering much US trade law, particularly concerning antidumping and countervailing duties. We could add to the mix the Departments of Agriculture, Labor, and Energy (see Pigman 2004). Even this portrait of bureaucratic competition for leadership on external economic relations leaves aside the myriad US regulatory agencies with their overwhelmingly (some might say myopically) domestic focus.

At the same time, crucially, protectionism seems to be gaining ground on both sides of the aisle in the US Congress. In part this trend is due to the almost complete disappearance of the centrist coalition in the House of Representatives that in earlier eras instinctively favored free trade and could be counted on to deliver 'fast track' (see Destler 2005: 28–30).[7] In 2001, the Bush administration won TPA for what became the Doha Round only by exploiting the shadow of September 11, 2001, exerting heavy pressure on House Republicans, and even then barely winning three excruciatingly close votes (none by more than three votes).

Although it is possible (especially in Europe) to overestimate the role of campaign finance in US trade policy (see Smith 2004), there is no question that one of the effects of steadily more expensive political campaigns is a steadily weaker USTR. Institutionally, it finds it increasingly difficult to resist pressure from members of Congress (to which it is ultimately accountable) to act as lawyer for firms or industries that are large campaign contributors. More generally, trade and other economic issues on Capitol Hill increasingly are 'seen as weapons for combat with the other-party enemy. Less and less are they considered dispassionately, on their own substantive terms, with recognition that neither political side has a monopoly on truth and wisdom' (Destler 2005: 305). There is no other single factor that places greater limits on the statesmanship the USA can show in economic diplomacy than the rise of intense partisanship in American politics.

US trade policy institutions, therefore, are ill-suited to tackling the types of issues at the heart of the transatlantic economic agenda. Destler's persistence (2005: 6) in labeling the American system of trade policymaking as the '1934

---

[7] An important cause is 'redistricting', which involves the redrawing of House constituencies on a partisan basis. It usually results in more 'safe' seats that only one party has any hope of winning. One effect is that party primaries are often more competitive than general elections, and candidates are more dependent on traditional party 'clients' for support and funding (business for the Republicans and trade unions for the Democrats), thus reinforcing clientalism in trade policy.

system' hints at how far behind the times it has fallen. And there is little evidence of political will to modernize it.

The EU: Expanded Agenda, Loss of Control

There are uncanny echoes of America's archaic trade policy system in the EU system. The 1957 Treaty of Rome called for the creation of a customs union, which itself demanded that the EU negotiate as a single entity in international trade, at least with respect to goods, with the Commission—particularly the EU Trade Commissioner—in the lead. The resulting CCP, based on Article 113 (later Article 133), combined three elements: First, it gave the EU (technically the EC) exclusive, 'hard' competence in commercial policy on trade in goods. Second, Council of Ministers decisions under the CCP were (formally, at least) subject to QMV. Third, the EP was given no scrutiny role whatsoever.

The EU's trade policy competence has expanded over time, albeit more slowly and less completely than the changing international trade agenda (see Young 2002). Despite the changes introduced in the 2001 Treaty of Nice, competence over 'new' trade issues—particularly FDI, intellectual property, and some services—has not been resolved to the satisfaction of the Commission, as the EU must continue to share power in these areas with the member states (see Meunier 2005: 29–32). The effect is often to make the EU an unwieldy partner in trade negotiations.

In the best of circumstances, the EU Trade Commissioner often reinforces some of the more general prejudices of Washington, a political capital in which power is highly personalized. Like other representatives of international organizations, the Commissioner is another 'unelected bureaucrat', but in this case he wields formidable power to cause the USA (in this case, economic) pain. Ultimately, however, the Commission may enjoy even less 'agency slack', or ability to wield its delegated authority with autonomy, vis-à-vis EU member states than the USTR does with the powers it wields on behalf of Congress, because national European capitals often intervene so directly in terms of negotiating tactics and final packages (Woolcock 2005: 389–90). From an American perspective, the EU Trade Commissioner often embodies the worst possible combination of power and powerlessness.

More generally the EU's trade policy institutions have not changed very much despite the expansion of the Union's responsibility for foreign economic exchange. In the transatlantic context, the most significant change has been that, with the 1992 Treaty of Maastricht, the EP acquired the right of assent (i.e. veto rights) on trade agreements that affect internal rules adopted under the codecision procedure, including many single market regulations. The EU's Constitutional Treaty, if ratified, would have further increased the EP's role in trade policy by giving it rights of codecision over 'the framework for implementing policy'.

The EP's formal role in trade policy, however, remains far short of what it (and others) consider appropriate. Consequently, the EU's system for trade policy is increasingly under duress from a restive EP, particularly its new Committee on International Trade.[8]

An additional problem is that many of the regulatory issues that create the most acute transatlantic tensions directly involve EU member states. Many disputes touch directly upon distinct national rules, especially with regard to services, or highlight the important role national governments play in implementing EU directives. Thus transatlantic institutions, in which the Commission usually leads for the EU as a whole, sideline actors who can contribute significantly to transatlantic trade tensions, or resolution of them.

The broad trade agenda has also raised concerns about the EU's regulatory autonomy. For example, US complaints in the WTO about the EU's ban on hormone-treated beef and moratorium on the approval of genetically modified crops contributed significantly to the politicization of trade policy in the EU. Both disputes brought more actors into the trade policy process and fuelled the expectations of parliaments, national and European, and NGOs, who now generally demand more powerful roles in a more transparent and open policy process (Young and Peterson 2006). At present, the Commission is ill-equipped to meet such expectations, and increasingly is unable to control the deep trade policy agenda. This agenda now extends well beyond the EU's exclusive competences. It also provokes politically charged choices that are ill-suited to technocratic decision-making.

Historical Institutionalism and Transatlantic Institutions

Our empirical narrative lends itself to several important theoretical insights. Both EU and US trade policy institutions were 'present at the creation' of European integration itself and of the international trading system in the American case. Most scholarly accounts of European integration or US trade politics seem unable to explain why these institutions have carried on essentially unaltered against a backdrop of revolutionary change in their policy area. However, an HI account, to a considerable extent, offers an exception.

Crucially for our purposes, Pierson (2004: 6) contends that the goal of studying 'politics in time' is to identify social mechanisms: frequently observed phenomena that have the power of causation. For HIs, these might include timing and sequence, conjunctures ('interaction effects between distinct causal sequences'; Pierson 2004: 12), 'threshold effects' (what happens when a social process reaches a 'tipping point'), and path dependence. Each of these mechanisms is a source of causation in transatlantic economic relations.

[8] The Committee was created in 2004 after a five-year experiment (which apparently failed) of having the EP's Industry Committee handle trade.

Timing and sequence are clearly important: trade policy institutions were created on both sides long before globalization 'existed', yet they have survived essentially unaltered. It is possible to identify several important conjunctures, particularly for transatlantic institutions, not least when the EU emerged as a geopolitical magnet at the same time as step-level changes in cross-border economic flows began to reveal themselves in the 1990s, thus producing a significant spur to the institutionalization of the USA–EU dialogue. The threshold effects of globalization are crucial: by the time new transatlantic institutions were created in the mid-1990s, it was already 'too late' in that economics were running so far and fast ahead of politics that there was little prospect of public power effectively 'governing' globalization (see Peterson 2004; Berger et al. 2006).

Perhaps above all, we find powerful path dependencies of two different types. The first arises from the self-perpetuating dynamic of penetration by each 'side' of the economy of the other in the early twenty-first century. The second is reflected in trade policy institutions that are now anachronistic. The depth of the transatlantic economic relationship, however, has not yet created pressures strong enough to propel reform of domestic and international trade policy institutions.

Conclusion

To bring this analysis full circle, we might return to the questions posed at the beginning. How and how much are transatlantic relations mediated by the institutional setting(s) in which they take place? We have focused almost exclusively on the US–EU institutional track, and said little or nothing about other important ones (such as NATO, the G8, the OECD, the WTO, and so on). Even working under this restriction, we find something of a forest of different, mostly specialized institutional dialogues. What is striking is how weak are mechanisms for coordinating them or hierarchies for subjecting them to political control. These problems are exacerbated by the US and EU trade policy institutions that were designed to handle a shallow trade agenda and simpler trade politics than those that now arise from a far deeper and more complex economic relationship.

The NTA was partly a response to the broadening of the bilateral economic agenda to include a wide range of regulatory issues. But the dialogue has remained a low-key and technocratic one that only 'works' in the sense of facilitating open flows of trade and investment up to the point where these flows touch upon anything remotely controversial or politicized. At that point, because the US–EU dialogue commands such a low profile, officials usually cannot expect the agreements they make to manage or solve disputes to receive political backing. Meanwhile, the trading relationship per se (especially as it is dominated by bilateral disputes) has mostly shifted into a separate USTR–Commission dialogue, even though the Commissioner for Trade and USTR have both lost political authority and (often) the ability to resolve conflicts when they arise. The deep trade agenda itself is left mostly unsupervised.

Do bilateral institutions facilitate effective governance of transatlantic economic relations? Again, the glass could be seen as either half-empty or half-full. Trade policy institutions on both sides seem badly in need of reform. Put baldly, there is no 'Transatlantic Economic Partnership', and the optimism of the mid-1990s about regulatory cooperation seems mostly to have dissipated. There exists almost no strategic dialogue in the context of the NTA about major political questions such as (say) the collapse of the Doha Round. On the other hand, bilateral institutions keep regulators and trade officials on both sides talking to one another. Transatlantic institutions may be so weak or fragmented that the economic relationship between Europe and America just stumbles on from day-to-day, without (paradoxically) much if any political profile but also little capacity to solve teeth-grinding disputes. But it still manages to generate enormous wealth and profits.

Institutional change has not kept pace with the rise of new obstacles to trade—mostly occurring 'behind the border'—that are changing the nature of trade politics. Usually, existing institutions, including the WTO, are able—*just*—to manage most trade tensions, but not to prevent them from recurring. It is not clear, however, that the sort of radical institutional change that would be required to eliminate most transatlantic trade disputes would bring sufficient gains in the form of increased economic exchange to outweigh the costs of dealing with hard questions about legitimacy, should such change even be possible. Given the incentives for cooperation stemming from their large markets and the relative similarity of their policy preferences, the failings of transatlantic economic cooperation bode ill for the prospects of global economic governance.

For now, the USA and EU still enjoy an extraordinarily coherent economic relationship, given all the obstacles and barriers it must surmount. But to confront our question about how much light is shed on this case by historical institutionalism: its concern with how institutions are created, and how they change and affect behavior are obviously key to our story. Few of today's trade policy institutions were designed to cope with a deep trade agenda. This agenda is very deep in the case of the transatlantic relationship given the intensity of economic activity, the regulatory activism of both polities, and their large and comparable markets. The USA and EU each behave as an economic actor in ways that are clearly and powerfully determined by domestic and bilateral institutions.

A broader question, beyond the scope of this short contribution, is whether the depth and intensity of the transatlantic economy helps preserve a true alliance between Europe and America. A partial answer to the question, at least, is that rising economic interdependence between the USA and EU has not led to the creation (or redesign) of powerful institutions that protect transatlantic economic exchange from all threats, and thus buttress a political partnership. There are new tricks that these two old dogs have yet to learn. This result would not surprise many historical institutionalists.

17

From EU Model to External Policy? Promoting Regional Integration in the Rest of the World

MARY FARRELL[1]

Introduction

To what extent is the EU seeking to replicate the European model of regional integration elsewhere in the world? Statements by senior European officials suggest the policy is being developed with serious intent. Romano Prodi, the former president of the European Commission was vocal in his claim:

Our European model of integration is the most developed in the world. Imperfect though it is, it nevertheless works on a continental scale. Given the necessary institutional reforms, it should continue to work well after enlargement, and I believe we can make a convincing case that it would also work globally (Romano Prodi, president of the European Commission, 2000—cited in Rosamond 2002: 473).

Javier Solana, the EU High Representative for the CFSP was similarly forthright:

In Europe we have learned the hard way that sustainable peace and security require regional cooperation and integration. Managing crises is not the same as building security. That is why supporting regional cooperation is such a 'growth area' in our efforts. The African Union, Mercosur, ASEAN: these are all examples of strengthening regional regimes, explicitly taking their inspiration from the EU. We are deepening our relations with these other regional players and, where possible and relevant, we are giving our support for their further development. In the years ahead, these inter-regional dialogues will steadily reshape the nature of international politics and forge new mechanisms to manage global interdependence and tackle cross-border problems (2005).

European regional integration has evolved considerably since the Treaty of Rome.[2] Today, it is considered by many analysts to be distinctive in its institutional arrangements, the patterns of reiterative cooperation, the extent of common

---

[1] I wish to thank Sophie Meunier and Kathleen McNamara for comments on an earlier draft of this chapter. All remaining errors are my responsibility.

[2] There is a vast literature on the historical development and the current state of European integration, with contributions from various disciplinary perspectives, including economics, history, political science, legal theory, and international relations. From a very broad field, see

policies and economic liberalization, and the nature of the European legal order (Wallace, Wallace, and Pollack 2004; Wiener and Diez 2004). Whether it represents a case of successful regional integration is another matter, and a question that is beyond the scope and remit of this chapter.[3] Nonetheless, the political community and its governance model is recognized both within the EU and beyond for the achievements and results that have been produced over the past fifty years (Dinan 1994; Moravcsik 1998; Scharpf 1998). The central questions of this chapter are to what extent has the EU been able to 'sell' the model to other regional communities, how it has proceeded to do so, and to what result.

Across the globe, regional integration and cooperation arrangements have increased in number, exhibiting a diversity in the scope and strength of regional integration while so far showing no particular tendency toward a common model (Fawcett and Hurrell 1995; Mattli 1999; Farrell and Hettne 2005). The renewed activity in European integration as a result of the Single Market program launched in the 1980s gave rise to fears of a 'fortress Europe' and prompted other countries to react by initiating or strengthening their own regional integration arrangements (Cameron 1992). However, some of this proliferation is the direct result of an active promotion of regional integration by the EU.

The policy of promoting regional integration in other parts of the world coincided with the attempt to define Europe's place in the world (Wallace 1995; Grugel 2004; Hill and Smith 2005). Despite its significant (and indeed growing) economic weight in the global economy, the EU has continued to struggle with a more overtly political role in international affairs. Promoting regional integration as an external policy raises much less controversy among the member states, since there is no perceived challenge to national sovereignty and no significant budgetary implications. The Commission has played a leading role in this aspect of EU external relations, since the external relations and trade directorates, as well as the development directorate, have to a greater or lesser extent all advocated regional integration as part of the international relations portfolio.

This chapter analyzes three ways in which the EU can influence regional integration processes. First, enlargement of the EU provides a very direct and comprehensive way of expanding regional integration, spreading the regulatory system and its legal order to new member states, and resulting in a process

---

Dinan (1994), Wallace, Wallace, and Pollack (2004), Milward (1992), Weiler (1991), and Hill and Smith (2005).

[3] I do not put forward the view that the EU is the best, 'most advanced' regional integration project, nor wish to propose that the EU should be treated as the standard against which all other regional integration schemes can be evaluated. Regional integration is after all a political process, and the degree of integration will be the subject of negotiation, compromise, and bargaining among social actors within a particular region. It is also an evolutionary process. With regard to Europe, one can say that the European model works for the Europeans, at least some of the time—or, perhaps more accurately, works for some people, some of the time. See also Warleigh and Rosamond (2005).

of endogenous growth. Second, it is possible for the EU to influence regional integration in a broad or general way through normative suasion, where other regional communities adopt certain practices, institutional arrangements, or other forms of governance modeled on the European governance. In this context, the role of ideas and norms in shaping outcomes is also a potentially important factor (Goldstein and Keohane 1993; Manners 2002; Youngs 2004), so that the EU need not have a specific policy, agreement, or other form of intervention targeted at the region in order to exert influence. Yet some analysts remain skeptical that a normative Europe can overcome the more realist tendencies of states (Nicolaïdis and Howse 2002; Smith, K. E. 2004).[4]

A third kind of influence emanates from the interregional agreements that the EU has established with other regional groupings, such as the Asia–Europe meeting (ASEM), or the Cotonou Agreement with the African, Caribbean, and Pacific (ACP) group. Interregionalism constitutes a distinct set of processes, involving cooperation between two distinct regions (Alecu de Flers and Regelsberger 2005). Following Aggarwal and Fogarty (2004), this chapter recognizes the varieties of interregional arrangements, distinguishing between pure interregional cooperation (involving formal regional groupings, such as EU–Mercosur), and hybrid interregionalism (cooperation between a formal regional bloc and a group of countries that do not constitute a formal regional grouping). It is useful to make this distinction between the different forms of interregional cooperation in order to arrive at a more precise assessment of the EU influence on other regional groupings. Bloc-to-bloc regional cooperation can in practice take different forms, however interregionalism has the potential to support (or restrict) intraregional integration (Rüland 2001; Ravenhill 2004).

Bloc-to-bloc regional cooperation is characterized by diverse institutional arrangements, and motivated by various factors. The highly institutionalized arrangements that supported EU–ACP cooperation from the earliest days were not indicative of increasing influence on the African side, or of continued interest in this partnership on the European side. By contrast, the recent development in EU–Asia cooperation, through the ASEM summits, features less formal arrangements, reflecting the Asian countries' preference for less institutionalized frameworks. In an international system where states are still influential players, interregional cooperation presents a new challenge for IR theorists, but also a possible alternative to global governance. While it is still to early to judge how interregional

---

[4] The role of ideas in shaping institutions is now widely accepted in international relations theory, and international political economy. Ideas refer to common understandings of what is (either as a factual reality or as an imagined better state of affairs), and can be a strong force for change and/or to initiate political action. 'Ideas do not freely remake the world in their image, but they are inestimably effectual. Ideas are a form of power, and are often a partner to other forms of power—and this, in intricate ways—.' D. Philpott (2001). *Revolutions in Sovereignty. How Ideas Shaped Modern International Relations*. Princeton: Princeton University Press, 47.

cooperation may shape international governance, there is already some indication of a spillover from the international arena to the regional level. One such mechanism occurs through specific policy initiatives on the part of the EU designed actively to promote intraregional cooperation, for instance through the use of the conditionality clauses inserted in the Economic Partnership Agreements (EPAs) currently under negotiation between the EU and African and Caribbean states. In this case, interregional cooperation is used as a conduit for influencing intraregional cooperation and integration processes, to deepen and strengthen institutional mechanisms of cooperation *within* the formal region.

The first section of this chapter analyzes the rationales behind the EU's efforts to transpose its integration model elsewhere, focusing in particular on its limited panoply of foreign policy tools. Next, I analyze the three main ways in which the EU has sought to export its model: through enlargement; by exercising normative influence and via the power of example; using active policies that support regional cooperation and integration directly or indirectly. The chapter assesses the relative success of these three strategies, and concludes with a review of the likely trajectory of policy and the possibility of exporting the European model of regional integration. The question has particular resonance in the contemporary context of, on the one hand, rising internal criticism directed toward European integration, growing Euroskepticism, and increasing ambivalence toward future enlargements while, on the other hand, there is the continued, if uncertain, influence of globalization, increasing criticism of global governance systems and, more generally, the rising anti-Americanism in the world.

Historical Perspectives

The story of the EU's origins has been well documented, even if there remain significant disagreements over the nature of the political community that has emerged (Dinan 1994; Milward 1992). Regional integration emerged from the broad consensus around the need to restore and maintain peace, an objective that reflected the shared and common interests of many European governments with the support (even if it was implicit) of the European public. The idea of creating a security community by economic means (effectively a common market) may not be radical, but it certainly seemed so at the time.

It was not only the memories of war that spurred a collective consciousness about the need for common action, but also the earlier memories of how the tariff wars and reactionary protectionism during the 1930s had fomented the conditions in which nationalism ultimately led to that war. Even earlier, the harsh conditions attached to the reparations agreement imposed on the defeated German government after World War I sowed the seeds of a resentment that would simmer over into more serious bellicose attitudes, and was a reminder to the victorious countries in 1945 of the need to show more empathy with the defeated Germany. Also, there was the lesson of the failed League of Nations, a pointed reminder of how collective action is dependent upon both politics and the right institutions.

Understanding the lessons of the past, the founding member states adopted a set of formal institutional arrangements that were at once intergovernmental and supranational; the European Commission's responsibilities in agenda setting, implementing policy, monitoring policy implementation by the member states, and handling external trade relations gave it an influential role that was the embodiment of supranationality. To the extent that the proposed new supranational institutional structure would be concerned with external relations, it would do so through the European Commission and largely through trade policy.[5]

National interests were overseen in the Council of the EU, the institution charged with the executive and legislative responsibilities in the European system of governance. In deference to national sensitivities, the broad panoply of what is generally understood as foreign and security policy would remain under the exclusive competence of the member state governments. Consequently, the European integration process was internally oriented and inward-looking over the four decades since its inception, focused on the goal of eliminating the conflicts and divisions that had torn apart the continent for much of the twentieth century, while external relations were characterized principally in an expansion in the number and range of trade agreements under the leadership of the European Commission.

When and why did the EU seek to promote regional integration as part of external relations policy? Prior to the introduction of the CFSP under the Maastricht Treaty, the character of the EU's external projection had been structured by the institutional arrangements of the Treaty of Rome. European Community support for regional integration beyond its own borders was fitful and piecemeal, running the gamut of trade and development policies directed at countries and regions for which the member states retained some degree of strategic or postcolonial interest, while selectively exporting regional integration through a gradual process of enlargement from six to fifteen countries in Western Europe. Historical ties of individual countries largely determined the pattern of interregional cooperation right up until the 1980s (Holland 2002)—the Lomé Agreements with the African countries, a short-lived Euro–Arab dialogue that was initiated as a result of the Arab–Israeli conflict, and the beginnings of dialogue with ASEAN and with Central America (Alecu de Flers and Regelsberger 2005).

An HI inquiry as to why the EU initially adopted a low-key stance in advocating regional integration as part of its external relations policy would suggest that we

---

[5] Even the more recently created European Central Bank has a remit that is limited to the maintenance of internal stability within the euro area, and though it has extensive powers with which the ECB seeks to direct the financial management policies of the member states there is no obligation to manage the external value of the euro through intervention on foreign exchange markets.

should look at how the institutions (formal and informal) shape the policymakers' preferences and policy outcomes (Hall and Taylor 1996; Pierson 1996; Pierson 2000). Formal institutions and informal rules increasingly interacted to form a novel and multidimensional European regional governance model capable of balancing the interests of the different actors—preserving the sovereignty of the member states while exercising the Community method, promoting internal economic liberalization (competition policy) and balancing this with a redistributive system (regional policy).

Without a supranational foreign policy, the principal line of action in external affairs was confined to the economic arena, and specifically to matters of trade where the European Commission had legal competence to act on behalf of the community as a whole—a right most often exercised in the successive rounds of GATT negotiations. In foreign policy, as well as in development and aid policy, member states still retained the sovereign right of action to pursue activities in countries and regions of the world according to individual national political and geostrategic priorities. The interregional cooperation of EU–ACP (under Yaoundé and the successor Lomé agreements) exemplified how the historical arrangements of the Treaty of Rome influenced outcomes designed to retain old ties in a postcolonial world, with the European Commission adopting a leadership role to act as the agent of the member states (Ravenhill 2004).

From the 1990s, a new dynamism reinforced the European support for regional integration and interregional cooperation generally. Three distinct yet interlinked factors explain the resurgence of interest among the EU member states in exporting the regional governance model fashioned over the preceding four decades: the collapse of the Soviet Union initiated concerns about security and possible instability on the EU's borders, raising the question of how to manage relations with the newly democratizing states; the Maastricht Treaty established the basis for a EFP and reignited the debates over the EU's capacity and means as an international actor; new European geostrategic priorities were emerging and served to underline the need for new actions and programs located in the strategic priorities of the EU, rather than of individual member states.

Though the preservation of regional order and the search for global presence had always been important goals for the European states, the EU had reached a stage of development in its own regional integration that required a more strategic approach toward external relations particularly since a foreign policy of the more traditional kind would not be readily forthcoming. The debate over the capability–expectations gap revolved around the question how the EU might usefully and effectively engage with the rest of the world (Hill 1993; Ginsberg 2001). And the representation of the EU as a civilian or normative power, in contrast to the traditional military power capable of influencing other international actors by force or threat of force (epitomized in realist international relations), pointed to a possible alternative foreign policy based on the EU values such as democracy, rule of law, respect for human rights, and the role of multilateral institutions (Nye 2004).

The external promotion of regional integration was a way to export the EU model of governance, to exercise international influence through the spread of EU values and strengthen the identity of the EU without compromising the national interests of the individual member states (Caporaso and Jupille 1998). Even the most Euroskeptic member state would find it hard to oppose such an external policy, since it is difficult to criticize the club to which it belongs without risk to their own credibility. The next section examines how the EU approach has developed in practice.

Exporting Regional Governance

How does the EU actually seek to export regional integration? And is it practical to speak about exporting a model that is acknowledged to be *sui generis*, a product of the historical, political, and social conditions of a time and a place? Additionally, this model has evolved through the political processes of cooperation, bargaining, compromise, and negotiation among the member states, marked sometimes by the big bargains between countries interspersed with the multitude of agreements worked out among the national negotiators in Brussels.

But the EU is also a governance model based on institutionalized decision-making, with legal rules that support such principles of regional integration as competition, liberalization, mutual recognition, and subsidiarity, and a set of normative values based on democracy, the rule of law, respect for human rights, and multilateralism. Although the political processes identified above are clearly not exportable, the EU has adopted a range of other policy tools and political strategies with the aim of expanding the rule-based system and the political processes that support regional cooperation among sovereign states. However, there are differences in the processes and the outcomes associated with the enlargement of the EU on the one hand, and other cases where the use of normative suasion or conditionality clauses in trade and other political agreements with third countries and regional groups has formed the basis of interregional cooperation policy. The terms of EU external engagement are emerging as a set of highly differentiated bargains between the EU and other regional communities.

Regional Integration through Enlargement

The collapse of communism raised the possibility of instability on the EU's eastern border and reawakened concerns about security. In this regard, the eventual decision to offer membership to the eight countries of Central and Eastern Europe can be seen as an understandable action by a community that itself originated from a desire to construct a security community. If integration and economic interdependence had worked to restore peace and stability for the west European countries, then there was a good justification to extend the model eastward.

Once the European Council approved the decision on enlargement in 1993 and adopted the Copenhagen criteria as the basic eligibility conditions for each applicant, the process of extending European integration was in place. Regional integration in this instance relied heavily on a series of conditionality instruments. The approach toward the single largest phase of EU enlargement was based on the leadership of the European Commission that blended carrot-and-stick mechanisms to engender domestic political changes in the applicant countries, in return for eventual membership.

Conditionality operated at two levels: the broad principles set out in the Copenhagen criteria; and the general requirements related to the adoption of and adaptation to the *acquis communautaire*. By requiring the applicant countries to consolidate democratic systems, establish the institutions guaranteeing the rule of law, respect for human rights and for minorities, and for a functioning market economy able to withstand competitive pressures, the EU outlined the governance model that accession would ultimately demand. If these conditions were more explicit than under previous phases of enlargement, they were also a recognition that the applicant countries were about to embark on a distinct ideological and political route.

While the Copenhagen criteria applied to all eight applicant countries, the EU negotiated on the other conditions of membership with each applicant individually. Karen Smith suggests that this bilateralism-within-regionalism approach toward enlargement allowed the EU to apply economic and political conditionality, and to differentiate between the fast and slow reformers, even if at the risk of exacerbating the tensions among the countries of the region (2005*a*). The goal of eventual membership might have compensated somewhat for the political adjustment costs that burdened many of the countries as they pursued the 'moving target' of what was an 'evolving process that is highly politicized, especially on the EU side' (Grabbe 2001).

But the use of conditionality in the enlargement process served the purpose of enforcing the EU rules and shaping the institutions in the applicant states toward the EU model. In a similar vein, the use of conditionality was 'a strategy of reinforcement by reward', where the European Commission engaged in protracted material bargaining with the applicant states (Schimmelfennig, Engert, and Knobel 2003).

Conditionality was coercive, with the intent to secure compliance with a policy or institutional outcome. But its use was also ambiguous and ambivalent, allowing the Commission to apply conditionality rules in a selective manner (Hughes, Sasse, and Gordon 2004). This was not a case of actions characterized by transparency and fairness, nor by the consistent and coherent application of rules and norms over the course of time. While the Commission engaged in a highly politicized negotiation process, the individual applicant states were obliged to adopt the enormous body of rules, regulations, standards, and policies in the *acquis communautaire*. There were no opt-outs for the accession states, though the existing (EU-15) member states were allowed certain opt-outs, most notably in the restrictions placed on migrant labor from the accession states. For instance all the accession states were required to adopt measures to prepare for the eventual introduction of the euro, though three of the EU-15 (Britain, Sweden, and Denmark) had secured exemption from the single currency zone. The politicized nature of conditionality did allow some room for maneuver by the applicant state, depending on the existing level of integration and the respective policy area, as well as the negotiating capacity of the applicant.

Enlargement is the most comprehensive form of expanding regional integration. But it is also a process that created insiders and outsiders, with the possibility of initiating further instability and tension between the enlarged EU and its neighbors. The big-bang approach to enlargement that brought the accession of ten Central and Eastern European countries all at the same time was largely attributable to security considerations. Countries of Southern and Eastern Europe excluded from membership by virtue of lack of preparedness, or their strategic location, or their political problems were still targeted by the reforming zeal of the European Commission, which proposed that these countries should be offered increased economic integration and closer political cooperation with the EU under the ENP.

The ENP was rooted in EU concern to surround itself with a zone of stability, which the European Security Strategy (December 2003) highlighted quite clearly, 'Our task is to promote a ring of well governed countries to the East of the EU and on the borders of the Mediterranean with whom we can enjoy close and cooperative relations' (European Council 2003: 9). The ENP brought the east and south regions into one framework, and aimed to reinforce the Barcelona Process through a deepening dialogue and a series of action plans (European Commission 2003*a*).[6] The wide geographic scope of the ENP was matched by the mix of bilateralism (EU agreements with individual countries), multilateralism (dialogue with all partners, EU-25 and the sixteen Mediterranean countries), and regionalism (a Mediterranean free trade area). But in practice, it was confined to bilateralism, based on action plans with individual countries (Smith 2005*b*).

The ultimate aim of the ENP to encourage economic and political reforms in accordance with the benchmarks set by the EU was in line with the policy of exporting integration—not the full-scale model of governance to be found

---

[6] Sixteen 'neighbors' were involved in the ENP— Algeria, Armenia, Azerbaijan, Belarus, Egypt, Georgia, Israel, Jordan, Lebanon, Libya, Moldova, Morocco, Palestinian Authority, Syria, Tunisia, and Ukraine.

internally, but components of it (Kelley 2006). Since the origin of Euro–Med cooperation at the Barcelona European Council summit (1995), the aim had been to promote regional economic integration among the Mediterranean countries— and to enhance the reciprocal trade relations with the EU.[7] However, membership of the EU is not on offer to the ENP countries though conditionality is still a key feature of the European Commission's dialogue and negotiations. Instead, the offer is a 'privileged partnership' in exchange for 'mutual commitment to common values', including democracy and human rights, with the promise of deepening trade and economic relations, and the possibility of moving beyond cooperation toward a stake in the EU's internal market.

Normative Suasion

The representation of the EU as a normative power is based on the claim that the EU is different, that this difference is reflected in its pursuit of norms and values, and that the EU has the capability to 'shape conceptions' of what is 'normal' in international affairs (Manners 2002). While this perspective on the EU's international role fits well with recent scholarship on the significance of norms in international politics generally, and indeed also with observable directions in external relations policy (the emphasis on good governance, human rights, and democratization), there remains the question of how to define objective standards against which normative judgments can be assessed.

The EU itself embodies many of the values that it seeks to transmit internationally—a political community where the right of membership is conditional on democracy, respect for the rule of law and for human rights, and with a strong belief in international institutions to manage cooperation. Within the EU, norms are *enforced* and *reinforced* through the EU legal order, the *acquis communautaire*, and the political process of dialogue. Externally, enforcement is reliant on whatever capacity the EU can bring to bear through conditionality and other political or economic incentives. In the case of EU enlargement, the notable success in norm transfer was due in large measure to the character of the EU institutions, and the requirement that applicant states meet the conditions imposed by the EU prior to accession. As Vachudova argues convincingly in this volume, enlargement succeeded as a democracy-promotion program. Whether democracy promotion can achieve the same results for the ENP, or through the EU's support for regional integration in other parts of the world is uncertain. The precise set of conditions do not hold for the countries in the ENP, or with the African countries negotiating EPAs. However, the EU's capacity to wield influence through

[7] The Barcelona declaration, on which the Euro–Mediterranean partnership was initiated, was adopted by Algeria, Morocco, Tunisia, Egypt, Israel, Gaza/West Bank, Jordan, Lebanon, Syria, Malta, Cyprus, and Turkey. Since then, Cyprus and Malta have acceded to the EU, while Turkey was granted the status of accession candidate.

the judicious mix of threats and incentives, backed up by its trade/economic power is likely over the long term to produce results (Meunier and Nicolaïdis 2006).

It should be remembered that the same policy approach is not adopted for all regional groupings and individual countries, so that the EU's effectiveness as a norm exporter will be determined by the nature of each arrangement and how the target region interacts with the EU. Agreements that are politically rather than legally binding tend effectively to commit the contracting parties only if there is a strong interest at stake. Where non-compliance with EU norms and values is not sanctioned, the adherence to agreements is purely voluntary. Turkey responded to EU demands for constitutional reforms required to meet the Copenhagen criteria even before starting the accession negotiations. In the case of the ENP countries, there is not the same pressure for democratic change in those Arab states which still lack universal suffrage, free and recurrent elections, multiparty systems, and alternative sources of public information.

The effectiveness of EU policy on democracy promotion is influenced by the political will of national and regional actors to effect change, and to adopt democratic norms. By itself, the EU cannot be a successful exporter of democratic norms. As the recent experience in Iraq suggests, democracy cannot be imposed from the outside by an external actor or international organization. This reality need not preclude the EU from continuing its self-appointed role as a promoter of democracy, but it does indicate the need to think about the nature and substance of policies in this area. Furthermore, the problems over the democratic legitimacy of the EU itself, which have been identified in chapter one of this volume, can undermine the credibility of the EU as democracy promoter in the wider world.

Since 1992 all EU agreements with third countries contain a clause defining respect for human rights and democracy as 'essential elements' in the EU's relationship, so the EU can suspend the agreement (under international law) where there is a breach of the agreement evidenced by human rights infringements. This approach was further elaborated in the Cotonou Agreement signed in 2000, with clauses regarding respect for human rights, democratic principles and the rule of law, and good governance (Farrell 2005). The clause effectively marks a sea change in the way that the EU relates to many third countries (and regional groupings), particularly on the African continent where it is regarded as a new coercive element in the negotiations for EPAs, though the EU has not so far availed of this option (Nwobike 2005).

While the weak states of Africa have been vulnerable to the EU pressures, the Asian states were in a much stronger position economically and politically to stress their commitment to the principle of non-intervention (Jones and Smith 2006). Ever since 1993 when the EU began to push its human rights clause, the Asian countries have challenged European attempts to raise human rights issues, viewing such efforts as 'soft imperialism' and, worse still, irrelevant to the regional context where 'Asian values' were directly instrumental in raising development and cutting poverty (Gilson 2004).

These differences have continued to characterize EU–ASEAN relations, particularly since Myanmar joined the Asian community, and testing the resolve of the European states to observe human rights law against their desire to increase trade with the region (Gilson 2005). Though the Asian countries continued to maintain their position that sensitive or controversial issues should be avoided at the Asia–Europe summit meetings (ASEM), the ASEAN countries themselves worked out an arrangement for the ASEM Hanoi meeting in 2005, which allowed Myanmar to attend the summit meeting as observer but not make any public statements. Subsequently, Myanmar agreed to forgo its turn holding the ASEAN presidency.

At the EU institutional level, it is the European Commission that takes the lead in promoting the democracy and human rights provisions in agreements and negotiations with regional groupings, a role which has expanded across the Commission's action in the field of external relations generally, development policy, and the activities to promote regional economic integration. In line with Treaty demands, the Commission also works to ensure the consistency of EP and Council activity in these areas which often involves the reconciliation of the intergovernmental–supranational divide and institutional positions. However, the notion that the EU's promotion of values and norms is a force for goodness in international society has frequently been regarded with some skepticism, where self-interest, strategic considerations, or even the inevitable tussle between intergovernmentalism and supranationalism shape actors' motivations across such areas as human rights, participation in the UN system, or in regard to relations with Africa (Youngs 2004; Farrell 2005; Laatikainen and Smith 2006).

Regional Cooperation as Policy

By 1995 regional cooperation was a significant objective in EU foreign policy, with the community dealing increasingly with third countries primarily on a regional basis, thereby distinguishing its approach from that of other international actors. Since then, the regional approach has developed a whole array of actions, including aid programs, regional strategies, regional trade agreements, and support for regional integration. Bloc-to-bloc regional cooperation agreements exist with the ACP countries, the Andean Community, ASEAN, the Central American community, and the Gulf Cooperation Council, while an agreement is currently under negotiation with Mercosur. De Flers and Regelsberger (2005) identify nineteen interregional agreements, varying in their substantive nature and the degree of strategic significance, ranging from dialogue partners to strategic partners (sometimes of little more than symbolic significance), and trade partners.

The genesis of these agreements is a shift in the EU's strategic priorities, and geographic proximity serves to prioritize the regions of greatest importance.

As we have seen, the Central and Eastern European grouping was the priority in the 1990s until absorbed in the enlargement process, followed by the ENP grouping. Though relations with the African-regional grouping (ACP) date back to the 1960s, since the Cotonou Agreement was signed in 2000 the EU priorities have shifted toward Asia. Relations with ASEAN have been strengthened, and the ASEM summit meetings provide a platform for interregional dialogue across a whole range of issues. Similarly, dialogue frameworks are important in the ENP.

Generally, the interregional cooperation agreements cover a whole range of issues, though the respective agreements also contain specified objectives—for instance, the Cotonou Agreement with the ACP countries provides for development and trade issues, the conclusion of EPAs between the EU and groups of African countries, to assist with the integration of the countries into the global economy, and provisions on democracy and human rights. This agreement also specifies the EU support for regional integration within Africa, while other agreements support regional integration in Latin America and Asia. However, there is no standard approach by the EU in all cases of interregional cooperation, rather the outcome is the result of bargaining and negotiation between both sides.

The argument here is that the EU can shape regional integration elsewhere by direct policy intervention or through its own experience and the power of example. In the EPAs, the EU is negotiating a set of reciprocal trade agreements with six groups of countries in the ACP bloc (SADC—southern Africa; ESA—east Africa; west Africa—ECOWAS; central Africa—CEMAC; Caribbean—CARIFORM/CARICOM; and the Pacific Forum). EPAS must be compatible with WTO rules, requiring the signatory countries to commit to the liberalization of trade in 'substantially all products', generally understood as 90 percent of total trade. Alongside, the EU is encouraging regional integration *among* the countries in the subregional grouping, while insisting on the objective of integrating the African countries into the global economy. In substance, this policy involves the EU in a major program of trade liberalization, with the democracy and human rights clauses discussed earlier added on.

In the course of the EPA negotiations, issues such as market access, trade in services, trade barriers, customs, rules of origin, and competition will be addressed—many of these items are at the heart of the EU system of (internal) regional governance, and while the protracted EU–Africa negotiations will expose the African countries to the EU negotiation style, there is also the reverse influence on systems of governance in the African subregions. Is this about exporting the EU model of governance? No, if we think of European governance in its totality of rules, institutions, laws, and structures. But, as has already been mentioned, the EU governance is multidimensional, and a significant aspect is the trade liberalization which comes with a series of informal and formal rules to maintain an open and liberal trading order. The EPA negotiation process and its eventual outcome will undoubtedly reflect much of the EU model of governance.

The EU model has in fact been a template for recent African efforts at regional integration.[8] Unlike the Asian case, discussed below, African regional integration embodies a strong element of supranational institution-building. The African Union (established in 2002) will have an extensive institutional structure, including an assembly in the form of a pan-African Parliament, a Commission, Executive Council of Ministers, Permanent Representatives Committee, a Court of Justice, a Peace and Security Council, Financial Institutions (to include eventually an African Central Bank, African Monetary Fund, and African Investment Bank) as well as a number of lesser supranational entities—all of these supranational institutions mirror the EU structure.

The proposal for West African monetary integration adopted many of the elements of the European model, including a set of convergence criteria covering public borrowing, inflation, and interest rates, as well as establishing the West African Monetary Institute, and proposed a phased approach toward the introduction of the single currency, the eco—the deadline, like its European counterpart, has now been put back by several years. The Constitutive Act of the AU sets out three key ideas on continental unity—political integration should be the *raison d'être* of the AU, the objective being to achieve a USA of Africa in the long run; the integration process should be geared to stimulating and reenergizing the role of the states; and regional integration processes should incorporate the interests not only of government representatives, but also involve parliamentarians, political parties, economic actors, and civil society representatives. The Constitutive Act proposed also that regional integration would build on the foundations of existing regional groupings and proceed along the path of unity at variable speed.

In the African case, what is missing is the political will on the part of national political leaders to delegate sovereignty to these supranational institutions they have created, and to 'think regional' when it comes to resolving issues in security, development, trade, and economic growth.

To what extent has the EU been a model for regional integration in Asia? Unlike the case of Africa discussed in the previous section, the EU's use of political conditionality in Asia has been more limited since power asymmetries are fewer in the case of EU–Asia interregionalism. The EU has not sought to push through political and economic reforms to the same extent, though it has continually raised concerns about human rights and democracy in bilateral discussions, as well as through the ASEM forum. Recent Commission publications confine proposals for direct support of regional integration to the SAARC region (European Commission 2005c). Indirectly, the EU has been a force for regional identity building in East and Southeast Asia since the countries were obliged to 'think regionally' in

---

[8] The concept of regional integration has been the subject of debate in Africa since independence, and was most commonly discussed in the visions of African unity proposed by Ghana's first postindependence leader, Kwame Nkrumah.

preparing common positions for dialogue with the EU (Hemmer and Katzenstein 2002).

However, the history of Asian regionalism is not entirely separate from that of the European experience. Even those who argue that the historical experiences are too different to allow for comparison or even any discussion of the exportability of the European model can identify common concerns over security, and also the economic dynamic that is shaping regional cooperation (Beeson 2005). Contexts do change, forcing actors and institutions to adapt and even to change their preferences. This has been true for the EU, most recently in the definition of an Asia strategy.

The revised EU (2001*c*), *Europe and Asia: A Strategic Framework for Enhanced Partnerships*, was rooted in the discourse of globalization, uncertainty, instability, and global interdependence, and the need for partnership. The mutual interests of Europe and Asia lay, according to this European strategy, in their shared interest in promoting global peace and security, enhancing the effectiveness of the UN, and addressing global environmental challenges. Security in its many dimensions, it was argued, presented an opportunity for the two regions to work together, in the multilateral institutions, as well as bilaterally (European Commission 2003*b*).

However, the core objective of the EU's new Asia strategy was explicit—to strengthen the EU's political and economic presence across the region, and to raise this to a level commensurate with the global weight of an enlarged EU (European Commission 2001*c*: 3). Asia had become a major trading partner for the EU, and China in particular was an emerging regional power as well as a significant importer and exporter in global terms. While much of China's trade was with America, it had also become in a very short time one of the EU's main trade partners. China is the EU's second largest trading partner, and the EU is China's third trading partner with its 1980s surplus toward China turning into a deficit of €44.6 billion in 2000.

The Asian financial crisis was a defining moment for the countries of the Asian region. The impact of financial instability showed the degree of dependence on the global economy, and the limited capacity of states to protect against the ravages of unexpected short-term capital movements. Gradually those same states came to accept the need for a regional architecture to manage issues of regional concern, and to act as a collective polity. Even countries formerly not inclined to support regional cooperation and integration, notably Japan and China, have now endorsed regional integration. Regional strategic crises, such as the financial crisis or the 'war on terrorism' have shifted attitudes and beliefs, and opened the way for institutional adaptation (Jones and Smith 2006). The recent proposals for deepening Asian regional economic and monetary integration can be seen in this light (Dieter and Higgott 2003). However, the current picture of countries rushing to sign free trade agreements with other countries in the region may have more to do with the slow progress on the Doha Development Round, and pressure from the USA and indeed the EU to push ahead with bilateralism (Ravenhill 2003).

Conclusion

This chapter looked at the export of the European governance model in the promotion of regional integration in other parts of the world. It is evident that the European Commission has played the leadership role in this regard, pushing ahead with a series of highly differentiated approaches to the export of regional integration, and that internal growth through enlargement has resulted in the most comprehensive expansion of the EU governance system. The external promotion of regional integration was differentiated geographically and institutionally, the result of which was a preference for a denser form of regional integration and cooperation with the countries closest to the EU. Further afield, regional integration was promoted in the form of economic liberalization (notably in the EPAs currently being negotiated with the African and Caribbean group), and in a loose form of regional cooperation and dialogue with ASEAN.

The empirical puzzle of concern here is to explain this particular outcome, and to ask if and how the historical development of European integration might impact on the contemporary institutions and actors now engaged in the external promotion of regional integration. Following the line of enquiry in this volume, we can ask if the tools of historical institutionalism can explain the path of development in European integration?

At its foundation, the EC was intended to be a security community and indeed was so recognized by the member states who, anxious to retain as much sovereignty as possible, adopted an institutional structure that attempted to reconcile the tensions between supranationality and intergovernmentalism. The institutional structure allowed for both sets of interests, in the European Commission and the Council of Ministers. In like manner, creating a common market set the economic community on a path toward integration without the risk of confrontation with concerns of high politics. With the Treaty of Rome (1957), the authority to represent the EC externally was vested in the European Commission, though confined largely to trade. When this economic/security community faced new security challenges on its eastern border some four decades later, the contemporary EU responded in the way that a security community believing in economic integration as the route to stability might be expected to.

Indeed, there were few options available to the EU by way of response to the potential instability on its eastern frontier other than enlargement. Despite the institutional development and regulatory expansion over the decades, the foreign policy and security mechanisms remained in the hands of the member states, leaving the EU ill-equipped to deal with external relations on those terms. Adopting an HI analysis, we can pinpoint the role played by the European Commission as a key political actor with the capability to develop the enlargement strategy so as to take account of member state and Community interests in the accession negotiations.

At the global level, the strategy of promoting regional integration combines two fundamental elements of the EU model of integration, the economic one involving trade liberalization and a norm-driven support for the values of democracy, the rule of law, protection of human rights, and multilateralism. As this chapter suggests, the regional integration strategy can fit emerging EU strategic priorities (development through trade, shaping the multilateral order, strengthening economic ties with Asia, etc.) and reflect the nature of the European regional governance model internationally and globally. How to define the EU role in international relations remains one of the vexing questions facing integration theorists and policy analysts alike, but it is a question that can generate more fruitful exploration if we can look at it in terms of a 'regional governance model within a broader global exchange of governance methodologies' (Rosamond 2005: 474). This would of course mean taking up the challenge, referred to by Romano Prodi at the beginning of this chapter, to make a convincing case for the EU model of governance at the global level.

BIBLIOGRAPHY

(2006). 'MEPS Unveil Free Market in Services', *Contractor UK News*. Available at: www.contractoruk.com/news/002522.html

(2005). 'Slimming Costs with Cheaper Fats', *Confectionery News*.

(2003). *Interview with European Parliamentarian*. Brussels.

(1975). 'The "All Saints" Day Manifesto for European Monetary Union', *The Economist*, 1 November; Reprinted in M. Fratianni and T. Peeters (eds.) (1978). *One Money for Europe*. London: Macmillan, pp. 37–43.

Addison, J. and Siebert, W. S. (1997). 'The Course of European-Level Labor Market Regulation', in J. Addison and W. S. Siebert (eds.), *Labor Markets in Europe: Issues of Harmonization and Regulation*. London: Dryden Press, pp. 28–34.

Aggarwal, V. K. and Fogarty, E. (eds.) (2004). *EU Trade Strategies. Between Regionalism and Globalism*. Basingstoke, UK: Palgrave.

Alecu de Flers, N. and Regelsberger, E. (2005). 'The EU and Inter-regional Cooperation', in C. Hill and M. Smith (eds.), *International Relations and the European Union*. Oxford: Oxford University Press, pp. 317–42.

Alford, D. 'The Lamfalussy Process and EU Bank Regulation: Another Step on the Road to Pan-European Regulation?' *Annual Review of Banking and Financial Law*, forthcoming.

Algieri, F. and Janning, J. (1996). 'The German Debate', in F. Algieri, H. Grabbe, K. Hughes, J. Janning, R. Lindahl, and F. Rodrigo (eds.), *The 1996 IGC—National Debates (2): Germany, Spain, Sweden and the UK*. London: Royal Institute of International Affairs, pp. 1–21.

Allen, D. (1977). 'Policing or Policy-Making? Competition Policy in the European Communities', in H. Wallace, W. Wallace, and C. Webb (eds.), *Policy-Making in the European Communities*, 1st edn. London: John Wiley & Sons, pp. 91–112.

——— Smith, M. (1996). 'The European Union's Presence in the European Security Order: Barrier, Facilitator, or Manager?' Paper delivered at the Tenth International Conference of Europeanists, Chicago, IL, March 14–16, 1996.

Almer, J. and Rotkirch, M. (2004). *European Governance: An Overview of the Commission's Agenda for Reform*. Stockholm: Swedish Institute for European Policy Studies.

Alter, K. (2001). *Establishing the Supremacy of European Law: The Making of an International Rule of Law in Europe*. Oxford: Oxford University Press.

——— Vargas, J. (2000). 'Explaining Variation in the Use of European Litigation Strategies'. *Comparative Political Studies*, 33/4: 452–82.

Andenas, M. and Woolridge, F. (2005). *European Comparative Company Law*. New York: Cambridge University Press.

Andonova, L. (2003). *Transnational Politics of the Environment. The EU and Environmental Policy in Central and Eastern Europe.* Cambridge: MIT Press.

Andrews, D. M. (ed.) (2005). *The Atlantic Alliance Under Stress.* Cambridge: Cambridge University Press.

Ansell, C. and Di Palma, G. (2004). *Restructuring Territoriality: Europe and the United States Compared.* New York: Cambridge University Press.

Armitage, Jr., D. T. and Moisan, A. M. (2005). 'Constabulary Forces and Postconflict Transition: The Euro-Atlantic Dimension', *Strategic Forum, Institute for National Strategic Studies, National Defense University,* 218: 1–3.

Armstrong, K. and Bulmer, S. (1998). *The Governance of the Single European Market.* Manchester, UK: Manchester University Press.

Art, R. J. (1996). 'Why Western Europe Needs the United States and NATO', *Political Science Quarterly,* 111: 1–39.

Article 29 Data Protection Working Party (2002). *Opinion 5/2002 on the Statement of the European Data Protection Commissioners at the International Conference in Cardiff on mandatory systematic retention of telecommunications traffic data.* Brussels: European Community.

——(2004). *Opinion 9/2004 on a draft Framework Decision on the storage of data processed and retained for the purpose of providing electronic public communications networks with a view to the prevention, investigation, detection, and prosecution of criminal acts, including terrorism.* Brussels: European Community.

Askari, H. and Chatterjee, J. (2005). 'The Euro and Financial Market Integration', *Journal of Common Market Studies,* 43/1: 1–11.

Aspinwall, M. D. and Schneider, G. (2001). 'Institutional Research on the European Union: Mapping the Field', in M. Aspinwall and G. Schneider (eds.), *The Rules of Integration: Institutionalist Approaches to the Study of Europe.* Manchester, UK: Manchester University Press, pp. 1–18.

——(2000). 'Same Menu, Separate Tables: The Institutionalist Turn in Political Science and the Study of European Integration', *European Journal of Political Research,* 38/1: 1–36.

Authers, J. and Gangahar, A. (2006). 'The Battle of the Bourses', *Financial Times,* 23 May.

Axelrod, R. (1984). *The Evolution of Cooperation.* New York: Basic Books.

Balassa, B. (1961). *The Theory of Economic Integration.* London: George Allen and Unwin.

Baldwin, M., Peterson, J., and Stokes, B. (2003). 'Trade and Economic Relations', in J. Peterson and M. A. Pollack (eds.), *Europe, America, Bush: Transatlantic Relations in the 21st Century.* London and New York: Routledge, pp. 29–46.

Baldwin, R. and Daintith, T. (1992). 'The European Framework', in R. Baldwin and T. Daintith (eds.), *Harmonization and Hazard: Regulating Workplace Health and Safety in the EC.* London: Graham and Trotman.

Ball, R. (2004). 'Corporate Governance and Financial Reporting at Daimler-Benz (Daimler-Chrysler) AG: From a "Stakeholder" toward a "Shareholder Value" Model', in C. Leuz, D. Pfaff, and A. Hopwood (eds.), *The Economics and Politics of Accounting: International Perspectives on Research Trends, Policy, and Practice.* Oxford: Oxford University Press, pp. 103–44.

Barnett, D. F. (1986). *Up from the Ashes: The Rise of Steel Minimill in the United States.* Washington, DC: Brookings Institution.

——Crandall, R. W. (2002). 'Steel: Decline and Renewal', in L. L. Duetsch (ed.), *Industry Studies*, 3rd edn. New York: M. E. Sharpe, pp. 124–46.

Barnett, M. and Finnemore, M. (2004). *Rules for the World: International Organizations in Global Politics.* Ithaca, NY: Cornell University Press.

Barre Report (1969). *Memorandum from the Commission to the Council on the Coordination of Economic Policies and Monetary Cooperation within the Community.* COM 69/150 Bulletin of the EEC, supplement 3.

Bartels, L. (2001). 'An Agenda for Voting Research', in E. Katz and Y. Warshel (eds.), *Election Studies: What's Their Use?* Boulder, CO: Westview Press, pp. 59–81.

Beach, D. (2004). 'The Unseen Hand in Treaty Reform Negotiations: The Role and Impact of the Council Secretariat', *Journal of European Public Policy*, 11/3: 408–39.

Bednar, J. (2006). *The Robust Federation*, forthcoming. Available at: www-personal.umich.edu/~jbednar

——Eskridge, W., and Ferejohn, J. (2001). 'A Political Theory of Federalism', in J. Ferejohn, J. N. Rakove, and J. Riley (eds.), *Constitutional Culture and Democratic Rule.* New York: Cambridge University Press, pp. 223–70.

Beeson, M. (2005). 'Rethinking Regionalism: Europe and East Asia in Comparative Historical Perspective', *Journal of European Public Policy*, 12/6: 969–85.

Bennett, C. (1992). *Regulating Privacy: Data Protection and Public Policy in Europe and the United States.* Ithaca, NY: Cornell University Press.

——Raab, C. (2006). *The Governance of Privacy: Policy Instruments in Global Perspective.* Boston, MA: MIT Press.

Berger, S. and the MIT Industrial Performance Center (2006). *How We Compete.* New York: Currency Doubleday.

Berghahn, V. R. (1985). *Unternehmer und Politik in der Bundesrepublik.* Frankfurt am Main: Suhrkamp Verlag.

Bergström, C. F., Almer, J., Varone, F., and de Visscher, C. (2004). *Governance and the EU Securities Sector.* New Modes of Governance Project, CIT1-CT-2004-506392, 7/D1.

Berman, S. (2006). 'Europe's Choice', *Dissent*, 53/1: 100.

Bermeo, N. (2002). 'A New Look at Federalism', *Journal of Democracy*, 13/2: 96–110.

Beyers, J. (2005). 'Multiple Embeddedness and Socialization in Europe: The Case of Council Officials', *International Organization*, 59: 899–936.

Bignami, F. (2004). 'The Challenge of Cooperative Regulatory Relations After Enlargement', in G. Bermann and K. Pistor (eds.), *Law and Governance in an Enlarged European Union.* Oxford: Hart Publishing, 97–141.

Biscop, S. (ed.) (2005). *E Pluribus Unum? Military Integration in the European Union.* Brussels: Royal Institute for International Relations.

Blackwell, D. (2006). 'Nomad Sarbox Refugee Aims for Low-Cost London', *Financial Times*, 17 March.

Blanpain, R. (ed.) (2002). *Involvement of Employees in the European Union.* The Hague: Kluwer Law International.

Blondel, J., Sinnott, R., and Svensson, P. (1998). *People and Parliament in the European Union: Participation, Democracy, Legitimacy.* Oxford: Oxford University Press.

Bolkestein, F. (2002). 'The New European Company: Opportunity in Diversity', Speech at the University of Leiden, November 29.

——(2003). Letter. T. Ridge. Brussels. Available at: www.statewatch.com

Börzel, T. (2001). 'Non-compliance in the European Union', *Journal of European Public Policy*, 8/5: 803–24.

——Hosli, M. (2003). 'Brussels Between Bern and Berlin', *Governance*, 16/2: 179–202.

——et al. (2005). 'The Disparity of European Integration: Revisiting Neofunctionalism, Special Issue in Honour of Ernst Haas', *Journal of European Public Policy*, 12/2: 215–396.

Bostock, D. (2002). 'Coreper Revisited', *Journal of Common Market Studies*, 40/2: 215–34.

Brouard, S. and Tiberj, V. (2006). 'YES to the Europe I Want; NO to this One. Some Reflection on France's Rejection of the EU Constitution', *Political Science and Politics*, 39: 261–8.

Brusoni, S. and Orsenigo, L. (1997). 'State-Owned Enterprises and Managerial Structure: The Italian Experience in Steel and Oil', in C. Edquist (ed.), *Innovation Systems and European Integration (ISE)*. Bocconi University, mimeo. Available at: www.tema.liu.se/tema-t/sirp/PDF/324_4.pdf.

Bruun, N. (2001). 'The European Employment Strategy and the "Acquis Communautaire" of Labor Law', *The International Journal of Comparative Labor Law and Industrial Relations*, 17/2: 309–24.

Budden, P. M. (1994). The Making of the Single European Act: The United Kingdom and the European Community, 1979–1986, D.Phil. thesis, University of Oxford.

Bulmer, S. J. (1994). 'Institutions and Policy Change in the European Communities: The Case of Merger Control', *Public Administration*, 72/3: 423–44.

——(1998). 'New Institutionalism and the Governance of the Single Market', *Journal of European Public Policy*, 5/3: 365–86.

Burgess, K. and Postelnicu, A. (2005). 'Why Aim is Foreign Target of Choice', *Financial Times*, September 3.

Burley, A.-M. and Mattli, W. (1993). 'Europe before the Court: A Political Theory of Legal Integration', *International Organization*, 47/1: 41–76.

Büthe, T. (2002). 'Taking Temporality Seriously: Modeling History and the Use of Narratives as Evidence', *American Political Science Review*, 96/3: 481–93.

——Swank, G. T. (2006). *The Politics of Antitrust and Merger Review in the European Union: Institutional Change and Decisions from Messina to 2004*. CES Working Paper No. 142. Cambridge, MA: Minda de Gunzberg Center for European Studies, Harvard University, December 2006.

Buxbaum, R. M. and Hopt, K. J. (1988). *Legal Harmonization and the Business Enterprise*. New York: Walter de Gruyter.

Bzdera, A. (1993). 'Comparative Analysis of Federal High Courts', *Canadian Journal of Political Science*, 26/1: 3–29.

CAG [Competitiveness Advisory Group] (1995). *Enhancing European Competitiveness: First Report to the President of the Commission, the Prime Ministers and Heads of State*. Brussels, June.

Cameron, D. (1992). 'The 1992 Initiative: Causes and Consequences', in A. Sbragia (ed.), *Europolitics. Institutions and Policy-Making in the 'New' European Community*. Washington, DC: Brookings Institute, pp. 23–74.

—— (2003). 'The Challenges of Accession', *East European Politics and Societies*, 17/1: 24–41.

—— (2005). 'The Quality of Democracy in Postcommunist Europe', Presented at the Annual Meeting of the *American Political Science Association*, Washington, DC.

Campbell, A. (2003). *How Policies Make Citizens: Senior Political Activism and the American Welfare State*. Princeton, NJ: Princeton University Press.

Caporaso, J. (2000). *The European Union: Dilemmas of Regional Integration*. Boulder, CO: Westview Press.

—— Jupille, J. (1998). 'States, Agency and Rules: The EU in Global Environmental Politics', in C. Rhodes (ed.), *The European Union in the World Community*. Boulder, CO: Lynne Rienner, 213–31.

—— Keeler, J. (1995). 'The European Union and Regional Integration Theory', in C. Rhodes and S. Mazey (eds.), *The State of the European Union Volume 3: Building a European Polity?* Boulder, CO: Lynne Rienner, pp. 29–62.

—— Stone Sweet, A. (2001). 'Conclusion: Institutional Logics of European Integration', in A. Stone Sweet, W. Sandholtz, and N. Fligstein (eds.), *The Institutionalization of Europe*. Oxford: Oxford University Press, pp. 221–36.

Cappelletti, M., Seccombe, M., and Weiler, J. (eds.) (1986). *Integration Through Law*. Berlin and New York: Walter de Gruyter.

Carpenter, D. (2001). *Forging of Bureaucratic Autonomy: Reputations, Networks, and Policy Innovation in Executive Agencies, 1862–1928*. Princeton, NJ: Princeton University Press.

Casey, B. H. and Gold, M. (2005). 'Peer Review of Labor Market Programs in the European Union: What Can Countries Really Learn from One Another?' *Journal of European Public Policy*, 1/12: 23–43.

Casper, S. (2001). 'The Legal Framework for Corporate Governance: The Influence of Contract Law on Company Strategies in Germany and the United States,' in P. Hall and D. Soskice (eds.), *Varieties of Capitalism*. New York: Oxford University Press, pp. 387–416.

Cavendish, J. et al. (2006). 'Special Issue: Rating Enforcement', *Global Competition Review*, 9.

Cederman, L. (2000). 'Nationalism and Bounded Integration', Working paper RSC, 2000/34. Fiesole: European University Institute.

Checkel, J. (2005*a*). *International Institutions and Socialization in Europe*. New York: Cambridge University Press.

—— (2005*b*). 'International Institutions and Socialization in Europe', *International Organization*, 59/4: 801–26.

Chhibber, P. and Kollman, K. (2004). *The Formation of National Party Systems*. Princeton, NJ: Princeton University Press.

Choudhry, S. (2001). 'Citizenship and Federations', in K. Nicolaïdis and R. Howse (eds.), *The Federal Vision: Legitimacy and Levels of Governance in the US and the EU*. Oxford: Oxford University Press, pp. 377–402.

Christensen, T., Jørgensen, K. E., and Wiener, A. (1999). 'The Social Construction of Europe', *Journal of European Public Policy*, 6/4: 528–44.

—— —— —— (eds.) (2001). *The Social Construction of Europe*. London: Sage.

Cichowski, R. A. (2002). *Litigation, Mobilization, and Governance: The European Court and Transnational Activists*. Cambridge: Cambridge University Press.

Cini, M. (1996). 'La Commission Européenne lieu d'émergence de cultures administratives: L'exemple de la DG IV et de la DG XI', *Revue Française de Science Politique*, 46/3: 457–72.

—— (2001). 'The Soft Law Approach: Commission Rule-Making in the EU's State Aid Regime', *Journal of European Public Policy*, 8/2: 192–207.

—— McGowan, L. (1998). *Competition Policy in the European Union*. New York: St. Martin's Press.

Cohen, J. and Sabel, S. 'Global Democracy?' *New York University Journal of International Law and Policy*, (forthcoming).

Cohen-Tanugi, L. (1996). 'The French Debate', in L. Cohen-Tanugi, S. Fagiolo, M. Kwast-van Duursen, and A. C. G. Stubb (eds.), *The 1996 IGC—National Debates (1) Finland, France, Italy and the Netherlands*. London: Royal Institute of International Affairs, pp. 23–35.

Collins, D. (1975). *The European Communities: The Social Policy of the First Phase, the European Coal and Steel Community 1951–1970*. London: Martin Robertson.

Corbett, R. (1992). *The Treaty of Maastricht. From Conception to Ratification: A Comprehensive Reference Guide*. Essex, UK: Longman.

—— (1998). *The European Parliament's Role in Closer EU Integration*. Basingstoke, UK: Palgrave.

—— (2000). 'Academic Modeling of the Codecision Procedure: A Practitioner's Puzzled Reaction', *European Union Politics*, 1/3: 373–81.

—— (2001). 'A Response to a Reply to a Reaction (I Hope Somebody is Still Interested!)', *European Union Politics*, 2/3: 361–6.

Council Legal Service (1995). 'Study of Council Practice Regarding Statements for the Minutes in Connection with Openness', Council document, 6879/95.

Council of Europe (1981). *Convention for the Protection of Individuals with Regard to Automatic Processing of Personal Data*. Strasbourg: Council of Europe.

Cox, R. and Jacobson, H. (1973). *The Anatomy of Influence: Decision-Making in Industrial Organizations*. New Haven, CT: Yale University Press.

Craig, P. and de Burca, G. (2003). *EU Law: Text, Cases and Material*. Oxford: Oxford Univeristy Press.

Cremona, M. (2003). 'State Aid Control: Substance and Procedure in the Europe Agreements and the Stabilisation and Association Agreements', *European Law Journal*, 9/3: 265–87.

Daley, A. (1996). *Steel, State, and Labor: Mobilization and Adjustment in France*. Pittsburgh: University of Pittsburgh Press.

Davignon Group [Group of Experts] (1997). *European Systems of Worker Involvement: With Regard to the European Company Statute and other Pending Proposals*. Brussels, May.

Deakin, S. (1997). 'Integration through Law? The Law and Economics of European Social Policy', in J. T. Addison and S. W. Siebert (eds.), *Labor Markets in*

Europe: Issues of Harmonization and Regulation. London: Dryden Press, pp. 118–51.

De Burca, G. (2003). 'The Constitutional Challenge of New Governance in the European Union', *European Law Review,* 28: 814.

Deeg, R. (1999). *Finance Capital Unveiled: Banks and the German Political Economy.* Ann Arbor, MI: University of Michigan Press.

De Figueiredo, R. and Weingast, B. (2005). 'Self-Enforcing Federalism', *Journal of Law, Economics and Organization,* 21/1: 103–35.

De Grauwe, P. and Polan, M. (2005). 'Globalization and Social Spending', *Pacific Economic Review,* 10: 105–23.

Delors Report (1989). *Report on Economic and Monetary Union in the European Community.* Committee for the Study of Economic and Monetary Union. Luxembourg: Office for Official Publications of the EC.

Dermine. J. (1999). 'European Capital Markets: Does the Euro Matter?' in J. Dermine and P. Hillion (eds.), *European Capital Markets with a Single Currency.* Oxford: Oxford University Press, pp. 1–32.

―― Hillion, P. (eds.) (1999). *European Capital Markets with a Single Currency.* Oxford: Oxford University Press.

De Ruyt, J. (1989). *L'Acte Unique Européen.* Brussels: Institut d'Etudes Européen.

De Schoutheete de Tervarent, P. (1980). *La Coopération Politique Européenne.* Brussels: F. Nathan Editions Labor.

Destler, I. M. (2005). *American Trade Politics.* Washington, DC: Institute for International Economics.

Deutsch, K. W. (1957). *Political Community and the North Atlantic Area.* Princeton, NJ: Princeton University Press.

Devuyst, Y. (2000). 'Toward a Multilateral Competition Policy Regime?' *Global Governance,* 6/2: 319–38.

―― (2001). 'Transatlantic Competition Relations', in M. Pollack and G. C. Shaffer (eds.), *Transatlantic Governance in the Global Economy.* Boulder, CO: Rowman and Littlefield, pp. 127–52.

Dewing, I. P. and Russell, P. O. (2004). 'Accounting, Auditing and Corporate Governance of the European Listed Countries: EU Policy Developments Before and After Enron', *Journal of Common Market Studies,* 42/2: 289–319.

Diebold, W. (1959). *The Schuman Plan: A Study in Economic Cooperation 1950–1959.* New York: Praeger.

Dieter, H. and Higgott, R. (2003). 'Exploring Alternative Theories of Economic Regionalism: From Trade to Finance in Asian Co-operation', *Review of International Political Economy,* 10/3: 430–54.

Dinan, D. (1994). *Ever Closer Union? An Introduction to the European Community.* Boulder, CO: Lynne Rienner.

―― (2004a). *Ever Closer Union? An Introduction to the European Community.* Boulder, CO: Lynne Rienner.

―― (2004b). *Europe Recast: A History of the European Union.* Boulder, CO: Lynne Rienner.

Dolvik, J. E. (1997). *Redrawing Boundaries of Solidarity? ETUC, Social Dialogue and the Europeanisation of Trade Unions in the 1990s.* Oslo: ARENA and FAFO.

Dolvik, J. E. and Visser, J. (2001). 'ETUC and European Social Partnership: A Third Turning Point?' in H. Compston and J. Greenwood (eds.), *Social Partnership in the European Union*. Basingstoke, UK: Palgrave, pp. 72–100.

Dombey, D. (2004). 'Report Queries Need for EU Financial Regulation', *Financial Times*, May 7.

Donahue, J. and Pollack, M. (2001). 'Centralization and its Discontents', in K. Nicolaïdis and R. Howse (eds.), *The Federal Vision: Legitimacy and Levels of Governance in the US and the EU*. Oxford: Oxford University Press, pp. 73–117.

Dowding, K. (2000). 'Institutionalist Research on the European Union: A Critical Review', *European Union Politics*, 1: 125–44.

Duchêne, F. (1994). *Jean Monnet: The First Statesman of Interdependence*. New York: Norton.

Duchesne, S. and Frognier, A. (1995). 'Is there a European Identity?' in O. Niedermayer and R. Sinnott (eds.), *Public Opinion and Internationalized Governance*. Oxford: Oxford University Press, pp. 193–225.

Dudley, G. and Richardson, J. (1999). 'Competing Advocacy Coalitions and the Process of "Frame Reflection": A Longitudinal Analysis of EU Steel Policy', *Journal of European Public Policy*, 6: 225–48.

Duff, A. (2006). *The Struggle for Europe's Constitution*. London.

Dumez, H. and Jeunemaître, A. (1996). 'The Convergence of Competition Policies in Europe: Internal Dynamics and External Imposition', in S. Berger and R. Dore (eds.), *National Diversity and Global Capitalism*. Ithaca, NY: Cornell University Press, pp. 216–38.

Dumoulin, M. (1988). 'La Belgique et Les Débuts du Plan Schuman (Mai 1950-Février 1952)', in K. Schwabe (ed.), *Die Anfänge des Schuman-Plans, 1950/51*. Baden-Baden: Nomos, pp. 271–84.

Dymond, W. D. and Hart, M. M. (2000). 'Post-Modern Trade Policy: Reflections on the Challenges to Multilateral Trade Negotiations After Seattle', *Journal of World Trade*, 34/3: 21–38.

Dyson, K. (1994). *Elusive Union: The Process of Economic and Monetary Union in Europe*. London: Longman.

——Featherstone, K. (1999). *The Road to Maastricht: Negotiating Economic and Monetary Union*. Oxford: Oxford University Press.

Economist (2001). 'A Ragbag of Reform', March 3: 63–5.

Egan, M. (2001*a*). *Constructing a European Market: Standards, Regulation, and Governance*. Oxford and New York: Oxford University Press.

——(2001*b*). 'Mutual Recognition and Standard Setting: Public and Private Strategies for Governing Markets', in M. A. Pollack and G. C. Shaffer (eds.), *Transatlantic Governance in the Global Economy*. Boulder, CO: Rowman and Littlefield, pp. 179–211.

Egeberg, M. (1999). 'Transcending Intergovernmentalism?' *Journal of European Public Policy*, 6: 456–74.

Eichener, V. (1992). *Social Dumping or Innovative Regulation: Processes and Outcomes of European Decision-Making in the Sector of Health and Safety at Work Harmonization*. Florence: European University Institute.

Eilstrup-San Giovanni, M. (2006). *'Binding Hegemons'—How Regional Power Transition Promotes Integration*. MS: University of Cambridge.

Elazar, D. (1987). *Exploring Federalism*. Tuscaloosa: University of Alabama Press.

_____(2001). 'The United States and the European Union: Models for Their Epochs', in K. Nicolaïdis and R. Howse (eds.), *The Federal Vision: Legitimacy and Levels of Governance in the United States and the European Union*. Oxford and New York: Oxford University Press, pp. 31–53.

Elgström, O. and Smith, M. (2006). *The European Union's Roles in International Politics: Concepts and Analysis*. Oxford: Routledge.

Elster, J. (1992). 'Arguing and Bargaining in the Federal Convention and the Assemblée Constituante', in R. Malnes and A. Underdal (eds.), *Rationality and Institutions: Essays in Honour of Knut Midgaard*. Oslo: Universitetsforlaget, pp. 13–50.

Epstein, R. (2006). 'Cultivating Consensus and Creating Conflict: International Institutions and the (De)Politicization of Economic Policy in Post-communist Europe', *Comparative Political Studies*, forthcoming.

Esser, J. and Fach, W. (1989). 'Crisis Management "Made in Germany": The Steel Industry', in P. Katzenstein (ed.), *Industry and Politics in West Germany: Toward the Third Reich*. Ithaca, NY: Cornell University Press, 221–48.

EU (2000). *Treaty of Nice*.

EU Observer (2006). 'Western Europe Remains Wary of New Member State Workers', available at: http://euobserver.com/9/21469/?rk=1.

European Coal and Steel Community (1953). *Recueil Statistique de la Communauté Européenne du Charbon et de l'Acier*. Luxembourg: Haute Autorité.

European Commission (1970). 'Vorschlag einer Verordnung des Rates über das Statut für europäische Aktiengesellschaften', *Amtsblatt* C 124/1, 10 October.

_____(1975a). 'Amended Proposal for a Council Regulation on the Statute for European Companies', *Official Journal* COM 75/150 final. Luxembourg, 30 April.

_____(1975b). *Towards European Citizenship*, Supplement 7/75: Bull. EC.

_____(1978). *La Cooperation Au Developpment et le Respect de Certaines Normes Internationales en Matière de Conditions de Travail*. Brussels.

_____(1979). Proposal for a Council Directive on a Right of Residence for Nationals of Member States in the Territory of Another Member State. COM 79/215.

_____(1980). *Towards a European Stock Exchange: Symposium*. XV/231/81, Brussels, 13–14 November.

_____(1983). *Financial Integration*. COM 83/207, April.

_____(1985a). 'Completing the Internal Market: White Paper from the Commission to the European Council', *Official Journal* COM 85/ 310 final, 14 June.

_____(1985b). *EC Bulletin*. Brussels.

_____(1988). *Social Europe: The Social Dimension of the Internal Market. Interim Report of the Interdepartmental Working Party, Special Edition*. Luxembourg.

_____(1989a). 'Proposal for a Council Regulation on the Statute for a European Company', *Official Journal* C 263/07, 16 October.

_____(1989b). 'Proposal for a Council Directive Complementing the Statute for a European Company with Regard to the Involvement of Employees in the European Company', *Official Journal* C 263/08, 16 October.

_____(1989c). *Proposal for a Council Directive on the Right of Residence*. COM 89/275. Brussels.

European Commission (1991a). 'Amended Proposal for a Council Regulation (EEC) on the Statute for a European Company', *Official Journal* COM 176/01, 8 July.

———(1991b). 'Amended Proposal for a Council Directive Complementing the Statute for a European Company with Regard to the Involvement of Employees in the European Company', *Official Journal* COM 91/174 final, 29 May.

———(1993). *Community-Wide Framework for Employment*. Brussels: Commission of the European Communities.

———(1994). *Proposal for a Council Directive Laying Down Detailed Arrangements for the Exercise of the Right to Vote and to Stand as a Candidate to Municipal Elections by Citizens of the Union Residing in a Member State of Which They Are not Nationals.* COM 94/38. Brussels.

———(1995). *Accounting Harmonisation: A New Strategy vis-à-vis International Harmonisation.* COM 95/508 EN.

———(1997). *The 1998 Employment Guidelines. Council Resolution of 15 December 1997.* Brussels: Directorate-General for Employment, Industrial Relations, and Social Affairs.

———(1998a). *Financial Services: Building a Framework for Action.* Ip/98/941, 28 October.

———(1998b). *Risk Capital: A Key to Job Creation in the European Union.* SEC (1998): 552.

———(1999). *Financial Services. Implementing the Framework for Financial Markets: Action Plan.* COM (1999): 232.

———(2001a). 'On the Statute for a European Company (SE)', *Council Regulation (EC)* No 2157/2001, 8 October.

———(2001b). *The Treaty of Nice: A Comprehensive Guide.* Brussels.

———(2001c). *Europe and Asia: A Strategic Framework for Enhanced Partnerships.* COM (2001): 469 final, 4 September.

———(2002). *Taking Stock of Five Years of the European Employment Strategy: Communication from the Commission to the Council, the European Parliament, the Economic and Social Committee, and the Committee of the Regions.* Brussels.

———(2003a). *Wider Europe—Neighborhood: A New Framework for Relations with Our Eastern and Southern Neighbors.* COM (2003): 104 final.

———(2003b). *Communication from the Commission to the Council and the European Parliament. The European Union and the United Nations: The Choice of Multilateralism.* COM (2003): 526 final.

———(2004). *The Transitional Arrangements for the Free Movement of Workers from the New Member States Following Enlargement of the European Union on 1 May 2004.* Brussels: Employment, Social Affairs, and Equal Opportunities DG.

———(2005a). *Financial Integration Monitor, 2005.* SEC (2005): 927.

———(2005b). *Communication from the Commission to the Council and the European Parliament Common Actions for Growth and Employment: The Community Lisbon Program.* Brussels.

———(2005c). *Strategy Paper and Indicative Programme for Multi-country Programmes in Asia 2005–2006.* Brussels.

———(2005d). *Review of the Framework for Relations between the European Union and the United States: An Independent Study.* Available at: http://europa.eu.int/comm/ external_relations/us/revamping/final_report_260405.pdf

____(2006a). *Amended Proposal for a Directive of the European Parliament and of the Council on Services in the Internal Market.* Brussels: Commission of the European Communities.

____(2006b). *European Globalisation Fund.* Brussels.

____(2006c). *Single Market in Financial Services Progress Report, 2004–2005.* SEC (2006) 17, 5 January.

____(2006d). 'The Future of Europe', *Eurobarometer,* 251.

____(2006e). *Eurobarometer,* 64.

European Convention (2002a). 'Communication from the Commission to the Convention, 22 May 2002: A Project for the European Union', CONV 229/02.

____(2002b). Contribution Submitted by E. Hernandez-Soro, J. Chabert, M. Dammeyer, P. Dewael, C. Du Granrut, and C. Martini, Observers of the Committee of the Regions and Members of the Convention. CONV 195/02.

____(2002c). *Preliminary Draft Constitutional Treaty.* CONV 369/02.

European Council (1968a). *Directive 68/360 of 15 October 1968 on the Abolition of Restrictions on Movement and Residence within the Community for Workers of Member States and their Families.*

____(1968b). *Regulation 1612/68 of 15 October 1968 on Freedom of Movement for Workers within the Community.*

____(1985). *New Approach to Technical Harmonization and Standardization.* Council Resolution 7.5.1985 COM (85): 310 final. Brussels.

____(1990). *Presidency Conclusions, Dublin European Council, 25 and 26 April 1990.* Bulletin EC: 6-1990, 15–16.

____(1994). *Meeting on 9 and 10 December 1994.* Essen: Presidency Conclusions.

____(1995). *Madrid European Council 15 and 16 December 1995: Presidency Conclusions.*

____(1998). *Cardiff European Council, 15 and 16 June 1998, Presidency Conclusions.* SN 150/1/98 REV 1 EN.

____(2000). *Presidency conclusions Lisbon European Council 23 and 24 March 2000.*

____(2001a). *The Future of the European Union: Laeken Declaration.*

____(2001b). 'On the Statute for a European Company (SE)', Council Regulation (EC) No 2157/2001 (8 October 2001).

____(2001c). Council Directive 2001/86/EC. *Official Journal* 294/22 (10 November 2001).

____(2003). 'A Secure Europe in a Better World', in *European Security Strategy, Adopted by the Heads of State and Government at the European Council.* Brussels, 12 December.

European Parliament (1977). *Resolution on the Granting of Special Rights to the Citizens of the European Community* (16 November). OJ C 299, 12 December.

____(1979). *Proceedings of the Round Table on 'Special Rights and a Charter of the Rights of the Citizens of the European Community' and Related Documents.* Luxembourg: European Parliament.

____(1984). *Resolution on the Draft Treaty establishing the European Union.* OJ C 77, 19 March: 53.

____(1988). *Resolution on the Results Obtained from Implementation of the Single Act (Graziani Report).* OJ C 309, 27 October.

European Parliament (1991*a*). *Resolution on Union citizenship (14 June)*. OJ C 183, 15 July: 473.

———(1991*b*). *Report of the Committee on Institutional Affairs of the European Parliament on Union Citizenship (Bindi Report)*. Doc A3-0300/91, PE 153.099/fin, 6 November.

———(1996). *White Paper on the 1996 Intergovernmental Conference: Summary of Positions of the Member States of the European Union with a View to the 1996 Intergovernmental Conference*. Brussels.

———(1998). *Resolution on the Second Commission Report on Citizenship of the Union (2 July)*. OJ C 226, 20 July: 61.

———(2001). *Draft Report on the Treaty of Nice and the future of the European Union*. Committee on Constitutional Affairs, PE 294.755.

Everts, S. et al. (2004). *A European Way of War*. London: Centre for European Reform.

Fabbrini, S. (ed.) (2005). *Federalism and Democracy in the European Union and the United States*. London: Routledge.

Falkner G. (1998). *EU Social Policy in the 1990s: Towards a Corporatist Policy Community*. London: Routledge.

———(1999). 'European Social Policy: Towards Multi-level and Multi-actor Governance', in R. Eising and B. Kohler-Koch (eds.), *The Transformation of Governance in the European Union*. London: Routledge, pp. 83–97.

———(2002). 'How Intergovernmental are Intergovernmental Conferences? An Example from the Maastricht Treaty', *Journal of European Public Policy*, 9/1: 98–119.

———Hartlapp, M., Leiber, S., and Treib, O. (2004). 'Non-Compliance with EU Directives in the Member States: Opposition through the Backdoor?' *West European Politics*, 27/3: 452–73.

Farrell, H. (2003). 'Constructing the International Foundations of E-commerce: The EU–US Safe Harbor Arrangement', International Organization, 2: 277–306.

———Heritier, A. (2003). 'Formal and Informal Institutions Under Codecision: Continuous Constitution Building in Europe', *Governance: An International Journal of Policy*, 16/4: 577–600.

Farrell, M. (2005). 'A Triumph of Realism over Idealism? Cooperation between the European Union and Africa', *Journal of European Integration*, 27/3: 263–83.

———Hettne, B. (2005). *Global Politics of Regionalism. Theory and Practice*. London: Pluto Press.

Fawcett, L. and Hurrell, A. (1995). *Regionalism in World Politics: Regionalism and World Order*. Oxford: Oxford University Press.

——— ———(1999). *Regionalism in World Politics: Regionalism and World Order*. Oxford: Oxford University Press.

FESE (2000). *Report and Recommendations on European Regulatory Structures*. Brussels.

Filippov, M., Ordeshook, P., and Shvetsova, O. (2004). *Designing Federalism*. New York: Cambridge University Press.

Fioretos, O. (2001). 'The Domestic Sources of Multilateral Preferences: Varieties of Capitalism in the European Community', in P. A. Hall and D. Soskice (eds.), *Varieties of Capitalism*. New York: Oxford University Press, pp. 213–44.

Flaherty, D. (1989). Protecting Privacy in Surveillance Societies. Chapel Hill: University of North Carolina Press.

Fligstein, N. (1997). 'Social Skill and Institutional Theory', *American Behavioral Scientist*, 40/4: 397–405.

_____ (2001). *The Architecture of Markets: An Economic Sociology of Twenty-first Century Capitalist Societies*. Princeton, NJ: Princeton University Press.

_____ Mara-Drita, I. (1996). 'How to Make a Market: Reflections on the Attempt to Create a Single Market in the European Union', *American Journal of Sociology*, 102/1: 1–33.

_____ Sandholtz, W., and Stone Sweet, A. (2001). *The Institutionalization of Europe*. Oxford: Oxford University Press.

Fogarty, E. A. (2004). 'Be Careful What You Wish For: The European Union and North America', in V. K. Aggarwal and E. A. Fogarty (eds.), *EU Trade Strategies: Between Regionalism and Globalism*. Houndsmills: Palgrave, pp. 180–206.

Franck, T. (ed). (1968). *Why Federations Fail*. New York: NYU Press.

Friedman-Goldstein, L. (2001). *Constituting Federal Sovereignty*. Baltimore, MD: Johns Hopkins University Press.

Friedrich, C. (1969). *Trends of Federalism in Theory and Practice*. New York: Praeger.

FT (2004). 'Work in Progress', *Financial Times*, Editorial, 10 May: 12.

GAO (2006). *Sarbanes-Oxley Act: Consideration of Key Principles Needed in Addressing Implementation for Smaller Public Companies*. Washington, DC: GAO-06-361.

Garbarino, N. and Heisenberg, D. unpublished manuscript.

Gardner, A. (1997). *A New Era in US-EU Relations? The Clinton Administration and the New Transatlantic Agenda*. Aldershot, UK: Ashgate.

Garrett, G. (1993). 'The Politics of Maastricht', *Economics and Politics*, 5:2, 105–25.

_____ (1995). 'The Politics of Legal Integration in the European Union', *International Organization*, 49: 181–91.

_____ Tsebelis, G. (1996). 'An Institutional Critique of Intergovernmentalism', *International Organization*, 50/2: 269–90.

_____ Weingast, B. (1993). 'Ideas, Interests and Institutions: Constructing the EC Internal Market', in J. Goldstein and R. Keohane (eds.), *The Role of Ideas in Foreign Policy*. Ithaca, NY: Cornell University Press, pp. 173–206.

Gegout, C. (2005). 'Causes and Consequences of the EU's Military Intervention in the DRC: A Realist Explanation', *European Foreign Affairs Review*, 10/3: 427–43.

Gerber, D. J. (1998). *Law and Competition in Twentieth Century Europe: Protecting Prometheus*. Oxford, UK: Clarendon Press.

Giavazzi, F., Baldwin, R., Berglof, E., and Widgren, M. (2001). *Nice Try: Should the Treaty of Nice Be Ratified?* London: Centre for Economic Policy Research (CEPR).

Giddens, A. (1985). *The Nation-State and Violence, Volume Two of A Contemporary Critique of Historical Materialism*. Cambridge: Polity Press.

Gillingham, J. (1991). *Coal, Steel, and the Rebirth of Europe, 1945–1955: The Germans and French from Ruhr Conflict to Economic Community*. Cambridge, UK, and New York: Cambridge University Press.

Gilson, J. (2004). 'Weaving a New Silk Road: Europe meets Asia', in V. K. Aggarwal and E. Fogarty (eds.), *EU Trade Strategies. Between Regionalism and Globalism*. Basingstoke, UK: Palgrave, pp. 64–92.

_____ (2005). 'New Inter-regionalism? The EU and East Asia', *Journal of European Integration*, 27/3: 307–26.

Ginsberg, R. H. (1989). *Foreign Policy Actions of the European Community: The Politics of Scale.* Boulder, CO: Lynne Rienner.

——(2001). *The European Union in International Politics: Baptism by Fire.* Lanham: Rowman and Littlefield.

——(2007). 'European Union Common Foreign and Security Policy', in *Demystifying the European Union: The Enduring Logic of Regional Integration.* Lanham: Rowman and Littlefield.

Gold, M. (1998). 'Social Partnership at the EU Level: Initiatives, Problems and Implications for Member States', in D. Hine and H. Kassim (eds.), *Beyond the Market: The EU and National Social Policy.* London: Routledge, pp. 107–33.

Goldstein, J. and Keohane, R. O. (1993). *Ideas and Foreign Policy: Beliefs, Institutions and Political Change.* Ithaca, NY: Cornell University Press.

——Kahler, M., Keohane, R. O., and Slaughter, A.-M. (2000). 'Introduction: Legalization and World Politics', *International Organization,* 54/3: 385–99.

Golub, J. (1999). 'In the Shadow of the Vote? Decision Making in the European Community', *International Organization,* 53/4: 733–64.

Goodman, J. (1991). 'The Politics of Central Bank Independence', *Comparative Politics,* 23/3: 329–49.

Gordon, P. H. (1997–98). 'Europe's Uncommon Foreign Policy', *International Security,* 22: 74–100.

——Shapiro, J. (2004). *Allies at War: America, Europe and the Crisis Over Iraq.* New York: McGraw-Hill.

Gourevitch, P. (1978). 'The Second Image Reversed: The International Sources of Domestic Politics', *International Organization,* 32: 881–911.

Goyder, D. G. (2003). *EC Competition Law,* 4th edn. Oxford: Oxford University Press.

Grabbe, H. (2001). 'How Does Europeanisation Affect CEE Governance? Conditionality, Diffusion and Diversity', *Journal of European Public Policy,* 8/6: 1013–31.

——(2006). *The EU's Transformative Power: Europeanization through Conditionality in Central and Eastern Europe.* New York: Palgrave Macmillan.

Grant, R. W. and Keohane, R. (2005). 'Accountability and Abuses of Power in World Politics', *American Political Science Review,* 99: 1–15.

Grieco, J. M. (1995). 'The Maastricht Treaty, Economic and Monetary Union and the Neorealist Research Programme', *Review of International Studies,* 21/1: 21–40.

Groeben, H.v.d. (2002). 'Europäische Integration aus historischer Erfahrung: Ein Zeitzeugengengespräch mit Michael Gehler', *Zentrum für europäische Integrationsforschung (ZEI) Discussion Paper,* C108/2002: 1–78.

Groenendijk, N. and Gert, H. (2002). 'A Requiem for the European Coal and Steel Community', *De Economist,* 150: 601–12.

Gros, D. (1998). 'EMU and Capital Markets: Big Bang or Glacier?' *International Finance,* 1/1: 3–34.

Gruber, L. (2000). *Ruling the World: Power Politics and the Rise of Supranational Institutions.* Princeton, NJ: Princeton University Press.

Grugel, J. (2004). 'New Regionalism and Modes of Governance—Comparing US and EU Strategies in Latin America', *European Journal of International Relations,* 10/4: 603–26.

Grunert, T. (1987). 'Decision-Making Processes in the Steel Crisis Policy of the EEC: Neocorporatist or Integrationist Tendencies?' in Y. Meny and V. Wright (eds.), *The Politics of Steel: Western Europe and the Steel Industry in the Crisis Years (1974–1984)*. Berlin: Walter de Gruyter, pp. 222–308.

Guersent, O. (2003). 'The Fight Against Horizontal Agreement in the EC Competition Policy', in B. Hawk (ed.), *International Antitrust Law & Policy*. New York: Fordham University Corporate Law Institute, 43–62.

Guigou, E. (1994). *Pour les Européens*. Paris: Flammarion.

Guiraudon, V. (2004). 'Immigration and Asylum: A Political Equilibrium?' Paper presented at *The European Union and the New Constitution: A Stable Political Equilibrium* Conference, Princeton, 10 November 2004.

Haas, E. ([1958] 2004). *The Uniting of Europe: Political, Social and Economic Forces. 1950–1957*. Notre Dame: University of Notre Dame Press.

——(1961). 'International Integration: The European and the Universal Process', *International Organization*, 15: 366–92.

——(1964). *Beyond the Nation-State: Functionalism and International Organization*. Stanford, CA: Stanford University Press.

Haas, P. (1992). 'Introduction: Epistemic Communities and International Policy Coordination', *International Organization*, 46/1: 1–35.

Habermas, J. (2001). 'Why Europe Needs a Constitution', *New Left Review*, 11: 5–26.

——(2005). 'Nach den Abstimmungs-Debakeln. Europa ist uns über die Köpfe hinweggerollt', *Süddeutsche Zeitung*. Available at: www.sueddeutsche.de/kultur/artikel/ 383/54329/.

Hall, P. A. and Soskice, D. (eds.) (2001). *Varieties of Capitalism: The Institutional Foundations of Comparative Advantage*. New York: Oxford University Press.

Hall, P. A. and Taylor, R. (1996). 'Political Science and the Three New Institutionalisms', *Political Studies*, 44/5: 936–57.

Hall, P. A. and Thelen, K. (2005). 'Institutional Change in Varieties of Capitalism', Paper presented at the *American Political Science Association*, Washington, DC, 1 September– 3 September 2005.

Halligan, B. (1997). 'Issues for Ireland', in B. Tonra (ed.), *Amsterdam: What the Treaty Means*. Dublin: Institute of European Affairs, 183–200.

Hallstein, W. (1972 (1969)). *Europe in the Making*. London: Allen and Unwin.

Haltern U. (2002). 'Pathos and Patina: The Failure and Promise of Constitutionalism in the European Imagination', *Constitutionalism Web-Papers, ConWEB*, 6/2002. Available at: http://les1.man.ac.uk/conweb.

Handoll, J. (1995). *Free Movement of Persons in the EU*. New York: John Wiley & Sons.

Harding, C. and Joshua, J. (2003). *Regulating Cartels in Europe: A Study of Legal Control of Corporate Delinquency*. New York: Oxford University Press.

Harris, A. W. (1983). *US Trade Problems in Steel: Japan, West Germany and Italy*. Praeger: New York.

Hayes-Renshaw, F. and Wallace, H. (1997). *The Council of Ministers*. New York: St. Martin's Press.

—— Van Aken, W. and Wallace, H. (2005). 'When and Why the Council of Ministers of the EU Votes Explicitly', *Journal of Common Market Studies*, 44/1: 161–94.

Hayes-Renshaw, F., Van Aken, W. and Wallace, H. (2006). 'When and Why the EU Council of Ministers Votes Explicitly', *Journal of Common Market Studies*, vol. 44, issue 1: 161–94.

Heipertz, M. and Verdun, A. (2004). 'The Dog that Would Never Bite? On the Origins of the Stability and Growth Pact', *Journal of European Public Policy*, 11/5: 765–80.

—— —— (2005). 'The Stability and Growth Pact—Theorizing a Case in European Integration', *Journal of Common Market Studies*, 43/5: 985–1008.

Heisenberg, D. (2005*a*). 'The Institution of "Consensus" in the European Union: Formal Versus Informal Decision-Making in the Council', *European Journal of Political Research*, 44: 65–90.

—— (2005*b*). Negotiating Privacy: The European Union, the United States, and Personal Data Protection. Boulder, CO: Lynne Rienner.

Hemmer, C. and Katzenstein, P. (2002). 'Why Is There No NATO in Asia? Collective Identity, Regionalism, and the Origins of Multilateralism', *International Organization*, 56/3: 575–608.

Henning, C. R. (1994). *Currencies and Politics in the United States, Germany, and Japan.* Washington, DC: Institute for International Economics.

—— (1998). 'Systemic Conflict and Regional Monetary Integration: The Case of Europe', *International Organization*, 52: 537–73.

Hentschel, V. (2002). *Ludwig Erhard: Ein Politikerleben.* München: Olzog Verlag.

Heritier, A. (2001). 'Overt and Covert Institutionalization in Europe', in A. Stone Sweet, W. Sandholtz, and N. Fligstein (eds.), *The Institutionalization of Europe.* Oxford: Oxford University Press, pp. 56–70.

Hermann, R., Risse, T. et al. (2004). *Transnational Identities: Becoming European in the EU.* Lanham: Rowman and Littlefield.

Hill, C. (ed.) (1993). 'The Capability-Expectations Gap, or Conceptualizing Europe's International Role', *Journal of Common Market Studies*, 31/3: 305–28.

—— (ed.) (1996). *The Actors in Europe's Foreign Policy.* London: Routledge.

—— Smith, M. (eds.) (2005). *The International Relations of the European Union.* Oxford: Oxford University Press.

Hix, S. (2005). *The Political System of the European Union*, 2nd edn. New York: St. Martin's Press.

—— Noury, A. G. (2006). 'After Enlargement: Voting Patterns in the Sixth European Parliament', Paper presented at the *Federal Trust Conference on The European Parliament and the European Political Space*, London, 30 March 2006.

—— —— Roland, G. (forthcoming). *Democratic Politics in the European Parliament*, Cambridge University Press.

—— Raunio, T., and Scully, R. (2003). 'Fifty Years On: Research on the European Parliament', *Journal of Common Market Studies*, 41: 191–202.

Hocking, B. (2004). 'Beyond Seattle: Adapting the Trade Policy Process', in B. Hocking and S. McGuire (eds.), *Trade Politics*, 2nd edn. London and New York: Routledge, pp. 263–75.

Hoffmann, S. (1966). 'Obstinate or Obsolete? The Fate of the Nation-State and the Case of Western Europe', *Daedalus*, 95: 862–915.

—— (2000). 'Towards a Common European Foreign and Security Policy?' *Journal of Common Market Studies*, 38: 189–98.

—— Keohane, R. O. (1991). *The New European Community: Decision-making and Institutional Change*. Boulder, CO: Westview Press.

Holland, M. (2002). *The European Union and the Third World*. Basingstoke, UK: Palgrave.

Hölscher, J. and Stephan, J. (2004). 'Competition Policy in Central Eastern Europe in Light of EU Accession', *Journal of Common Market Studies*, 42/2: 321–45.

Hondius, F. (1975). Emerging Data Protection in Europe. New York: Elsevier.

Hooghe, L. (2003). *Europe Divided?: Elites vs. Public Opinion on European Integration*. Vienna: Institute for Advanced Studies.

—— (2005). 'Several Roads Lead to International Norms, But Few Via International Socialization: A Case Study of the European Commission', *International Organization*, 59/4: 861–98.

—— Marks, G. (2006). 'Europe's Blues: Theoretical Soul-Searching after the Rejection of the European Constitution', *Political Science and Politics*, 39: 247–50.

Hopt, K. J. (1994). 'Labor Representation in Corporate Boards: Impacts and Problems for Corporate Governance and Economic Integration in Europe', *International Review of Law and Economics*, 14: 203–14.

Horowitz, D. (1985). *Ethnic Groups in Conflict*. Berkeley, CA: University of California Press.

Howarth, D. (2000). *The French Road to European Monetary Union*. Basingstoke, UK: Macmillan.

Howell, T. R., Noellert, W. A., Kreier, J. G., and Wolff, A. W. (1988). *Steel and the State: Government Intervention and Steel's Structural Crisis*. Boulder, CO: Westview Press.

Hug, S. and König, T. (2002). 'In View of Ratification: Governmental Preferences and Domestic Constraints at the Amsterdam Intergovernmental Conference', *International Organization*, 56: 447–76.

Hughes, J., Sasse, G., and Gordon, C. (2004). 'Conditionality and Compliance in the EU's Eastward Enlargement: Regional Policy and the Reform of Sub-national Government', *Journal of Common Market Studies*, 42/3: 523–51.

Idema, T. and Kelemen, R. D. (2006). 'New Modes of Governance, the Open Method of Coordination and other Fashionable Red Herrings', *Perspectives on European Politics and Society*, forthcoming.

Ikenberry, G. J. (1988). Reasons of the State: Oil Politics and the Capacities of American Government. Ithaca, NY: Cornell University Press.

—— (2001). *After Victory: Institutions, Strategic Restraint, and the Rebuilding of Order After Major Wars*. Princeton, NJ: Princeton University Press.

ILO (1956). *Social Aspects of European Collaboration (Ohlin Report)*. Geneva: ILO Studies and Reports (New Series).

Imig, D. and Tarrow, S. (2001). *Contentious Europeans: Protest and Politics in an Emerging European Polity*. Lanham, MD: Rowman and Littlefield.

Iversen, T., Pontusson, J., and Soskice, D. (eds.) (1999). 'Unions, Employers, and Central Banks: Macroeconomic Coordination and Institutional Change in Social Market Economics', Cambridge, UK. Unpublished paper.

Jabko, N. (1999). 'In the Name of the Market: How the European Commission Paved the Way for Monetary Union'. Journal of European Public Policy, 6/2: 475–95.

—— (2006). *Playing the Market: A Political Strategy for Uniting Europe, 1985–2005*. Ithaca, NY: Cornell University Press.

Jachtenfuchs, M. (2002). *Die Konstruktion Europas. Verfassungsideen und Institutionelle Entwicklung.* Baden-Baden, Germany: Nomos.

Jacobs, L. R. and Shapiro, R. Y. (2000). *Politicians Don't Pander: Political Manipulation and the Loss of Democratic Responsiveness.* Chicago, IL: Chicago University Press.

Jacoby, W. (2004). *The Enlargement of the European Union and NATO: Ordering from the Menu in Central Europe.* Cambridge: Cambridge University Press.

Joerges, C. and Vos, E. (eds.) (1999). *EU Committees: Social Regulation, Law and Politics.* Oxford, UK: Oxford University Press.

Johnson, A. (2005). *European Welfare States and Supranational Governance of Social Policy.* Houndmills, Hampshire, UK: Palgrave Macmillan.

Jones, D. M. and Smith. M. L. R. (2006). *ASEAN and East Asian International Relations: Regional Delusions.* Cheltenham, UK: Edward Elgar.

Jones E., Frieden, J., and Torres, F. (eds.) (1998). *Joining Europe's Monetary Club. The Challenges for Smaller Member States.* New York: St Martin's Press.

Jones, K. A. (1979). 'Forgetfulness of Things Past: Europe and the Steel Cartel', *The World Economy*, 2: 139–54.

Jones, K. (1986). *Politics vs. Economics in the World Steel Trade.* Allen & Unwin: London.

Jupille, J. H. (2004). *Procedural Politics: Issues, Influence, and Institutional Choice in the European Union.* Cambridge and New York: Cambridge University Press.

Kahler, M. (1995). *Regional Futures and Transatlantic Economic Relations.* New York: Council on Foreign Relations.

Kagan, R. (2002). 'Power and Weakness', *Policy Review*, 113: 3–28.

⸺(2003). *Of Paradise and Power: America vs. Europe in the New World Order.* New York: Knopf.

Katzenstein, P. J. (1987). *Policy and Politics in West Germany: The Growth of a Semisovereign State.* Philadelphia, PA: Temple University Press.

Katznelson, I. (1997). 'Structure and Configuration in Comparative Politics', in M. I. Lichbach and A. S. Zuckerman (eds.), *Comparative Politics: Rationality, Culture, and Structure.* Cambridge: Cambridge University Press, pp. 81–112.

Kelemen, R. D. (2003). 'The Structure and Dynamics of EU Federalism', *Comparative Political Studies*, 36/1–2: 184–208.

⸺(2004). *The Rules of Federalism.* Cambridge, MA: Harvard University Press.

⸺(2006). 'Suing for Europe: Adversarial Legalism and European Governance', *Comparative Political Studies*, 39/1: 101–27.

Keller, B. (2002). 'The European Company Statute: Employee Involvement and Beyond'. Presented at the *IIRA/CIRA 4th Regional Congress of the Americas*: University of Toronto.

Kelley, J. (2004). *Ethnic Politics in Europe: The Power of Norms and Incentives.* Princeton, NJ: Princeton University Press.

⸺(2006). 'New Wine in Old Wineskins: Promoting Political Reforms Through the New European Neighborhood Policy', *Journal of Common Market Studies*, 44/1: 29–55.

Keohane, R. O. (2002). *Power and Governance in a Partially Globalized World.* London and New York: Routledge.

⸺Nye, J. ([1977] 2001). *Power and Interdependence.* Boston, MA: Little Brown.

————Hoffmann, S. (eds.) (1993). *After the Cold War: International Institutions and States Strategies in Europe, 1989–91*. Cambridge, MA: Harvard University Press.

Kerremans, B. (2002). 'Belgium: From Orthodoxy to Pragmatism', in F. Laursen (ed.), *The Amsterdam Treaty: National Preference Formation, Interstate Bargaining and Outcome*. Odense, Denmark: Odense University Press, pp. 71–92.

Kipping, M. (1996). 'Inter-Firm Relations and Industrial Policy: The French and German Steel Producers and Users in the Twentieth Century', *Business History*, 38: 1–25.

————Ruggero, R., and Dankers, J. (2001). 'The Emergence of New Competitor Nations in the European Steel Industry: Italy and the Netherlands', *Business History*, 43: 69–96.

Knorr, L. and Ebbers, G. (2001). 'IASC Individual Accounts', in D. Ordelheide and KPMG (eds.), *Transnational Accounting*. New York: Palgrave, 1451.

König, T. and Proksch, S. (2006). 'Exchanging and Voting in the Council: Endogenizing the Spatial Model of Legislative Politics', *Journal of European Public Policy*, 13/5: 647–69.

Kopstein, J. (2006). 'The Transatlantic Divide Over Democracy Promotion', *The Washington Quarterly*, 29/2: 85–98.

Kreppel, A. (2002). *The European Parliament and the Supranational Party System*. New York: Cambridge University Press.

Kreyssig, G. (1958). *Révision du Traité Instituant la Communauté Européenne du Charbon et de l'Acier*. Strasbourg, France: Communauté Européenne du Charbon et de l'Acier.

Krugman, P. (1991). 'History and Industry Location: The Case of the Manufacturing Belt', *American Economic Review*, 81/2: 80–3.

Kruse, D. C. (1980). *Monetary Integration in Western Europe: EMU, EMS, and Beyond*. London, UK: Butterworths.

Laatikainen, K. and Smith, K. (2006). *The European Union at the United Nations: Intersecting Multilateralisms*. Basingstoke, UK: Palgave.

Labeta, J. (2005). *Opting-out yet anchored in: The Dynamics of Differentiated Integration in the EU*. M.Phil thesis, Oxford University.

Lalone, N. W. (2005). 'An Awkward Partner: Explaining France's Troubled Relationship to the Single Market in Financial Services', *French Politics*, 3: 211–33.

Lambert, J. (1966). 'The Constitutional Crisis: 1965–1966', *Journal of Common Market Studies*, 4: 195–228.

Lamfalussy, A. (2000). *Initial Report of the Committee of Wise Men on the Regulation of European Securities Markets*. Brussels, Belgium, November.

————(2001). *Final Report of the Committee of Wise Men on the Regulation of European Securities Markets*. Brussels, Belgium, February.

Lamy, P. (2004). 'Europe and the Future of Economic Governance', *Journal of Common Market Studies*, 42/1: 5–21.

Larsson, A. (2002). *The New Open Method of Co-ordination: A Sustainable Way Between a Fragmented Europe and a European Supra State? A Practitioner's View*. Lecture given at Uppsala University.

Laursen, F. and Vanhoonacker, S. (eds.) (1992). *The Intergovernmental Conference on Political Union*. Maastricht, Netherlands: European Institute of Public Administration.

336   *Bibliography*

Leibfried, S. (1995). 'Multi-Tiered Institutions and the Making of Social Policy', in S. Leibfried and P. Pierson (eds.), *European Social Policy: Between Fragmentation and Integration*. Washington, WA: The Brookings Institution, pp. 1–40.

——Pierson, P. (1995). 'The Dynamics of Social Policy Integration', in S. Leibfried and P. Pierson (eds.), *European Social Policy: Between Fragmentation and Integration*. Washington, WA: The Brookings Institution, pp. 432–65.

Leigh, M. (2005). 'The EU's Neighborhood Policy', in E. Brimmer and S. Fröhlich (eds.), *The Strategic Implications of European Union Enlargement*. John Hopkins University, MD: Center for Transatlantic Relations, pp. 101–25.

Lemco, J. (1991). *Political Stability in Federal Governments*. New York: Praeger.

Leonard, M. (2005). *Why Europe Will Run the 21st Century*. London and New York: Fourth Estate.

Leslie, P. (2000). 'Abuses of Asymmetry', in K. Neunreither and A. Wiener (eds.), *European Integration After Amsterdam*. Oxford, UK: Oxford University Press, pp. 192–97.

Levi Sandri, L. (1968). *Free Movement of Workers in the European Community, Bull. EC 11/68*. Brussels, Belgium: Commission of the European Communities.

Levy, J. (1999). *Tocqueville's Revenge: State, Society, and Economy in Contemporary France*. Cambridge, MA: Harvard University Press.

——(2006). *The State After Statism*. Cambridge, MA: Harvard University Press.

Lewis, J. (1998). 'Is the Hard Bargaining Image of the Council Misleading? The Committee of Permanent Representatives and the Local Election Directive', *Journal of Common Market Studies*, 36/4: 479–504.

——(2000). 'The Methods of Community in EU Decision-Making and Administrative Rivalry in the Council's Infrastructure', *Journal of European Public Policy*, 7/2: 261–89.

——(2002). 'National Interests: Coreper', in J. Peterson and M. Shackleton (eds.), *The Institutions of the European Union*. Oxford, UK: Oxford University Press: pp. 277–98.

——(2005). 'Socialization and Decision Making in the European Union', *International Organization*, 59/4: 937–71.

——(2005). 'The Janus Face of Brussels: Socialization and Everyday Decision-Making in the European Union', *International Organization*, Fall 2005, vol. 59, no. 4: 937–71.

Lindberg, L. (1963). *Political Dynamics of European Integration*. Oxford, UK: Oxford University Press.

Lindner, J. and Rittberger, B. (2003). 'The Creation, Interpretation, and Contestation of Institutions—Revisiting Historical Institutionalism', *Journal of Common Market Studies*, 41/3: 445.

Lister, L. (1960). *Europe's Coal and Steel Community*. New York: Twentieth Century Fund.

Long, J. W. and Quek, M. P. (2002). 'Personal Data Privacy Protection in an Age of Globalization: The US-EU Safe Harbor Compromise', *Journal of European Public Policy*, 9/3: 325–44.

Ludlow, P. (1982). *The Making of the European Monetary System. A Case Study of the Politics of the European Community*. London, UK: Butterworth.

——(2002). *The Laeken Council*. Brussels, Belgium: Eurocomment.

——(2004). *The Making of the New Europe: The European Councils in Brussels and Copenhagen 2002*. Brussels, Belgium: EuroComment.

Maas, W. (2001). 'Grotius on Citizenship and Political Community', *Grotiana*, 21: 163–78.

―――(2005a). 'The Genesis of European Rights', *Journal of Common Market Studies*, 43: 1009–25.

―――(2005b). 'Freedom of Movement Inside "Fortress Europe"', in E. Zureik and M.B. Salter (eds.), *Global Surveillance: Borders, Security, Identity*. Portland: Willan, 233–245.

―――(2006). 'Free Movement after EU Enlargement', in J. Roy and R. Domínguez (eds.), *Towards the Completion of Europe: Analysis and Perspectives of the New European Union Enlargement*. Coral Gables, FL: University of Miami, Florida European Union Center.

―――(2007). *Creating European Citizens*. Lanham, MD: Rowman & Littlefield.

MacDougall Report. (1977). *Report of the Study Group on the Role of Public Finance in European Integration*, Volumes 1 and 2. Brussels, Belgium: Commission of the European Communities, Doc II/10/77.

Maes, I. and Verdun, A. (2005). 'The Role of Medium-sized Countries in the Creation of EMU: The Cases of Belgium and the Netherlands', *Journal of Common Market Studies*. 43/2: 27–48.

Magnette, P. (1999). *La Citoyenneté Européenne: Droits, Politiques, Institutions*. Brussels, Belgium: Éditions de l'Université de Bruxelles.

Majone, G. (1996a). Regulating Europe. New York: Routledge.

―――(1996b). 'The Future of Regulation in Europe', in G. Majone (ed.), *Regulating Europe*. London, UK: Routledge, pp. 265–83.

―――(1997). 'The New European Agencies: Regulation by Information', *Journal of European Public Policy*, 4/2: 262–75.

―――(2001). 'Two Logics of Delegation: Agency and Fiduciary Relations in EU Governance', *European Union Politics*, 2: 103–21.

―――(2005). *Dilemmas of European Integration: The Ambiguities and Pitfalls of Integration by Stealth*. Oxford, UK: Oxford University Press.

Manners, I. (2002). 'Normative Power Europe: A Contradiction in Terms?' *Journal of Common Market Studies*, 40/2: 234–58.

―――(2006). 'Normative Power Europe Reconsidered: Beyond the Crossroads', *Journal of European Public Policy*, 13/2: 182–99.

―――Whitman, R. G. (eds.) (2000). *The Foreign Policies of European Union Member States*. Manchester, UK: Manchester University Press.

Marcussen, M. (1998). *Ideas and Elites. Danish Macro-Economic Policy-Discourse in the EMU Process*. PhD. dissertation, Aalborg University, Institute for Development and Planning, ISP-Series: 226.

―――Risse, T., Engelmann-Martin, D., Knopf, H. J., and Roscher, K. (1999). 'Constructing Europe? The Evolution of French, British, and German Nation State Identities', *Journal of European Public Policy*, 6: 614–33.

Marjolin, Robert et al. (1975). *Report of the Study Group Economic and Monetary Union 1980* (The 'Marjolin Report'). Brussels, Belgium: Commission of the European Communities, Doc II/675/3/74.

Martin, L. (1993). 'International and Domestic Institutions in the EMU Process', *Economics and Politics*, 5/2: 125–43.

Mason, H. L. (1955). *The European Coal and Steel Community: Experiment in Suprana-tionalism*. The Hague, Netherlands: Martinus Nijhoff.

Mathieu, G. (1970). 'Dans l'Histoire de la CECA, Du Rose et Du Gris', *Le Monde*, 7,874 ed. Paris.

Mattila, M. and Lane, J. (2001). 'Voting in the EU Council of Ministers: Will Enlargement Change the Unanimity Pattern?' *European Union Politics*, 2/1: 31–52.

Mattli, W. (1999). *The Logic of Regional Integration: Europe and Beyond*. New York and Cambridge: Cambridge University Press.

——(2005). 'Ernst Haas' Evolving Thinking on Comparative Regional Integration: Of Virtues and Infelicities', *Journal of European Public Policy*, 12: 327–48.

Maur, J-C. (2005). 'Exporting Europe's Trade Policy', *World Economy*, 28/11: 1565–90.

Maurer, A. (2006). 'How Does the Council Work (or Not)?' in G. Durand (ed.), *After the Annus Horribilis: A Review of the EU Institutions*, EPC Working Paper 22. Available at: www.theepc.be/TEWN/pdf/119591455_JD%20template%20for% 20WPS.pdf

Mayhew, A. (1998). *Recreating Europe: The European Union's Policy towards Central and Eastern Europe*. Cambridge, UK: Cambridge University Press.

Mazey, S. and Richardson, J. (2001). 'Institutionalizing Promiscuity: Commission-Interest Group Relations in the EU', in A. Stone Sweet, W. Sandholtz, and N. Fligstein (eds.), *The Institutionalization of Europe*. Oxford, UK: Oxford University Press, pp. 71–93.

Mazzucelli, C. (1997). *France and Germany at Maastricht: Politics and Negotiations to Create the European Union*. New York: Garland.

McClenahan, W. (1991). 'The Growth of Voluntary Export Restraints and American For-eign Economic Policy 1956–1969', *Business and Economic History*, 20: 180–90.

McKay, D. (1999). *Federalism and European Union*. Oxford, UK: Oxford University Press.

——(2001). *Designing Europe: Comparative Lessons from the Federal Experience*. Oxford, UK: Oxford University Press.

McKinnon, R. (1963). 'Optimum Currency Areas', *American Economic Review*, 53 (Sep-tember): 717–25.

McLachlan, D. L. and Swann, D. (1967). *Competition Policy in the European Community: The Rules in Theory and Practice*. Oxford, UK: Oxford University Press.

McNamara, K. (1998). *The Currency of Ideas: Monetary Politics in the European Union*. Ithaca, NY: Cornell University Press.

——(2001). 'Where Do Rules Come From? The Creation of European Central Bank', in W. Sandholtz, N. Fligstein, and A. Stone Sweet (eds.), *The Institutionalization of Europe*. Oxford, UK: Oxford University Press, pp. 155–70.

——(2003). 'Making Money: Political Development, the Greenback, and the Euro', *Cen-ter for German & European Studies Working Paper*: University of California, Berkeley.

—— Meunier, S. (2006). 'Introduction', in K. McNamara and S. Meunier (eds.), *Making History: European Integration and Institutional Change at Fifty*. Oxford, UK: Oxford University Press.

McNeely, C. L. (1995). *Constructing the Nation-State: International Organization and Prescriptive Action*. Westport, CT: Greenwood Press.

Mearsheimer, J. (1991). 'Back to the Future: Instability in Europe After the Cold War', in S. M. Lynn-Jones (ed.), *The Cold War and After: Prospects for Peace*. Cambridge, MA: MIT Press, pp. 141–92.

Mehta, K. (2003). 'International Competition Policy Cooperation', in E-U. Petersmann and M. A. Pollack (eds.), *Transatlantic Economic Disputes*. Oxford, UK: Oxford University Press, pp. 281–96.

Mendelssohn, M. and Oliphant, R. (2004). 'The Arrival of the European Company: The Vehicle of the Future?' *Tax Planning International*, 6/9: 3–6.

Meng, W. (2003). '"Early Warning System" for Dispute Prevention in the Transatlantic Partnership: Experiences and Prospects', in E-U. Petersmann and M. A. Pollack (eds.), *Transatlantic Economic Disputes*. Oxford, UK: Oxford University Press, pp. 507–26.

Menon, A. and Schain, M. (2006). *The US and the EU in Comparative Perspective*. Oxford, UK: Oxford University Press.

Mény, Y. and Wright, V. (1987). *The Politics of Steel: Western Europe and the Steel Industry in the Crisis Years (1974–1984)*. Berlin, Germany: Walter de Gruyter.

Merlingen, M. and Ostrauskaite, R. (2005). 'ESDP Police Missions: Meaning, Context, and Operational Challenges', *European Foreign Affairs Review*, 10/2: 215–35.

Mestmäcker, E-J. (1999). 'Versuch einer kartellpolitischen Wende in der EU', *Europäische Zeitschrift für Wirtschaftsrecht*, 10/17: 523–29.

Mettler, S. (2002). 'Bringing the State Back in to Civic Engagement: Policy Feedback Effects of the G.I. Bill for World War II Veterans', *American Political Science Review*, 96/2: 351–65.

Meunier, S. (2003). 'Trade Policy and Political Legitimacy in the European Union', *Comparative European Politics*, 1/1: 67–90.

—— (2005). *Trading Voices: The European Union in International Commercial Negotiations*. Princeton and Oxford: Princeton University Press.

—— Nicolaïdis, K. (1999). 'Who Speaks for Europe? The Delegation of Trade Authority in the European Union', *Journal of Common Market Studies*, 37: 477–501.

—— Nicolaïdis, K. (2006). 'The European Union As a Conflicted Trade Power', *Journal of European Public Policy*, 13/6: 200–32.

Milward, A. S. (1984). *The Reconstruction of Western Europe 1945–1951*. London, UK: Methuen & Co. Ltd.

—— (1988). 'The Belgian Coal and Steel Industries and the Schuman Plan', in K. Schwabe (ed.), *Die Anfänge des Schuman-Plans, 1950/51*. Baden-Baden, Germany, Nomos, pp. 437–54.

—— (1992). *The European Rescue of the Nation-State*. London: Routledge.

—— et al. (1993). *The Frontier of National Sovereignty: History and Theory 1945–1992*. London, UK, Routledge.

Mitnick, B. M. (1980). *The Political Economy of Regulation: Creating, Designing, and Removing Regulatory Forms*. New York: Columbia University Press.

Moloney, N. (2002). *EC Securities Regulation*. Oxford, UK: Oxford University Press.

Moore, M. (2003). *A World Without Walls: Freedom, Development, Free Trade and Global Governance*. Cambridge and New York: Cambridge University Press.

Moran, M. (1991). *The Politics of the Financial Services Revolution: The USA, UK, and Japan*. New York: St. Martin's Press.

Moravcsik, A. (1991). 'Negotiating the Single European Act: National Interests and Conventional Statecraft in the European Community', *International Organization*, 45/1: 19–56.

Moravcsik, A. (1993). 'Preferences and Power in the European Community: A Liberal Intergovernmentalist Approach', *Journal of Common Market Studies*, 31/4: 473–524.

_____(1998). *The Choice for Europe: Social Purpose and State Power from Messina to Maastricht*. Ithaca, NY: Cornell University Press.

_____(1999). 'Supranational Entrepreneurs and International Cooperation', *International Organization*, 53/2: 267–306.

_____(2001). 'Federalism in the European Union: Rhetoric and Reality', in K. Nicolaïdis and R. Howse (eds.), *The Federal Vision: Legitimacy and Levels of Governance in the US and the EU*. Oxford, UK: Oxford University Press, pp. 161–87.

_____(2002). 'In Defence of the Democratic Deficit: Reassessing Legitimacy in the European Union', *Journal of Common Market Studies*, 40/4: 603–24.

_____(2003). 'Striking a New Transatlantic Bargain', *Foreign Affairs*, July/August.

_____(2004). 'Is There a "Democratic Deficit" in World Politics? A Framework for Analysis', *Government and Opposition*, 39: 603–24.

_____(2005a). 'Europe Without Illusions', *Prospect*, 112.

_____(2005b). 'The European Constitutional Compromise and the Neofunctionalist Legacy', *Journal of European Public Policy*, 12/2: 349–89.

_____(2005c). 'The European Constitutional Compromise', *European Union Studies Association*, 18/2: 1–7.

_____(2006). 'What Can We Learn from the Collapse of the European Constitutional Project?' *Politische Vierteljahresschrift*, 47/2: 219–41.

_____Vachudova, M. (2003). 'National Interests, State Power, and EU Enlargement', *East European Politics and Societies*, 17/1: 42–57.

Morgan, G. (2005). *The Idea of a European Superstate: Public Justification and European Integration*. Princeton, NJ: Princeton University Press.

Motta, M. (2004). *Competition Policy: Theory and Practice*. Cambridge: Cambridge University Press.

Möttölä, K. (ed.) (2006). *Transatlantic Relations and Global Governance*. Washington DC: Center for Transatlantic Relations.

Mowle, T. S. (2004). *Allies at Odds? The United States and European Union*. London, UK: Palgrave.

Mundell, R. A. (1961). 'A Theory of Optimum Currency Areas', *American Economic Review*, 51(4): 509–17.

Murithi, T. (2005). *The African Union: Pan-Africanism, Peace-building and Development*. Aldershot, UK: Ashgate.

Nagel, T. (2005). 'The Problem of Global Justice', *Philosophy and Public Affairs*, 33: 113–47.

Neumann, M. (2001). *Competition Policy: History, Theory, and Practice*. Northampton, MA: Edward Elgar.

Newman, A. (2003). 'When Opportunity Knocks: Economic Liberalization and Stealth Welfare in the United States', *Journal of Social Policy*, 32/2: pp. 179–97.

_____Zysman, J. (2006). 'Transforming Politics', in J. Zysman and A. Newman (eds.), *How Revolutionary was the Digital Revolution?* Palo Alto: Stanford University Press, pp. 391–411.

Neyer, J. (2004). 'Explaining the Unexpected: Efficiency and Effectiveness in European Decision-Making', *Journal of European Public Policy*, 11/1: 19–38.

Nicolaïdis, K. (2001). 'Conclusion: The Federal Vision Beyond the Federal State', in K. Nicolaïdis and R. Howse (eds.), *The Federal Vision: Legitimacy and Levels of Governance in the US and the EU*. Oxford, UK: Oxford University Press, pp. 439–81.

——(2004). 'We the Peoples of Europe', *Foreign Affairs*, 83/6: 97–110.

——(2005). 'The Power of the Superpowerless', in T. Lindberg (ed.), *Beyond Paradise and Power: Europe, America and the Future of a Troubled Partnership*. New York: Routledge: pp. 93–120.

——(2006). 'Europe and Beyond: Struggles for Recognition', *Open Democracy*. Available at: www.opendemocracy.net

——Egan, M. (2001). 'Transnational Market Governance and Regional Policy Externality: Why Recognize Foreign Standards?' *Journal of European Public Policy*, 8/3: 454–73.

——Howse, R. (2001). *The Federal Vision: Legitimacy and Levels of Governance in the United States and the European Union*. Oxford, UK: Oxford University Press.

————(2002). 'This is my EUtopia: the EU, the WTO, global governance, and global justice', *Journal of Common Market Studies*, 40(4): 767–89.

————(2003). ' "This is my EUtopia": Narrative as Power', *Journal of Common Market Studies*, 40/4: 767–92.

——Steffenson, R. (2005). 'Managed Mutual Recognition in the Transatlantic Marketplace', in D. M. Andrews, M. A. Pollack, G. C. Shaffer, and H. Wallace (eds.), *The Future of Transatlantic Economic Relations: Continuity Amid Discord*. Florence, Italy: European University Institute, Robert Schuman Centre for Advanced Studies, pp. 139–63.

——Vernon, R. (1997). 'Competition Policy and Trade Policy in the European Union', in E. M. Graham and J. D. Richardson (eds.), *Global Competition Policy*. Washington, D.C.: Institute for International Economics, pp. 271–309.

Norman, P. (2005). *The Accidental Constitution. The Story of the European Convention*. Brussels, Belgium: Eurocomment.

Norris, P. (2001). *The Global Generation: The Cohort Support for European Governance*. Available at: http://ksghome.harvard.edu/~pnorris/Acrobat/Global% 20Generation%20Brussels.pdf.

North, D. (1981). *Structure and Change in Economic History*. New York: W. W. Norton.

——(1990). *Institutions, Institutional Change, and Economic Performance*. New York: Cambridge University Press.

Nugent, N. (2003). *The Government and Politics of the European Union* (5th edn). Durham, NC: Duke University Press.

Nwobike, J. (2005). 'The Application of Human Rights in African Caribbean and Pacific-European Union Development and Trade Partnership', *German Law Journal*, 6/10: 1381–406.

Nye, J. (2004). *Soft Power: The Means to Success in World Politics*. New York: Public Affairs.

Occhipinti, J. D. (2003). *The Politics of EU Police Cooperation: Toward a European FBI?* Boulder, CO: Lynne Rienner.

——(2005). 'Policing across the Atlantic: EU–U.S. Relations and International Crime Fighting,' *Bologna Center of International Affairs*, 8 (Spring 2005): 1–12.

O'Leary, S. (1996). *The Evolving Concept of Community Citizenship: From the Free Movement of Persons to Union Citizenship.* The Hague, Netherlands: Kluwer Law International.

——(1999). 'The Free Movement of Persons and Services', in P. Craig and G. De Búrca (eds.), *The Evolution of EU Law.* Oxford, UK: Oxford University Press, pp. 377–416.

Organization for Economic Cooperation and Development (2000). *Trade and Regulatory Reform: Insights from the OECD Country Reviews and Other Analyses,* TD/TC/WP (2000) 21. Paris, France: Organization for Economic Cooperation and Development.

——(2005). *The Benefits of Liberalizing Product Markets and Reducing Barriers to International Trade and Investment: The Case of the United States and European Union.* Paris, France: Organization for Economic Cooperation and Development.

Page, B. I. and Shapiro, R. Y. (1992). *The Rational Public: Fifty Years of Trends in Americans' Policy Preferences.* Chicago, IL: University of Chicago Press.

Papapavlou, G. (1992). 'Latest Developments Concerning the EC Draft Data Protection Directives', in J. Dumortier (ed.), *Recent Developments in Data Privacy Law.* Leuven, Belgium: Leuven University Press.

Pape, R. A. (2005). 'Soft Balancing Against the United States', *International Security,* 30/1: 7–45.

Parsons, C. (2003). *A Certain Idea of Europe.* Ithaca, NY: Cornell University Press.

Partan, D. G. (1993). 'Merger Control in the EC: Federalism with a European Flavor', in A. W. Cafruny and G. G. Rosenthal (eds.), *The State of the European Community, Vol.2: The Maastricht Debates and Beyond.* Boulder, CO: Lynne Rienner Publishers, pp. 285–302.

Paul, T. V. (2005). 'Soft Balancing in the Age of U.S. Primacy', *International Security,* 30/1: 46–71.

Pelkmans, J. (1987). 'The New Approach to Technical Harmonization and Standardization', *Journal of Common Market Studies,* 25/3: 249–69.

Penska, S. E. (2006). 'Mandates, Decision-making Structures, and Individuals: The Implementation of ESDP in Bosnia and Herzegovina from 2003–2006'. Brussels: Centre for European Policy Studies Working Paper.

Pescatore, P. (1981). 'Les Travaux du "Groupe Juridique" Dans la Négociation des Traités de Rome', *Studia Diplomatica (Chronique de Politique Etrangère),* 34: 159–78.

Peterson, J. 'The Politics of Transatlantic Trade Relations', in B. Hocking and S. McGuire (eds.), *Trade Politics* (2nd edn). London and New York: Routledge, pp. 36–50.

——(1996). *Europe and America: The Prospects for Partnership.* London and New York: Routledge.

——Bomberg, E. (1999). *Decision-Making in the European Union.* New York: St. Martin's Press.

Pettit, P. (2004). 'Depoliticizing Democracy', *Ratio Juris,* 17: 52–65.

Pierson, P. (1993). 'When Effect Becomes Cause: Policy Feedback and Political Change', *World Politics,* 45/4: 595–628.

——(1994). *Dismantling the Welfare State? The Politics of Retrenchment in Britain and the United States.* Cambridge: Cambridge University Press.

——(1996). 'The Path to European Integration: A Historical Institutionalist Analysis', *Comparative Political Studies,* 29/2: 123–63.

_____(1998). 'The Path to European Integration: A Historical-Institutionalist Analysis', in W. Sandholtz and A. Stone Sweet (eds.), *European Integration and Supranational Governance*. Oxford, UK: Oxford University Press, pp. 27–58.

_____(2000). 'Increasing Returns, Path Dependence, and the Study of Politics', *American Political Science Review*, 94/2: 251–67.

_____(2004). *Politics in Time: History, Institutions and Social Analysis*. Princeton, NJ: Princeton University Press.

_____Leibfried, S. (eds.) (1995). *European Social Policy*. Washington DC.

_____Skocpol, T. (2002). 'Historical Institutionalism in Contemporary Political Science', in I. Katznelson and H. Milner (eds.), *Political Science: State of the Discipline*. New York: W.W. Norton, pp. 693–721.

Pigman, G. A. (2004). 'Continuity and Change in US trade policy, 1993–2003', in B. Hocking and S. McGuire (eds.), *Trade Politics* (2nd edn). London and New York: Routledge, pp. 304–16.

Platten, N. (1996). 'Background to and History of the Directive', in D. Bainbridge (ed.), EC Data Protection Directive. London: Butterworths, pp. 13–32.

Plender, R. (2004). 'Definition of Aid', in A. Biondi, P. Eeckhout, and J. Flynn (eds.), *The Law of State Aid in the European Union*. New York: Oxford University Press, pp. 3–39.

Pollack, M. (1996). 'The New Institutionalism and EC Governance: The Promise and Limits of Institutional Analysis', *Governance*, 9/4: 429–58.

_____(1997). 'Delegation, Agency, and Agenda Setting in the European Community', *International Organization*, 51/1: 99–154.

_____(1998). 'Constructivism, Social Psychology, and Elite Attitude Change: Lessons from an Exhausted Research Program', Unpublished Paper.

_____(eds) (2001). *Transatlantic Governance in the Global Economy*. Boulder, CO: Rowman and Littlefield.

_____(2003*a*). *Engines of European Integration: Delegation, Agency and Agenda-Setting in the European Union*. New York and Oxford: Oxford University Press.

_____(2003*b*). 'Managing System Friction: Regulatory Conflicts in Transatlantic Relations and the WTO', in E-U. Petersmann and M. A. Pollack (eds.), *Transatlantic Economic Disputes*. Oxford and New York: Oxford University Press, pp. 595–602.

_____(2004). 'The New Institutionalisms and European Integration', in A. Wiener and T. Diez (eds), *European Integration Theory*. Oxford and New York: Oxford University Press, pp. 137–56.

_____(2005*a*). 'The *JCMS* Lecture: The New Transatlantic Agenda at Ten', *Journal of Common Market Studies*, 43/5: 899–919.

_____(2005*b*). 'Theorizing the European Union: International Organization, Domestic Polity, or Experiment in New Governance?' *Annual Review of Political Science*, 8/1: 357–98.

_____Shaffer, G. C. (2005) 'Biotechnology Policy: Between National Fears and Global Disciplines', in H. Wallace, W. Wallace, and M.A. Pollack (eds.), *Policy-Making in the European Union* (5th edn). Oxford and New York: Oxford University Press, pp. 329–51.

Pontusson, J. (2006). *Inequality and Prosperity: Social Europe vs. Liberal America*. Ithaca, NY: Cornell University Press.

Posner, E. (2005*a*). 'Market Power Without a Single Market: The New Transatlantic Relations in Financial Services', in D. M. Andrews, M. A. Pollack, G. C. Shaffer, and H. Wallace (eds.), *The Future of Transatlantic Economic Relations: Continuity Amid Discord*. Florence, Italy: EUI, pp. 233–68.

—— (2005*b*). 'Sources of Institutional Change: The Supranational Origins of Europe's New Stock Markets', *World Politics*, 58: 1–40.

Pridham, G. (2005). *Designing Democracy: EU Enlargement and Regime Change in Postcommunist Europe*. New York: Palgrave Macmillan.

Priess, H-J. (1996). 'Recovery of Illegal State Aid: An Overview of Recent Developments in the Case Law', *Common Market Law Review*, 33/1: 69–91.

Prodi, R. (2001). 'For a Strong Europe, with a Grand Design and the Means of Action', *Speech by the President of the European Commission at the Institut d'Etudes Politiques*. Paris, 29 May.

Puetter, U. (2006). *The Eurogroup. How a Secretive Circle of Finance Ministers Shape European Economic Governance*. Manchester, UK: Manchester University Press.

Quaglia, L. (2007). 'The Politics of Financial Service Regulation and Supervision Reform in the European Union', *European Journal of Political Research*.

Quinlan, J. (2006). 'The Primacy of the Transatlantic Economy', in M. Zaborowski (ed.), *Friends Again? EU-US Relations After the Crisis*. Paris, France, European Union Institute for Security Studies.

Rabkin, J. (2005). *Law without Nations: Why Constitutional Government Requires Nation States*. Princeton, NJ: Princeton University Press.

Ravenhill, J. (2003). 'The New Bilateralism in the Asia-Pacific', *Third World Quarterly*, 24/2: 299–317.

—— (2004). 'Back to the Nest? Europe's Relations with the African, Caribbean and Pacific Group of Countries', in V. K. Aggarwal and Edward Fogarty (eds.), *EU Trade Strategies: Between Regionalism and Globalism*. Basingstoke, UK: Palgrave.

Rehbinder, M. (2004). 'Recent Developments in Commission State Aid Policy and Practice', in A. Biondi, P. Eeckhout and J. Flynn (eds.), *The Law of State Aid in the European Union*. New York: Oxford University Press, pp. 117–31.

Rhodes, M., Ferrera, M., and Hemerijck, A. (2001). 'The Future of the European "Social Model" in the Global Economy', *Journal of Comparative Policy Analysis*, 3: 163–90.

Riker, W. H. (1964). *Federalism: Origin, Operation, Significance*. Boston, MA: Little Brown.

—— (1996). 'European Federalism: The Lessons of Past Experience', in Jens Joachim Hesse and Vincent Wright, *Federalizing Europe? The Costs, Benefits and Preconditions of Federal Political Systems*. Oxford: Oxford University Press, pp. 9–24.

Riley, A. (2003*a*). 'EC Antitrust Modernisation: The Commission Does Very Nicely—Thank You! Part One: Regulation 1 and the Notification Burden', *European Competition Law Review*, 24/11: 604–15.

—— (2003*b*). 'EC Antitrust Modernisation: The Commission Does Very Nicely—Thank You! Part Two: Between The Idea and the Reality: Decentralisation under Regulation 1', *European Competition Law Review*, 24/12: 657–72.

Risse, T. (2001). 'A European Identity? Europeanization and the Evolution of Nation-State Identities', in T. Risse, J. Caporaso, and M. Cowles (eds.), *Transforming Europe*. Ithaca, NY: Cornell University Press, 198–216.

_____ (2003*a*). 'The Euro between National and European Identity', *Journal of European Public Policy*, 10/4: 487–503.

_____ (2003*b*). 'For a New Transatlantic—and European—Bargain', *Internationale Politik*, 3/4: 22–30.

Rittberger, B. (2001). 'Which Institutions for Post-War Europe? Explaining the Institutional Design of Europe's First Community', *Journal of European Public Policy*, 8/5: 673–708.

_____ (2005). *Building Europe's Parliament. Democratic Representation Beyond the Nation-State*. Oxford, UK: Oxford University Press.

_____ Schimmelfennig, F. (eds.) (2006). 'The Constitutionalization of the European Union', in *Journal of European Public Policy*, 1148–67.

Rodden, J. (2005). *Hamilton's Paradox: The Promise and Peril of Fiscal Federalism*. Cambridge: Cambridge University Press.

Rogoff, K. (2004). 'Europe's Quiet Leap Forward', *Foreign Policy Magazine*.

Romero, F. (1991). *Emigrazione e Integrazione Europea 1945–1973*. Rome: Edizioni Lavoro.

Rosamond, B. (2005). 'Conceptualizing the EU Model of Governance in World Politics', *European Foreign Affairs Review*, 10/4: 463–78.

Rosenthal, Glenda Goldstone (1975). *The Men Behind the Decisions: Cases in European Policy-Making*. Lexington, MA, Toronto and London: Lexington Books, D.C. Heath.

Ross, G. (1994). *Jacques Delors and European Integration*. Oxford, UK: Polity Press.

_____ (1995*a*). *Jacques Delors and European Integration*. Oxford, UK: Polity Press.

_____ (1995*b*). 'Assessing the Delors Era and Social Policy', in S. Leibfried and P. Pierson (eds.), *European Social Policy: Between Fragmentation and Integration*. Washington: The Brookings Institution, pp. 357–88.

Rubenfeld, J. (2003). 'The Two World Orders', *Wilson Quarterly*, 27: 22–36.

Ruggie, J. G. (1983). 'International Regimes, Transactions, and Change: Embedded Liberalism in the Postwar Economic Order', in S. D. Krasner (ed.), *International Regimes*. Ithaca, NY: Cornell University Press, pp. 195–231.

Rüland, J. (2001). 'ASEAN and the European Union: A Bumpy Interregional Relationship', *ZEI Discussion Paper*, C95.

Rydelski, M. S. (2004). 'The EEA State Aid Regime', in A. Biondi, P. Eeckhout, and J. Flynn (eds.), *The Law of State Aid in the European Union*. New York: Oxford University Press, pp. 189–204.

Sabel, C. F. and Zeitlin, J. (2006). 'Learning From Difference: The New Architecture of Experimentalist Governance in the European Union', *La Follette School Working Paper*, pp. 2006–18.

_____ 'Active Welfare, Experimental Governance, Pragmatic Constitutionalism: The New Transformation of Europe', Forthcoming. Available at: www2.law.columbia.edu/sabel/papers.htm.

Sally, R. (2004). 'The WTO in Perspective', in B. Hocking and S. McGuire (eds.), *Trade Politics* (2nd edn). London and New York: Routledge, pp. 105–19.

Salmon, T. (2005). 'The ESDP: Built on Rocks or Sand?' *European Foreign Affairs Review*, 10/3: 359–80.

Sanders, P. (1960). 'Vers une Société Anonyme Européenne?' *Le Droit Européen*: pp. 9–23.

Sanders, P. (1969). *European Stock Corporation: Text of Draft Statute with Commentary*. New York: Commerce Clearing House.

Sandholtz, W. (1993). 'Choosing Union: Monetary Politics and Maastricht', *International Organization*, 47/1: 1–39.

——Stone Sweet, A. (eds.) (1998). *European Integration and Supranational Governance*. Oxford, UK: Oxford University Press.

——Zysman, J. (1989). '1992: Recasting the European Bargain', *World Politics*, 42/1: 95–128.

Sassen, S. (2002). 'Economic Globalization and the Redrawing of Citizenship', in B. E. Hernández-Truyol (ed.), *Moral Imperialism: A Critical Anthology*. New York: New York University Press, pp. 135–50.

Sbragia, A. (ed.) (1992). *Euro-politics*. Washington, DC: Brookings.

——(ed.) (2006). 'Symposium: The EU Constitution: RIP?' *PS*. Available at: www.apsanet.org/content_30354.cfm

Scalingi, P. (1980). *The European Parliament: The Three-Decade Search for a United Europe*. London: Aldwych.

Scharpf, F. (1985). *The Joint-Decision Trap: Lessons from German Federalism and European Integration*. Berlin, Germany: Wissenschaftszentrum Berlin.

——(1988). 'The Joint Decision Trap', *Public Administration*, 66/3: 239–78.

——(1991). *Crisis and Choice in European Social Democracy*. Ithaca, NY: Cornell University Press.

——(1997). *Games Real Actors Play: Actor-Centered Institutionalism in Policy Research*. Boulder, CO: Westview Press.

——(1998). *Governing in Europe: Effective and Democratic?* Oxford, UK: Oxford University Press.

Scheingold, S. (1965). *The Rule of Law in European Integration*. New Haven, CT: Yale University Press.

——(1971). *The Law in Political Integration: The Evolution and Integrative Implications of Regional Legal Processes in the European Community*. Harvard University Center for International Affairs: Cambridge, Massachusetts.

Schickler, E. (2001). *Disjointed Pluralism: Institutional Innovation and the Development of the U.S. Congress*. Princeton, NJ: Princeton University Press.

Schimmelfennig, F. (2003a). *The EU, NATO and the Integration of Europe: Rules and Rhetoric*. Cambridge: Cambridge University Press.

——(2003b). 'Strategic Action in a Community Environment: The Decision to Expand the European Union to the East', *Comparative Political Studies*, 36: 156–83.

——(2006). 'Competition and Community. Constitutional Courts, Rhetorical Action, and the Institutionalization of Human Rights in the European Union', *Journal of European Public Policy*, 13: 1247–64.

——Sedelmeier, U. (eds.) (2005). *The Europeanization of Central and Eastern Europe*. Ithaca, NY: Cornell University Press.

——Engert, S., and Knobel, H. (2003). 'Costs, Commitment and Compliance: The Impact of EU Democratic Conditionality on Latvia, Slovakia, and Turkey', *Journal of Common Market Studies*, 41/3: 495–518.

_____ Rittberger, B., Bürgin, A., and Schwellnus, G. (2006). 'The Constitutionalization of the European Union: A Qualitative Comparative Analysis', *Journal of European Public Policy*, 13: 1168–90.

Schmidt, H. (1977). *Advantages and Disadvantages of an Integrated Market Compared with a Fragmented Market.* CEC Competition—Approximation of Legislation Series, 30.

Schmitter, P. (1969). 'Three Neo-Functional Hypotheses about International Integration', *International Organization*, 23: 161–66.

_____ (1996). 'Imagining the Future of the Euro-Polity with the Help of New Concepts', in G. Marks, F. Scharpf, P. Schmitter, and W. Streek (eds.), *Governance in the European Union.* London: Sage, pp. 121–50.

_____ (2000). *How to Democratize the European Union. And Why Bother?* Lanham, MD: Rowman and Littlefield.

_____ (2004). 'Neo-Neofunctionalism: Déjà Vu, or All Over Again?' in A. Wiener and T. Diez (eds.), *European Integration Theory*, New York: Oxford University Press, pp. 45–74.

Schmuck, O. (1987). 'The European Parliament's Draft Treaty Establishing the European Union', in R. Pryce (ed.), *The Dynamics of European Union.* London, UK: Croom Helm, pp. 188–216.

Schneider, G. (1995). 'The Limits of Self-Reform: Institution-Building in the European Union', *European Journal of International Relations*, 1/1: 59–86.

Scholl, B. (2005). *Der Einfluss nationaler Verfassungstraditionen auf die Konstitution-alisierungsdiskurse im Konvent zur Zukunft Europas.* Ph.D. dissertation (Cologne, 2005).

Schulz, H. and König, T. (2000). 'Institutional Reform and Decision-Making: Efficiency in the European Union', *American Journal of Political Science*, 44/4: 653–65.

Schwartz, E. (1993). 'Politics as Usual: The History of European Community Merger Control', *Yale Journal of International Law*, 18/2: 607–62.

Scitovsky, T. (1958). *Economic Theory and Western European Integration.* Stanford, CA: Stanford University Press.

Scully, R. (2005). *Becoming Europeans? Attitudes, Behaviour, and Socialization in the European Parliament.* Oxford, UK: Oxford University Press.

Sedelmeier, U. (2005). *Constructing the Path to Eastern Enlargement: The Uneven Policy Impact of EU Identity.* Manchester, UK: Manchester University Press.

Shaffer, G. C. (2003). 'Managing US-EU Trade Relations through Mutual Recognition and Safe Harbor Agreements: "New" and "Global" Approaches to Transatlantic Economic Governance?' in E-U. Petersmann and M. A. Pollack (eds.), *Transatlantic Economic Disputes.* Oxford and New York: Oxford University Press, pp. 297–325.

Shapiro, M. and Stone Sweet, A. (2002). *On Law, Politics, and Judicialization.* Oxford, UK: Oxford University Press.

Shaw, J. (2001). 'The Treaty of Nice: Legal and Constitutional Implications', *European Public Law*, 7/2: 195–215.

_____ (2003). 'Flexibility in a "Reorganized" and "Simplified" Treaty', *Common Market Law Review*, 40/2: 279–311.

Shaw, J. (2004). 'Flexibility and the Treaty establishing a Constitution for the European Union', available at: www.ecln.net/elements/conferences/prague/shawflex.pdf.

Sherrington, P. (2000). *The Council of Ministers: Political authority in the European Union*. London: Pinter.

Shonfield, A. (1969). *Modern Capitalism*. Oxford, UK: Oxford University Press.

Simitis, S. (1997). 'Data Protection in the European Union—The Quest for Common Rules', *Courses of the Academy of European Law*, 8/1: 95–142.

Sinnaeve, A. (2001). 'Block Exemptions for State Aid: More Scope for State Aid Control by Member States and Competitors', *Common Market Law Review*, 38: 1479–501.

Sissenich, B. (2003). *State Building by a Nonstate*. PhD. Dissertation (Cornell University, 2003).

Sjursen, H. (2006). 'What Kind of Power?' *Journal of European Public Policy*, 13: 169–81.

Skocpol, T. (1995). Protecting Soldiers and Mothers: The Political Origins of Social Policy in the United States. New York: Belknap Press.

Skowronek, S. (1982). *Building a New American State: The Expansion of National Administrative Capacities, 1877–1920*. Cambridge: Cambridge University Press.

Slaughter, A-M. (2004). *A New World Order*. Princeton, NJ: Princeton University Press.

Sloot, T. and Verschuren, P. (1990). 'Decision-Making Speed in the European Community', *Journal of Common Market Studies*, 29/1: 75–85.

Smith, K. E. (1999). *The Making of EU Foreign Policy: The Case of Eastern Europe*. London, UK: Macmillan.

—— (2004). 'Still "Civilian Power" EU'? Presented at *CIDEL Workshop on the theme: From civilian to military power: The European Union at a crossroads*? Oslo, October 22–23.

—— (2005a). 'The EU and Central and Eastern Europe: The Absence of Interregionalism', *Journal of European Integration*, 27/3: 347–64.

—— (2005b). 'The Outsiders: The European Neighborhood Policy', *International Affairs*, 81/4: 757–73.

Smith, M. E. (2003). *Europe's Foreign and Security Policy: The Institutionalization of Cooperation*. Cambridge: Cambridge University Press.

—— (2004a). 'Institutionalization, Policy Adaptation, and European Foreign Policy Cooperation', *European Journal of International Relations*, 10: 95–136.

—— (2004b). 'Toward a Theory of EU Foreign Policy-making: Multi-level Governance, Domestic Politics, and National Adaptation to Europe's Common Foreign and Security Policy', *Journal of European Public Policy*, 11: 740–58.

Smith, M. H. (2004). 'The European Union as a Trade Policy Actor', in B. Hocking and S. McGuire (eds.), *Trade Politics* (2nd edn). London and New York: Routledge, pp. 289–303.

Smith, M. P. (1996). 'Integration in Small Steps: The European Commission and Member-State Aid to Industry', *West European Politics*, 19/3: 563–82.

—— (1998). 'Autonomy by the Rules: The European Commission and the Development of State Aid Policy', *Journal of Common Market Studies*, 36/1: 55–78.

Solbes, M. P. (1991). 'La Citoyenneté Européenne', *Revue du Marché Commun*, 345: 168–70.

Soskice, D. (1999). 'Divergent Production Regimes: Coordinated and Uncoordinated Market Economies in the 1980s and 1990s', in H. Kitschelt et al. (eds.), *Continuity and*

Change in Contemporary Capitalism. New York: Cambridge University Press, pp. 101–34.

Steffenson, R. (2005). *Managing EU-US Relations: Actors, Institutions and the New Transatlantic Agenda*. Manchester, UK: Manchester University Press.

Steil, B. (1998). *Regional Financial Market Integration: Learning From the European Experience*. London, UK: Royal Institute of International Affairs.

Stein, E. (1981). 'Lawyers, Judges, and the Making of a Transnational Constitution', *American Journal of International Law*, 75: 1–27.

Steinberg, R. H. (2002). 'In the Shadow of Law or Power? Consensus-Based Bargaining and Outcomes in the GATT/WTO', *International Organization*, 56/2: 339–74.

Steinmo, S., Thelen, K., and Longstreth, F. (1992). *Structuring Politics: Historical Institutionalism in Comparative Analysis*. Cambridge: Cambridge University Press.

Stepan, A. (2001). *Arguing Comparative Politics*. Oxford: Oxford University Press, ch. 15.

Steunenberg, B. (1994). 'Decision-Making Under Different Institutional Arrangements: Legislation by the European Community', *Journal of Institutional and Theoretical Politics*, 150/4: 642–69.

Stiff, P. (2006). 'Italy Set for Collision with EU over Chocolate', *Food Navigator*.

Stone Sweet, A. (2000). *Governing with Judges: Constitutional Politics in Europe*. Oxford, UK: Oxford University Press.

——Caporaso, J. (1998). 'From Free Trade to Supranational Polity: The European Court and Integration', in W. Sandholtz and A. Stone Sweet (eds.), *European Integration and Supranational Governance*. New York: Oxford University Press, pp. 92–133.

——Fligstein, N., and W. Sandholtz (2001). 'The Institutionalization of European Space', in A. Stone Sweet, W. Sandholtz and N. Fligstein (eds.), *The Institutionalization of Europe*. Oxford, UK: Oxford University Press, pp. 1–28.

——Sandholtz, W., and Fligstein, N. (eds.) (2001). *The Institutionalization of Europe*. Oxford and New York: Oxford University Press.

Story, J. and Walter, I. (1997). *Political Economy of Financial Integration in Europe: The Battle of the Systems*. Cambridge: MIT Press.

Streeck, W. (1995). 'From Market-Making to State-Building: Reflections on the Political Economy of European Social Policy', in S. Leibfried, S. and P. Pierson (eds.), *European Social Policy: Between Fragmentation and Integration*. Washington: Brookings Institution, pp. 389–431.

Swenden, W. (2004). 'Is the EU in Need of a Competence catalogue?' *Journal of Common Market Studies*, 42/2: 371–92.

Tallberg, J. (2000). 'The Anatomy of Autonomy: An Institutional Account of Variation in Supranational Influence', *Journal of Common Market Studies*, 38/5: 843–64.

Tarrow, S. and Imig, D. (2001). *Contentious Europeans: Protest and Politics in a Europeanizing Polity*. Lanham, MD: Rowman and Littlefield.

Taschner, H. C. (1993). 'Free Movement of Students, Retired Persons and Other European Citizens—A Difficult Legislative Process', in H. G. Schermers (ed.), *Free Movement of Persons in Europe: Legal Problems and Experiences*. Dordrecht, Netherlands: Martinus Nijhoff, pp. 427–36.

Taylor, B. (2006). *Force and Federalism*. Unpublished MS, Syracuse University.

Taylor, P. (1983). *The Limits of European Integration*. New York: Columbia University Press.

Teichmann, C. (2003). 'The European Company: A Challenge to Academics, Legislatures, and Practitioners'. *German Law Review*, 4(1): 309–31.

Terada, T. (2003). 'Constructing an "East Asia" Concept and Growing Regional Identity: From EAEC to ASEAN+3', *Pacific Review*, 16/2: 251–77.

Thatcher, M. (2002). 'Regulation after Delegation: Independent Regulatory Agencies in Europe', *Journal of European Public Policy*, 9/6: 954–72.

Thelen, K. (1999). 'Historical Institutionalism and Comparative Politics', *Annual Review of Political Science*, 2: 369–404.

——(2003). 'How Institutions Involve: Insights from Comparative Historical Analysis', in J. Mahoney and D. Rueschemeyer (eds.), *Comparative Historical Analysis in the Social Sciences*. Cambridge: Cambridge University Press, pp. 208–40.

——(2004). *How Institutions Evolve: The Political Economy of Skills in Germany, Britain, Japan and the United States*. New York and Cambridge: Cambridge University Press.

——Steinmo, S. (1992). 'Historical Institutionalism in Comparative Politics', in S. Steinmo, K. Thelen, and F. Longstreth (eds.), *Structuring Politics: Historical Institutionalism in Comparative Politics*. Cambridge: Cambridge University Press, pp. 1–33.

Thielemann, E. R. (1999). 'Institutional Limits of a "Europe with the Regions": EC State-Aid Control Meets German Federalism', *Journal of European Public Policy*, 6/3: 399–418.

Thompson, D. (1969). *The Proposal for a European Company*. London: Chatham House.

Thomson, R. et al. (2005). *The European Union Decides*. Cambridge: Cambridge University Press.

Thorlakson, L. (2005). 'Federalism and the European Party System', *Journal of European Public Policy*, 12/3: 468–87.

——(2006). 'Building Firewalls or Floodgates? Constitutional Design for the European Union', *Journal of Common Market Studies*, 44/1: pp. 139–59.

Tiersky, R. (2003). *François Mitterrand: A Very French President*. Lanham, MD: Rowman & Littlefield.

Tinbergen, J. (1965). *International Economic Integration*. Amsterdam, Netherlands: Elsevier.

Tindemans, L. (1976). 'European Union, Report to the European Council of the European Communities', Brussels, Belgium: *Bulletin of the EC*, Supplement 1.

Töller, A. (2003). 'Dimensionen der Europäisierung—Das Beispiel des Deutschen Bundestages', Hamburg, Germany. Unpublished paper.

Torreblanca, J. (2001). *The Reuniting of Europe: Promises, Negotiations and Compromises*. Burlington, VT: Ashgate.

——(2002). 'Accomodating Interests and Principles in the European Union: The Case of Eastern Enlargement', in H. Sjursen (ed.), *Enlargement and the Finality of the EU. ARENA Report*, 7/2002: 7–33.

Tracy, M. (ed.) (1994). *Renationalisation of the Common Agricultural Policy: Risk or Remedy* Brussels, Belgium: Centre for European Policy Studies.

Trechsel, A. (ed.) (2005). 'Special Issue on EU Federalism', *Journal of European Public Policy*, 12/3.

Tsebelis, G. (1994). 'The Power of the European Parliament as a Conditional Agenda Setter', *The American Political Science Review*, 88/1: 128–42.

Tsoukalis, L. (1977). *The Politics and Economics of European Monetary Integration.* London: Allen and Unwin.

———— Strauss, R. (1985). 'Crisis and Adjustment in European Steel: Beyond Laisser-Faire', *Journal of Common Market Studies*, 23: 207–28.

—————— (1987). 'Community Policies on Steel 1974–1982: A Case of Collective Management', in Y. Meny and V. Wright (eds.), *The Politics of Steel: Western Europe and the Steel Industry in the Crisis Years (1974–1984).* Walter de Gruyter: Berlin, pp. 186–221.

Underhill, G. R. D. (1997). 'The Making of the European Financial Area: Global Market Integration and the EU Single Market for Financial Services', in G. R. D. Underhill (ed.), *The New World Order in International Finance.* New York: St. Martin's Press, pp. 101–23.

United Kingdom (1990). *Free Movement of People and Right of Residence in the European Community.* London: House of Lords Select Committee on the European Communities.

———— (1996a). *Proposal for Amendment of Articles 54, 57, and 118A, and for a Protocol Concerning Directive 93/104/EC (Working Time): Memorandum by the United Kingdom.*

———— (1996b). 'UK White Paper of 12 March 1996 on the IGC: "An association of nations"', in European Parliament (ed.), *White Paper on the 1996 Intergovernmental Conference: Summary of Positions of the Member States of the European Union with a View to the 1996 Intergovernmental Conference.* Brussels.

———— (1996c). *A Partnership of Nations: The British Approach to the European Union Intergovernmental Conference 1996.* London, UK: HMSO.

United States Trade Representative (2001). *2001 National Trade Estimate Report on Foreign Trade Barriers.* Washington, DC: United States Trade Representative.

Vachudova, M. A. (2005). *Europe Undivided: Democracy, Leverage and Integration After Communism.* Oxford, UK: Oxford University Press.

———— (2006). 'Democratization in Postcommunist Europe: Illiberal Regimes and the Leverage of International Actors'. Working Paper: Center for European Studies, Harvard University, forthcoming.

Van Hulle, K. (2004). 'From Accounting Directives to International Accounting Standards', in C. Leuz, D. Pfaff, and A. Hopwood (eds.), *The Economics and Politics of Accounting: International Perspectives on Research Trends, Policy, and Practice.* Oxford, UK: Oxford University Press, pp. 364–5.

Van Schendelen, M. P. C. M. (1996). '"The Council Decides": Does the Council Decide?' *Journal of Common Market Studies*, 34/4: 531–48.

Verdun, Amy (1996). 'An "Asymmetrical" Economic and Monetary Union in the EU: Perceptions of Monetary Authorities and Social Partners', *Journal of European Integration*, 20/1: 59–81.

———— (1999). 'The Role of the Delors Committee in the Creation of EMU: An Epistemic Community?' *Journal of European Public Policy*, 6/2: 308–28.

———— (2000a). *European Responses to Globalization and Financial Market Integration: Perceptions of Economic and Monetary Union in Britain, France, and Germany.* Basingstoke, UK: Macmillan; New York: St Martin's Press.

———— (2000b). 'Governing by Committee: The Case of the Monetary Committee', in T. Christiansen and E. Kirchner (eds.), *Committee Governance in the European Union.* Manchester, UK: Manchester University Press, pp. 132–45.

Vesterdorf, B. (2005). 'Standard of Proof in Merger Cases: Reflections in Light of Recent Case Law of the Community Courts', *European Competition Journal*, 1/1: 3–33.

Vignes, D. (1956). *La Communauté Européenne du Charbon et de l'Acier: Un Exemple d'Administration Économique Internationale*. Liège: Georges Thone.

Villa, P. (1986). *The Structuring of Labor Markets: A Comparative Analysis of the Steel and Construction Industries in Italy*. Oxford: Clarendon Press.

Vogel, D. (1995). *Trading Up*. Cambridge, MA: Harvard University Press.

——(1997). *Barriers or Benefits? Regulation in Transatlantic Trade*. Washington, DC: Brookings Institution Press.

——(2003). 'The Hare and the Tortoise Revisited: The New Politics of Consumer and Environmental Regulation in Europe', *British Journal of Political Science*, 33/4: 557–80.

Vogel, L. (1993). *Prevention at the Workplace: An Initial Review of how the 1989 Community Framework Directive is Being Implemented*. Brussels, Belgium: European Trade Union Technical Bureau for Health and Safety.

Vogel, S. K. (1996). *Freer Markets, More Rules: Regulatory Reform in Advanced Industrial Countries*. Ithaca, NY: Cornell University Press.

Wallace, H., Wallace, W., and Pollack, M. (eds.) (2004). *Policy-Making in the European Union* (5th edn). Oxford, UK: Oxford University Press.

Wallace, W. (1995). 'Regionalism in Europe. Model or Exception?' in L. Fawcett and A. Hurrell (eds.), *Regionalism in World Politics: Regional Organization and International Order*. Oxford, UK: Oxford University Press, pp. 201–27.

Waltz, K. N. (1993). 'The Emerging Structure of International Politics', *International Security*, 18: 44–79.

——(1999). 'Globalization and Governance', *PS: Political Science and Politics*, 32/December: pp. 693–700.

Warleigh, A. and Rosamond, B. (2005). 'Theorizing Regional Integration Comparatively: An Introduction.' Paper prepared for the ECPR Joint Sessions of Workshops (Workshop 10), Nicosia, Cyprus, April 25–30, 2006.

Warner, I. (1996). *Steel and Sovereignty: The Deconcentration of the West German Steel Industry, 1949–54*. Mainz: P. von Zabern.

Warren, K. (1975). *World Steel: An Economic Geography*. New York: David & Charles Newton Abbot, Crane, Russak.

Weber, K., Smith, M. E., and Baun, M. (eds.). (2007). *Governing Europe's New Neighborhood: Partners or Periphery?* Manchester, UK: Manchester University Press, forthcoming.

Weber, S. and Posner, E. (2000). 'Creating a Pan-European Equity Market: The Origins of the EASDAQ'. Review of the International Political Economy, 7/4: 529–73.

Wechsler, H. (1954). 'The Political Safeguards of Federalism', *Columbia Law Review*, 54: 543–60.

Weiler, J. (1981). 'The Community System: The Dual Character of Supranationalism', *Yearbook of European Law*, 1: 267–306.

——(1991). 'The Transformation of Europe', *Yale Law Journal, 100*: 2403–83.

——(1999). *The Constitution of Europe*. Cambridge: Cambridge University Press.

Weir, M., Orloff, A., and Skocpol, T. (1988). 'Introduction: Understanding American Social Policies', in M. Weir, A. Orloff, and T. Skocpol (eds.), The Politics of Social Policy in the United States. Princeton: Princeton University Press, pp. 3–35.

Werner Report (1970). 'Report to the Council and the Commission on the Realization by States of Economic and Monetary Union', *Council and Commission of the EEC Bulletin of the EC*: Supplement 11, Doc 16.956/11/70.

Wiebe, R. H. (2002). *Who We Are: A History of Popular Nationalism*. Princeton, NJ: Princeton University Press.

Wiener, A. (1998). *'European' Citizenship Practice: Building Institutions of a Non-State*. Boulder, CO: Westview Press.

—— Diez, T. (2004) *European Integration Theory*. Oxford, UK: Oxford University Press.

Wheare, K. C. (1964). *Federal Government* (4th edn). Oxford, UK: Oxford University Press.

Whitman, R. (1998). *From Civilian Power to Superpower? The International Identity of the European Union*. London: Palgrave-Macmillan.

Wighton, D. (2006). 'Selling the Attractions of Euronext', *Financial Times*, May 22: 30.

Wilks, S. (2005). 'Competition Policy: Challenge and Reform', in H. Wallace, W. Wallace, and M. A. Pollack (eds.), *Policy-Making in the European Union*, Fifth Edition. New York: Oxford University Press, pp. 113–39.

—— Bartle, I. (2002). 'The Unanticipated Consequences of Creating Independent Agencies', *West European Politics*, 25/1: 148–72.

—— McGowan, L. (1996). 'Competition Policy in the European Union: Creating a Federal Agency?' in S. Wilks and G. B. Doern (eds.), *Comparative Competition Policy: National Institutions in a Global Market*. Oxford, UK: Clarendon Press, pp. 225–67.

Winn, N. and Lord, C. (2001). *EU Foreign Policy Beyond the Nation-State: Joint Actions and Institutional Analysis of the Common Foreign and Security Policy*. London, UK: Palgrave-Macmillan.

Wolf, D. (1988). 'Principals, Bureaucrats, and Responsiveness in Clean Air Enforcement', *American Political Science Review*, 82: pp. 213–34.

—— (2004). 'State Aid Control at the National, European, and International Level', in M. Zürn and C. Joerges (eds.), *Law and Governance in Postnational Europe: Compliance Beyond the Nation-State*. Cambridge: Cambridge University Press, pp. 65–117.

Woolcock, S. (2005). 'Trade Policy: From Uruguay to Doha and Beyond', in H. Wallace, W. Wallace, and M. A. Pollack (eds.), *Policy-Making in the European Union* (5th edn). Oxford and New York: Oxford University Press, pp. 377–99.

Wuermeling, U. (1996). 'Harmonisation of European Union Privacy Law', *John Marshall Journal of Computer and Information Law*, 14/3: 411.

Young, A. R. (2002). *Extending European Cooperation: the European Union and the 'New' International Trade Agenda*. Manchester, UK: Manchester University Press.

—— Peterson, J. (2006). 'The New Trade Politics', *Journal of European Public Policy*, 13/6: 795–814.

Youngs, R. (2004). 'Normative Dynamics and Strategic Interests in the EU's External Identity', *Journal of Common Market Studies*, 42/2: 415–35.

Zeitlin, Jonathan (2005). 'Social Europe and Experimentalist Governance', EUROGOV Papers No. C-05-04.

Zeitlin, Jonathan, Pochet, P., and Magnusson, L. (eds.) (2005). *The Open Method of Coordination in Action: The European Employment and Social Inclusion Strategies.* Brussels, Belgium: Peter Lang Publishers, Inc.

Zielonka, J. (2006). *Europe as Empire: The Nature of the Enlarged European Union.* Oxford, UK: Oxford University Press.

Zweifel, T. (2002). *Democratic Deficit? Institutions and Regulation in the European Union, Switzerland and the United States.* Lanham, MD: Lexington Books.

——(2006). *International Organizations and Democracy.* Boulder, CO: Lynne Rienner.

Zysman, J. (1983). *Governments, Markets, and Growth: Financial Systems and the Politics of Industrial Change.* Ithaca, NY: Cornell University Press.

INDEX